GEGE AKUTAMI

Heart isn't in it.

D1501068

GEGE AKUTAMI published a few short
works before starting *Jujutsu Kaisen*, which began
serialization in *Weekly Shonen Jump* in 2018.

JUJUTSU KAISEN

VOLUME 5
SHONEN JUMP MANGA EDITION

BY GEGE AKUTAMI

TRANSLATION Stefan Koza
TOUCH-UP ART & LETTERING Snir Aharon
DESIGN Joy Zhang
EDITOR John Bae
CONSULTING EDITOR Erika Onabe

Printed in the U.S.A.

Published by VIZ Media, LLC
P.O. Box 77010
San Francisco, CA 94107

10 9 8 7 6 5
First printing, August 2020
Fifth printing, June 2021

VIZ MEDIA
viz.com

SHONEN JUMP

ratings.viz.com
RATED T+ OLDER TEEN

PARENTAL ADVISORY
JUJUTSU KAISEN is rated T+ for Older Teen and is recommended for ages 16 and up. This volume contains fantasy violence.

JUJUTSU KAISEN

5

KYOTO
SISTER-SCHOOL
GOODWILL
EVENT

STORY AND ART BY GEGE AKUTAMI

JUJUTSU KAISEN
CAST OF CHARACTERS

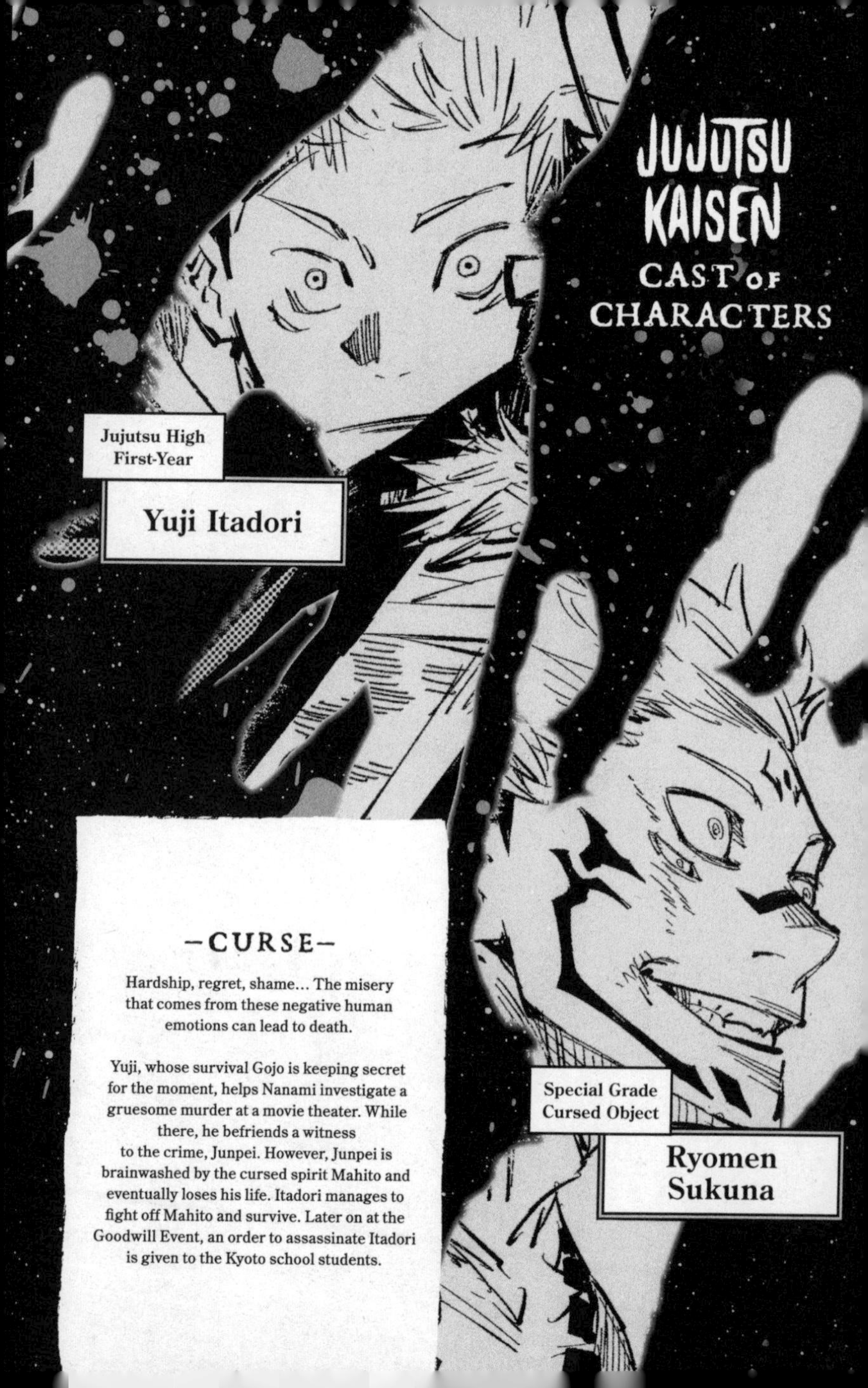
Jujutsu High First-Year
Yuji Itadori
Special Grade Cursed Object
Ryomen Sukuna

—CURSE—

Hardship, regret, shame... The misery that comes from these negative human emotions can lead to death.

Yuji, whose survival Gojo is keeping secret for the moment, helps Nanami investigate a gruesome murder at a movie theater. While there, he befriends a witness to the crime, Junpei. However, Junpei is brainwashed by the cursed spirit Mahito and eventually loses his life. Itadori manages to fight off Mahito and survive. Later on at the Goodwill Event, an order to assassinate Itadori is given to the Kyoto school students.

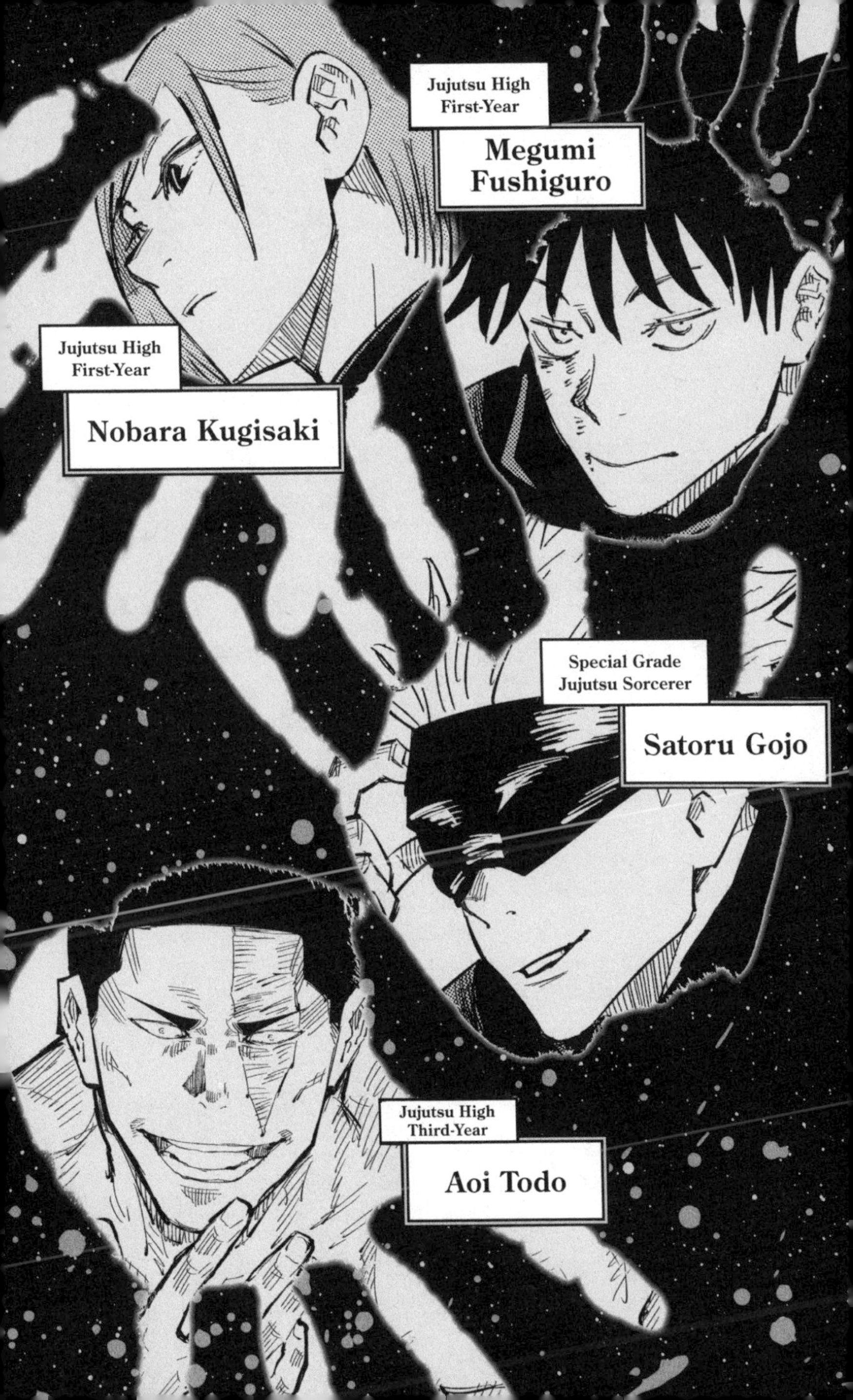
Jujutsu High First-Year
Megumi Fushiguro
Jujutsu High First-Year
Nobara Kugisaki
Special Grade Jujutsu Sorcerer
Satoru Gojo
Jujutsu High Third-Year
Aoi Todo

JUJUTSU KAISEN

5

KYOTO SISTER-SCHOOL GOODWILL EVENT

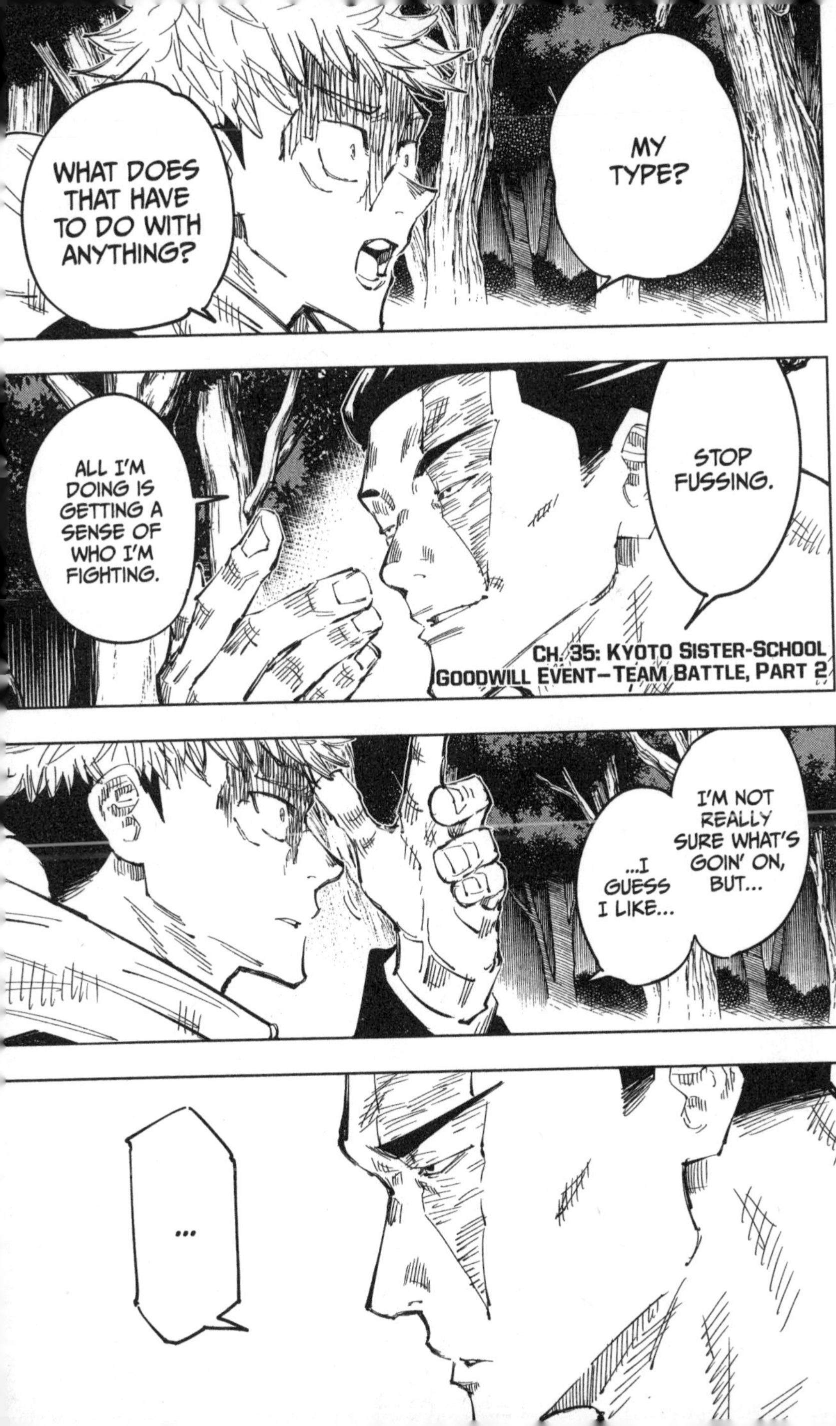
MY TYPE?
WHAT DOES THAT HAVE TO DO WITH ANYTHING?
STOP FUSSING.
ALL I'M DOING IS GETTING A SENSE OF WHO I'M FIGHTING.
CH. 35: KYOTO SISTER-SCHOOL GOODWILL EVENT—TEAM BATTLE, PART 2
I'M NOT REALLY SURE WHAT'S GOIN' ON, BUT...
...I GUESS I LIKE...
...

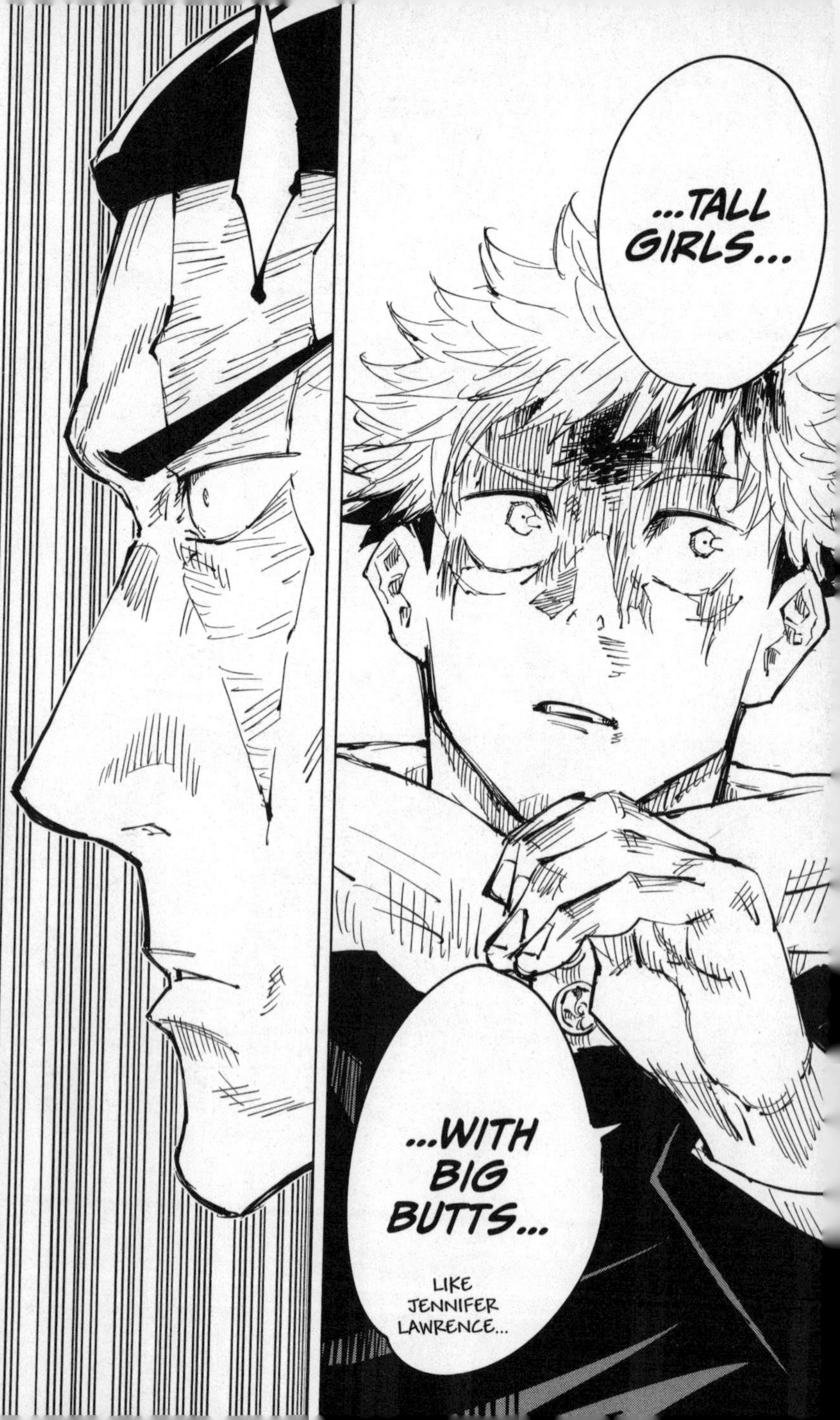
...TALL GIRLS...
...WITH BIG BUTTS...
LIKE JENNIFER LAWRENCE...

CHAPTER 35: KYOTO SISTER-SCHOOL GOODWILL EVENT—TEAM BATTLE, PART 2

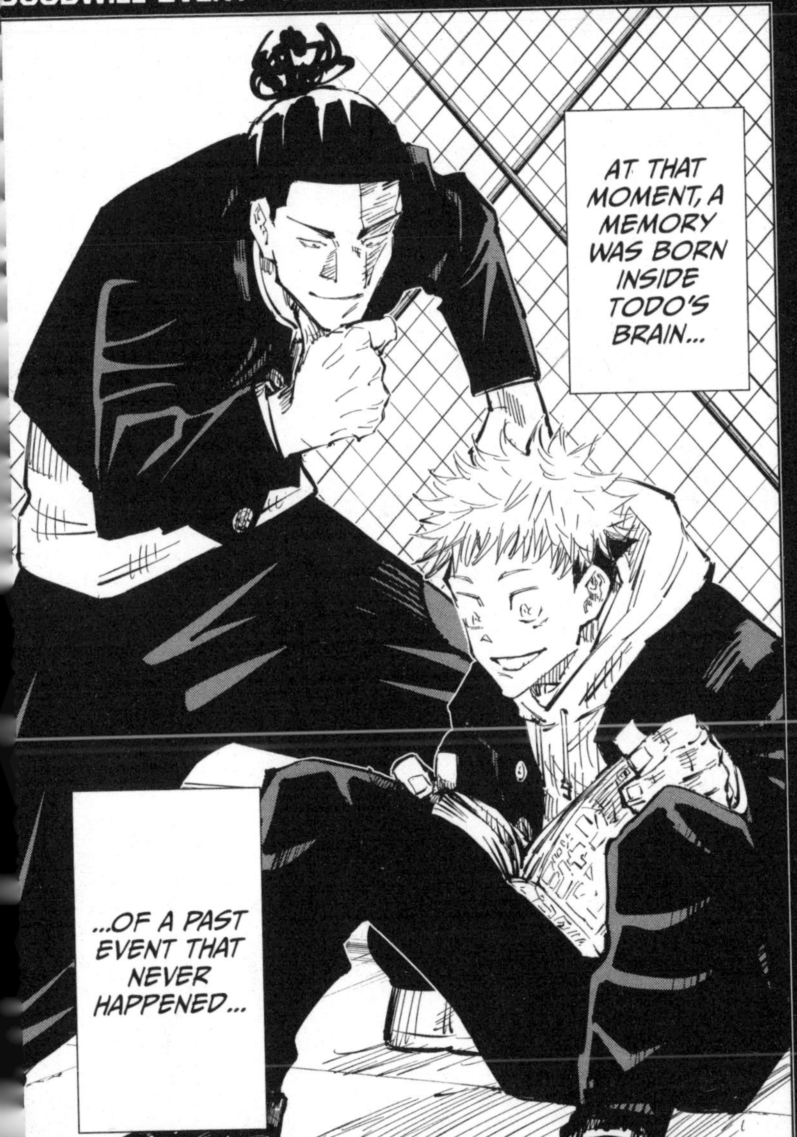
AT THAT MOMENT, A MEMORY WAS BORN INSIDE TODO'S BRAIN...
...OF A PAST EVENT THAT NEVER HAPPENED...

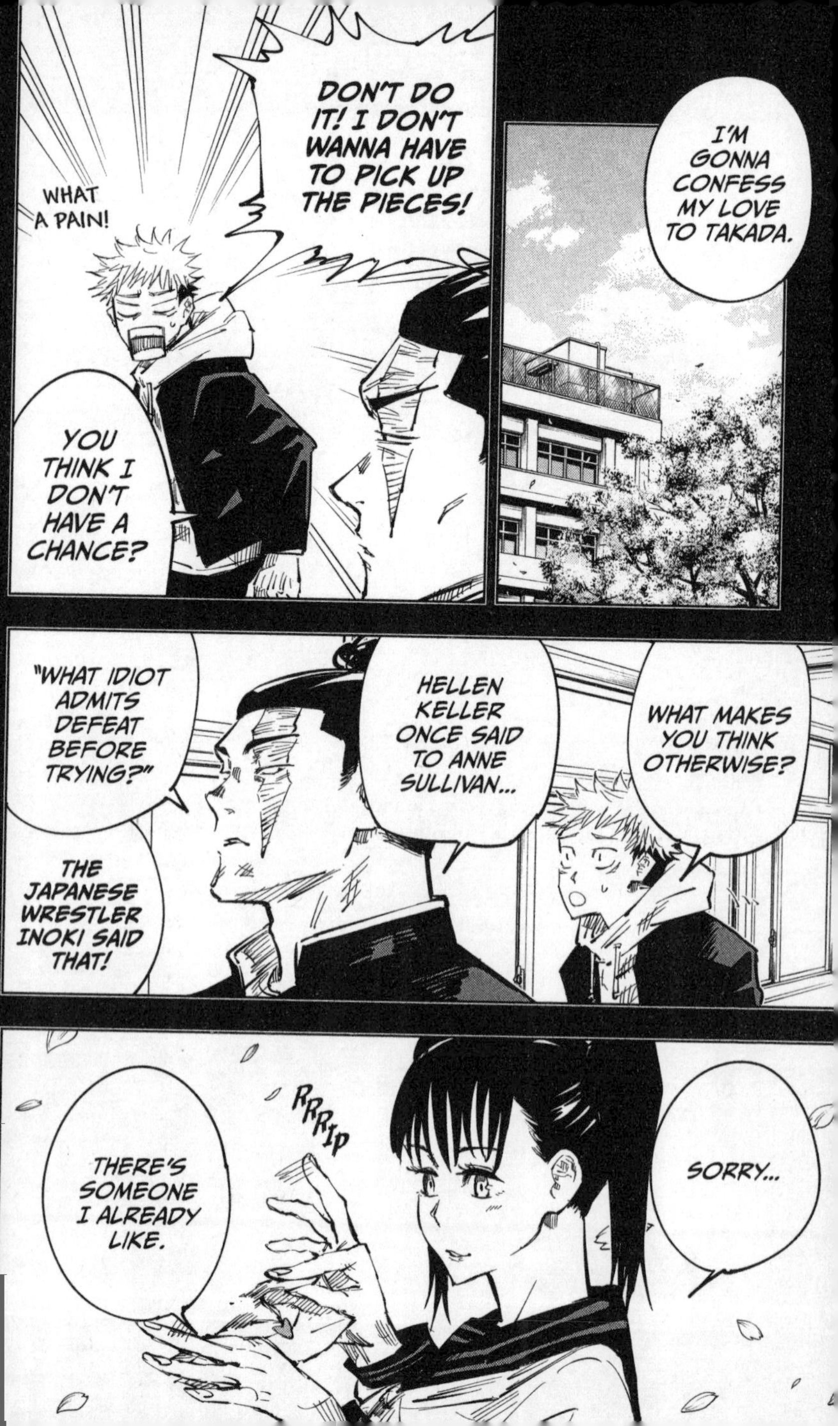
I'M GONNA CONFESS MY LOVE TO TAKADA.
DON'T DO IT! I DON'T WANNA HAVE TO PICK UP THE PIECES!
WHAT A PAIN!
YOU THINK I DON'T HAVE A CHANCE?
WHAT MAKES YOU THINK OTHERWISE?
HELLEN KELLER ONCE SAID TO ANNE SULLIVAN...
"WHAT IDIOT ADMITS DEFEAT BEFORE TRYING?"
THE JAPANESE WRESTLER INOKI SAID THAT!
SORRY...
RRRIP
THERE'S SOMEONE I ALREADY LIKE.

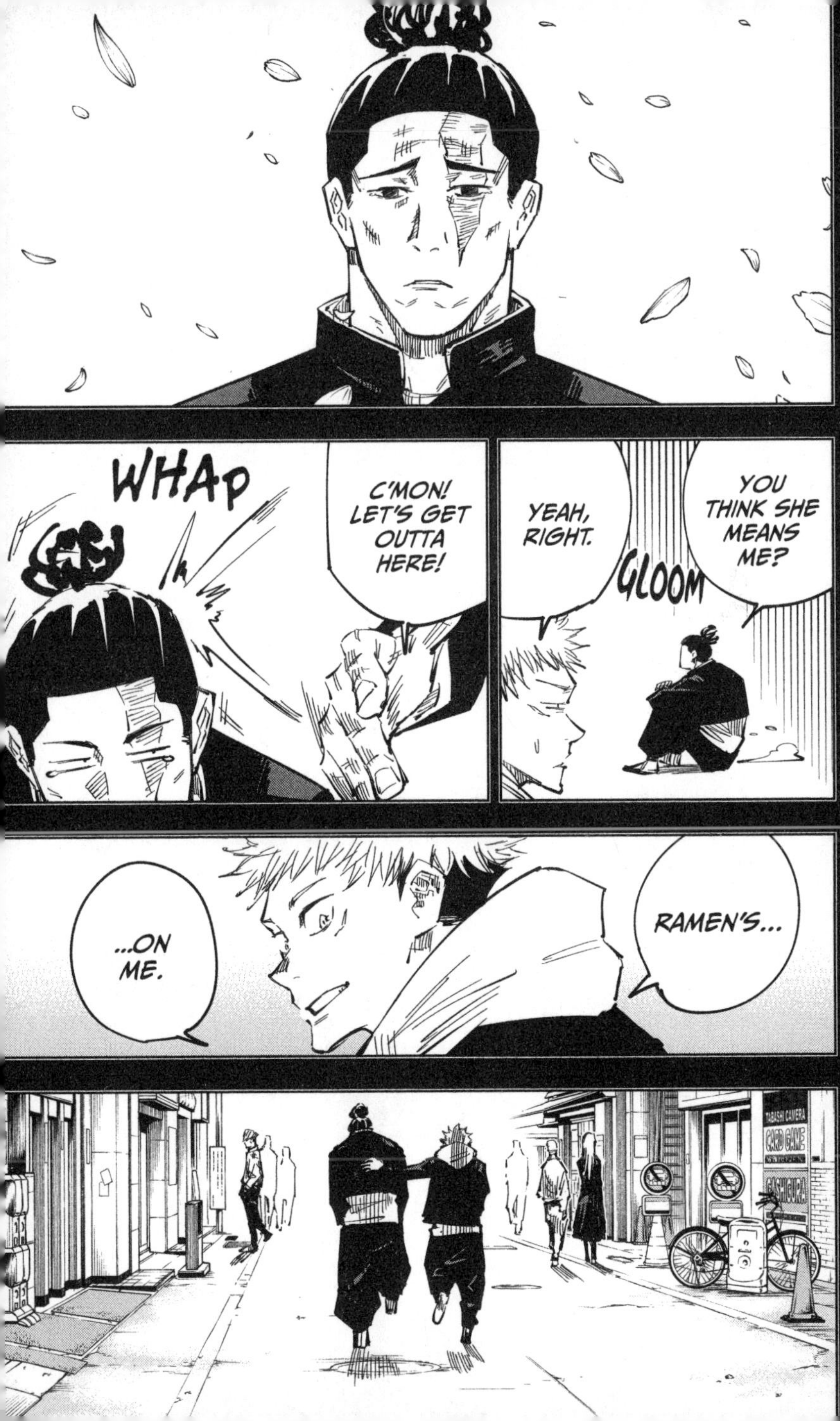
YOU THINK SHE MEANS ME?
GLOOM
YEAH, RIGHT.
C'MON! LET'S GET OUTTA HERE!
WHAP
RAMEN'S...
...ON ME.
CARD GAME

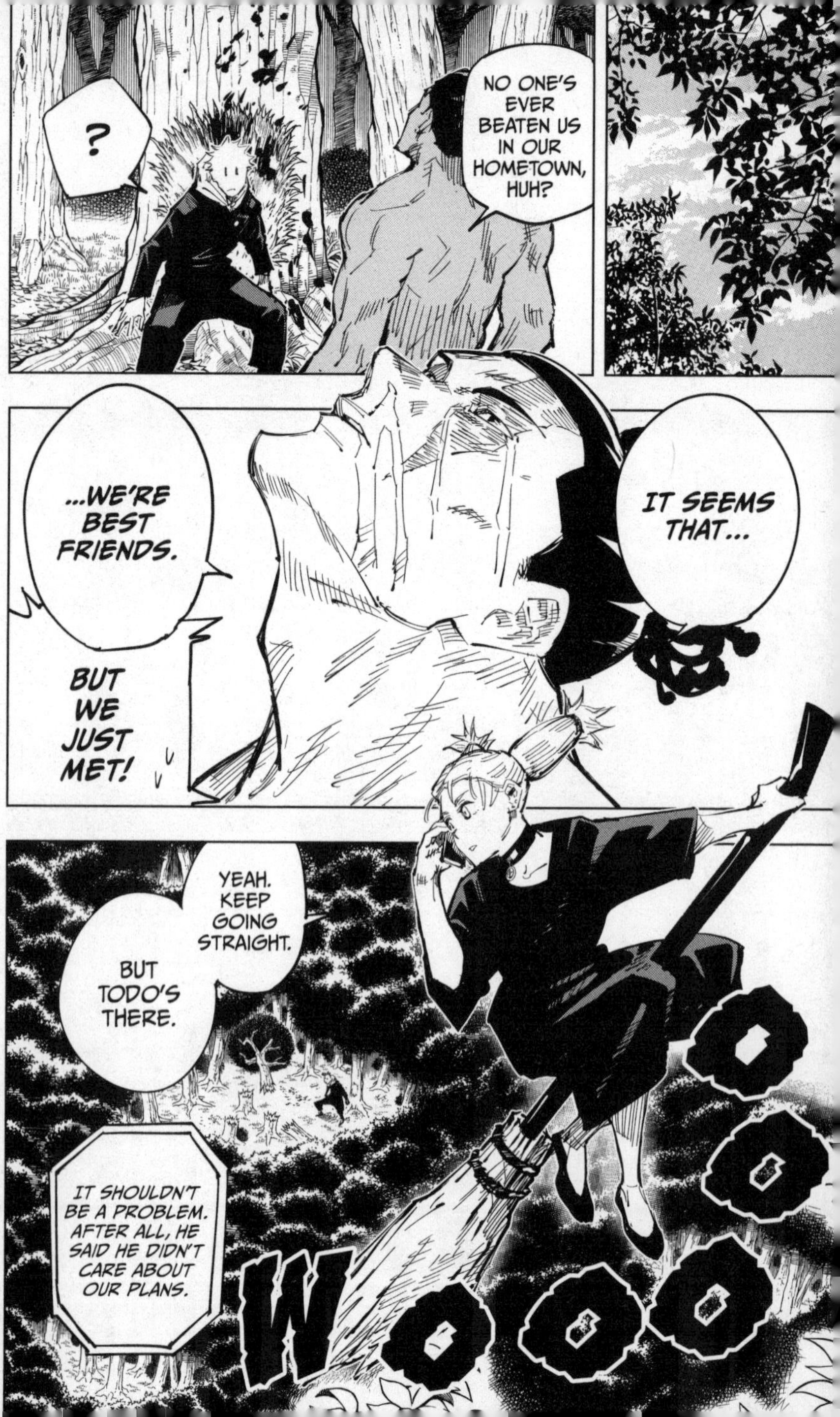
NO ONE'S EVER BEATEN US IN OUR HOMETOWN, HUH?
?
IT SEEMS THAT...
...WE'RE BEST FRIENDS.
BUT WE JUST MET!
YEAH. KEEP GOING STRAIGHT.
BUT TODO'S THERE.
IT SHOULDN'T BE A PROBLEM. AFTER ALL, HE SAID HE DIDN'T CARE ABOUT OUR PLANS.
WOOOOOO

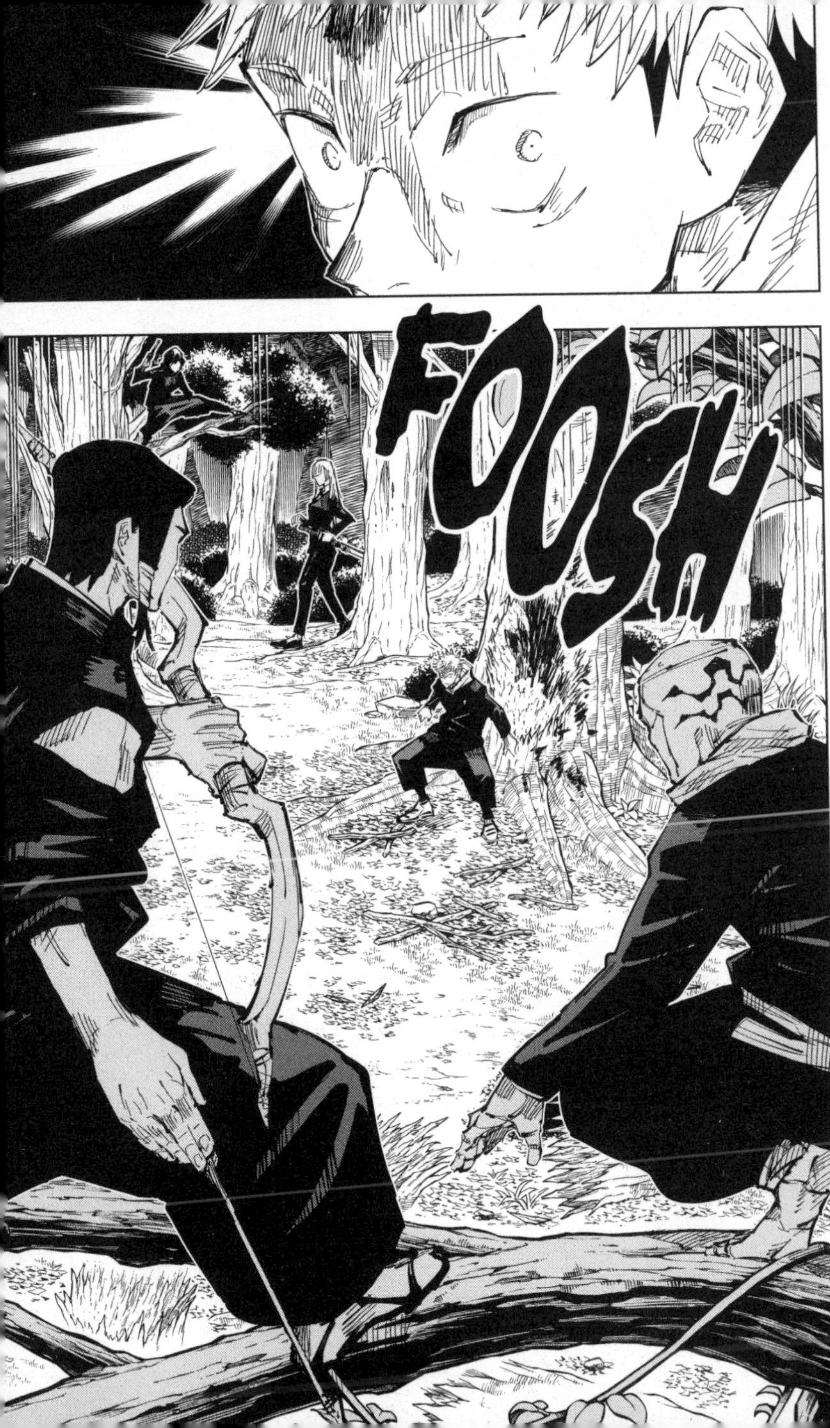
FOOSH

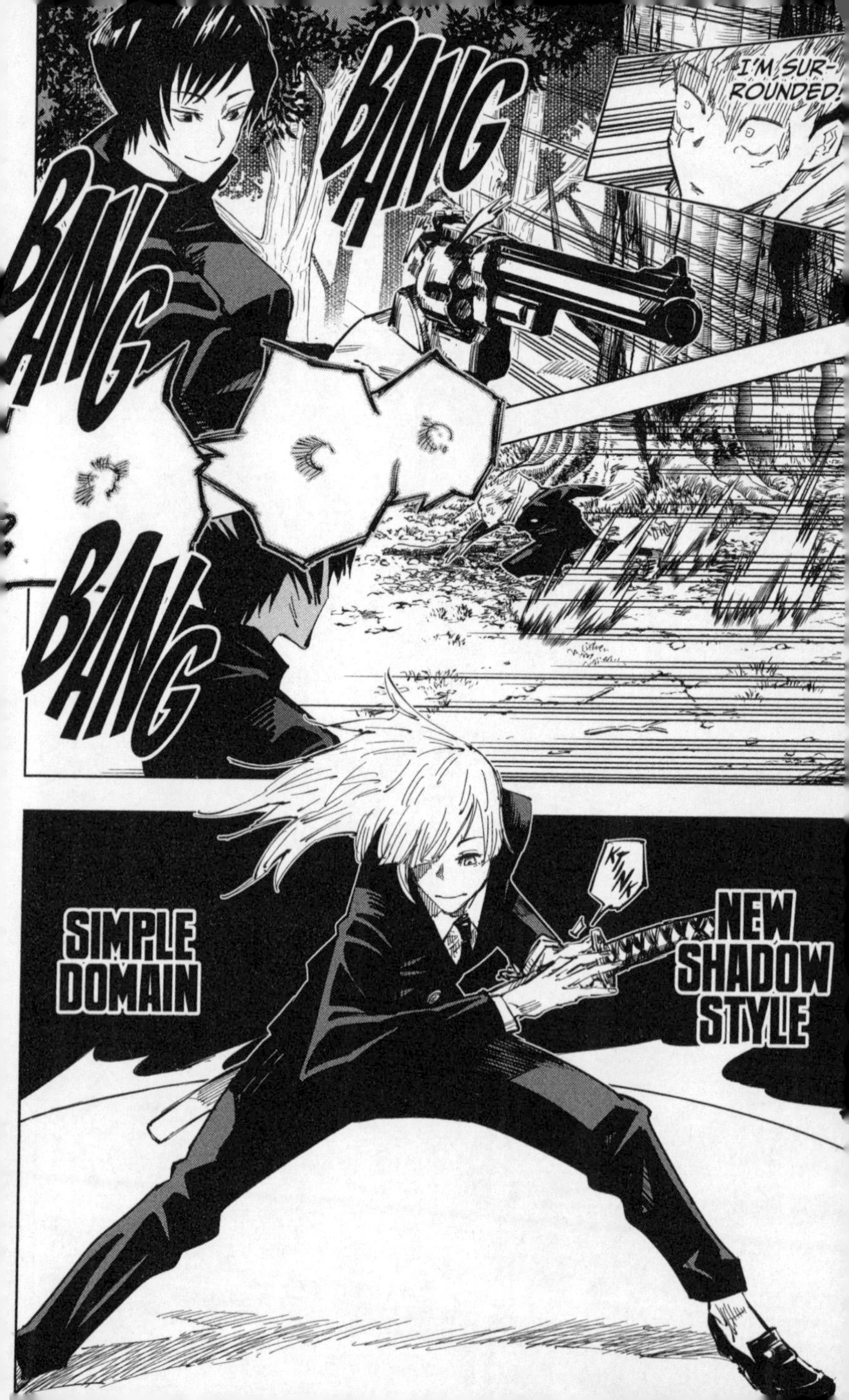

I'M SURROUNDED!
BANG
BANG
B-BANG
KTINK
NEW SHADOW STYLE
SIMPLE DOMAIN

SHF
BATTO SWORD DRAWING!
DUN
!!
WHAT QUICK REACTIONS! ALTHOUGH I DID HESITATE FOR A BIT, MY COUNTER DIDN'T EVEN TOUCH HIM!

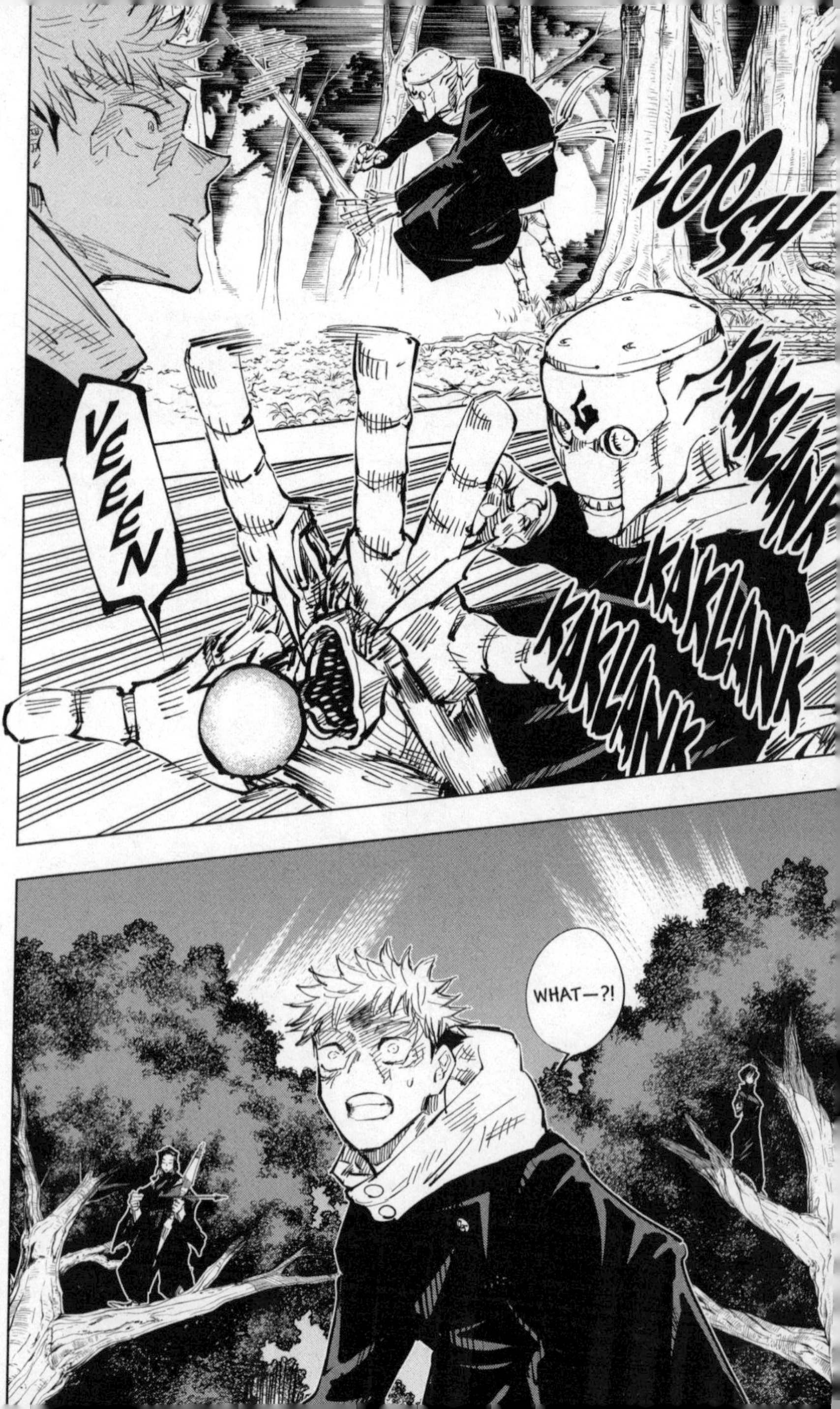
ZOOSH
KAKLANK
KAKLANK
KAKLANK
VEEEN
WHAT—?!

ARE THEY...

HUH?

...TRYING TO KILL ME?

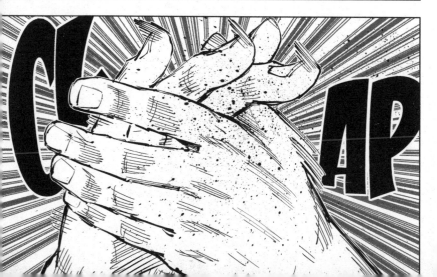

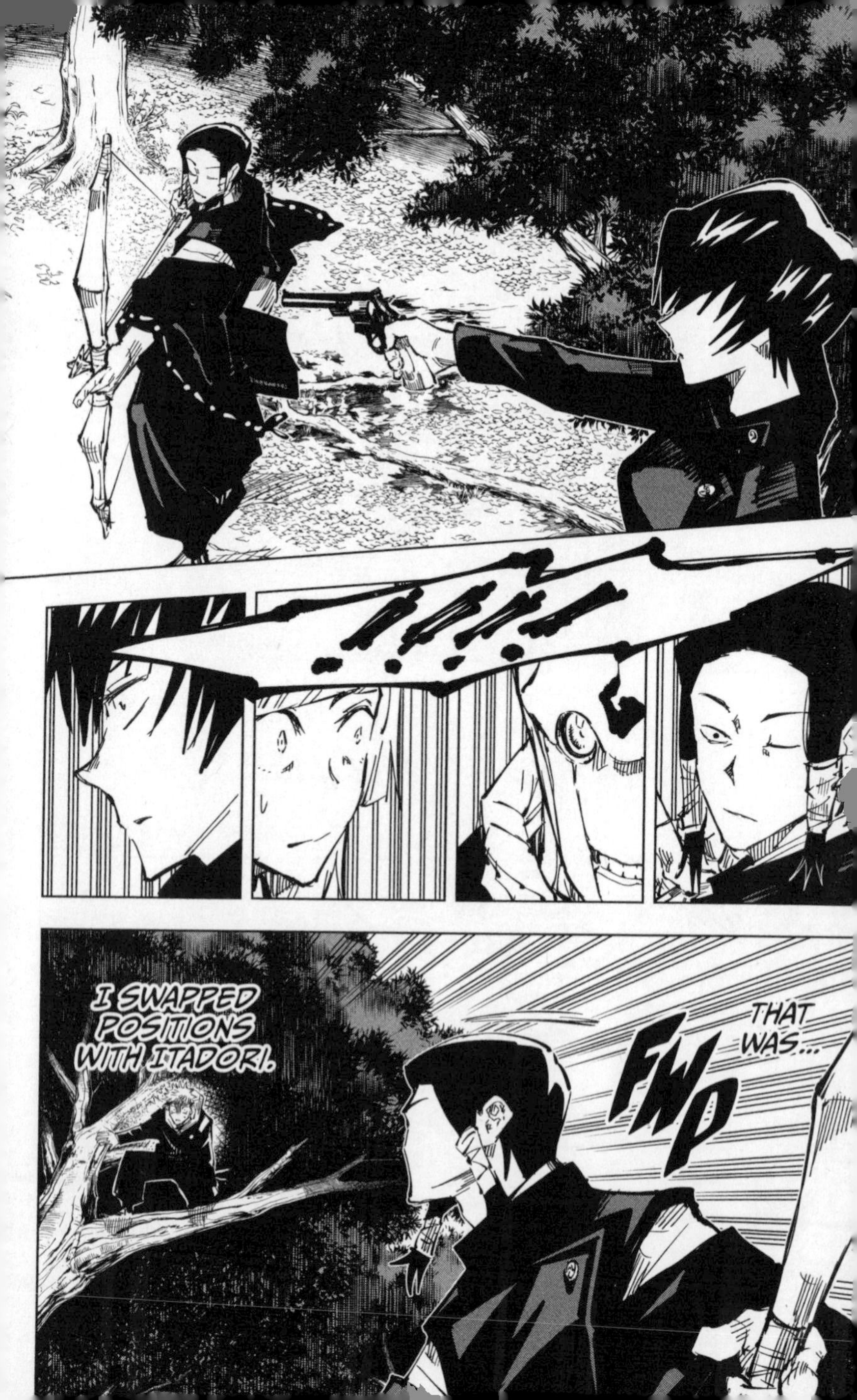
THAT WAS...
FWP
I SWAPPED POSITIONS WITH ITADORI.

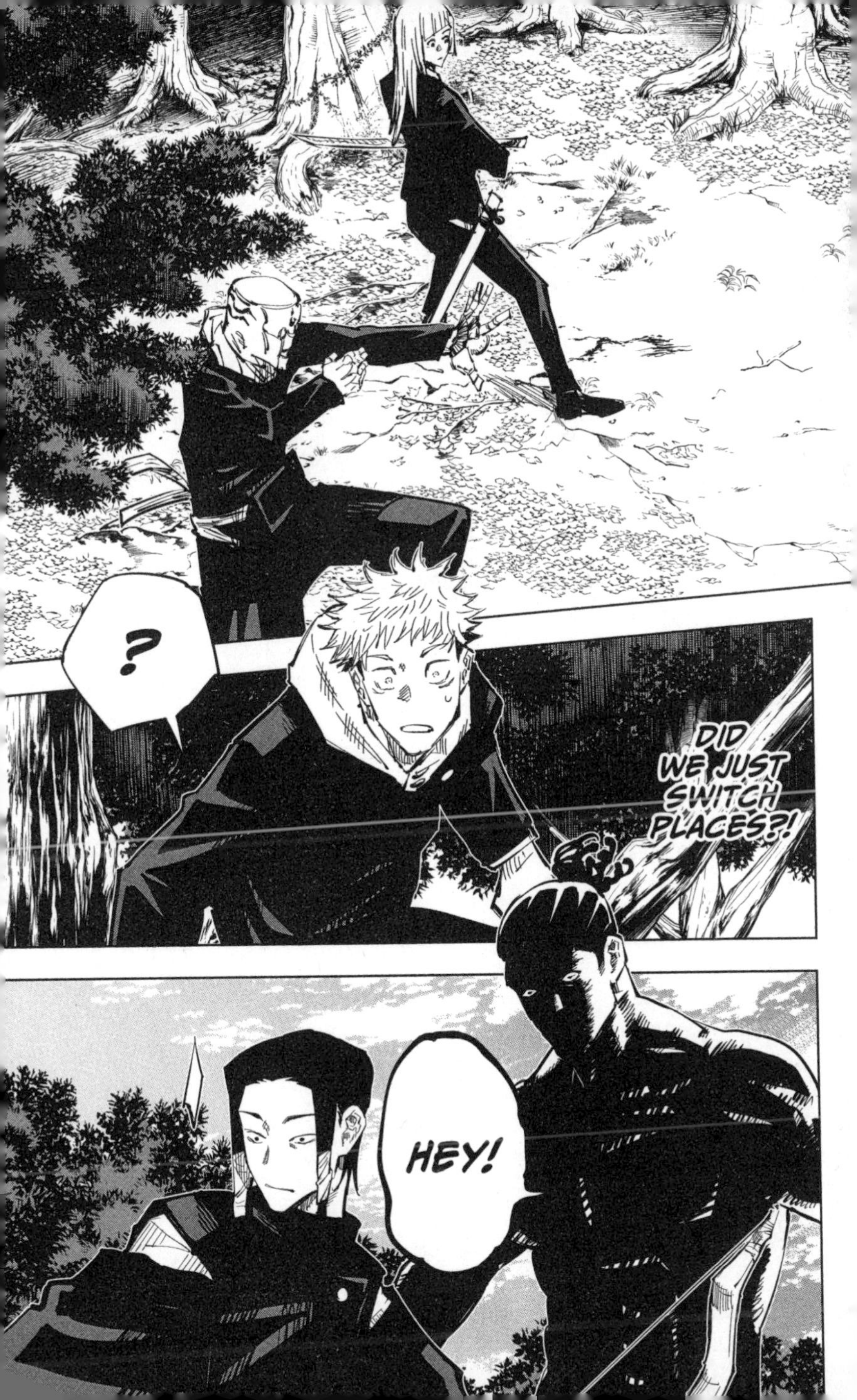
DID WE JUST SWITCH PLACES?!
?
HEY!

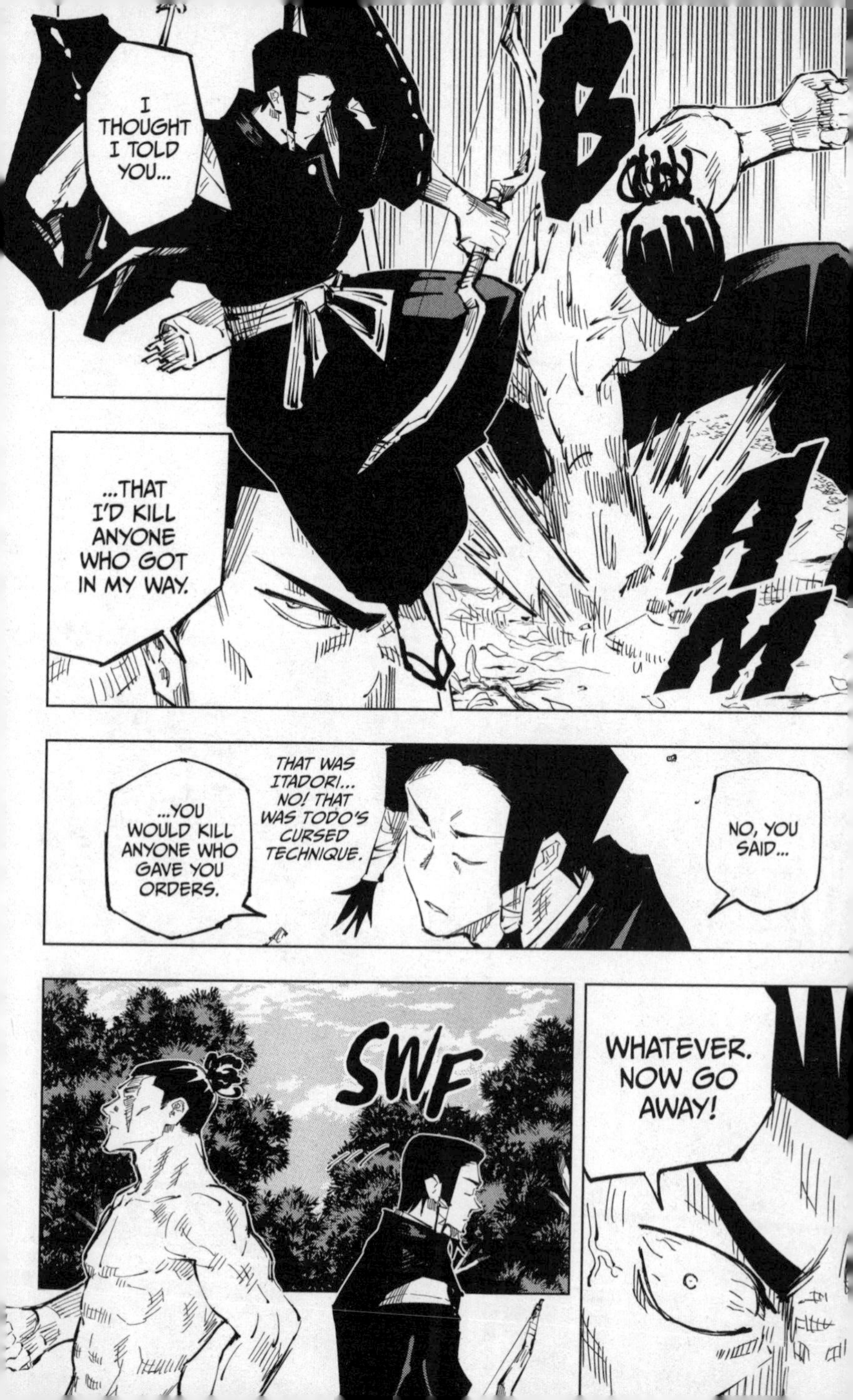
I THOUGHT I TOLD YOU...
BAM
...THAT I'D KILL ANYONE WHO GOT IN MY WAY.
NO, YOU SAID...
THAT WAS ITADORI... NO! THAT WAS TODO'S CURSED TECHNIQUE.
...YOU WOULD KILL ANYONE WHO GAVE YOU ORDERS.
WHATEVER. NOW GO AWAY!
SWF

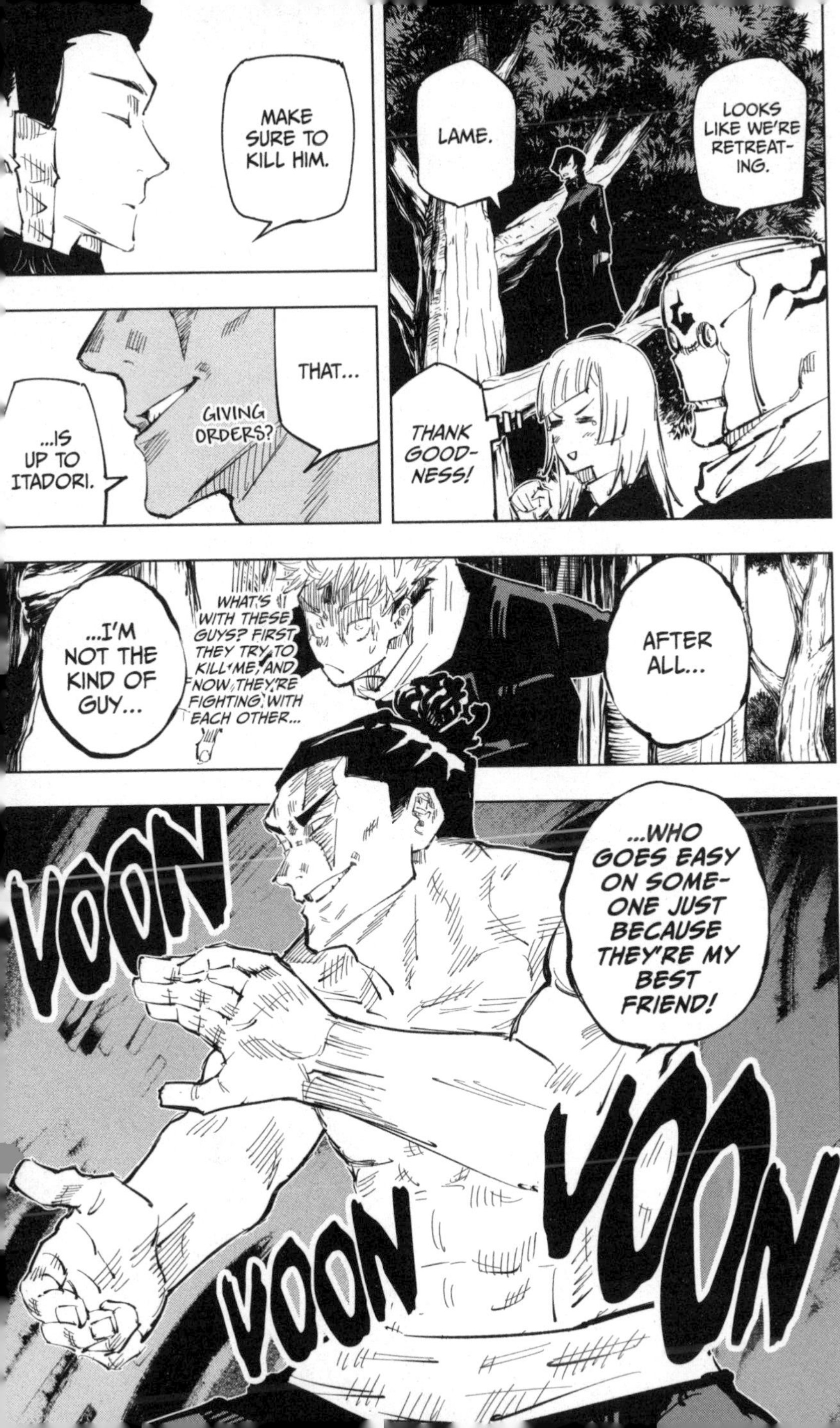
LOOKS LIKE WE'RE RETREATING.
LAME.
THANK GOODNESS!
MAKE SURE TO KILL HIM.
THAT...
GIVING ORDERS?
...IS UP TO ITADORI.
AFTER ALL...
WHAT'S WITH THESE GUYS? FIRST THEY TRY TO KILL ME, AND NOW THEY'RE FIGHTING WITH EACH OTHER...
...I'M NOT THE KIND OF GUY...
...WHO GOES EASY ON SOMEONE JUST BECAUSE THEY'RE MY BEST FRIEND!
VOON
VOON
VOON

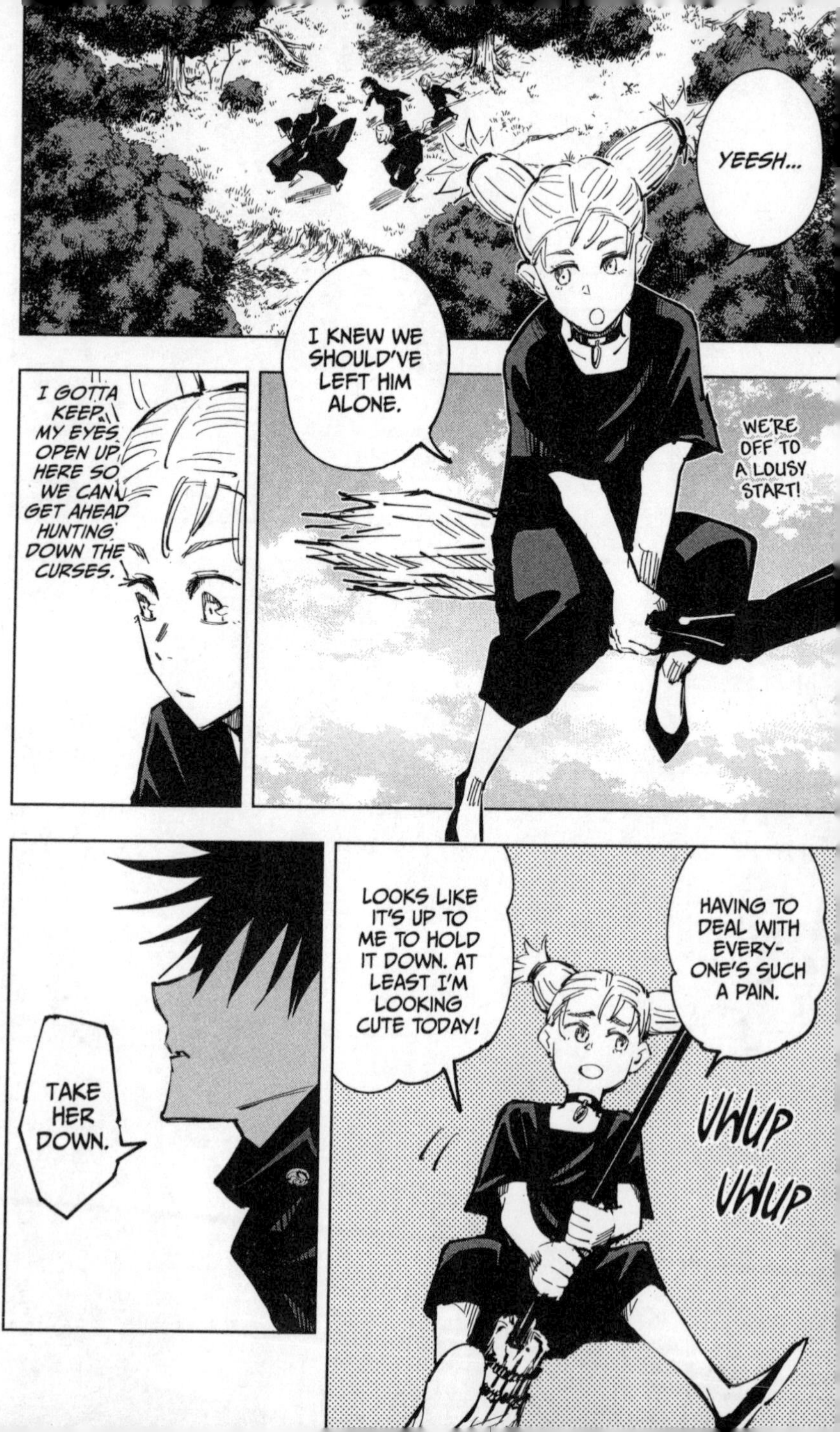
YEESH...
I KNEW WE SHOULD'VE LEFT HIM ALONE.
WE'RE OFF TO A LOUSY START!
I GOTTA KEEP MY EYES OPEN UP HERE SO WE CAN GET AHEAD HUNTING DOWN THE CURSES.
HAVING TO DEAL WITH EVERY-ONE'S SUCH A PAIN.
LOOKS LIKE IT'S UP TO ME TO HOLD IT DOWN. AT LEAST I'M LOOKING CUTE TODAY!
UWUP
UWUP
TAKE HER DOWN.

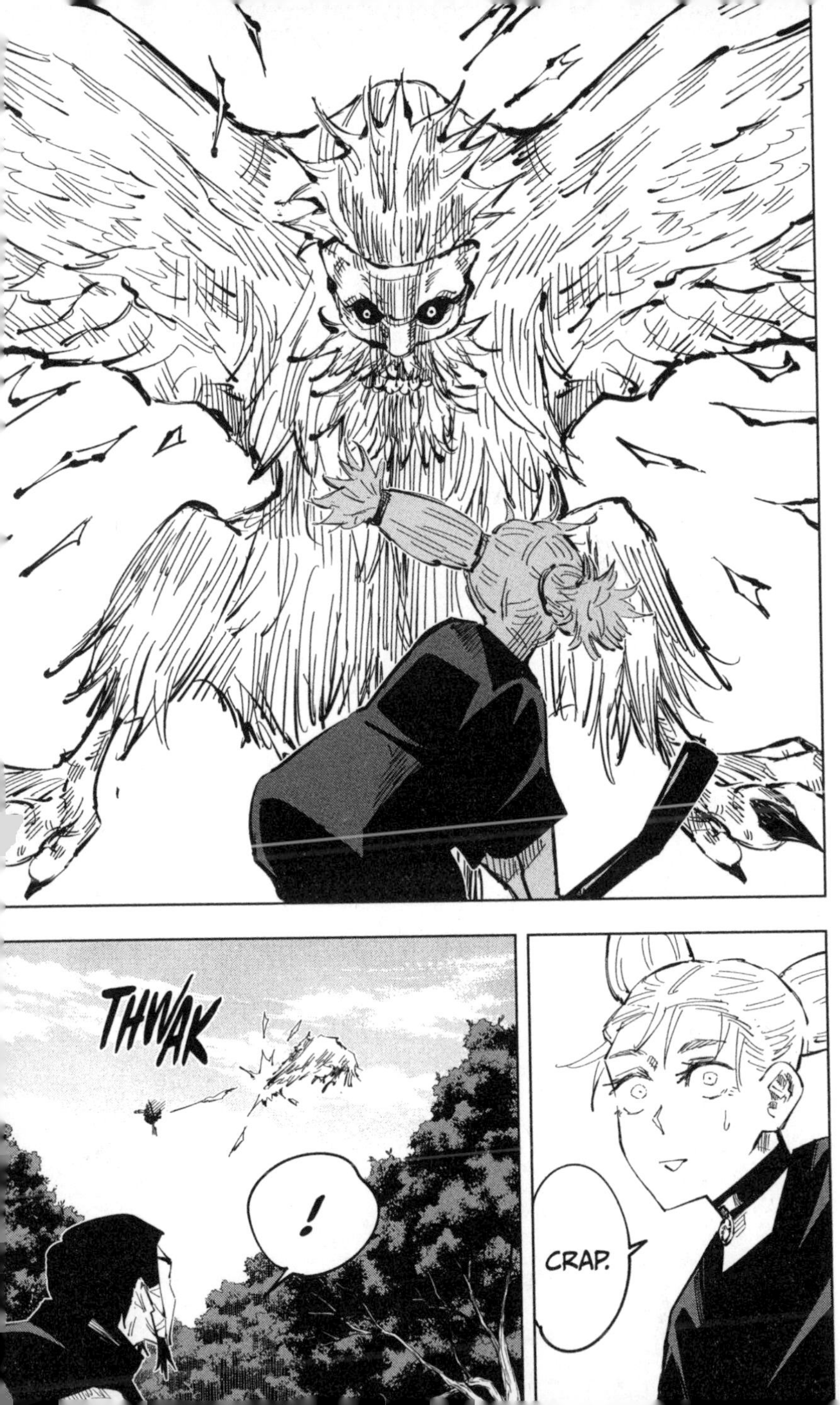
CRAP.
THWAK
!

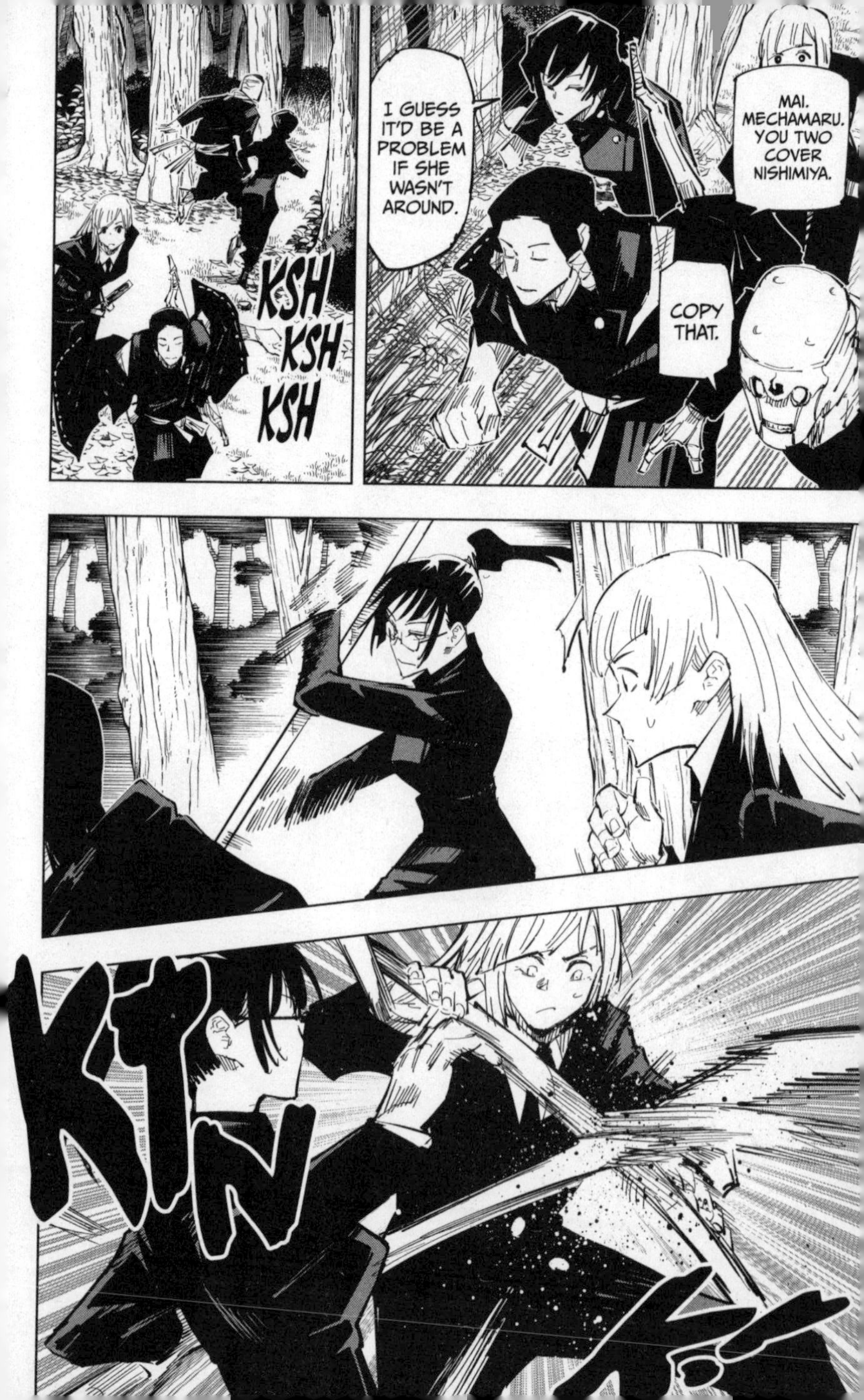
MAI. MECHAMARU. YOU TWO COVER NISHIMIYA.
I GUESS IT'D BE A PROBLEM IF SHE WASN'T AROUND.
COPY THAT.
KSH KSH KSH
KIN

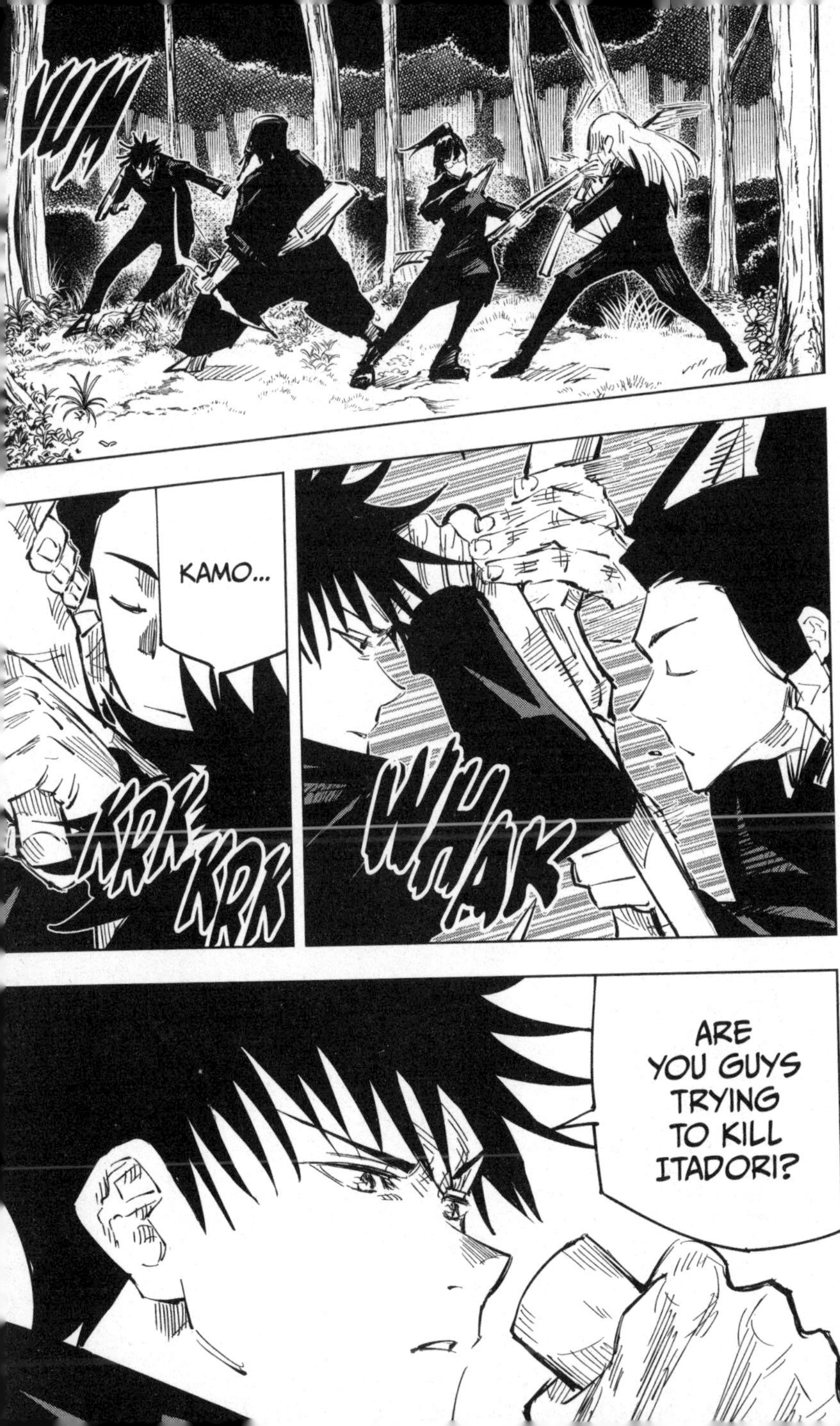
WHAK
KAMO...
KRK KRK
ARE YOU GUYS TRYING TO KILL ITADORI?

UTAHIME IORI
(31 YEARS OLD)

- The size of Utahime's ribbon changes according to Akutami Sensei's whim.

- Her hobbies inlcude watching sports and going to karaoke.

- She enjoys drinking alcohol (beer) and is friends with Ieiri, whom she wants to quit smoking.

- She hates Gojo most of the time.

AOI TODO

- Todo became a Grade 1 sorcerer as a student despite coming from a non-sorcerer family. He's like a highly skilled gorilla.

- Todo is meticulous about his appearance. He makes sure he's well groomed and has deodorant. He showered before the meet-and-greet event in volume 2. Todo always smells nice, which infuriarates the girls at the Kyoto school.

- He wants to marry Takada right now, so he's not a fan of the rule that bar idols from dating.

- Todo is about the same height as Gojo.

Chapter 36: Kyoto Sister-School Goodwill Event–Team Battle, Part 3

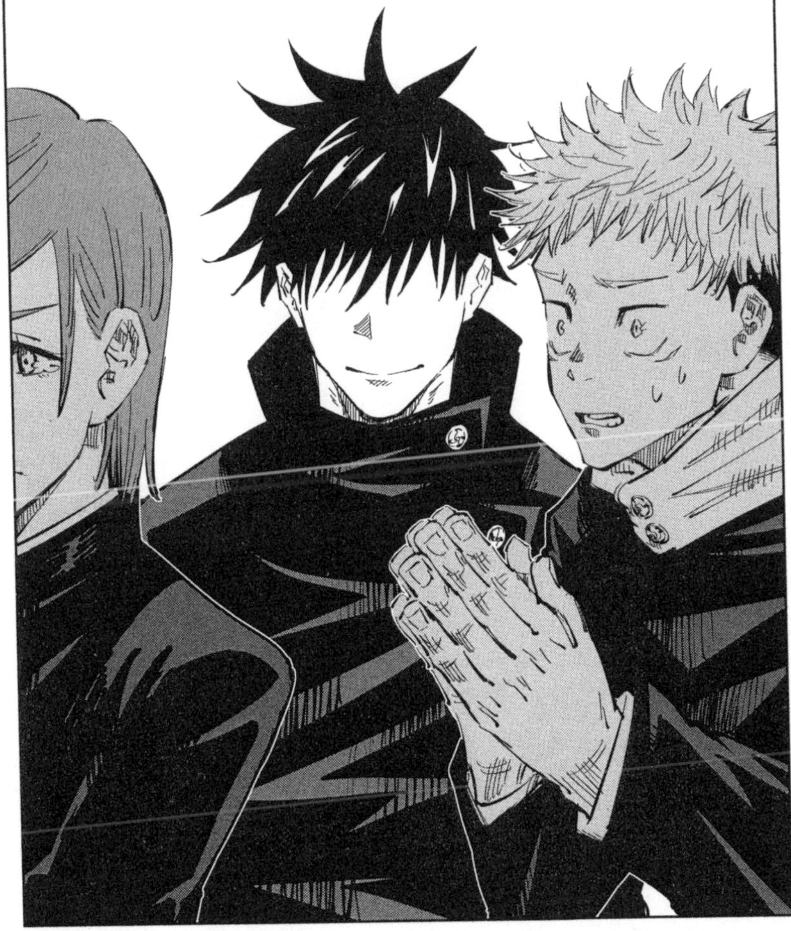

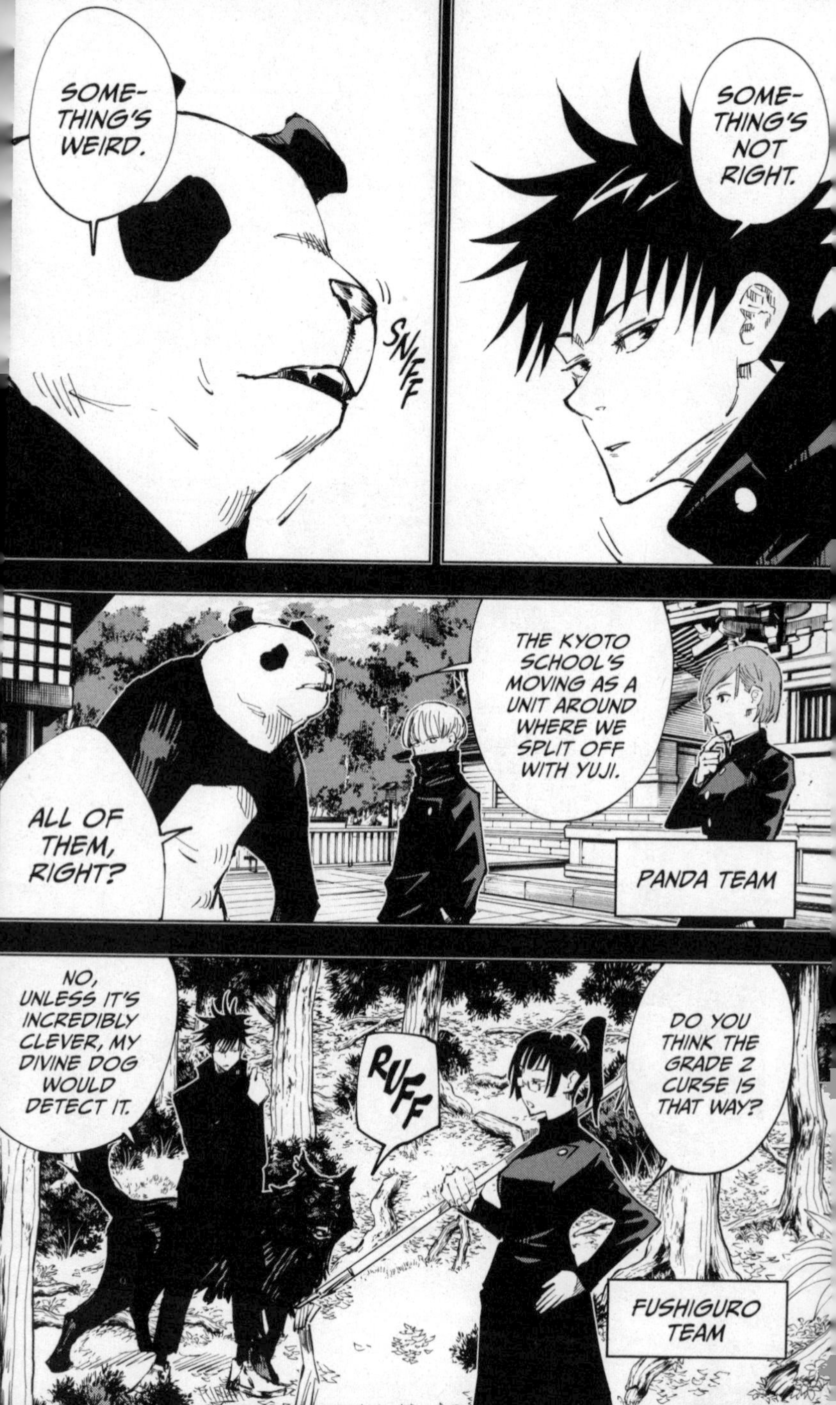
SOME-THING'S NOT RIGHT.
SOME-THING'S WEIRD.
SNIFF
THE KYOTO SCHOOL'S MOVING AS A UNIT AROUND WHERE WE SPLIT OFF WITH YUJI.
PANDA TEAM
ALL OF THEM, RIGHT?
DO YOU THINK THE GRADE 2 CURSE IS THAT WAY?
FUSHIGURO TEAM
RUFF
NO, UNLESS IT'S INCREDIBLY CLEVER, MY DIVINE DOG WOULD DETECT IT.

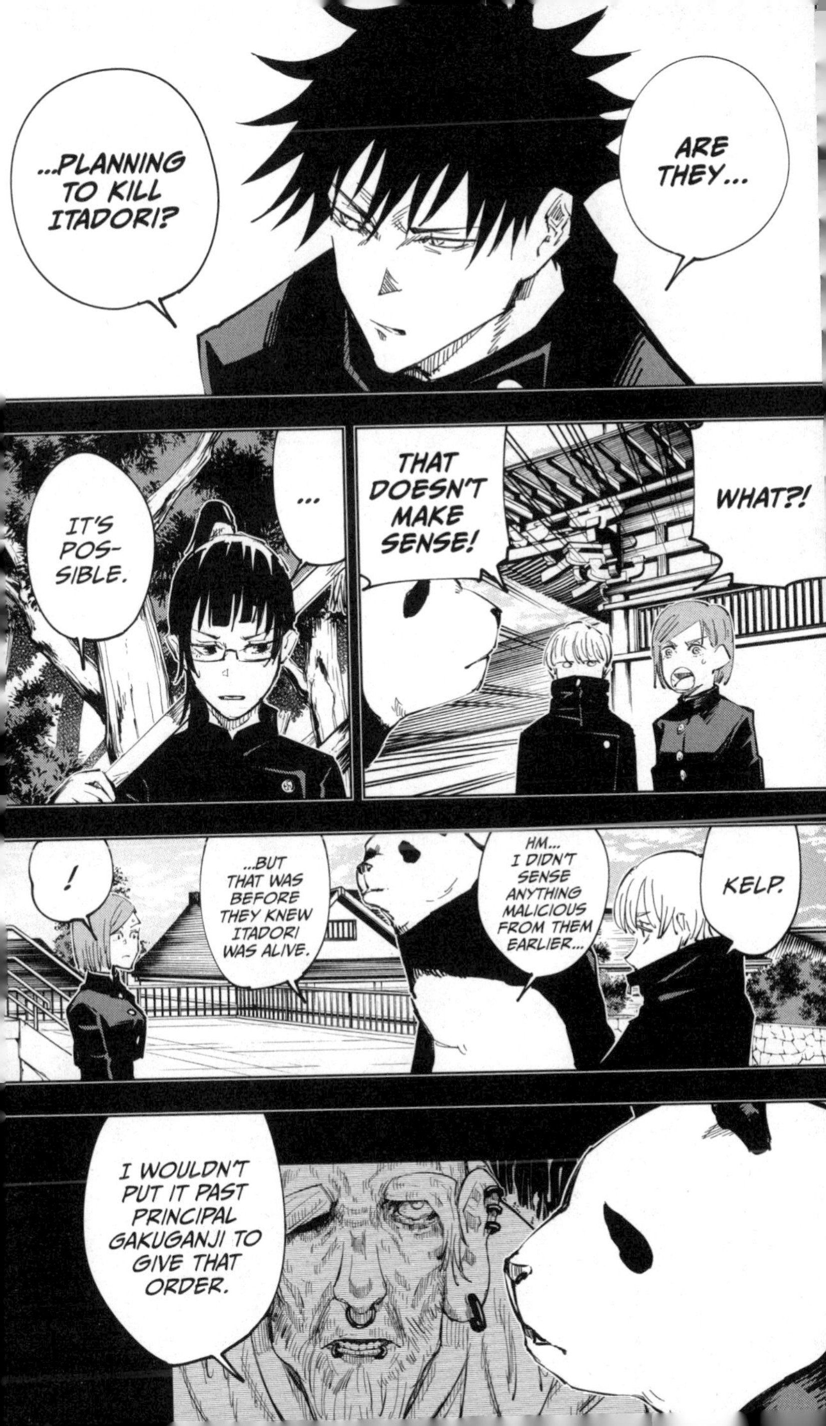
ARE THEY...
...PLANNING TO KILL ITADORI?
WHAT?!
THAT DOESN'T MAKE SENSE!
...
IT'S POS-SIBLE.
KELP.
HM... I DIDN'T SENSE ANYTHING MALICIOUS FROM THEM EARLIER...
...BUT THAT WAS BEFORE THEY KNEW ITADORI WAS ALIVE.
!
I WOULDN'T PUT IT PAST PRINCIPAL GAKUGANJI TO GIVE THAT ORDER.

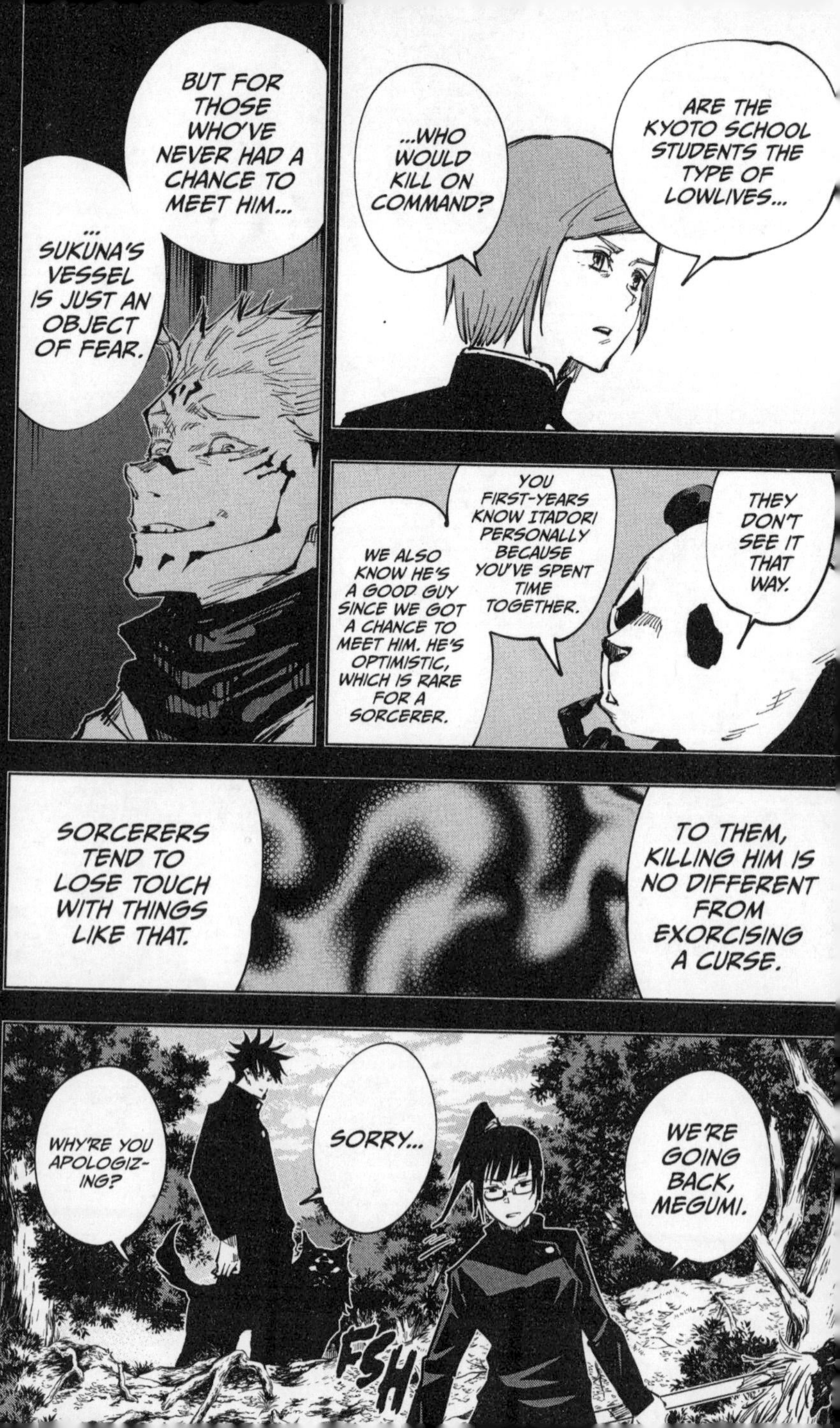
ARE THE KYOTO SCHOOL STUDENTS THE TYPE OF LOWLIVES...
...WHO WOULD KILL ON COMMAND?
THEY DON'T SEE IT THAT WAY.
YOU FIRST-YEARS KNOW ITADORI PERSONALLY BECAUSE YOU'VE SPENT TIME TOGETHER.
WE ALSO KNOW HE'S A GOOD GUY SINCE WE GOT A CHANCE TO MEET HIM. HE'S OPTIMISTIC, WHICH IS RARE FOR A SORCERER.
BUT FOR THOSE WHO'VE NEVER HAD A CHANCE TO MEET HIM...
... SUKUNA'S VESSEL IS JUST AN OBJECT OF FEAR.
TO THEM, KILLING HIM IS NO DIFFERENT FROM EXORCISING A CURSE.
SORCERERS TEND TO LOSE TOUCH WITH THINGS LIKE THAT.
WE'RE GOING BACK, MEGUMI.
SORRY...
WHY'RE YOU APOLOGIZING?
FSH

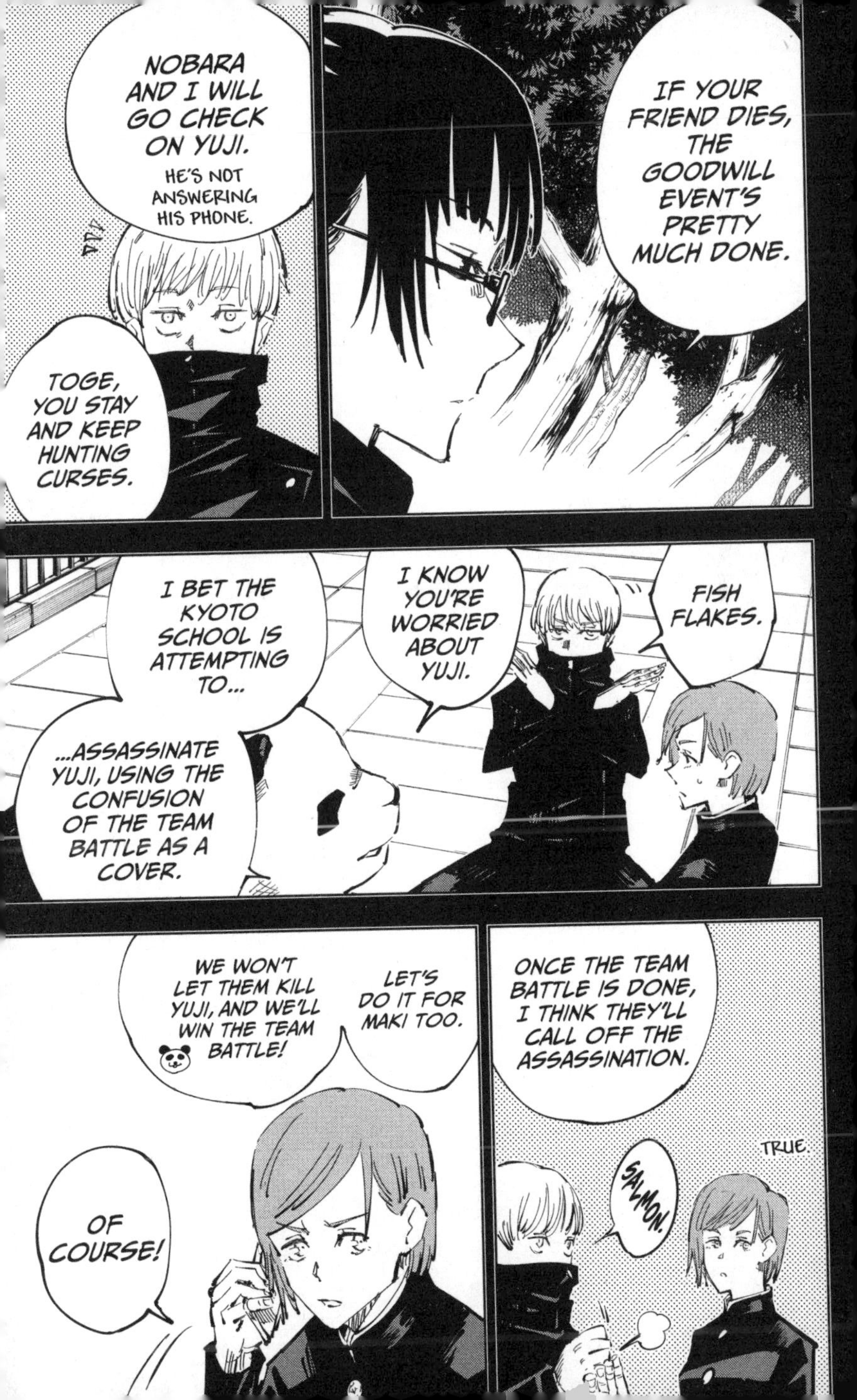
IF YOUR FRIEND DIES, THE GOODWILL EVENT'S PRETTY MUCH DONE.
NOBARA AND I WILL GO CHECK ON YUJI.
HE'S NOT ANSWERING HIS PHONE.
TOGE, YOU STAY AND KEEP HUNTING CURSES.
FISH FLAKES.
I KNOW YOU'RE WORRIED ABOUT YUJI.
I BET THE KYOTO SCHOOL IS ATTEMPTING TO...
...ASSASSINATE YUJI, USING THE CONFUSION OF THE TEAM BATTLE AS A COVER.
ONCE THE TEAM BATTLE IS DONE, I THINK THEY'LL CALL OFF THE ASSASSINATION.
TRUE.
SALMON.
LET'S DO IT FOR MAKI TOO.
WE WON'T LET THEM KILL YUJI, AND WE'LL WIN THE TEAM BATTLE!
OF COURSE!

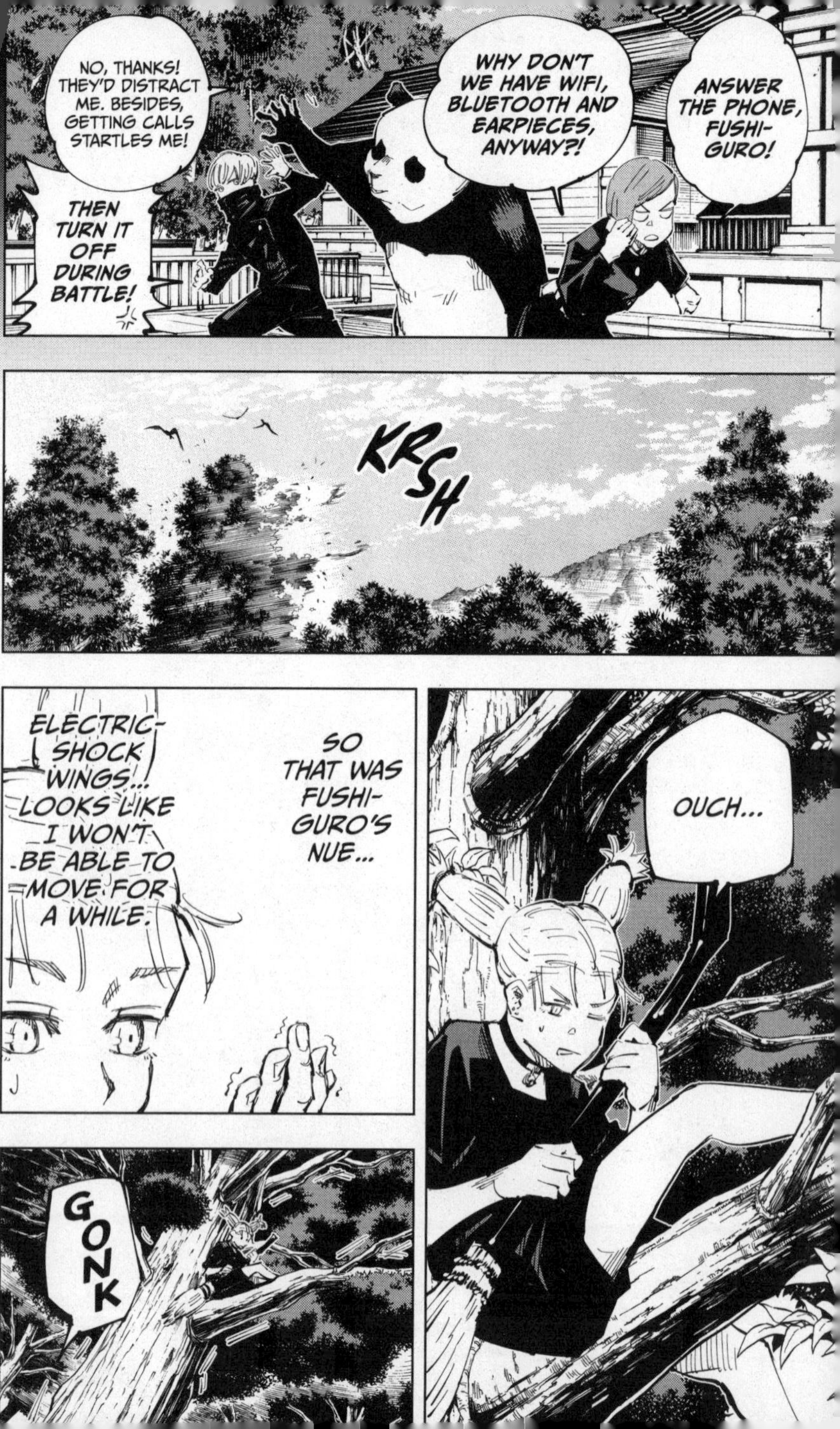
ANSWER THE PHONE, FUSHI-GURO!
WHY DON'T WE HAVE WIFI, BLUETOOTH AND EARPIECES, ANYWAY?!
NO, THANKS! THEY'D DISTRACT ME. BESIDES, GETTING CALLS STARTLES ME!
THEN TURN IT OFF DURING BATTLE!
KRSH
OUCH...
SO THAT WAS FUSHI-GURO'S NUE...
ELECTRIC-SHOCK WINGS... LOOKS LIKE I WON'T BE ABLE TO MOVE FOR A WHILE.
GONK

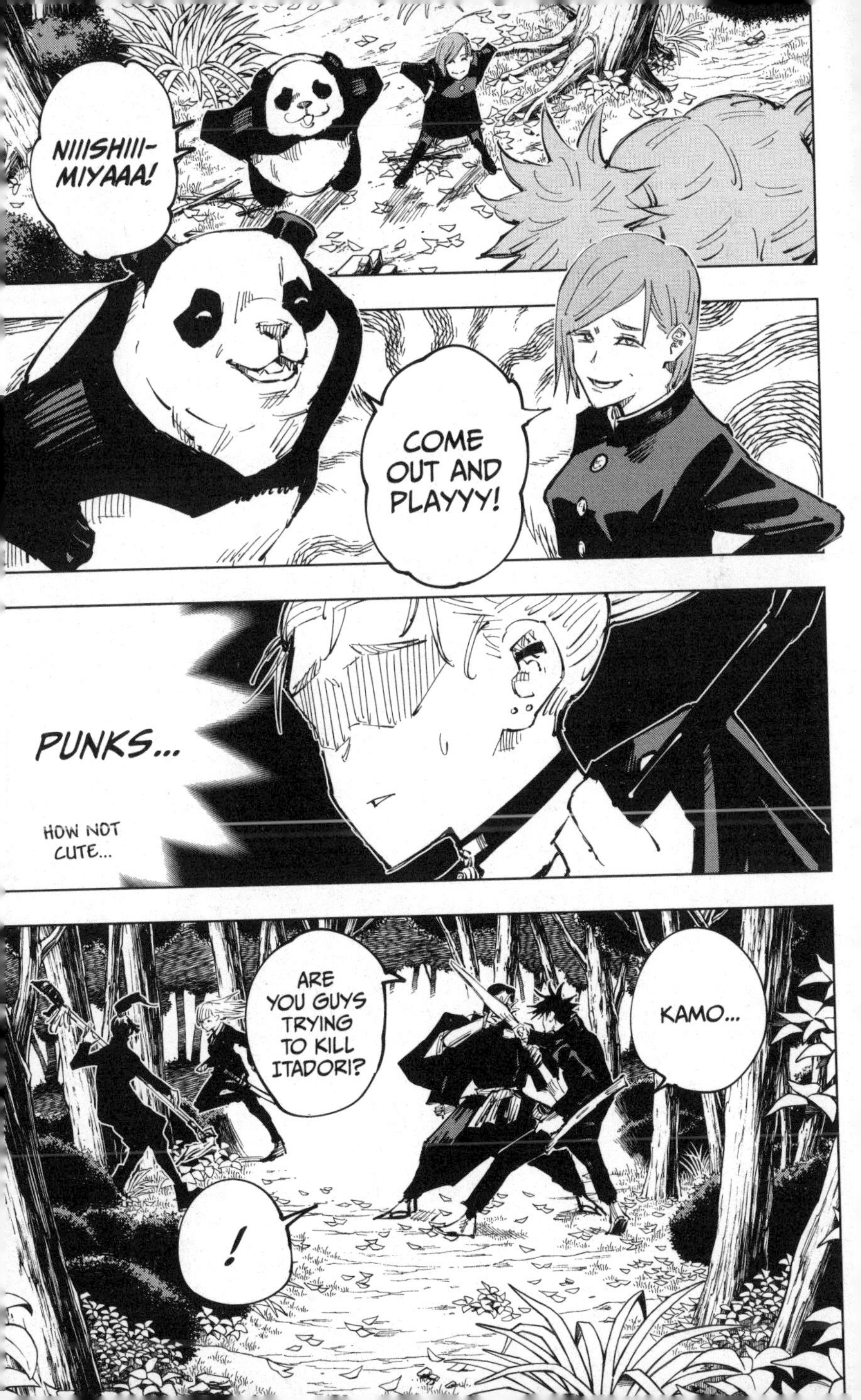
NIIISHIII-MIYAAA!
COME OUT AND PLAYYY!
PUNKS...
HOW NOT CUTE...
KAMO...
ARE YOU GUYS TRYING TO KILL ITADORI?
!

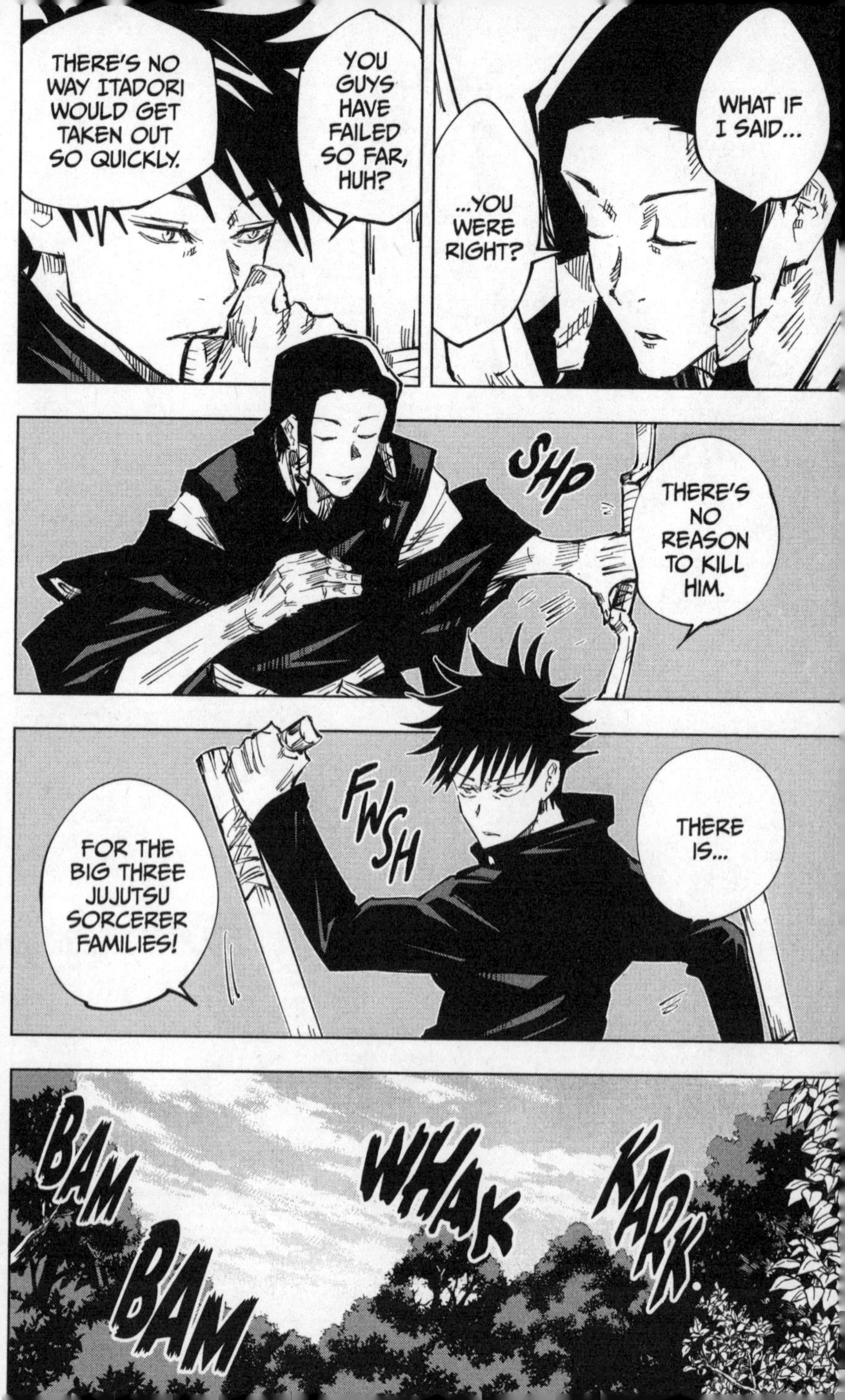
WHAT IF I SAID...
...YOU WERE RIGHT?
YOU GUYS HAVE FAILED SO FAR, HUH?
THERE'S NO WAY ITADORI WOULD GET TAKEN OUT SO QUICKLY.
THERE'S NO REASON TO KILL HIM.
SHP
THERE IS...
FWSH
FOR THE BIG THREE JUJUTSU SORCERER FAMILIES!
KARK.
WHAK
BAM
BAM

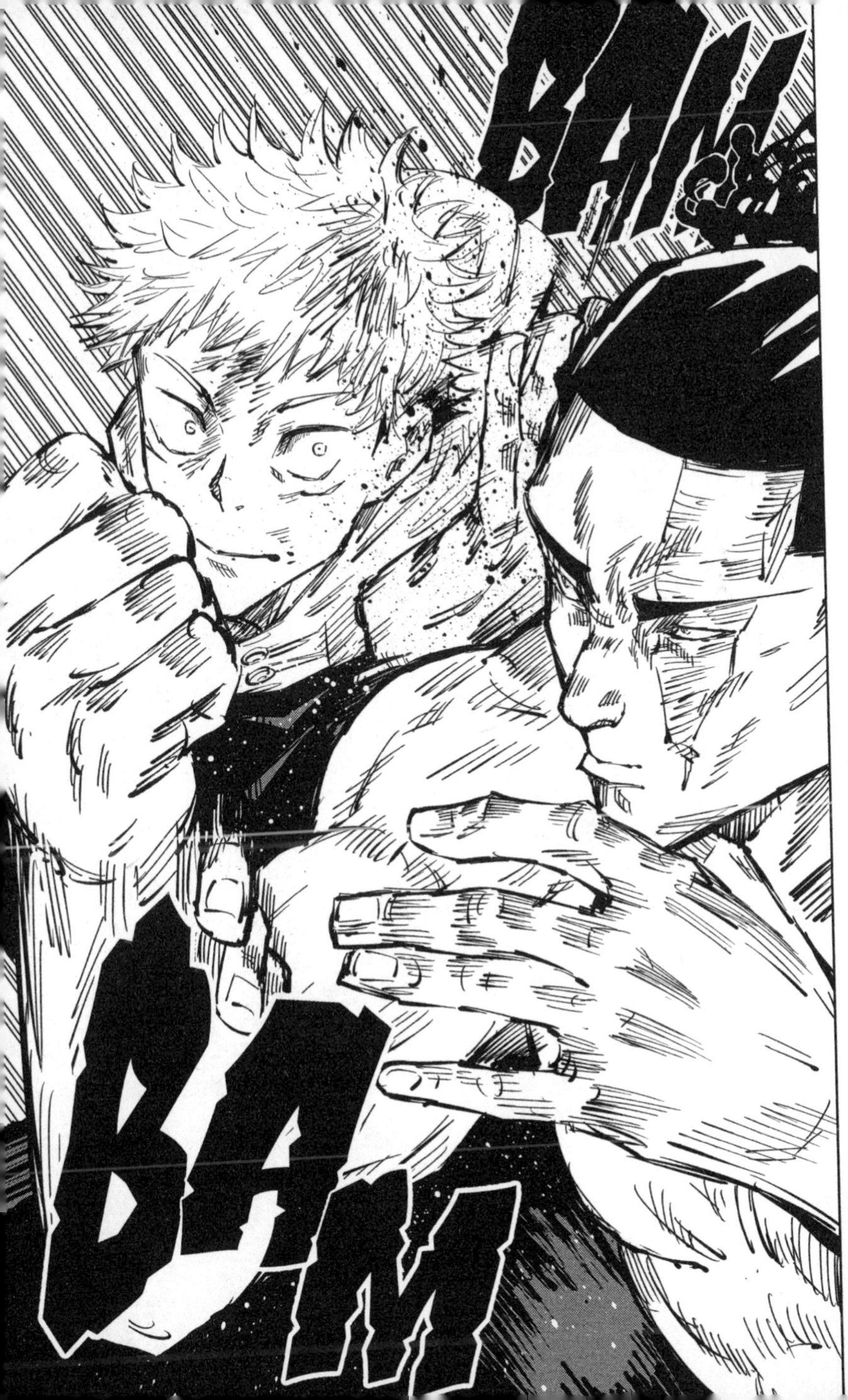
BAM
BAM

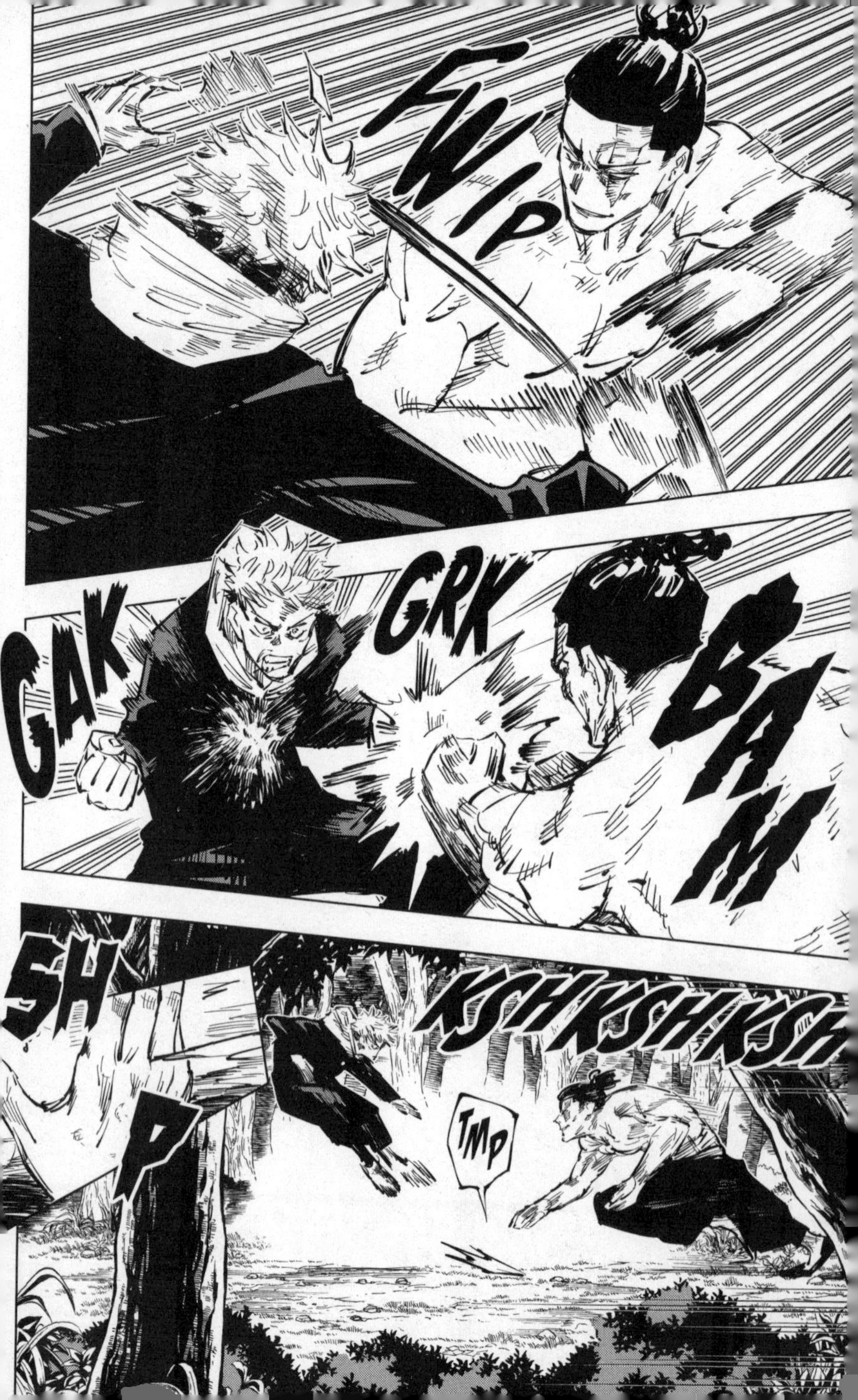
FWIP
BAM
GRK
GAK
KSHKSHKSH
TMP
SHP

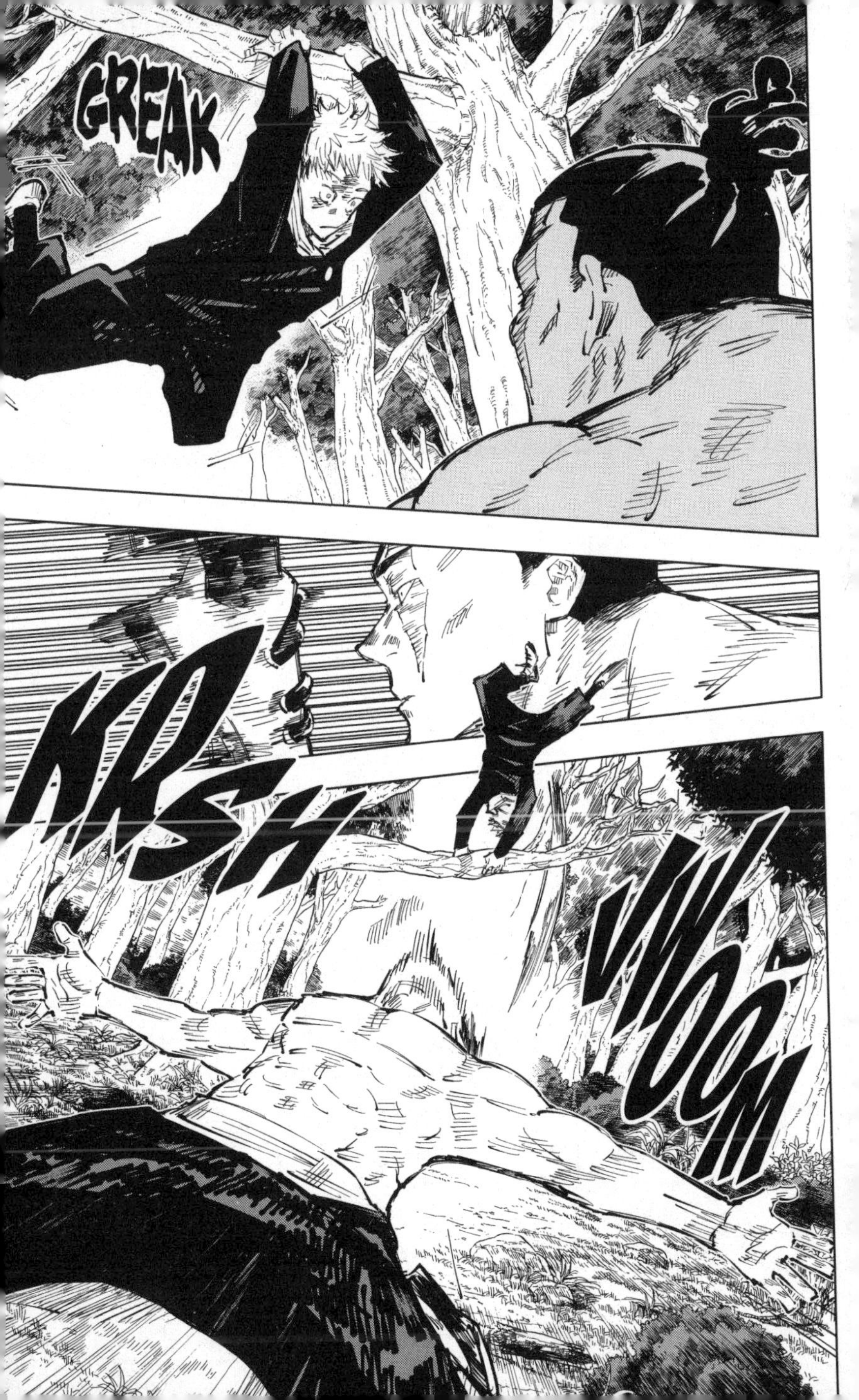
GREAK
KRSH
VWOOM

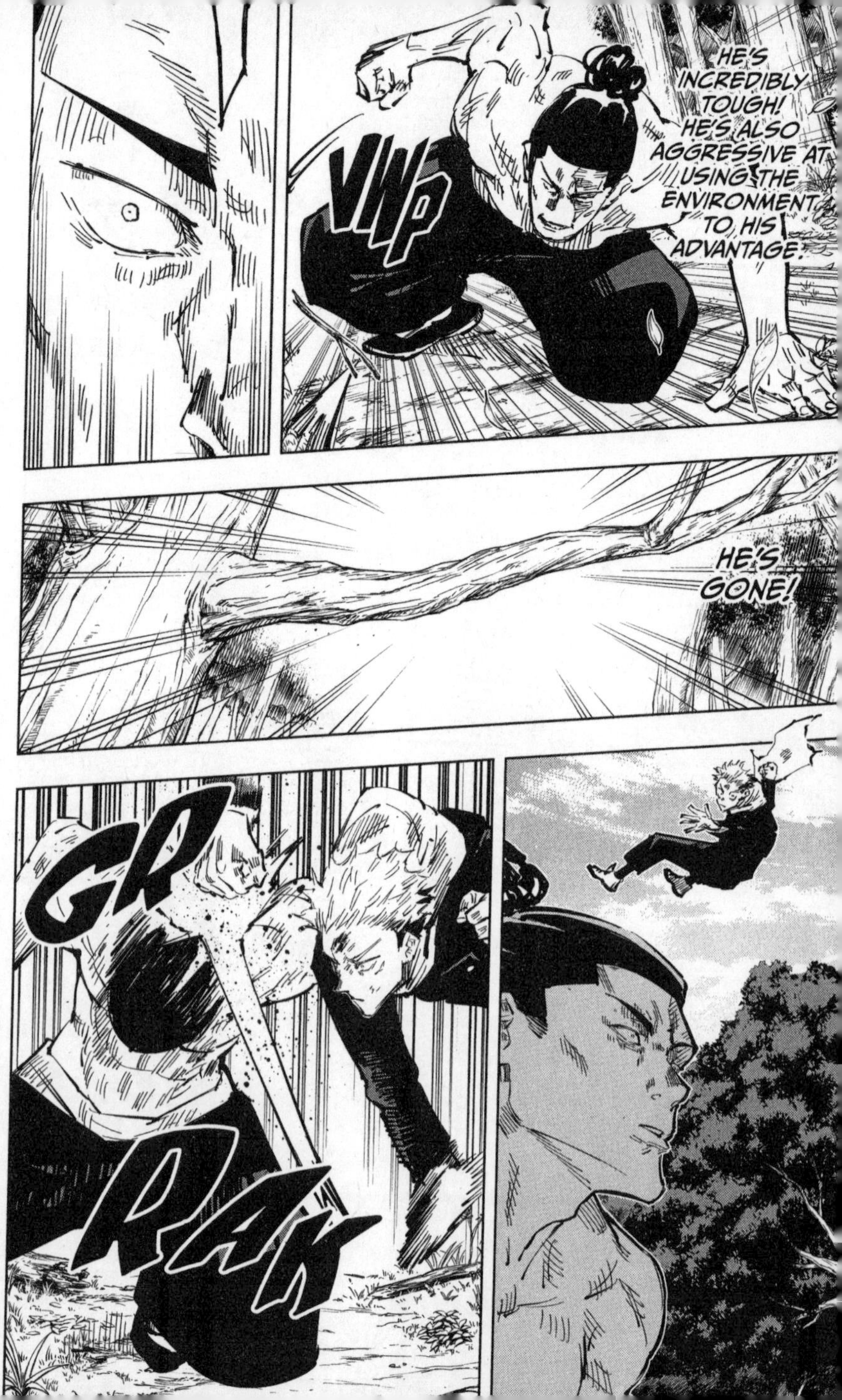
HE'S INCREDIBLY TOUGH! HE'S ALSO AGGRESSIVE AT USING THE ENVIRONMENT TO HIS ADVANTAGE.
VWP
HE'S GONE!
GR
RAK

HE'S ABLE TO THINK A STEP AHEAD!!

BLIND SPOT ①

BLIND SPOT ②

AND TO TOP IT ALL OFF...

FWAK

FWAK FWAK FWAK

FWAK

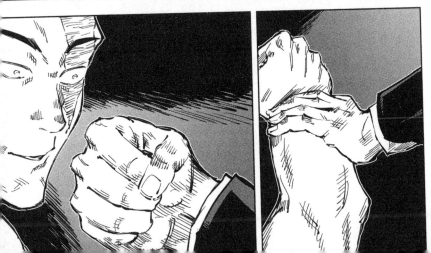

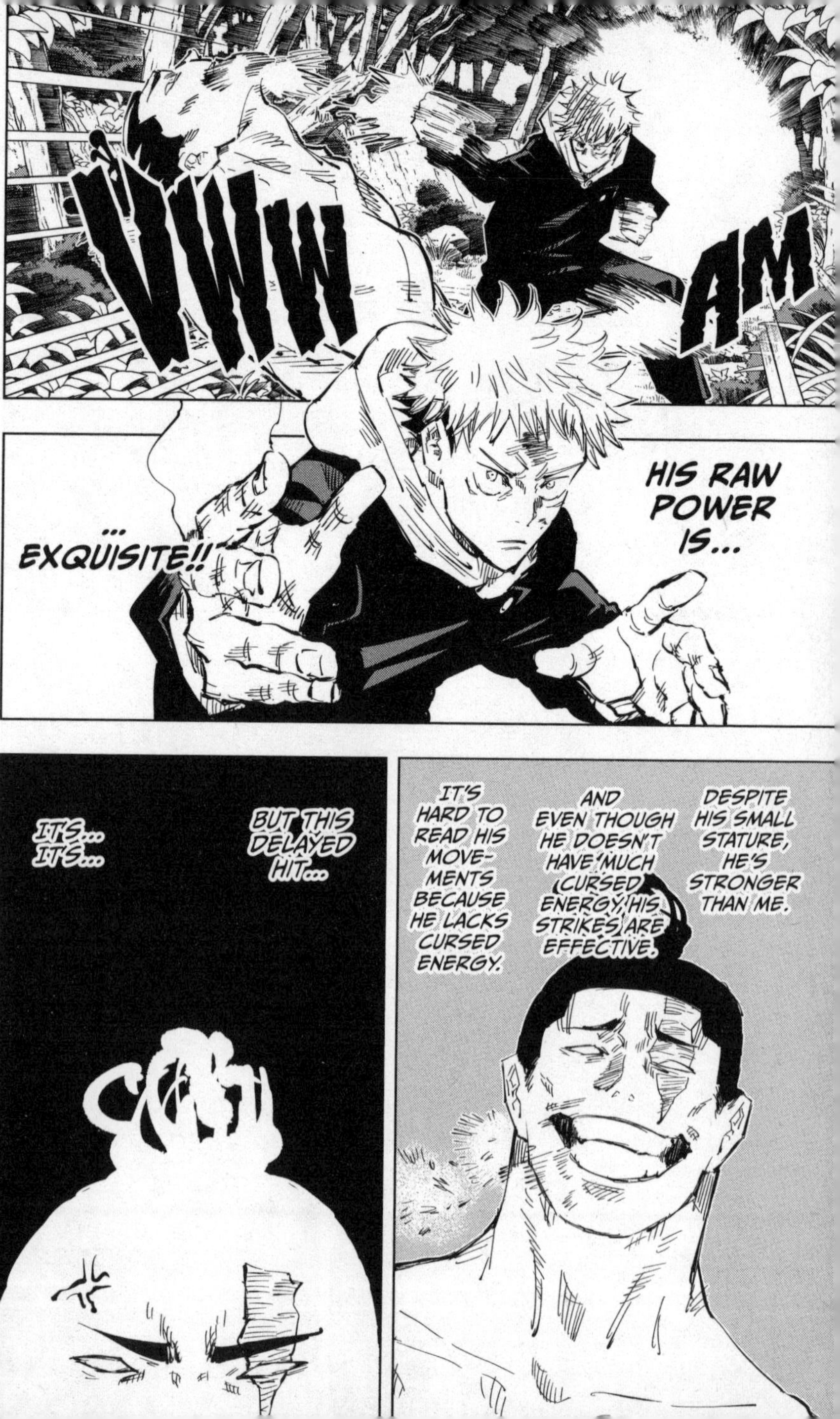
AM
VWW
HIS RAW POWER IS...
...EXQUISITE!!
DESPITE HIS SMALL STATURE, HE'S STRONGER THAN ME.
AND EVEN THOUGH HE DOESN'T HAVE MUCH CURSED ENERGY, HIS STRIKES ARE EFFECTIVE.
IT'S HARD TO READ HIS MOVEMENTS BECAUSE HE LACKS CURSED ENERGY.
BUT THIS DELAYED HIT...
IT'S... IT'S...

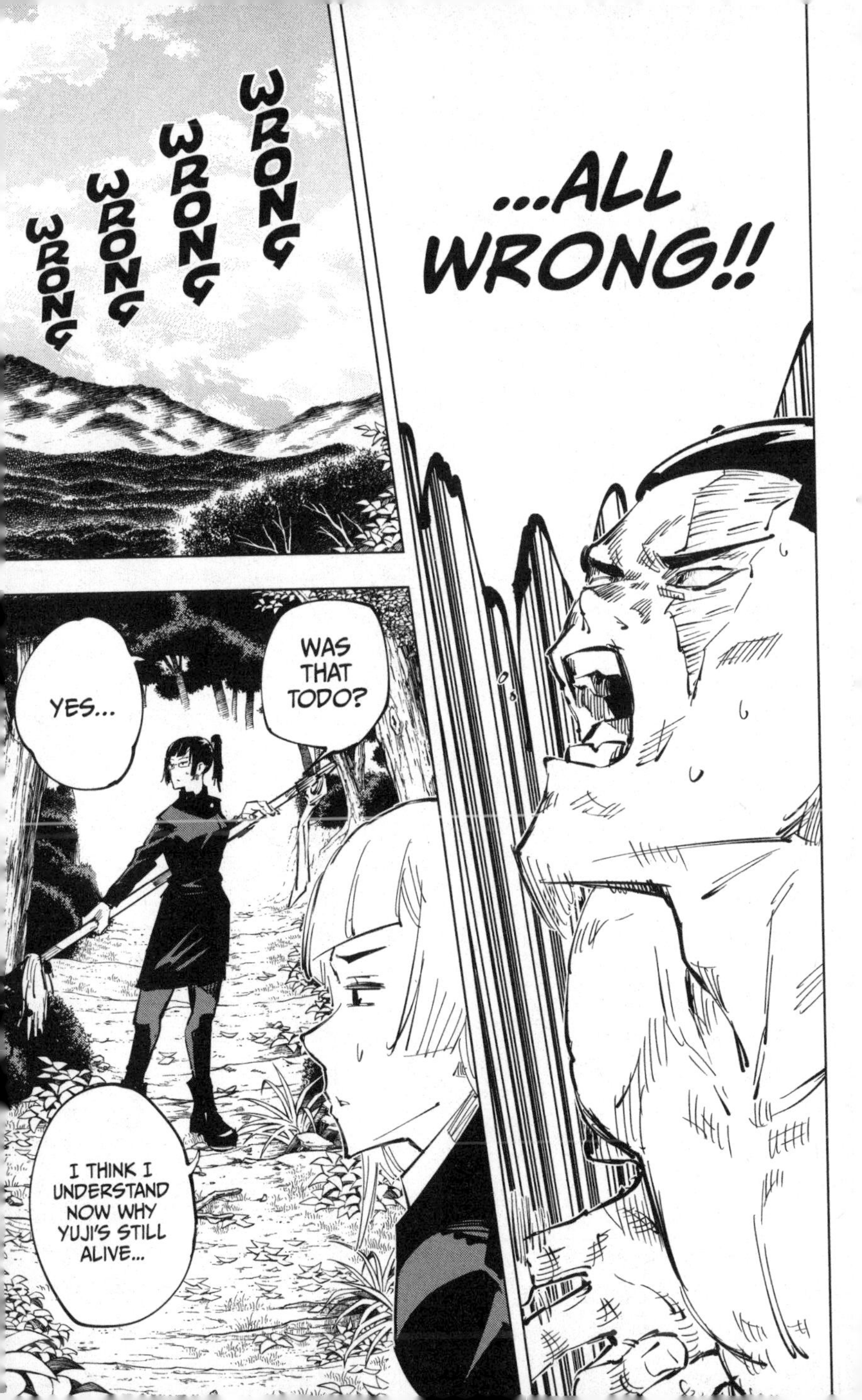
...ALL WRONG!!
WRONG WRONG WRONG WRONG
WAS THAT TODO?
YES...
I THINK I UNDERSTAND NOW WHY YUJI'S STILL ALIVE...

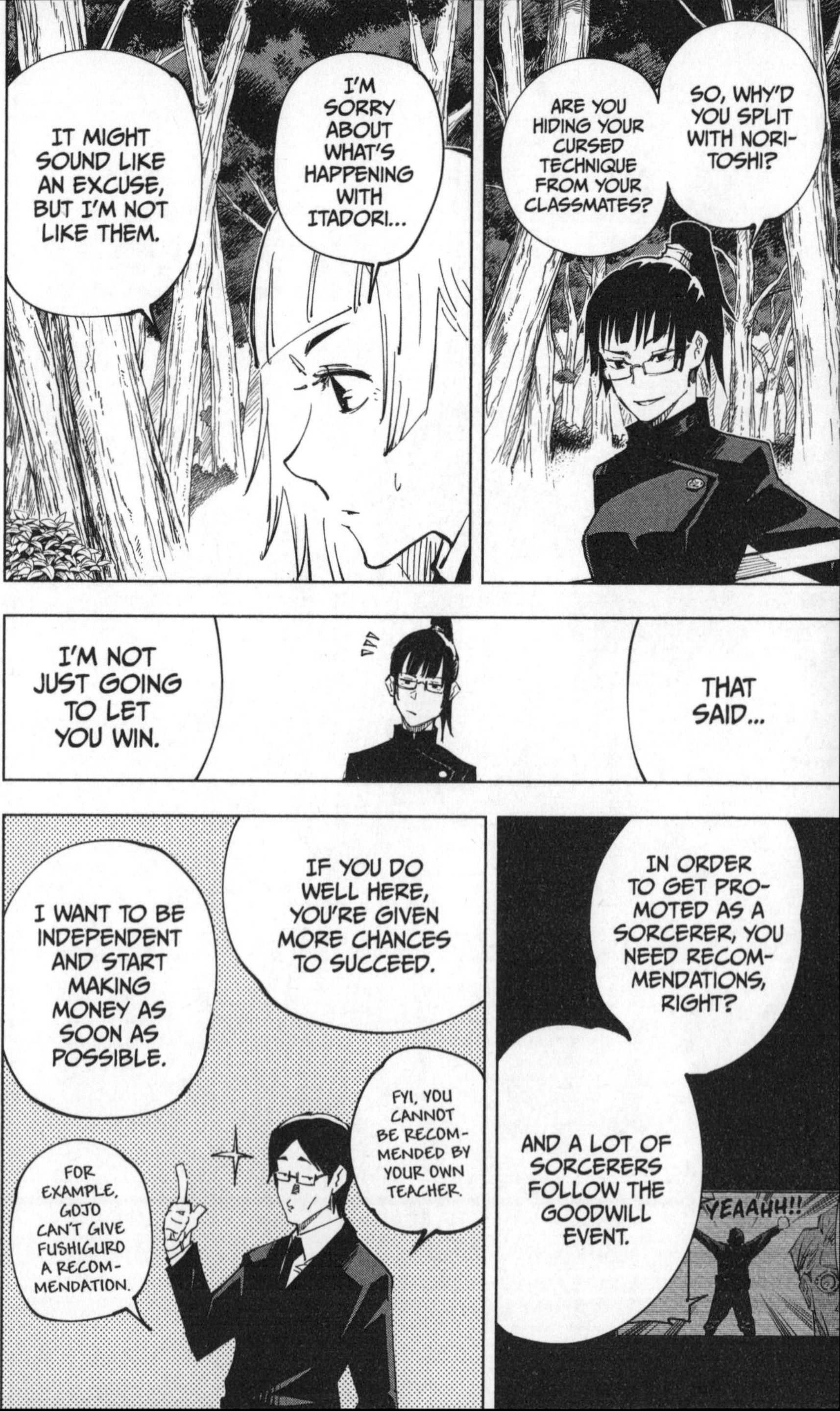
SO, WHY'D YOU SPLIT WITH NORI-TOSHI?
ARE YOU HIDING YOUR CURSED TECHNIQUE FROM YOUR CLASSMATES?
I'M SORRY ABOUT WHAT'S HAPPENING WITH ITADORI...
IT MIGHT SOUND LIKE AN EXCUSE, BUT I'M NOT LIKE THEM.
THAT SAID...
I'M NOT JUST GOING TO LET YOU WIN.
IN ORDER TO GET PRO-MOTED AS A SORCERER, YOU NEED RECOM-MENDATIONS, RIGHT?
AND A LOT OF SORCERERS FOLLOW THE GOODWILL EVENT.
YEAAHH!!
IF YOU DO WELL HERE, YOU'RE GIVEN MORE CHANCES TO SUCCEED.
I WANT TO BE INDEPENDENT AND START MAKING MONEY AS SOON AS POSSIBLE.
FYI, YOU CANNOT BE RECOM-MENDED BY YOUR OWN TEACHER.
FOR EXAMPLE, GOJO CAN'T GIVE FUSHIGURO A RECOM-MENDATION.

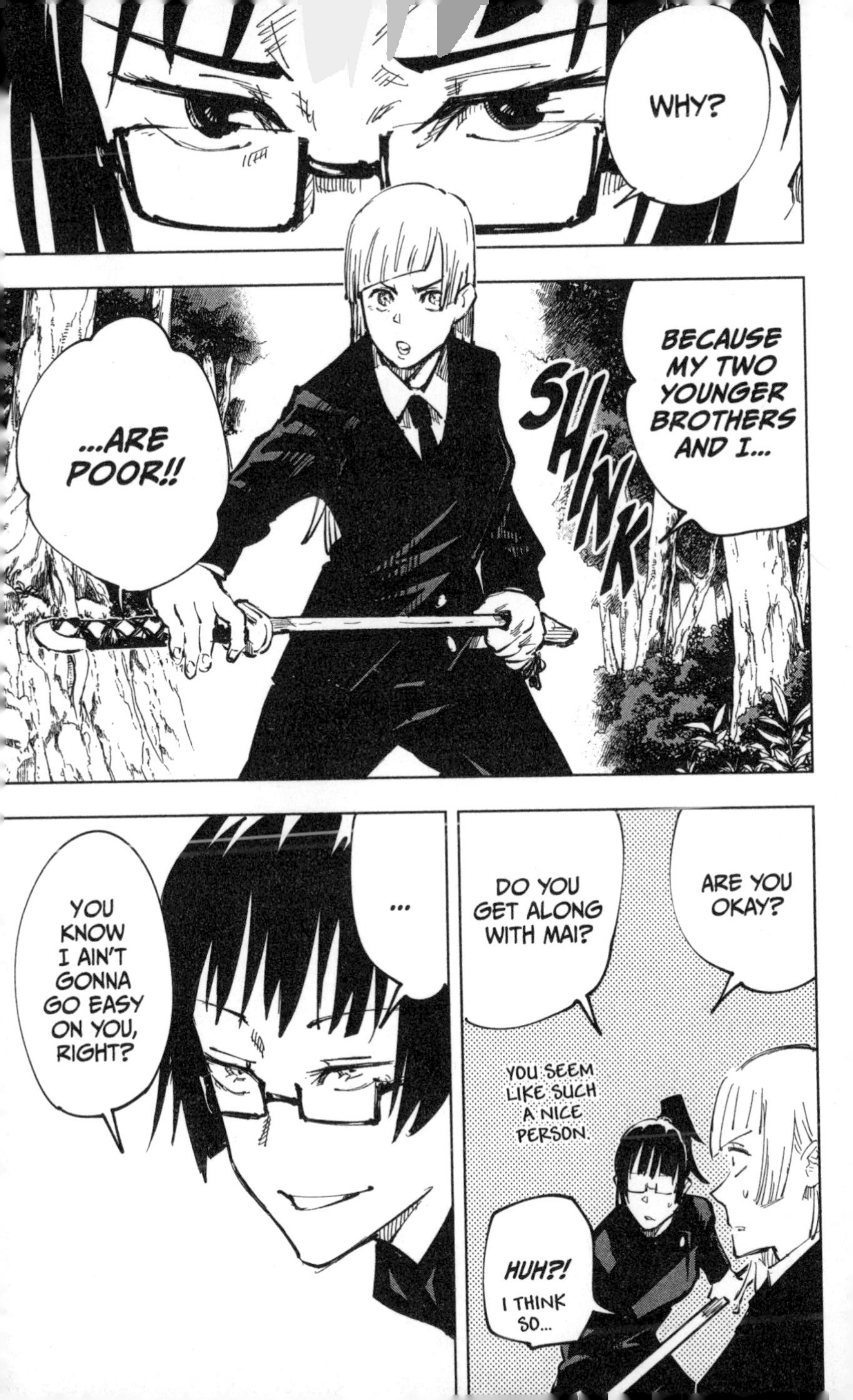
WHY?
BECAUSE MY TWO YOUNGER BROTHERS AND I...
SHINK
...ARE POOR!!
ARE YOU OKAY?
DO YOU GET ALONG WITH MAI?
YOU SEEM LIKE SUCH A NICE PERSON.
HUH?! I THINK SO...
...
YOU KNOW I AIN'T GONNA GO EASY ON YOU, RIGHT?

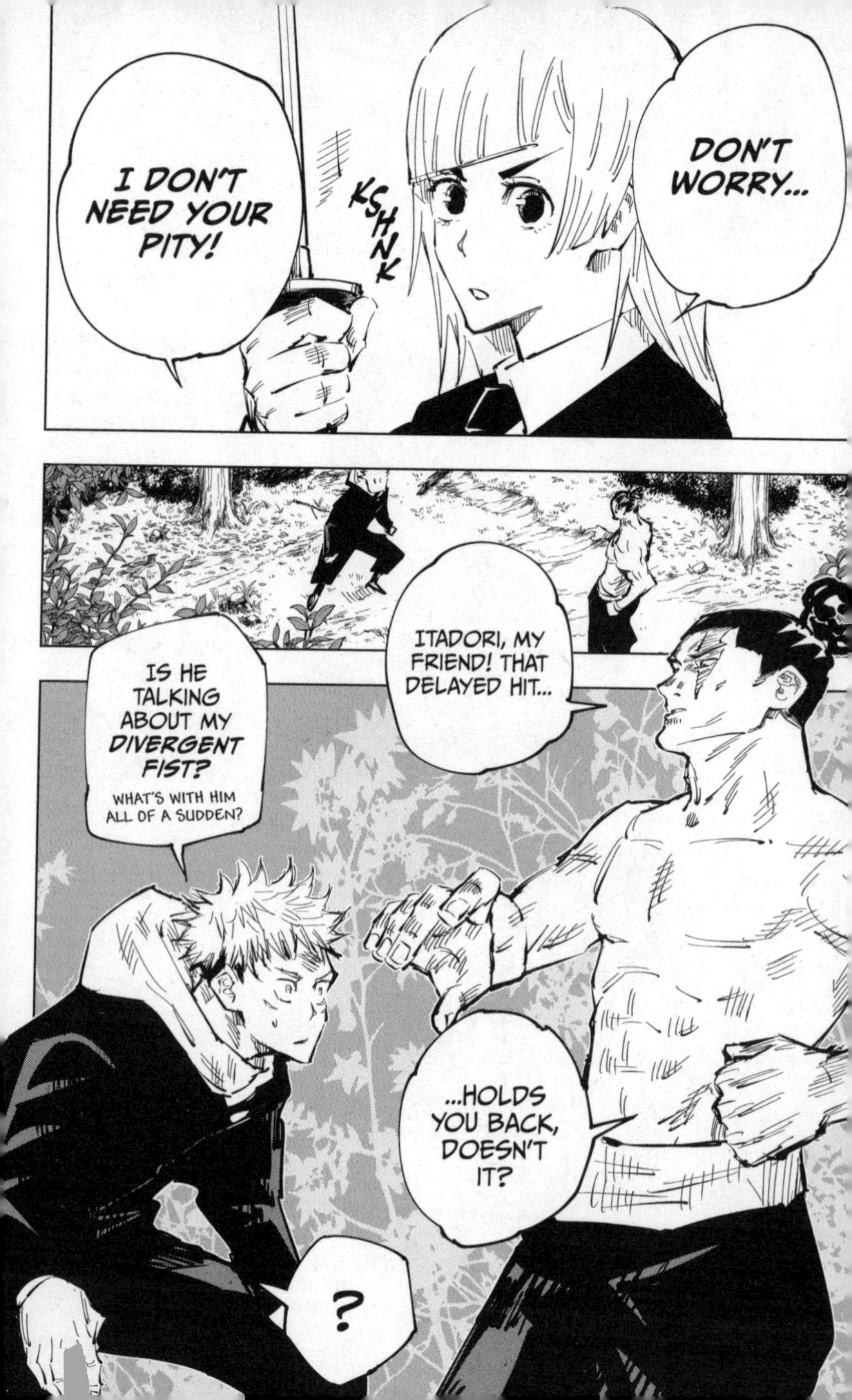
DON'T WORRY...
KSHNK
I DON'T NEED YOUR PITY!
ITADORI, MY FRIEND! THAT DELAYED HIT...
IS HE TALKING ABOUT MY *DIVERGENT FIST?*
WHAT'S WITH HIM ALL OF A SUDDEN?
...HOLDS YOU BACK, DOESN'T IT?
?

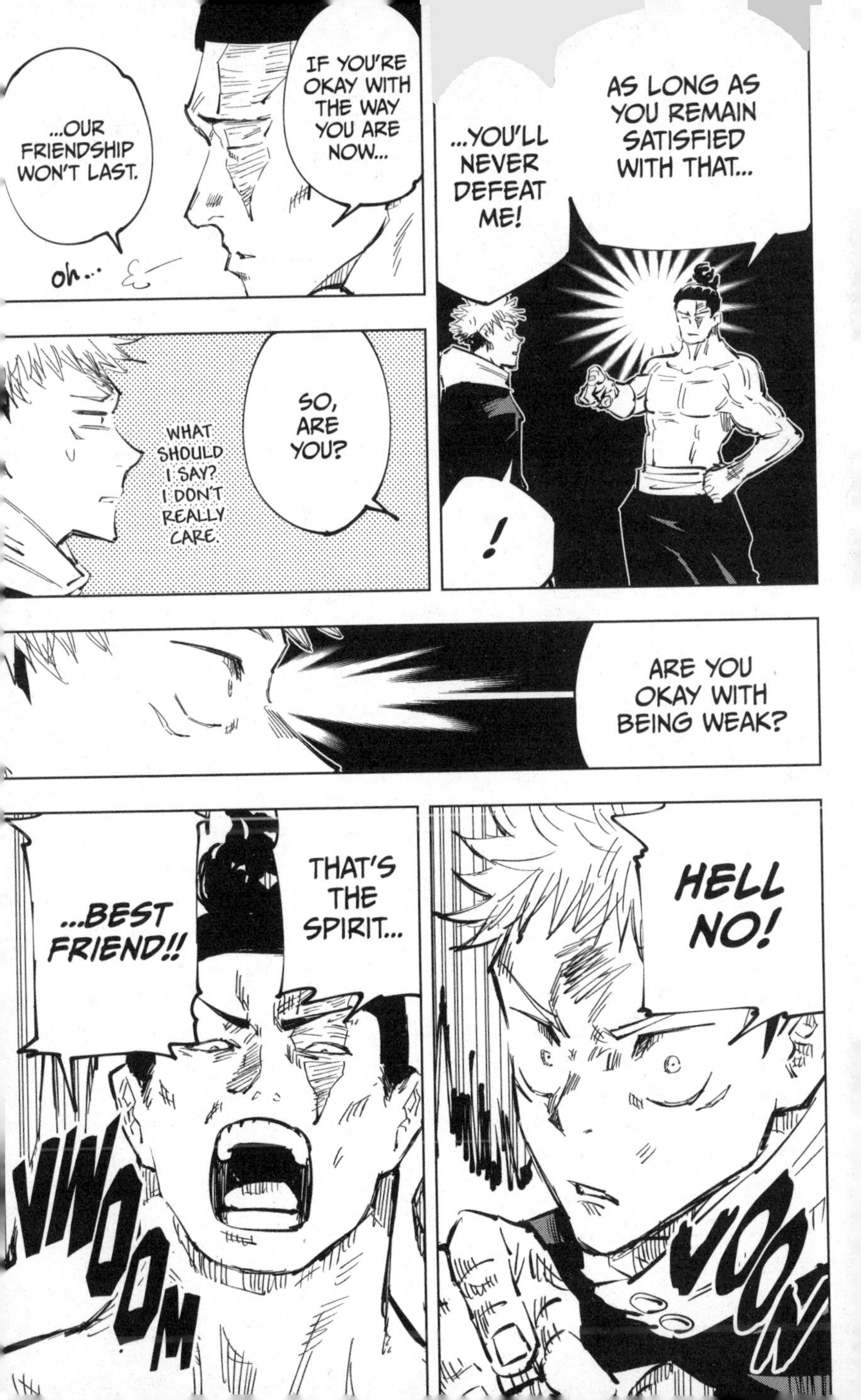
AS LONG AS YOU REMAIN SATISFIED WITH THAT...
...YOU'LL NEVER DEFEAT ME!
!
IF YOU'RE OKAY WITH THE WAY YOU ARE NOW...
...OUR FRIENDSHIP WON'T LAST.
oh...
SO, ARE YOU?
WHAT SHOULD I SAY? I DON'T REALLY CARE.
ARE YOU OKAY WITH BEING WEAK?
HELL NO!
VOOM
THAT'S THE SPIRIT...
...BEST FRIEND!!
VWOOM

MOMO NISHIMIYA

- Nishimiya is about 150 cm tall.

- She initially got piercings after being taken lightly because of her looks. Now she just enjoys them. (I also often forget to draw them.)

- Her hairstyle gives off a vibe that says, "I enjoy flying quietly."

- Her father is American.

- She enjoys cute things and going shopping with the second-year girls.

NORITOSHI KAMO

- Kamo was brought into the Kamo family as the heir at the age of six.

- Kamo, Zen'in (Fushiguro) and Gojo have been in contact even before Kamo entered Jujutsu High.

- Tried drawing him like the Japanese comedian Gor☆geous, but people often comment that he looks more like a member of KISS instead.

- He's a little taller than Fushiguro.

Chapter 37: Kyoto Sister-School Goodwill Event—Team Battle, Part 4

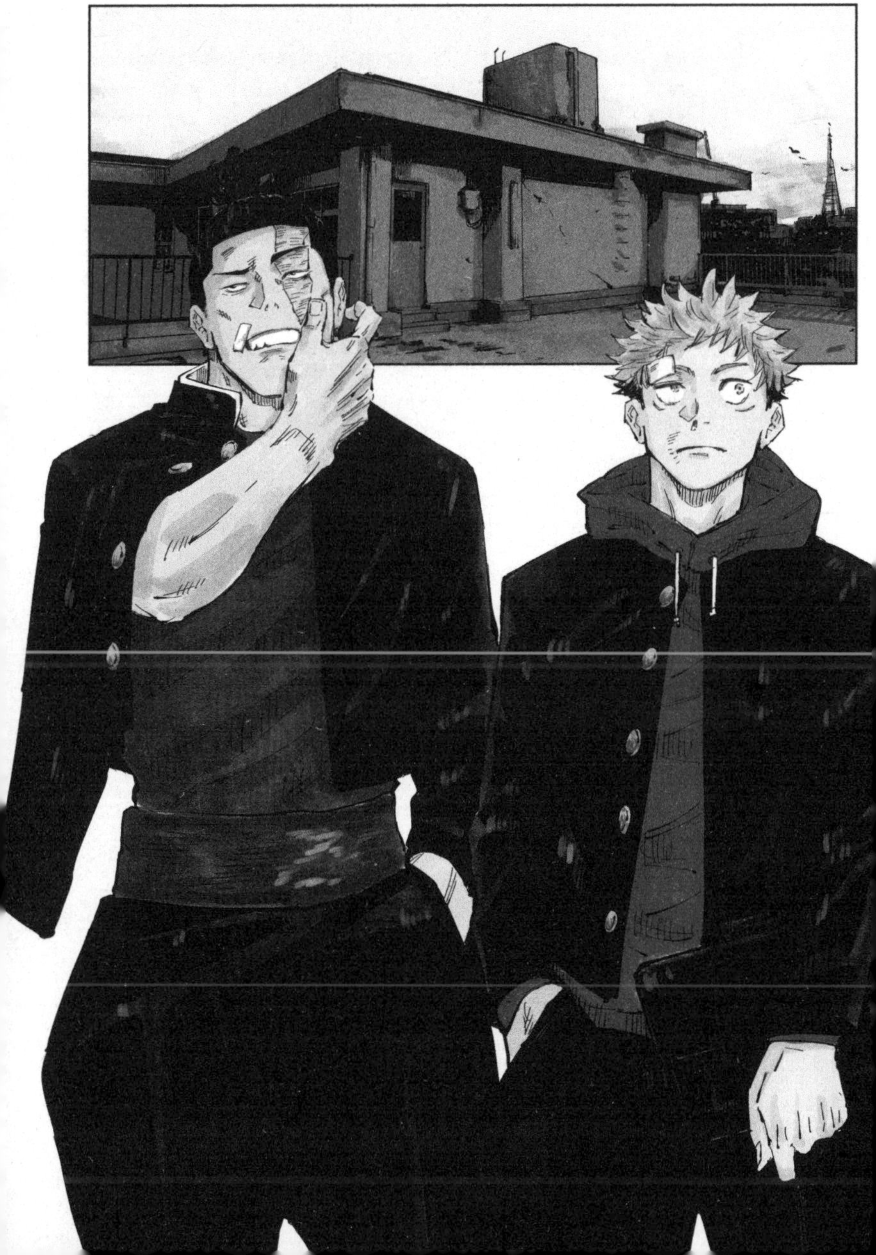

TOGE INUMAKI

- Inumaki's hairstyle was too similar to Itadori's, so we changed it and now it looks like Gojo's. What a conundrum!

- Inumaki is short.

- He doesn't look it next to Maki and Itadori, but he's extremely athletic.

- He loves trolling.

- His personal favorite rice ball ingredient is tuna mayo.

PANDA

- He's a panda.

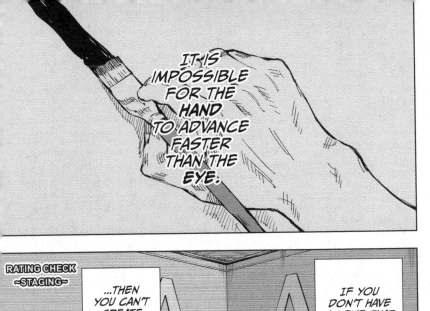

IT IS IMPOSSIBLE FOR THE **HAND** TO ADVANCE FASTER THAN THE **EYE**.

IF YOU DON'T HAVE AN **EYE** THAT CAN JUDGE QUALITY...

...THEN YOU CAN'T CREATE SOMETHING OF VALUE WITH YOUR **HAND**.

THAT IS A SAYING WITHIN THE ARTISTIC COMMUNITY.

CORRECT ANSWER ROOM

MANY DISCIPLINES ALSO BELIEVE THE SAYING TO BE TRUE.

THE RATE OF GROWTH FOR PEOPLE WHO POSSESS THIS **EYE** ECLIPSES THE RATE OF THOSE WHO DON'T.

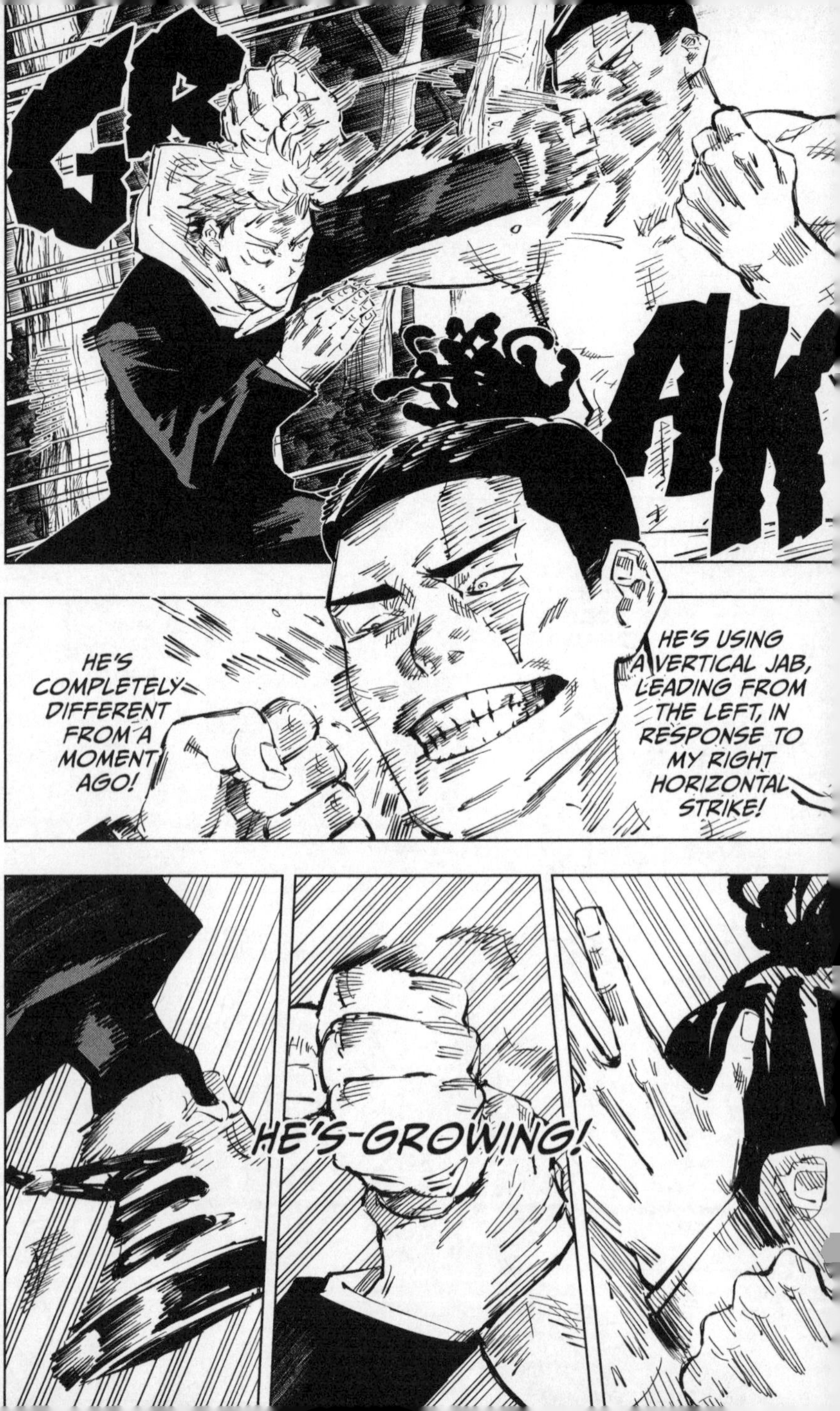
GR
AK
HE'S USING A VERTICAL JAB, LEADING FROM THE LEFT, IN RESPONSE TO MY RIGHT HORIZONTAL STRIKE!
HE'S COMPLETELY DIFFERENT FROM A MOMENT AGO!
HE'S GROWING!

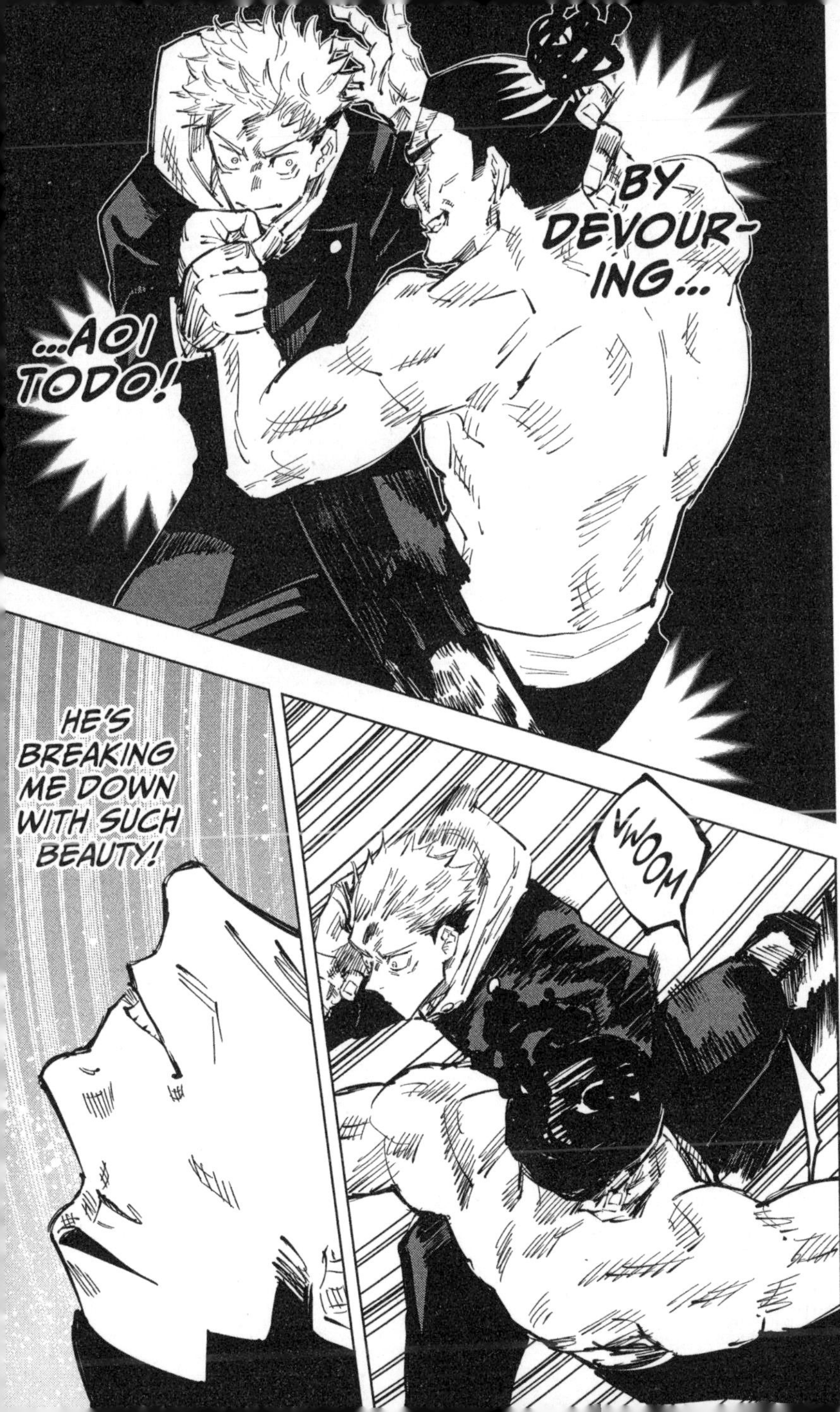
BY DEVOUR-ING...
...AOI TODO!
VWOOM
HE'S BREAKING ME DOWN WITH SUCH BEAUTY!

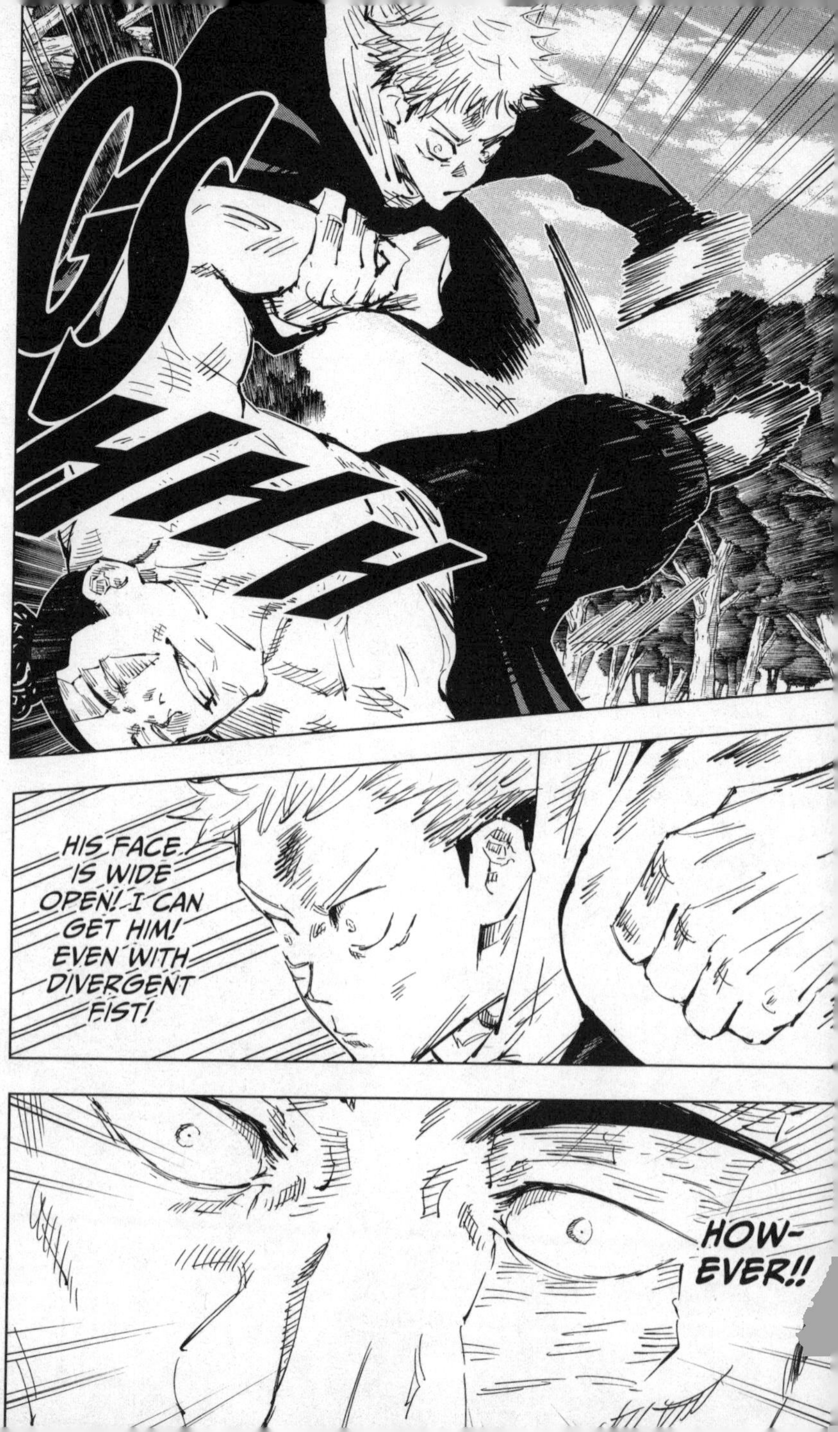
GO
HIS FACE IS WIDE OPEN! I CAN GET HIM! EVEN WITH DIVERGENT FIST!
HOW-EVER!!

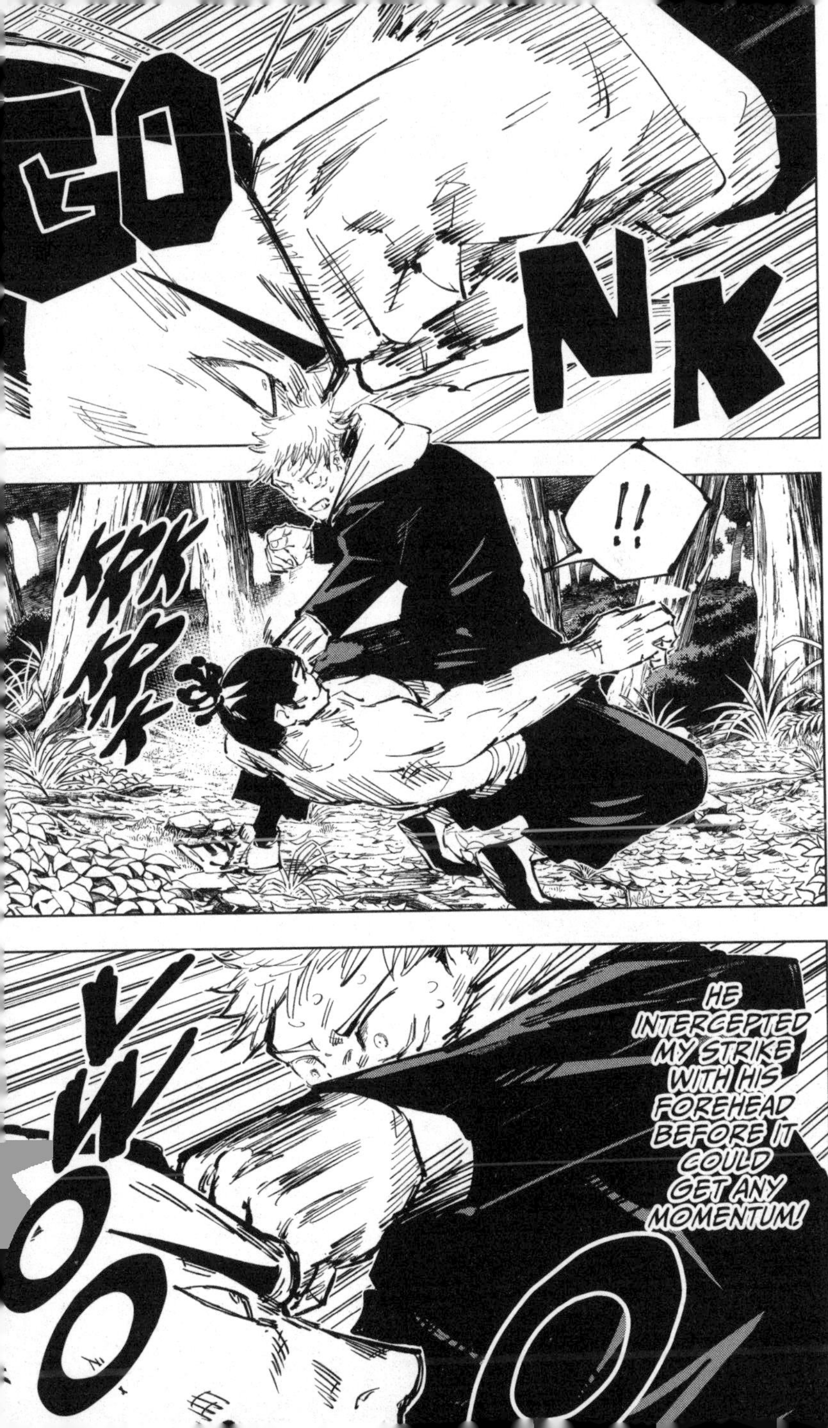
GONK
!!
KRK KRK
HE INTERCEPTED MY STRIKE WITH HIS FOREHEAD BEFORE IT COULD GET ANY MOMENTUM!
VWOO

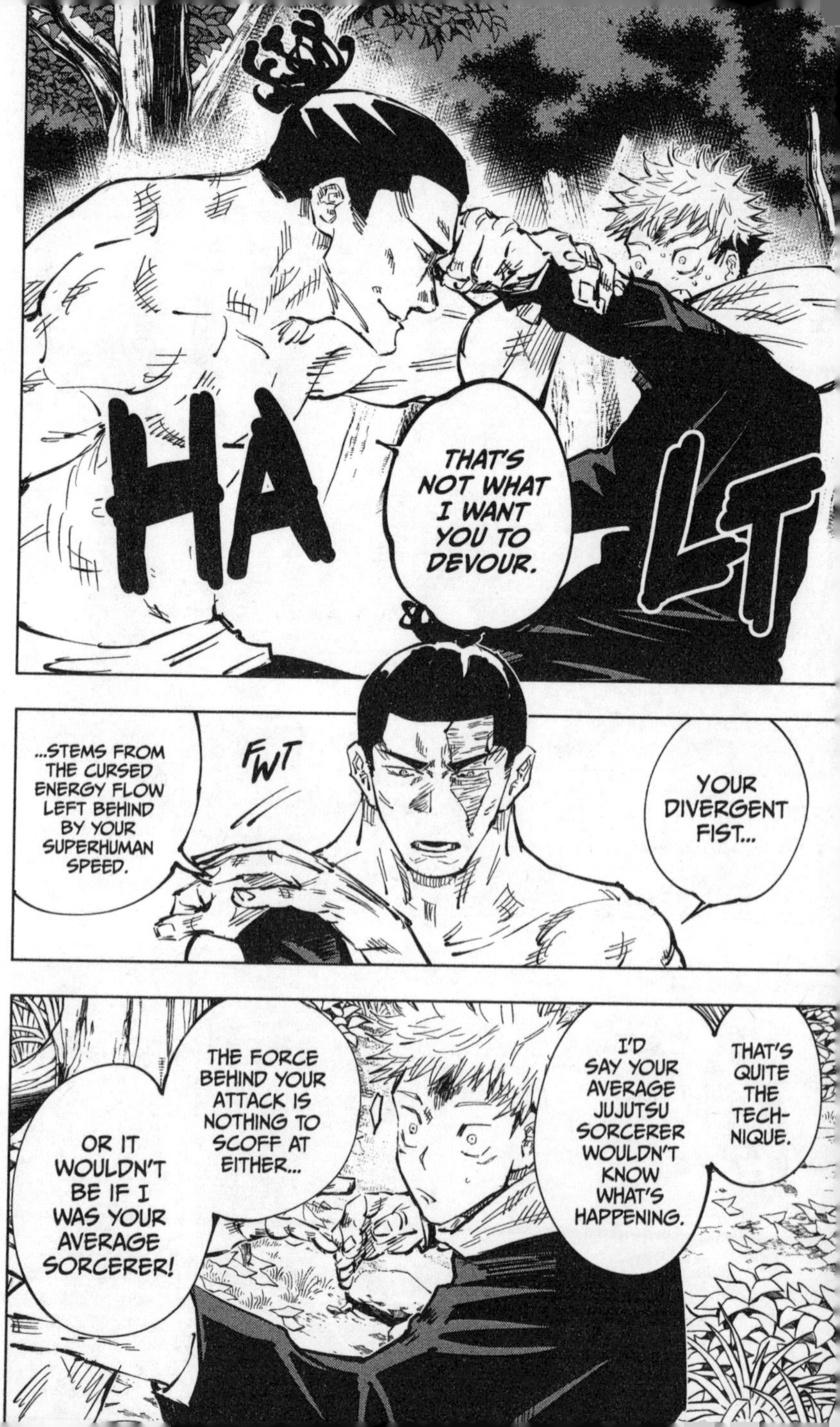
HALT
THAT'S NOT WHAT I WANT YOU TO DEVOUR.
YOUR DIVERGENT FIST...
FWT
...STEMS FROM THE CURSED ENERGY FLOW LEFT BEHIND BY YOUR SUPERHUMAN SPEED.
THAT'S QUITE THE TECH-NIQUE.
I'D SAY YOUR AVERAGE JUJUTSU SORCERER WOULDN'T KNOW WHAT'S HAPPENING.
THE FORCE BEHIND YOUR ATTACK IS NOTHING TO SCOFF AT EITHER...
OR IT WOULDN'T BE IF I WAS YOUR AVERAGE SORCERER!

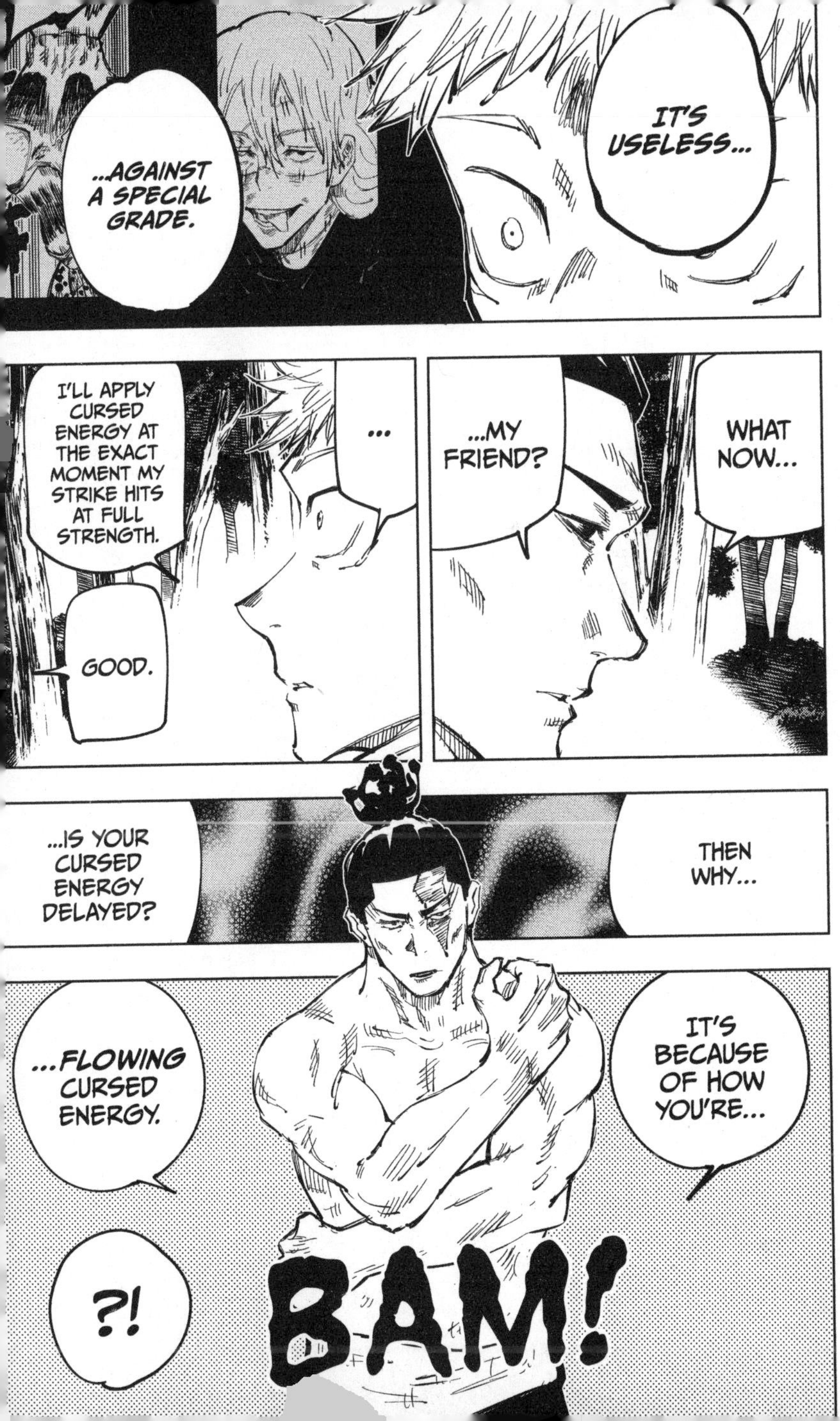
IT'S USELESS...
...AGAINST A SPECIAL GRADE.
WHAT NOW...
...MY FRIEND?
...
I'LL APPLY CURSED ENERGY AT THE EXACT MOMENT MY STRIKE HITS AT FULL STRENGTH.
GOOD.
THEN WHY...
...IS YOUR CURSED ENERGY DELAYED?
IT'S BECAUSE OF HOW YOU'RE...
...FLOWING CURSED ENERGY.
BAM!
?!

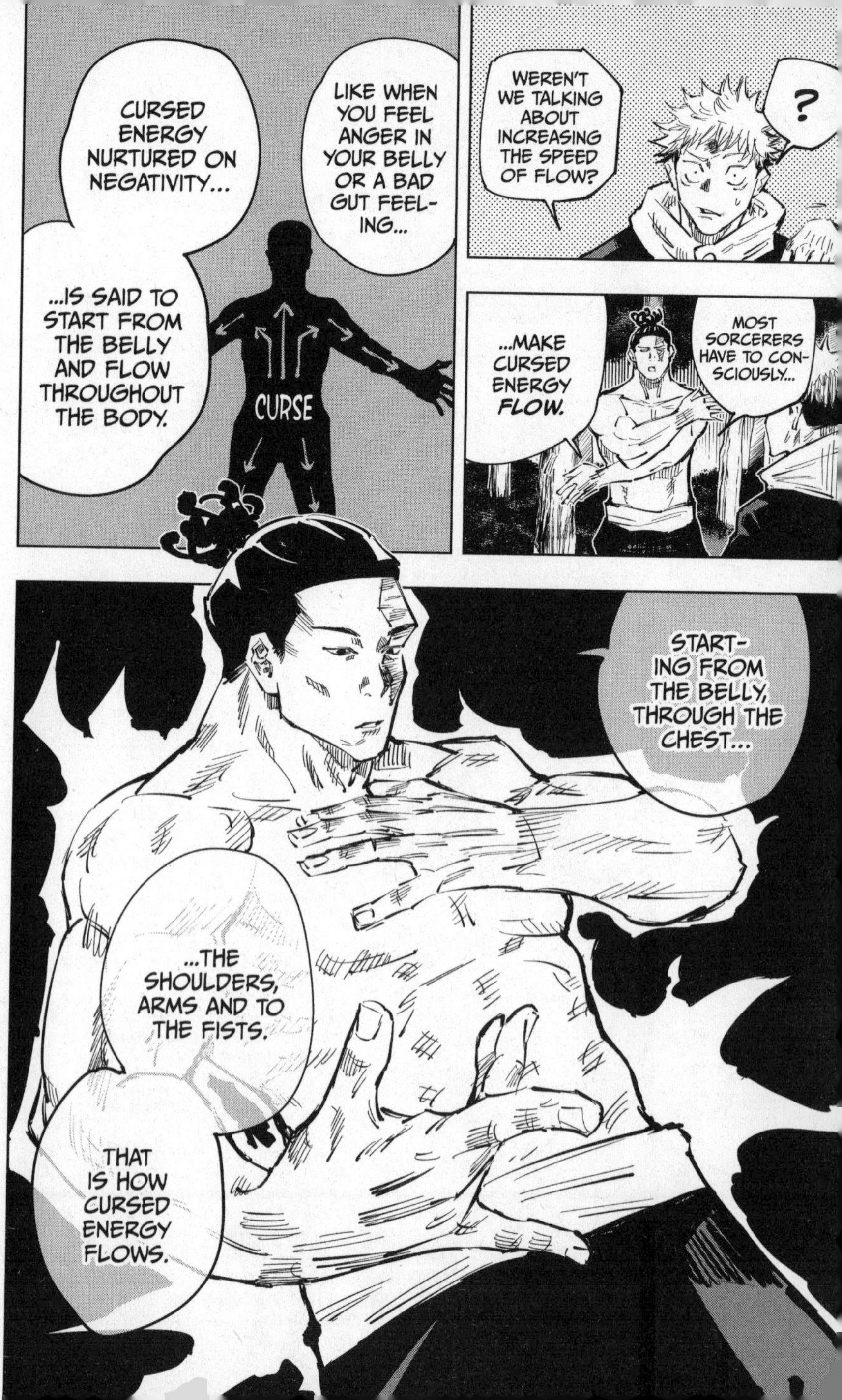
WEREN'T WE TALKING ABOUT INCREASING THE SPEED OF FLOW?
?
MOST SORCERERS HAVE TO CONSCIOUSLY...
...MAKE CURSED ENERGY *FLOW.*
LIKE WHEN YOU FEEL ANGER IN YOUR BELLY OR A BAD GUT FEEL-ING...
CURSED ENERGY NURTURED ON NEGATIVITY...
...IS SAID TO START FROM THE BELLY AND FLOW THROUGHOUT THE BODY.
CURSE
START-ING FROM THE BELLY, THROUGH THE CHEST...
...THE SHOULDERS, ARMS AND TO THE FISTS.
THAT IS HOW CURSED ENERGY FLOWS.

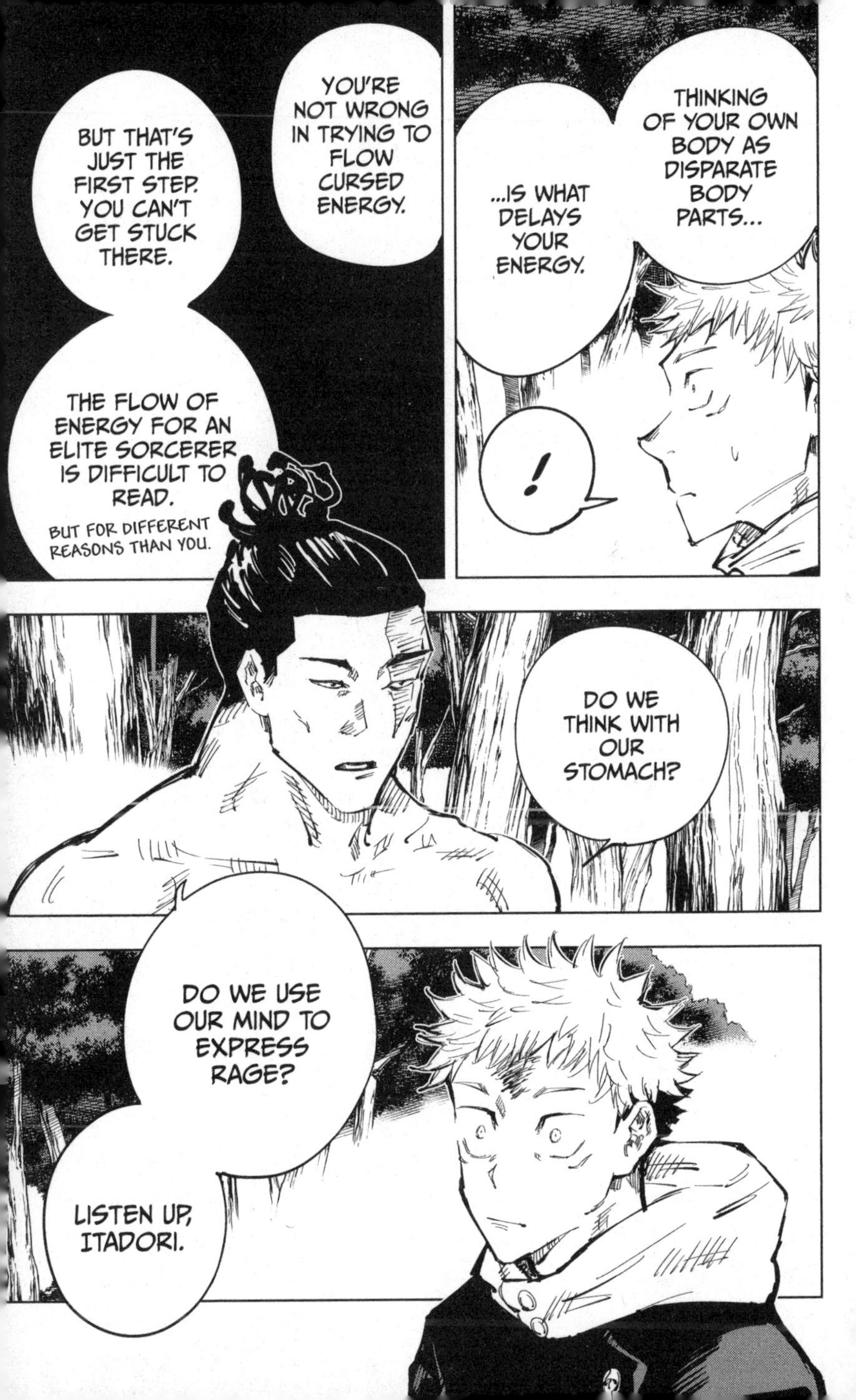
THINKING OF YOUR OWN BODY AS DISPARATE BODY PARTS...
...IS WHAT DELAYS YOUR ENERGY.
!
YOU'RE NOT WRONG IN TRYING TO FLOW CURSED ENERGY.
BUT THAT'S JUST THE FIRST STEP. YOU CAN'T GET STUCK THERE.
THE FLOW OF ENERGY FOR AN ELITE SORCERER IS DIFFICULT TO READ.
BUT FOR DIFFERENT REASONS THAN YOU.
DO WE THINK WITH OUR STOMACH?
DO WE USE OUR MIND TO EXPRESS RAGE?
LISTEN UP, ITADORI.

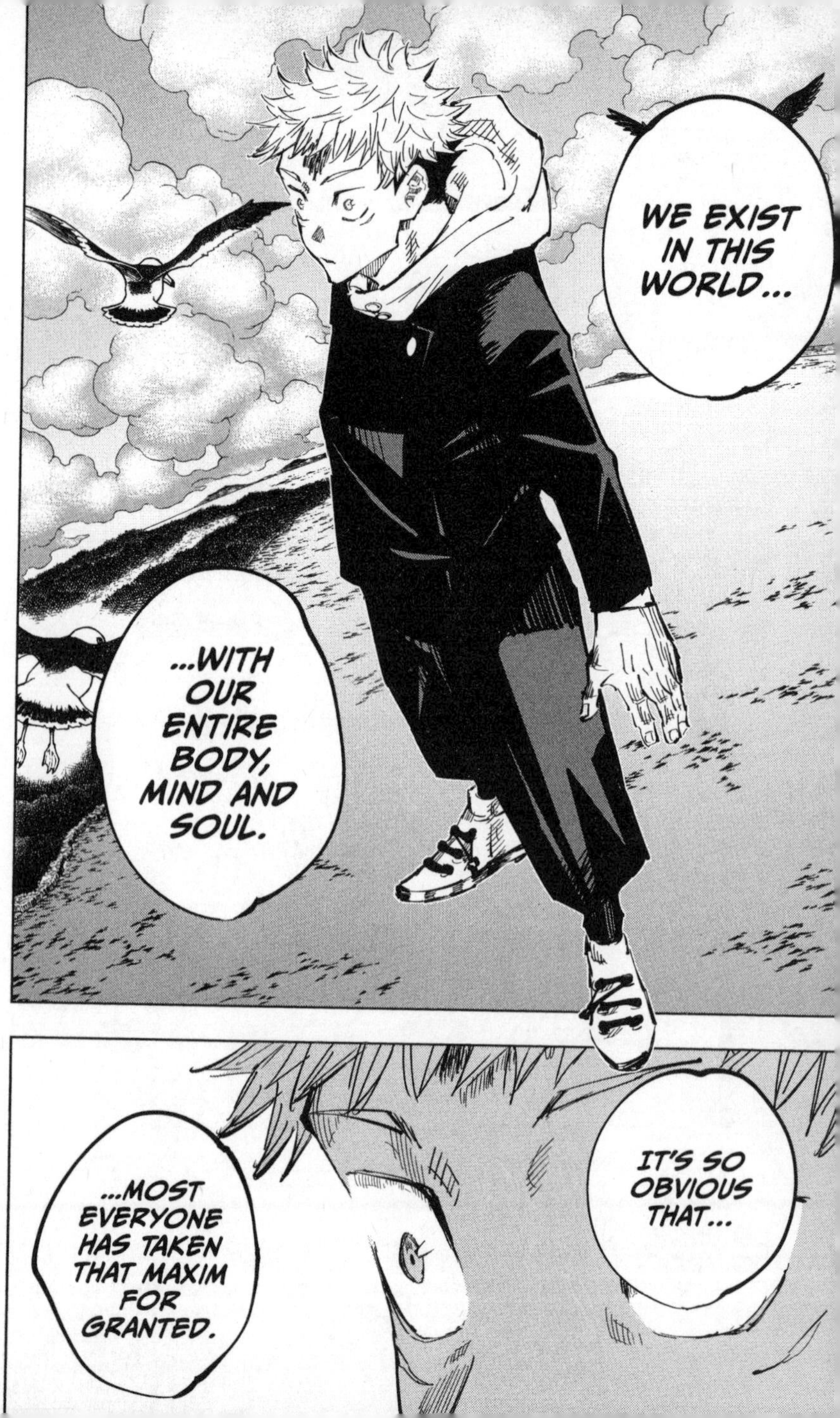
WE EXIST IN THIS WORLD...
...WITH OUR ENTIRE BODY, MIND AND SOUL.
IT'S SO OBVIOUS THAT...
...MOST EVERYONE HAS TAKEN THAT MAXIM FOR GRANTED.

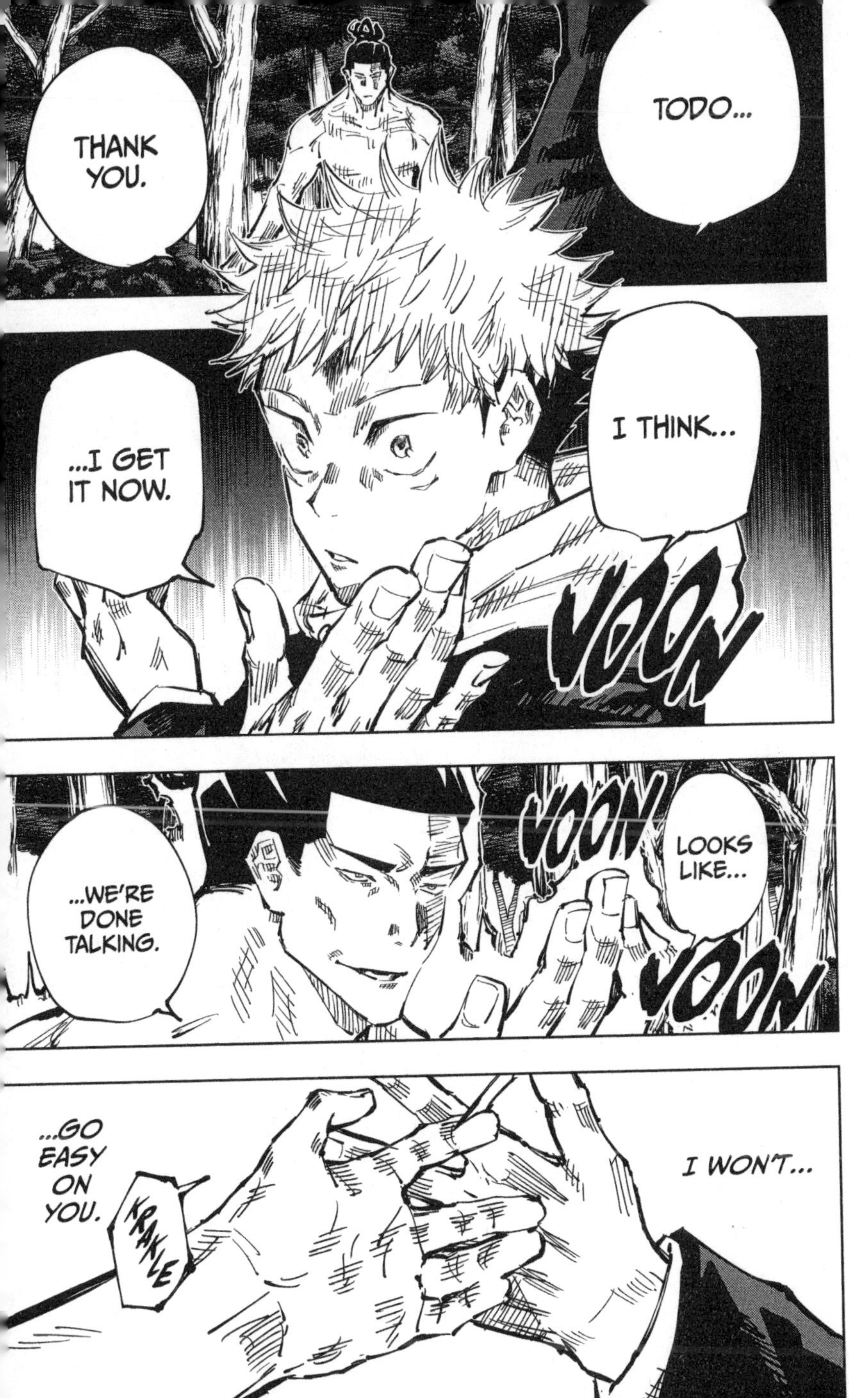
TODO...
THANK YOU.
I THINK...
...I GET IT NOW.
VOON
VOON
LOOKS LIKE...
...WE'RE DONE TALKING.
VOON
I WON'T...
KRAKLE
...GO EASY ON YOU.

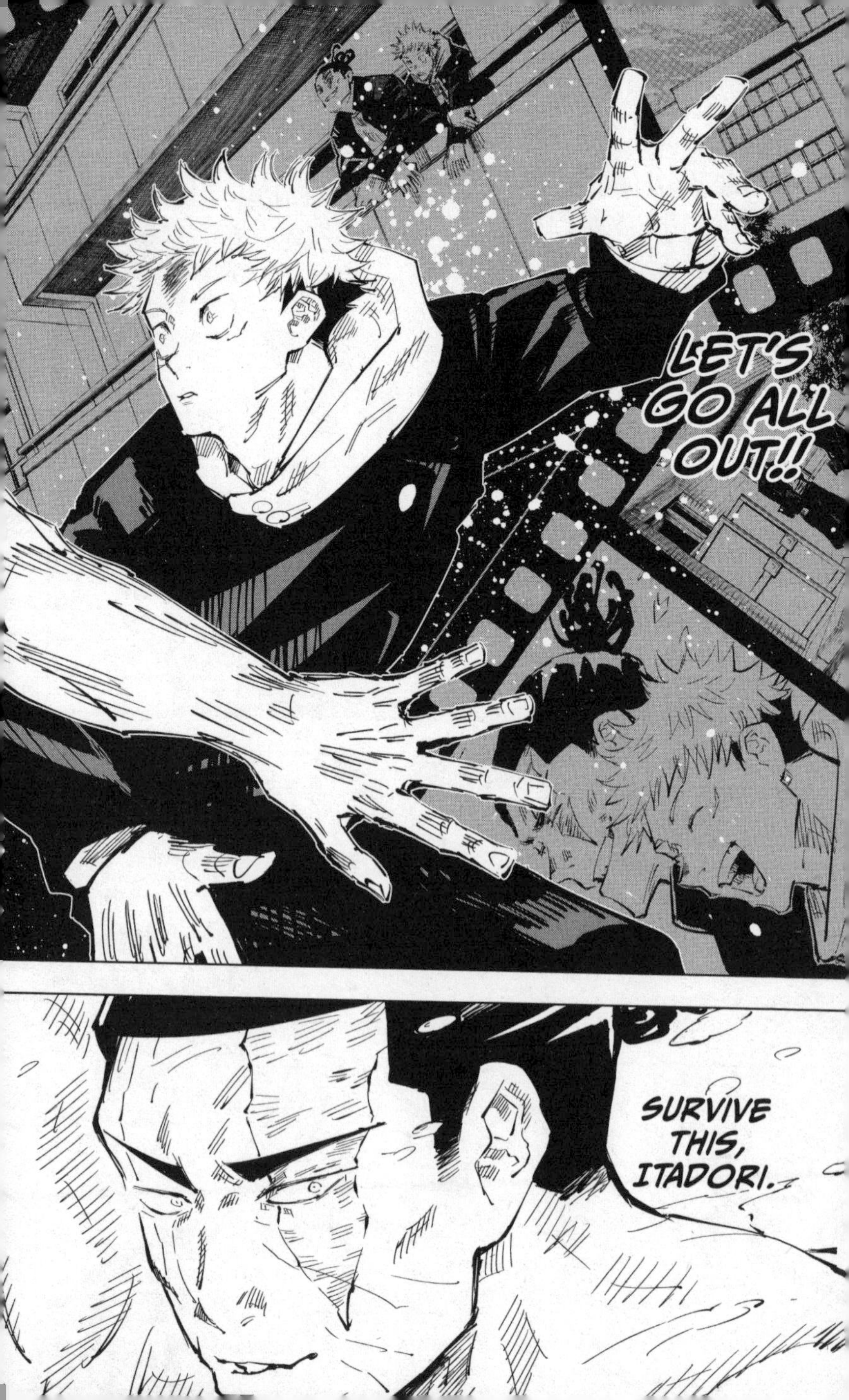
LET'S GO ALL OUT!!
SURVIVE THIS, ITADORI.

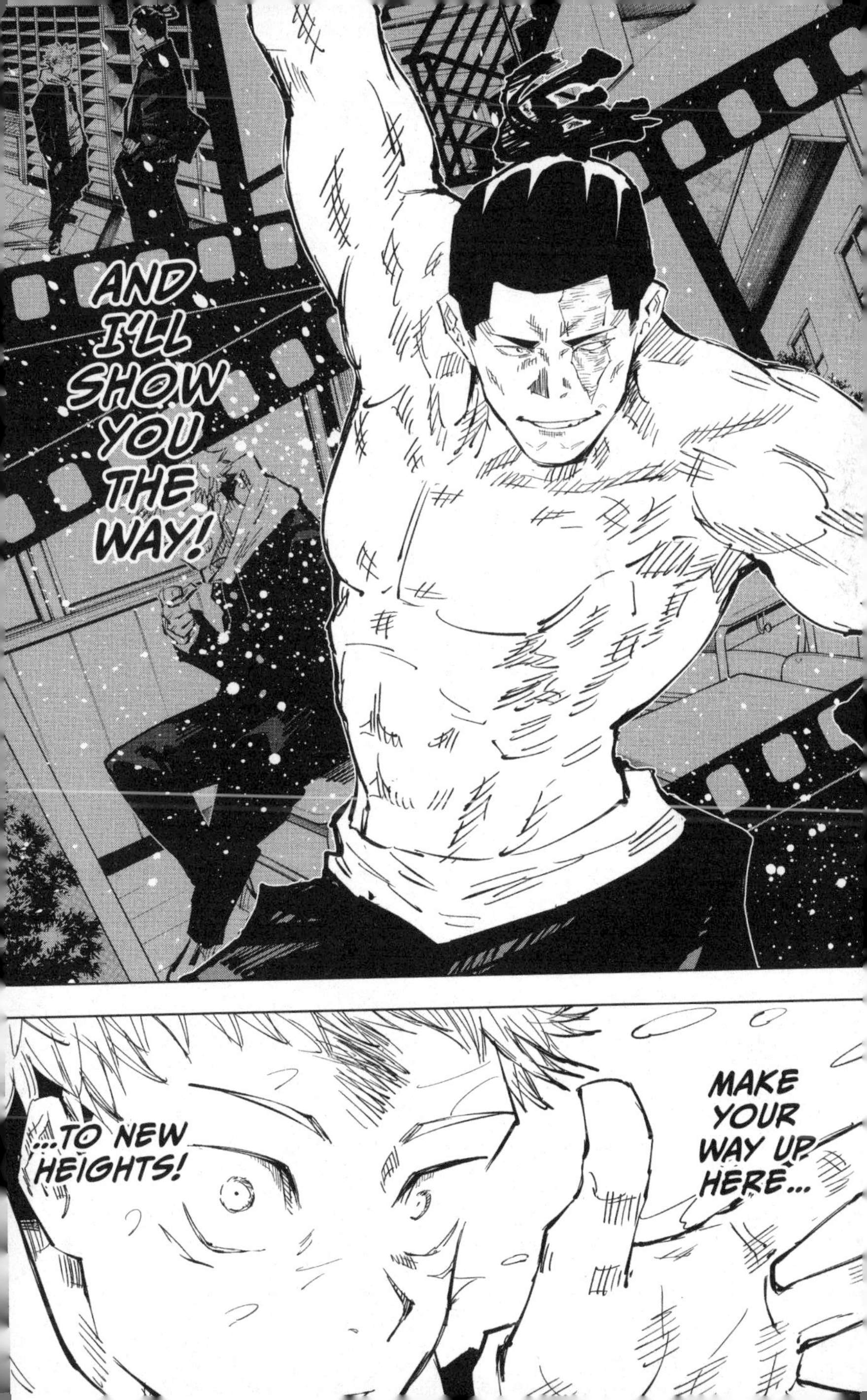
AND I'LL SHOW YOU THE WAY!
MAKE YOUR WAY UP HERE...
...TO NEW HEIGHTS!

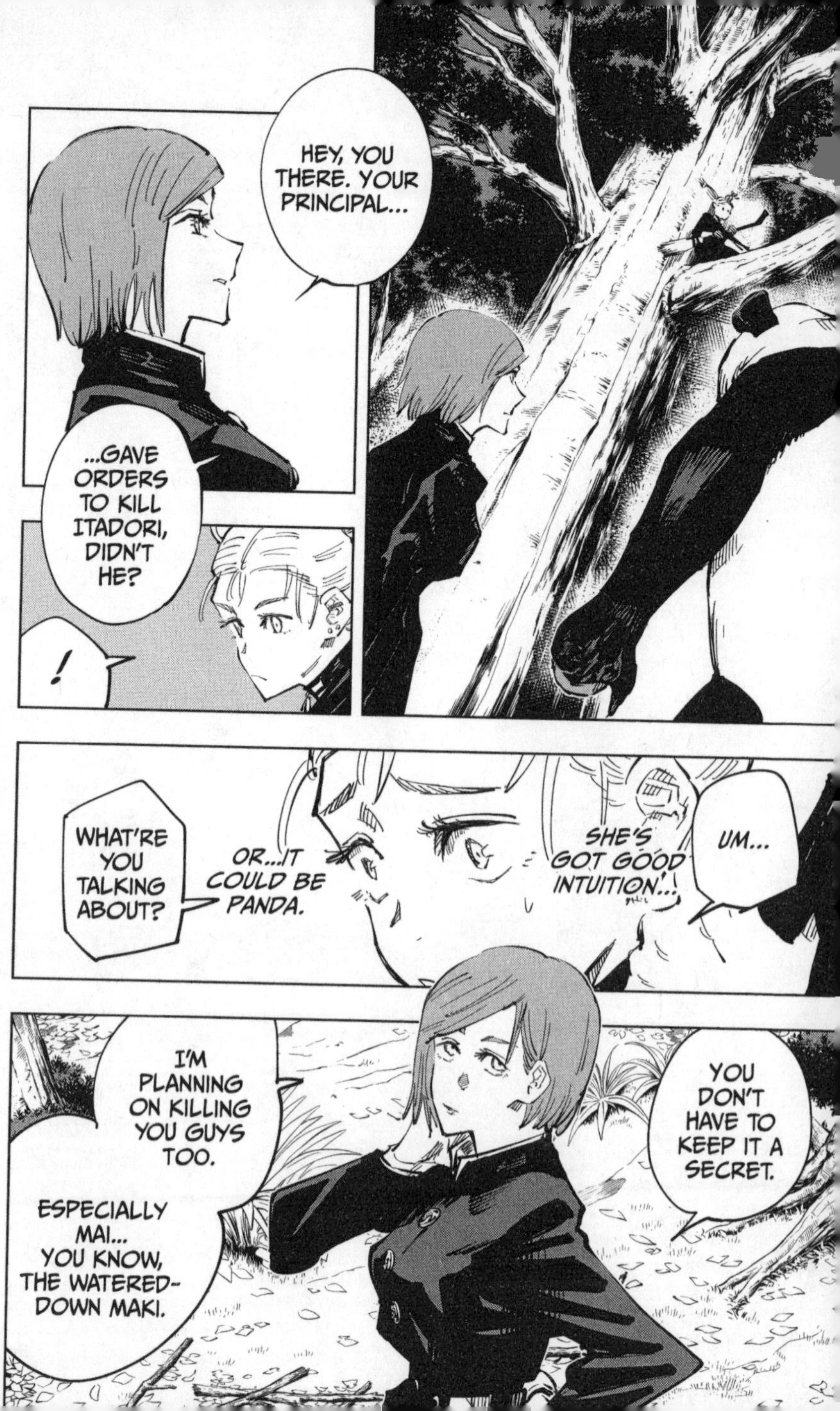
HEY, YOU THERE. YOUR PRINCIPAL...
...GAVE ORDERS TO KILL ITADORI, DIDN'T HE?
!
UM...
SHE'S GOT GOOD INTUITION...!
OR...IT COULD BE PANDA.
WHAT'RE YOU TALKING ABOUT?
YOU DON'T HAVE TO KEEP IT A SECRET.
I'M PLANNING ON KILLING YOU GUYS TOO.
ESPECIALLY MAI... YOU KNOW, THE WATERED-DOWN MAKI.

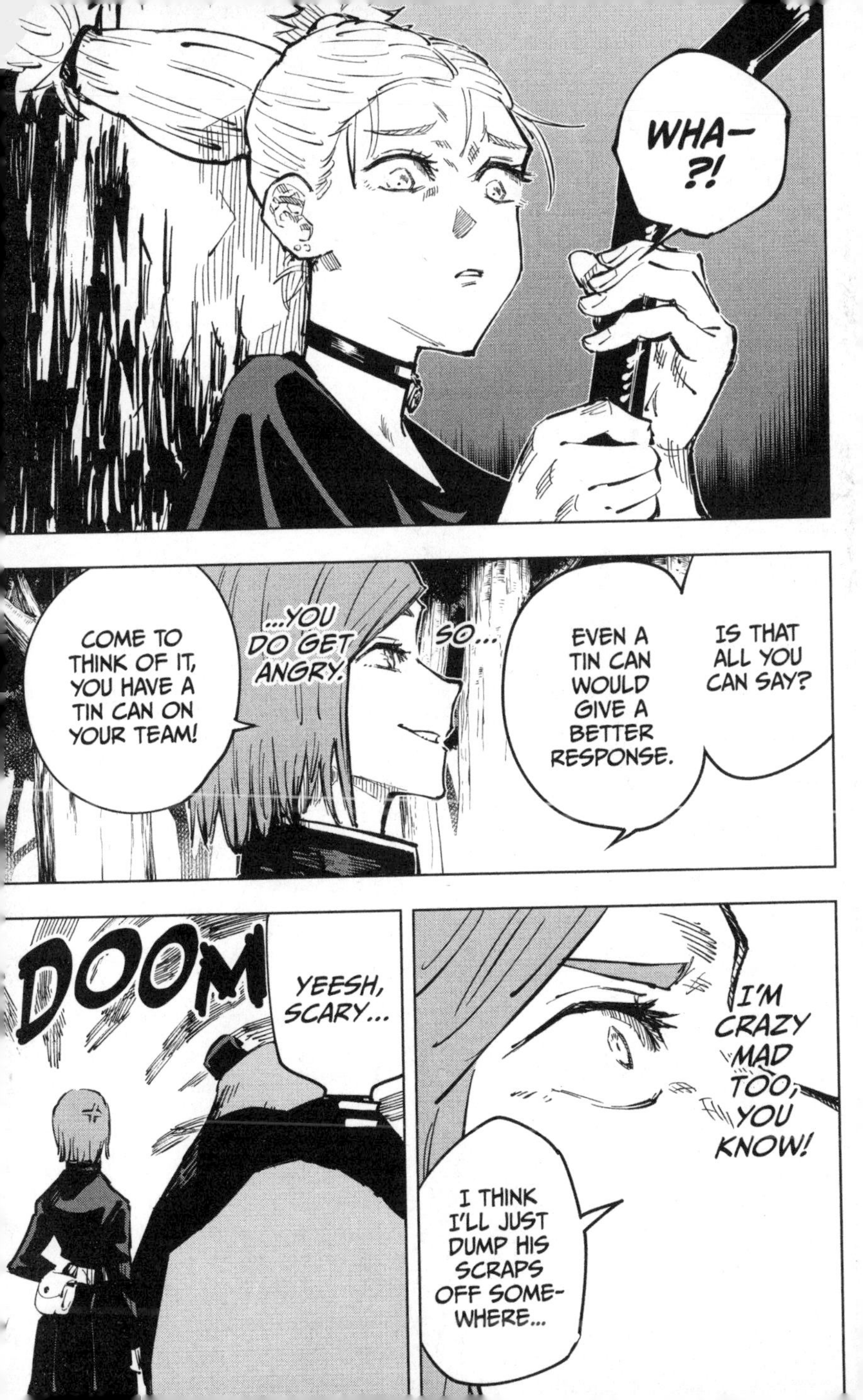
WHA- ?!
IS THAT ALL YOU CAN SAY?
EVEN A TIN CAN WOULD GIVE A BETTER RESPONSE.
SO...
...YOU DO GET ANGRY.
COME TO THINK OF IT, YOU HAVE A TIN CAN ON YOUR TEAM!
I'M CRAZY MAD TOO, YOU KNOW!
I THINK I'LL JUST DUMP HIS SCRAPS OFF SOME-WHERE...
YEESH, SCARY...
DOOM

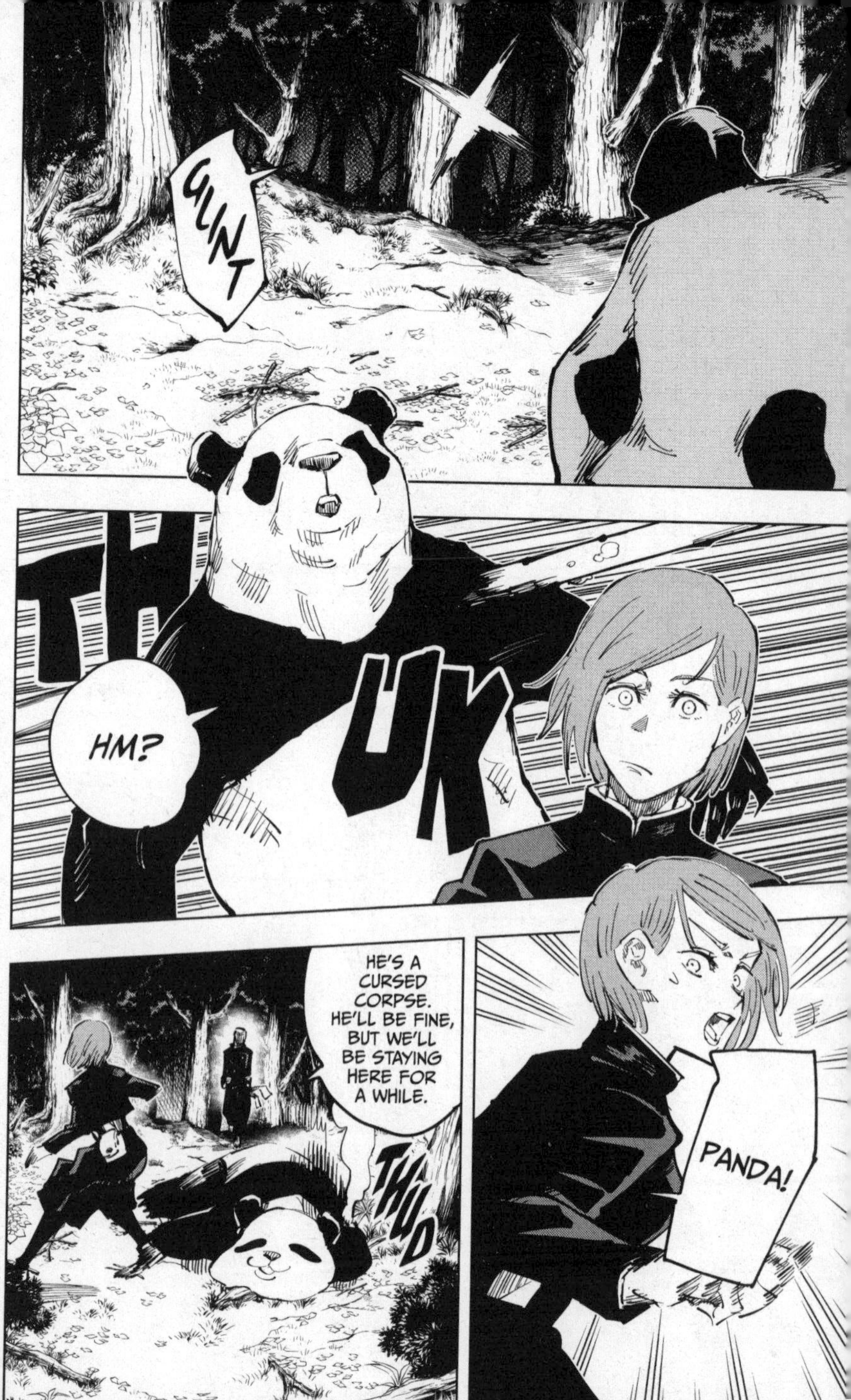
GLINT
THUNK
HM?
PANDA!
HE'S A CURSED CORPSE. HE'LL BE FINE, BUT WE'LL BE STAYING HERE FOR A WHILE.
THUD

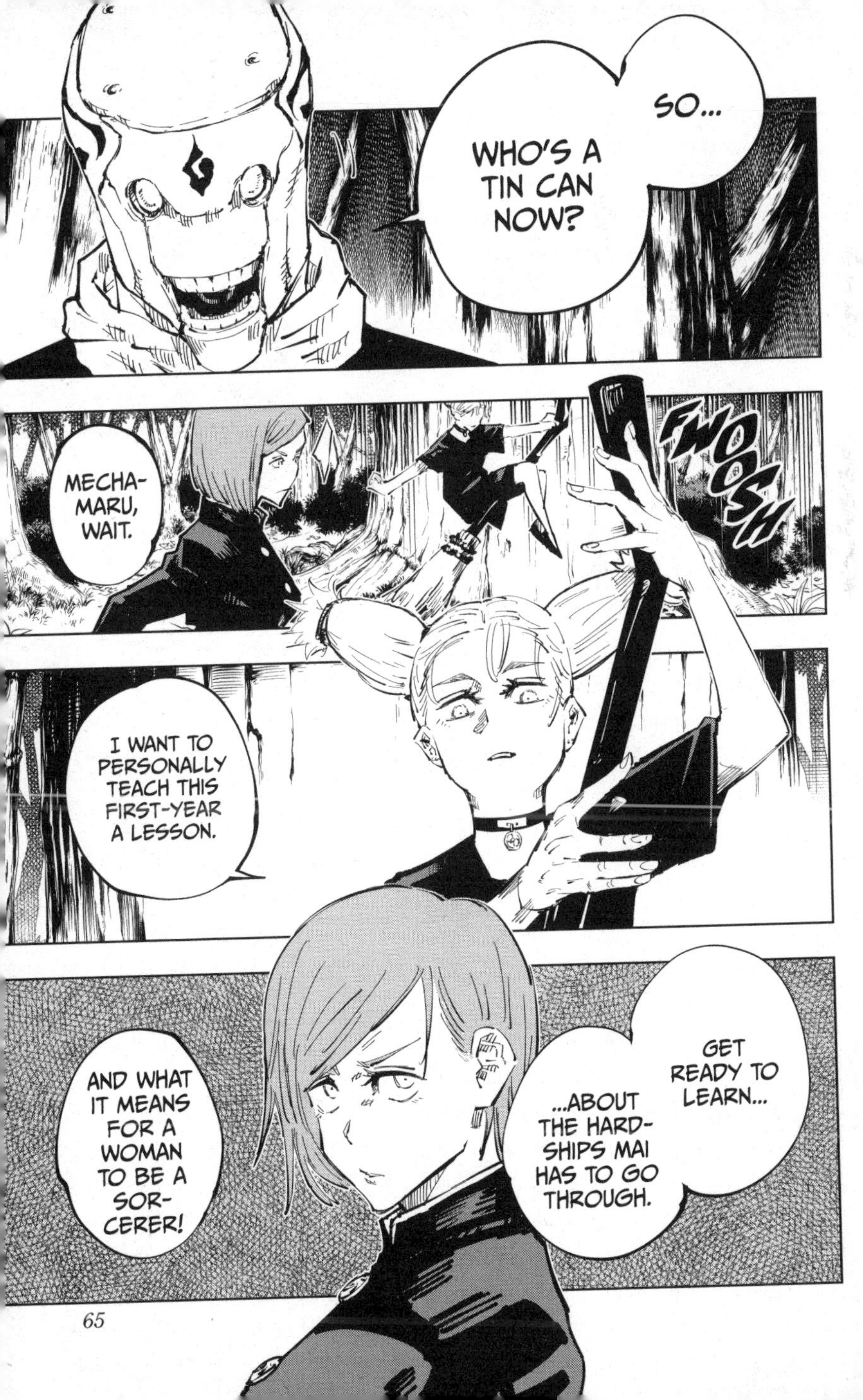
SO...
WHO'S A TIN CAN NOW?
FWOOSH
MECHA-MARU, WAIT.
I WANT TO PERSONALLY TEACH THIS FIRST-YEAR A LESSON.
GET READY TO LEARN...
...ABOUT THE HARD-SHIPS MAI HAS TO GO THROUGH.
AND WHAT IT MEANS FOR A WOMAN TO BE A SOR-CERER!

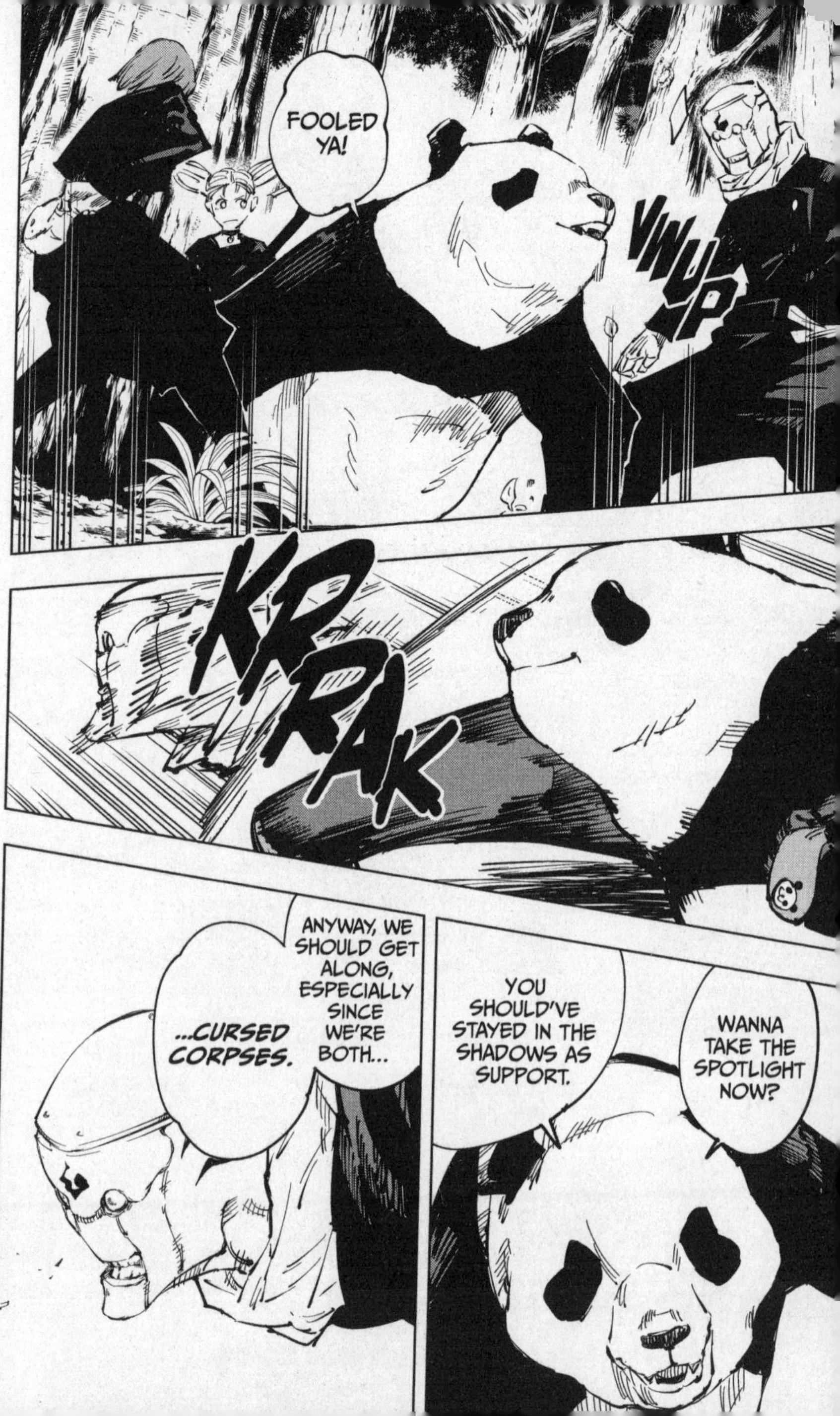
FOOLED YA!
VWUP
KRRAK
WANNA TAKE THE SPOTLIGHT NOW?
YOU SHOULD'VE STAYED IN THE SHADOWS AS SUPPORT.
ANYWAY, WE SHOULD GET ALONG, ESPECIALLY SINCE WE'RE BOTH...
...CURSED CORPSES.

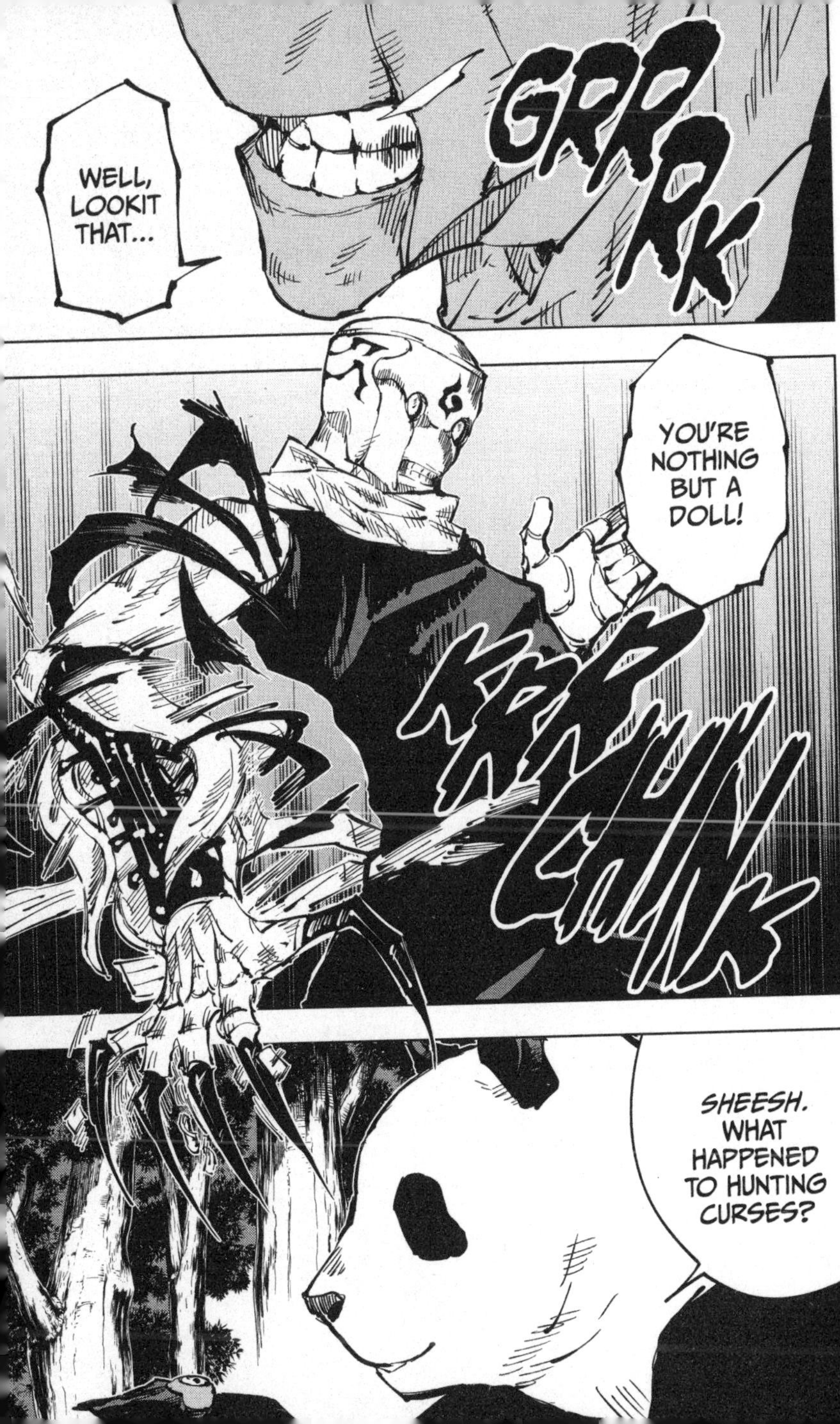
GRRRK
WELL, LOOKIT THAT...
YOU'RE NOTHING BUT A DOLL!
SHEESH. WHAT HAPPENED TO HUNTING CURSES?

MAI ZEN'IN

- Mai is a natural-born troublemaker.

- For some reason, whenever Mai interacts with another female character, you might wonder if they're dating.

- She and her twin are about 170 cm tall.

- Is her hairstyle okay?

MAKI ZEN'IN

- The length of her ponytail seems to change at Akutami Sensei's whim.

- Maki's hair is straighter than Mai's.

- She loves junk food.

- If you want to know more about Maki, buy read volume 0!

Chapter 38: Kyoto Sister-School Goodwill Event—Team Battle, Part 5

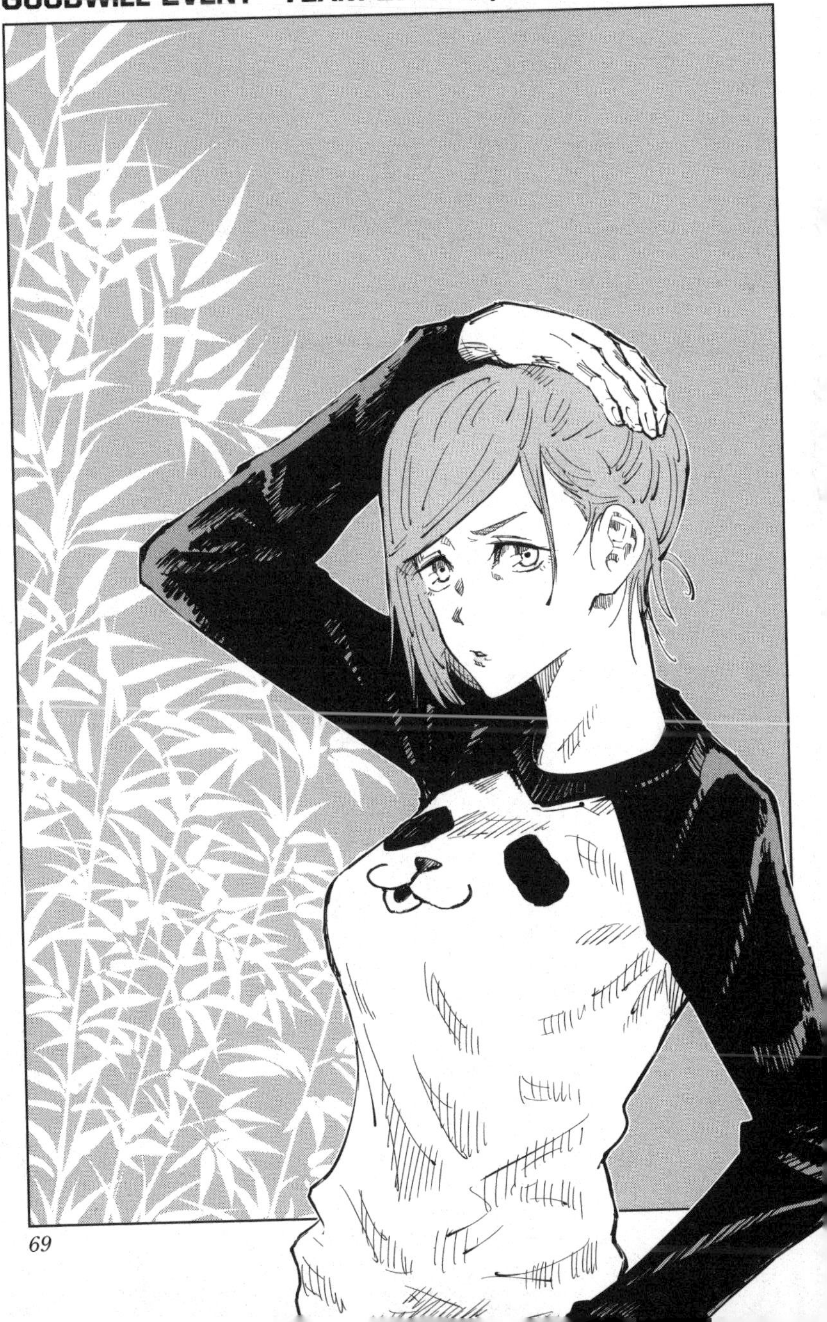

ANYWAY, WE SHOULD GET ALONG, ESPECIALLY SINCE WE'RE BOTH...

KSH...

...CURSED CORPSES.

KSSHH...

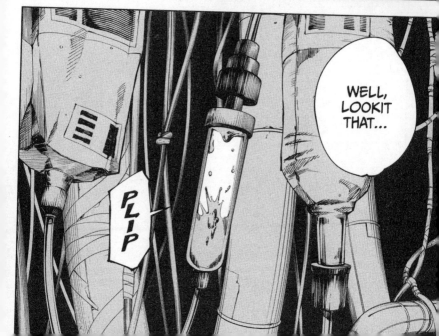

WELL, LOOKIT THAT...

PLIP

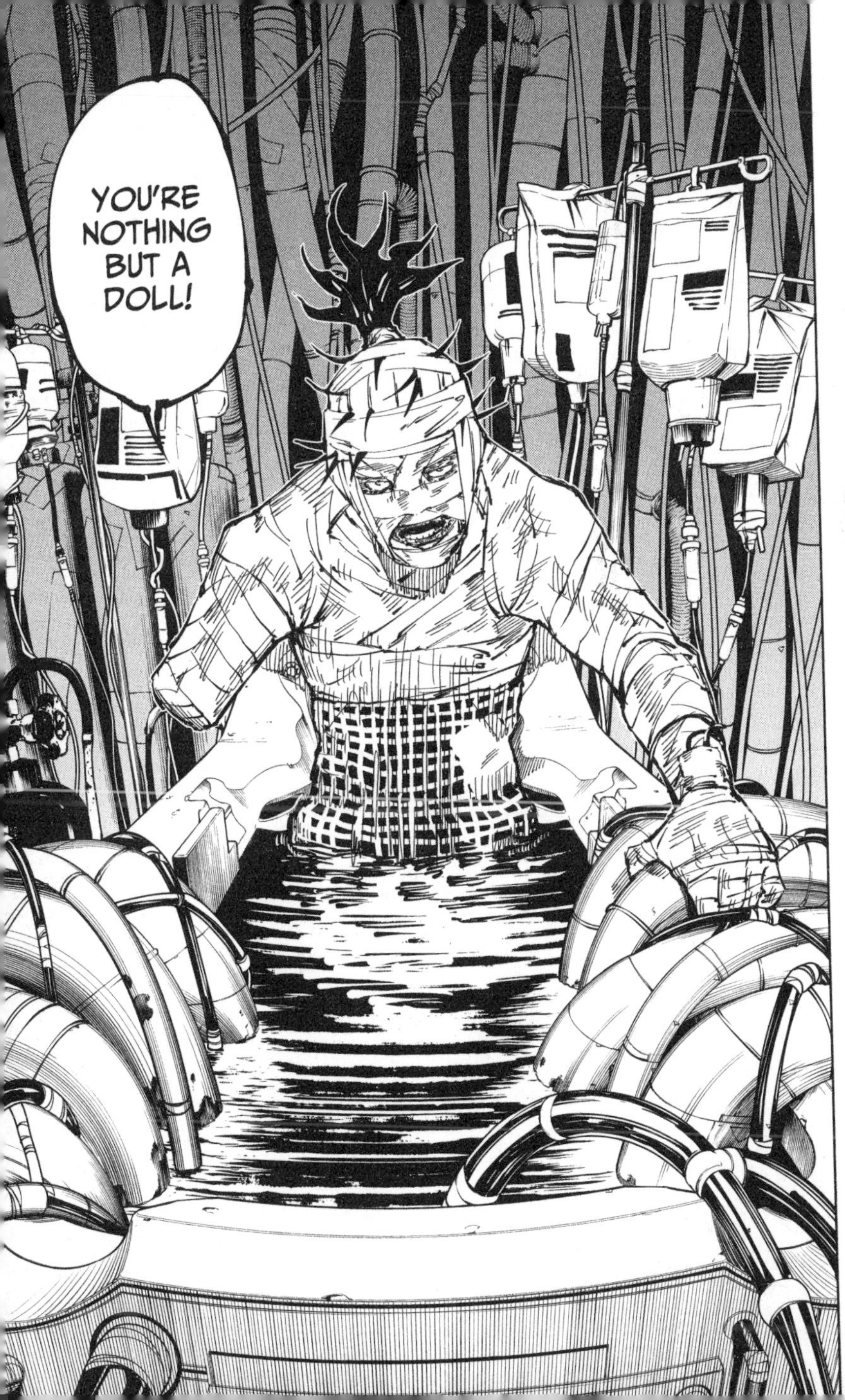
YOU'RE NOTHING BUT A DOLL!

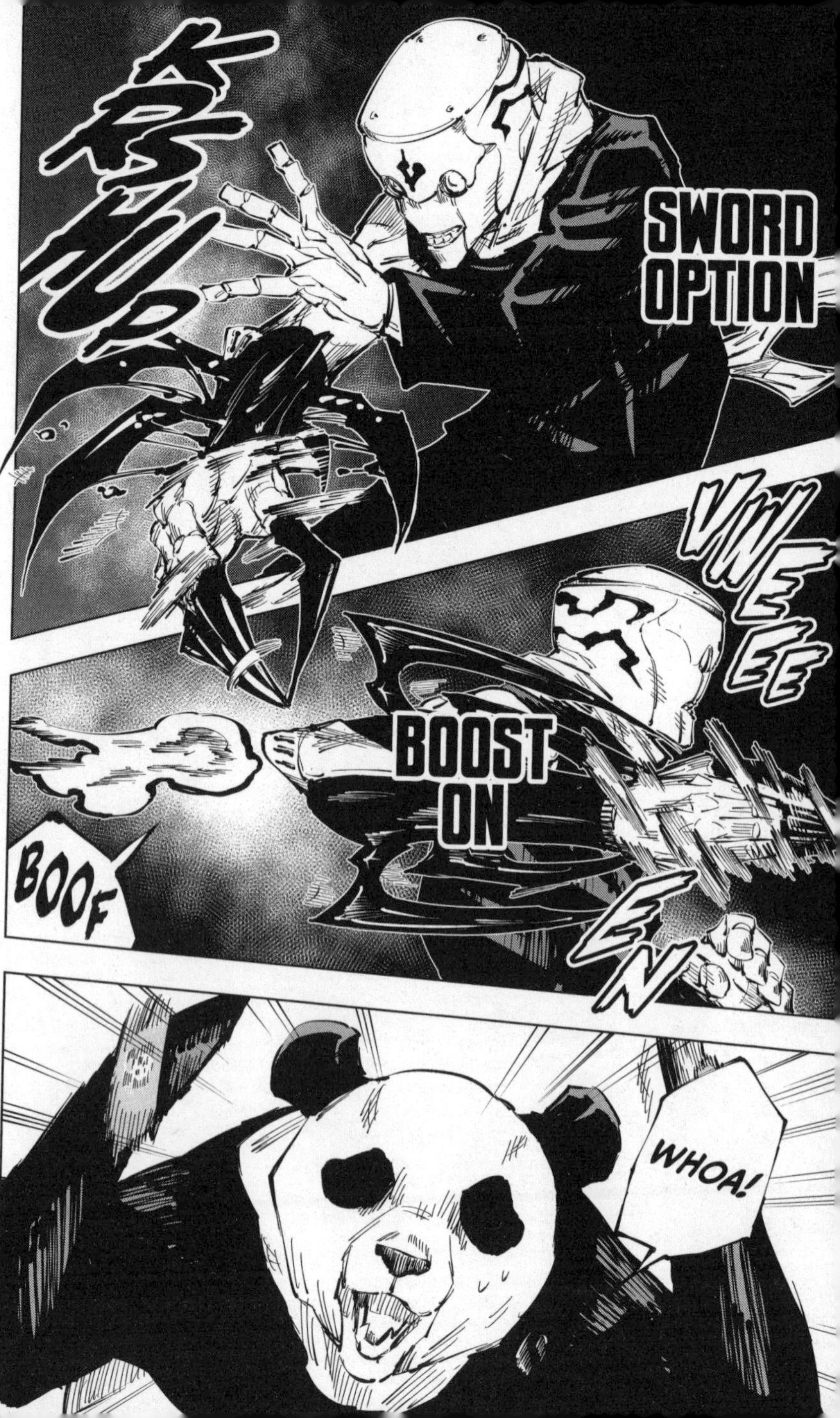
SWORD OPTION
KRSHUP
VWEEEEN
BOOST ON
BOOF
WHOA!

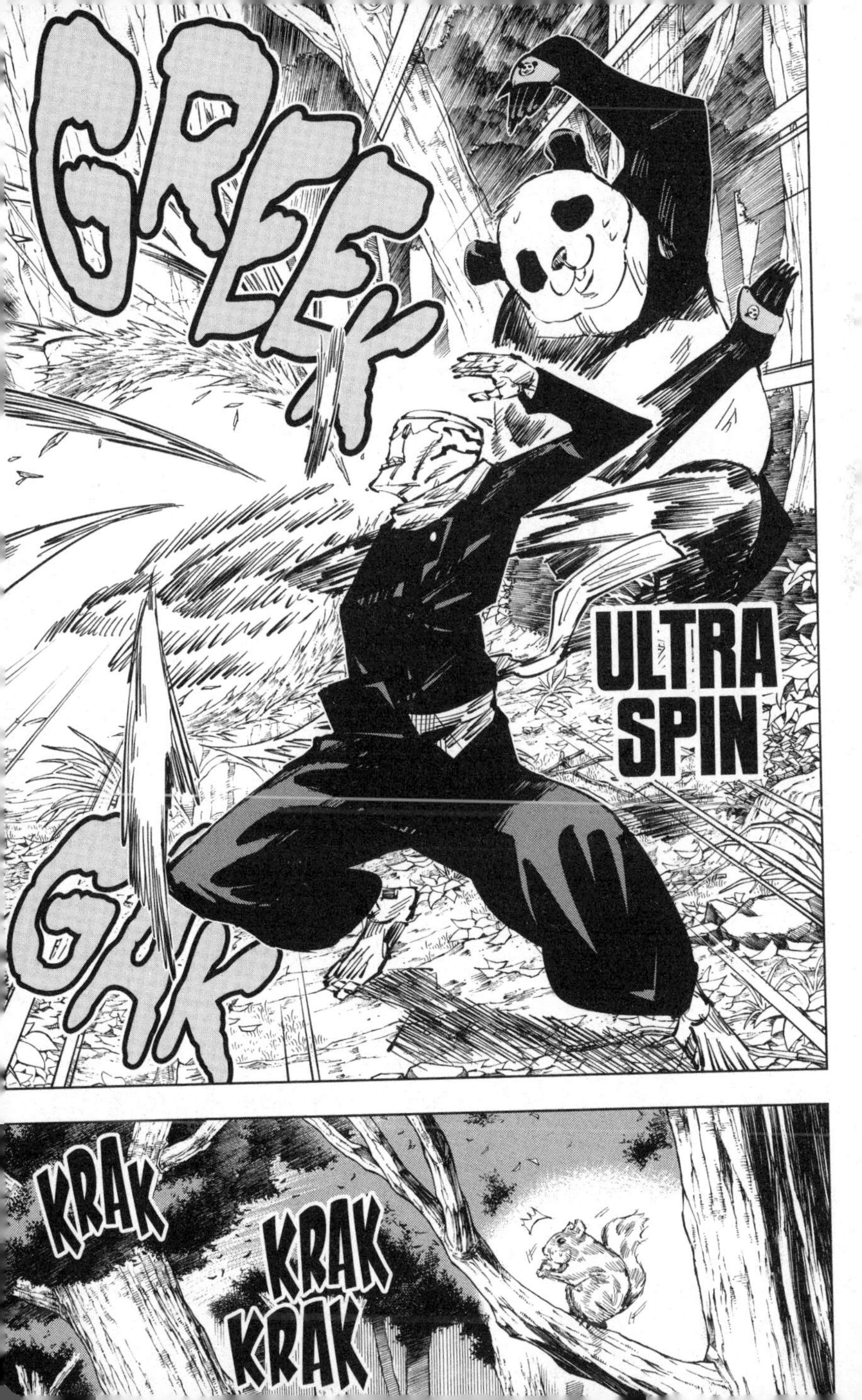
GREEK
ULTRA SPIN
GAK
KRAK KRAK
KRAK

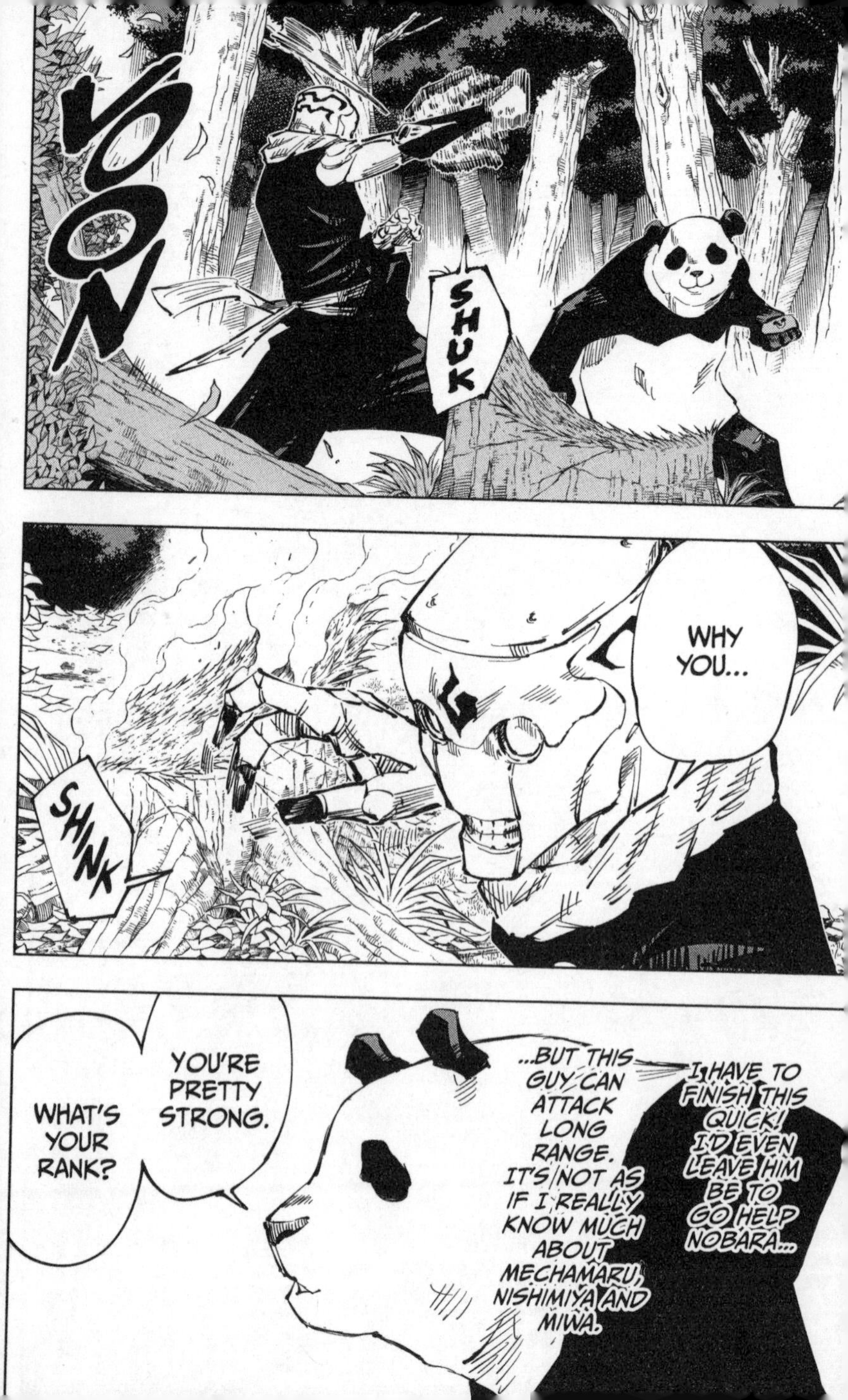
VOOON
SHUK
WHY YOU...
SHINK
I HAVE TO FINISH THIS QUICK! I'D EVEN LEAVE HIM BE TO GO HELP NOBARA...
...BUT THIS GUY CAN ATTACK LONG RANGE. IT'S NOT AS IF I REALLY KNOW MUCH ABOUT MECHAMARU, NISHIMIYA AND MIWA.
YOU'RE PRETTY STRONG.
WHAT'S YOUR RANK?

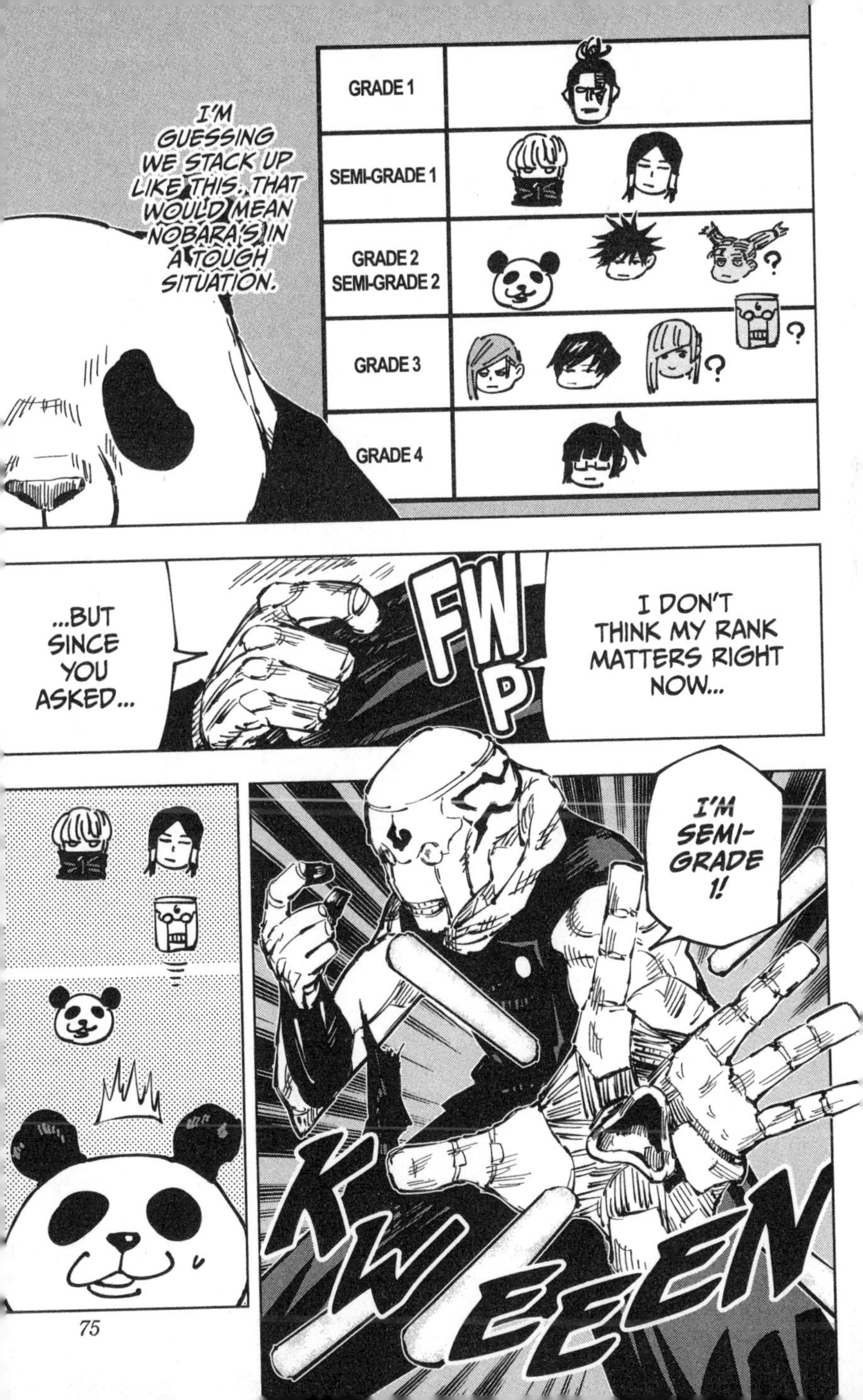
GRADE 1
SEMI-GRADE 1
GRADE 2
SEMI-GRADE 2
GRADE 3
GRADE 4
I'M GUESSING WE STACK UP LIKE THIS. THAT WOULD MEAN NOBARA'S IN A TOUGH SITUATION.
I DON'T THINK MY RANK MATTERS RIGHT NOW...
FWP
...BUT SINCE YOU ASKED...
I'M SEMI-GRADE 1!
KWEEEEN

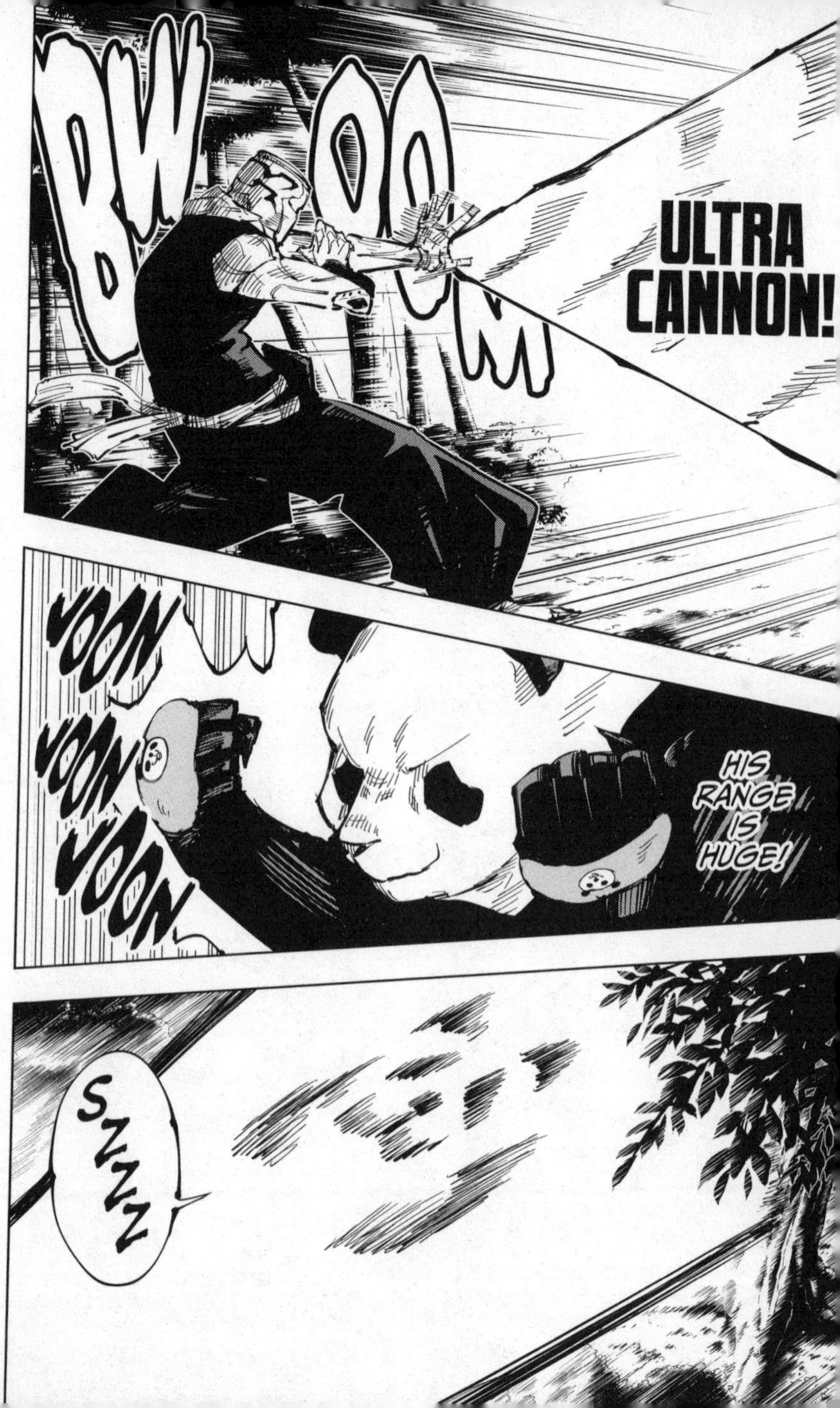
BWOOOM
ULTRA CANNON!
HIS RANGE IS HUGE!
JOON JOON JOON
SZZZ

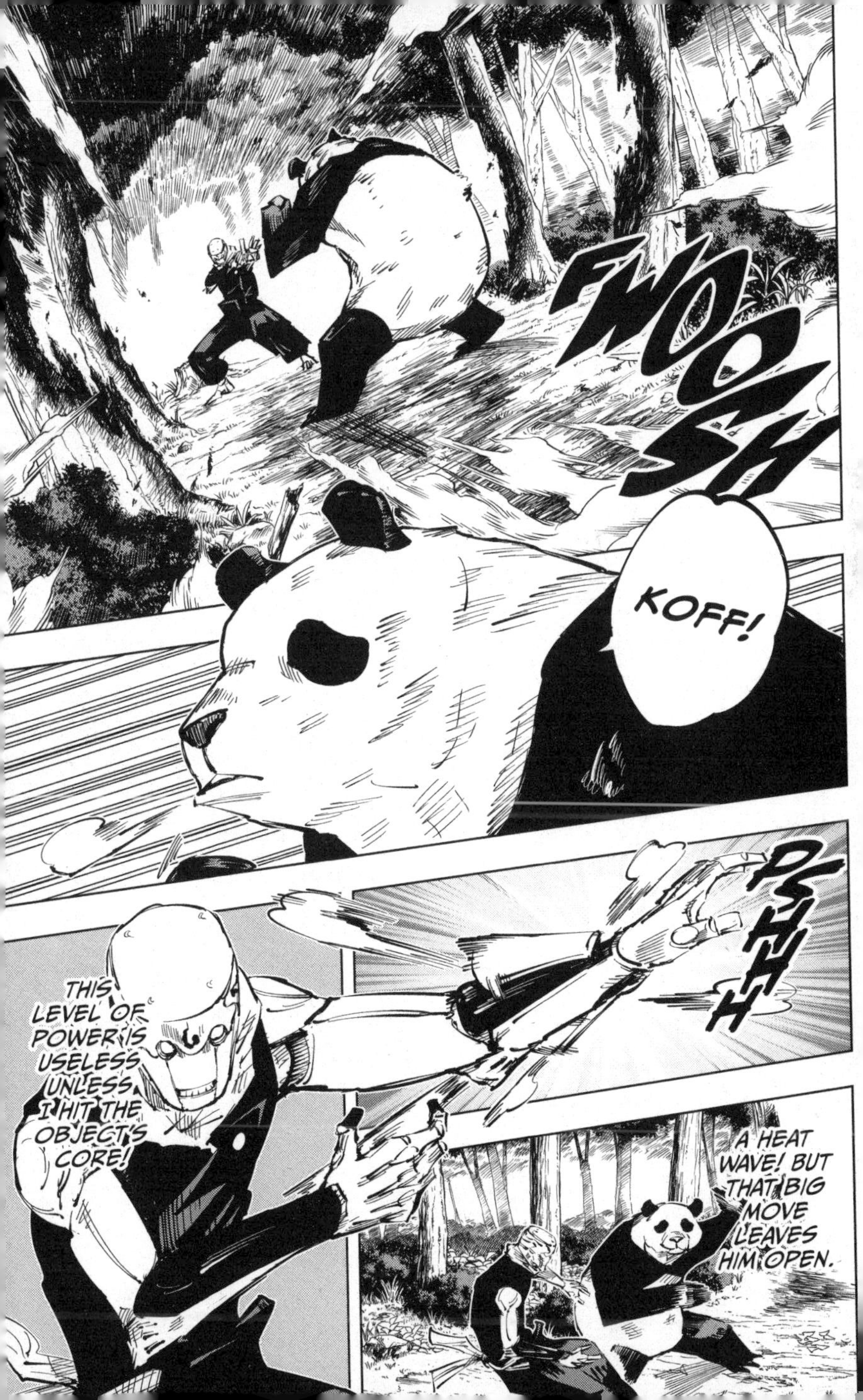
FWOOSH
KOFF!
PSHHH
THIS LEVEL OF POWER IS USELESS UNLESS I HIT THE OBJECT'S CORE!
A HEAT WAVE! BUT THAT BIG MOVE LEAVES HIM OPEN.

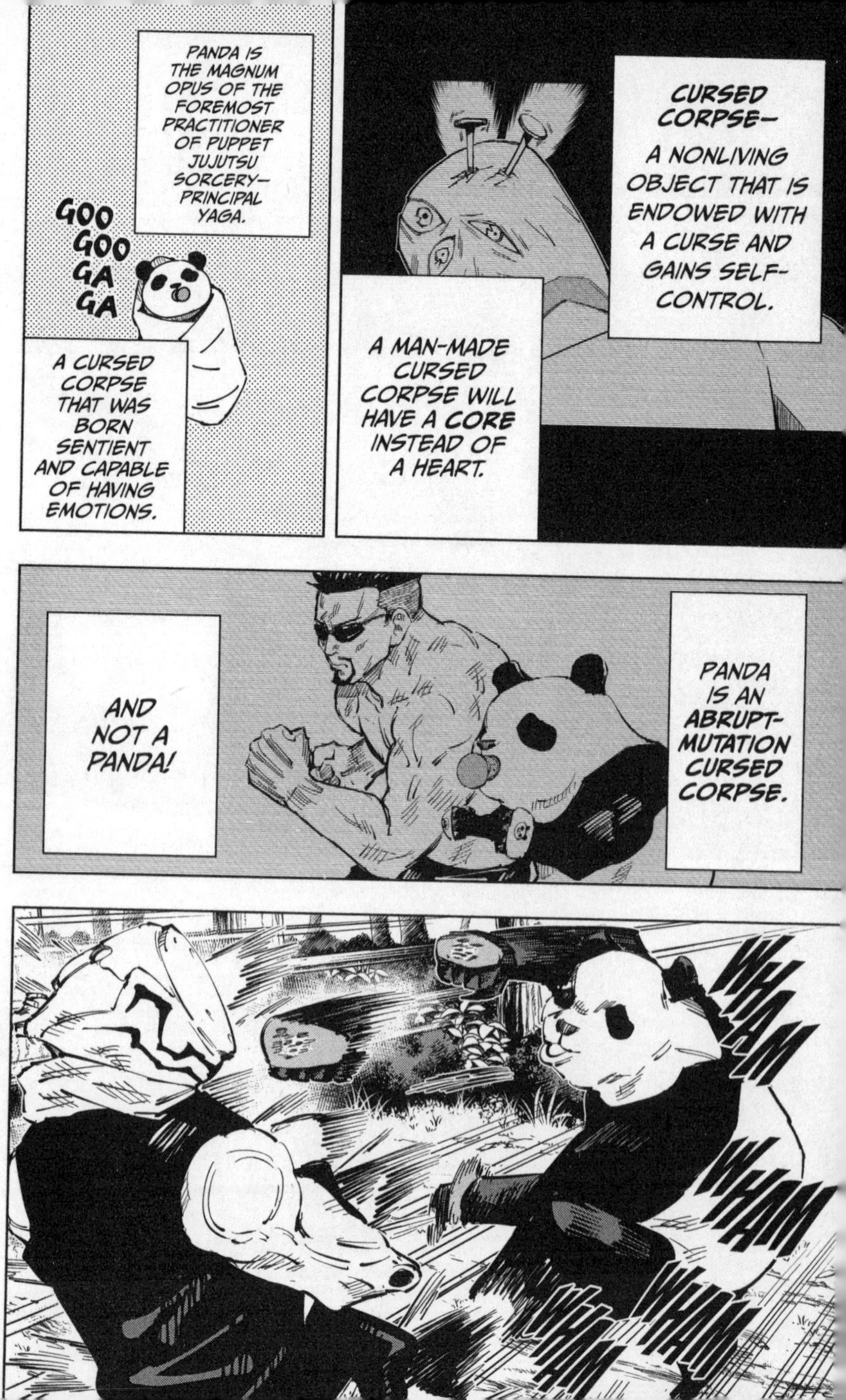
CURSED CORPSE— A NONLIVING OBJECT THAT IS ENDOWED WITH A CURSE AND GAINS SELF-CONTROL.
A MAN-MADE CURSED CORPSE WILL HAVE A CORE INSTEAD OF A HEART.
PANDA IS THE MAGNUM OPUS OF THE FOREMOST PRACTITIONER OF PUPPET JUJUTSU SORCERY— PRINCIPAL YAGA.
GOO GOO GA GA
A CURSED CORPSE THAT WAS BORN SENTIENT AND CAPABLE OF HAVING EMOTIONS.
PANDA IS AN ABRUPT-MUTATION CURSED CORPSE.
AND NOT A PANDA!
WHAM
WHAM
WHAM
WHAM

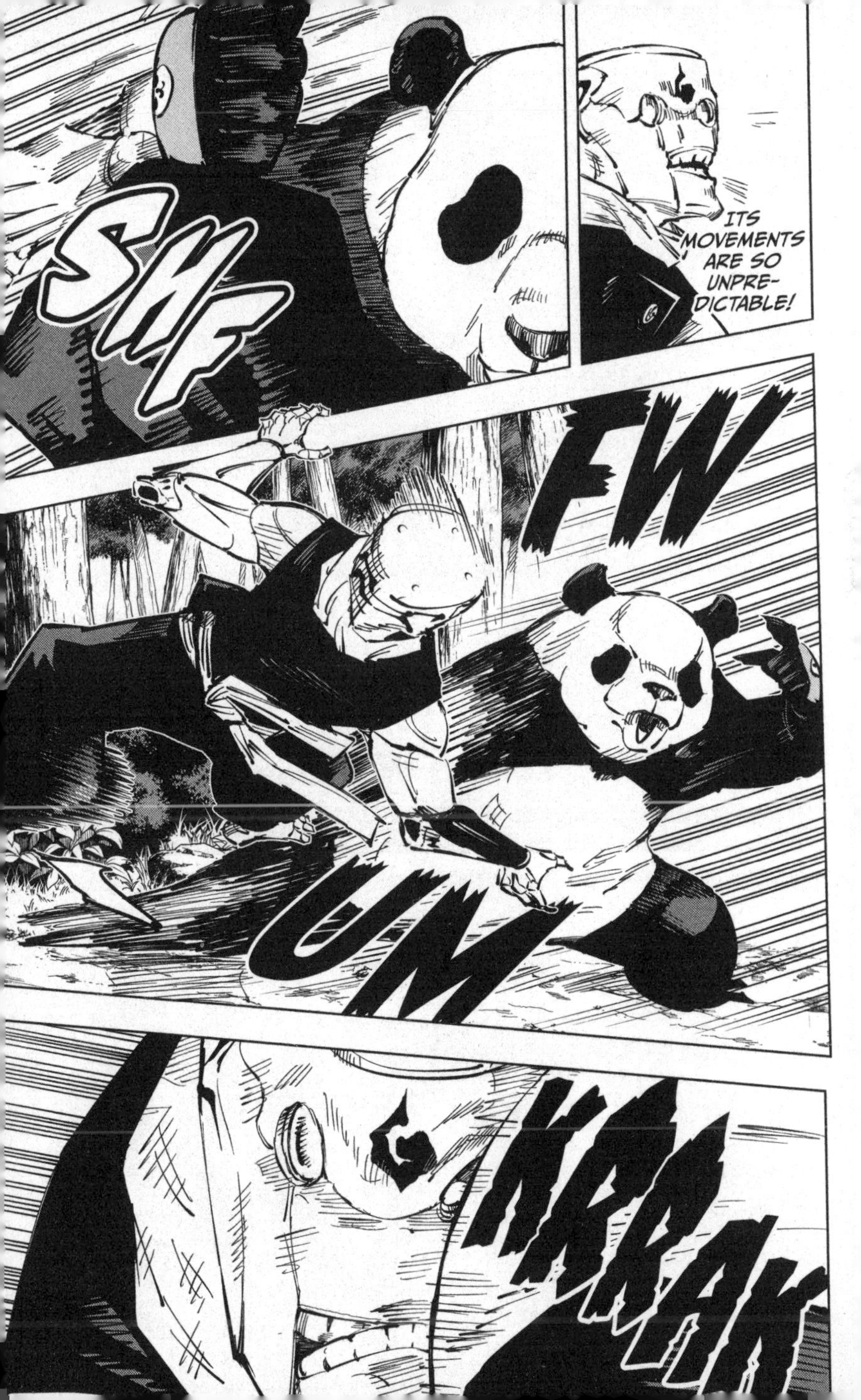
ITS MOVEMENTS ARE SO UNPRE-DICTABLE!
SHF
FW
UM
KRAK

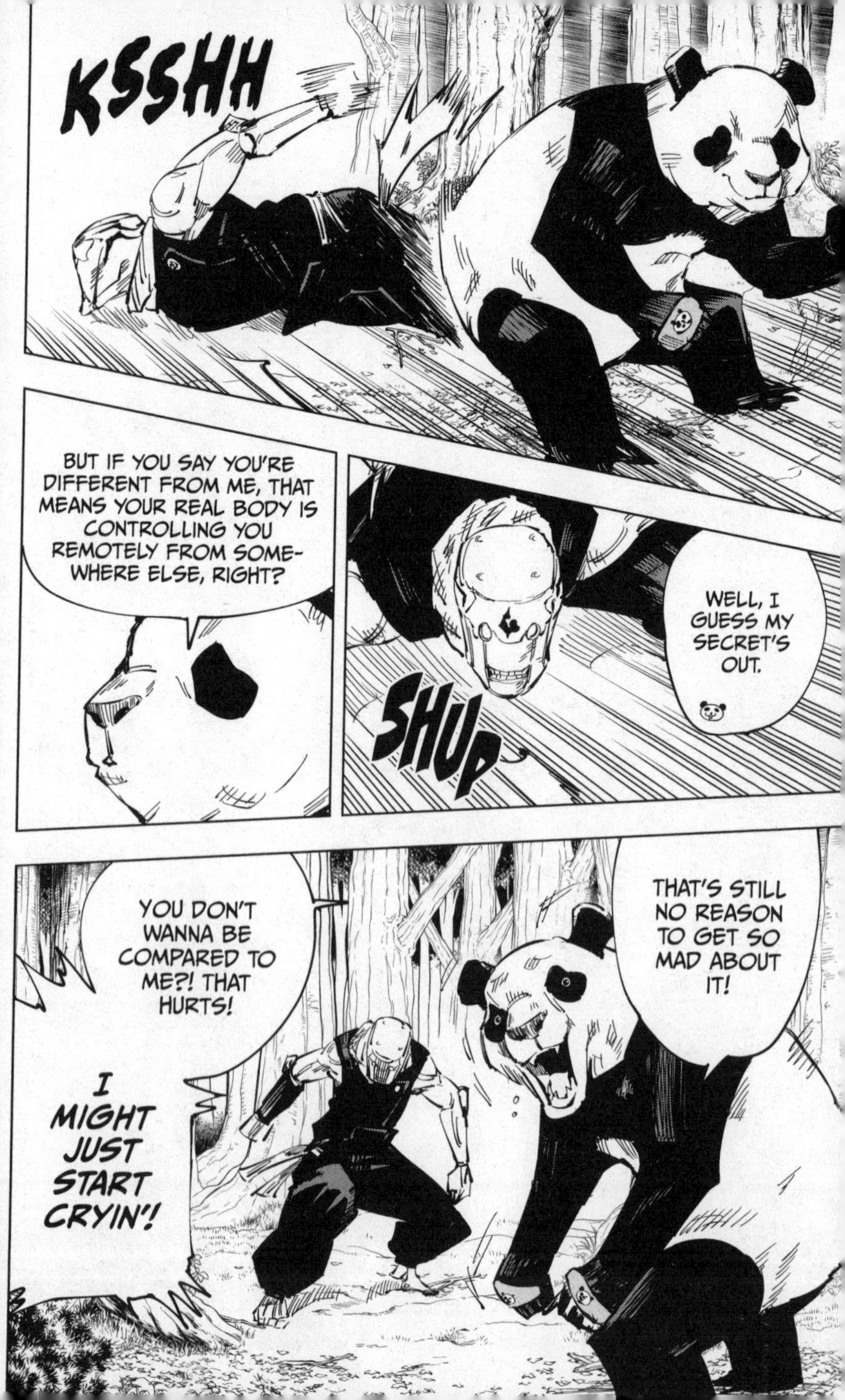
KSSHH
WELL, I GUESS MY SECRET'S OUT.
SHUD
BUT IF YOU SAY YOU'RE DIFFERENT FROM ME, THAT MEANS YOUR REAL BODY IS CONTROLLING YOU REMOTELY FROM SOME-WHERE ELSE, RIGHT?
THAT'S STILL NO REASON TO GET SO MAD ABOUT IT!
YOU DON'T WANNA BE COMPARED TO ME?! THAT HURTS!
I MIGHT JUST START CRYIN'!

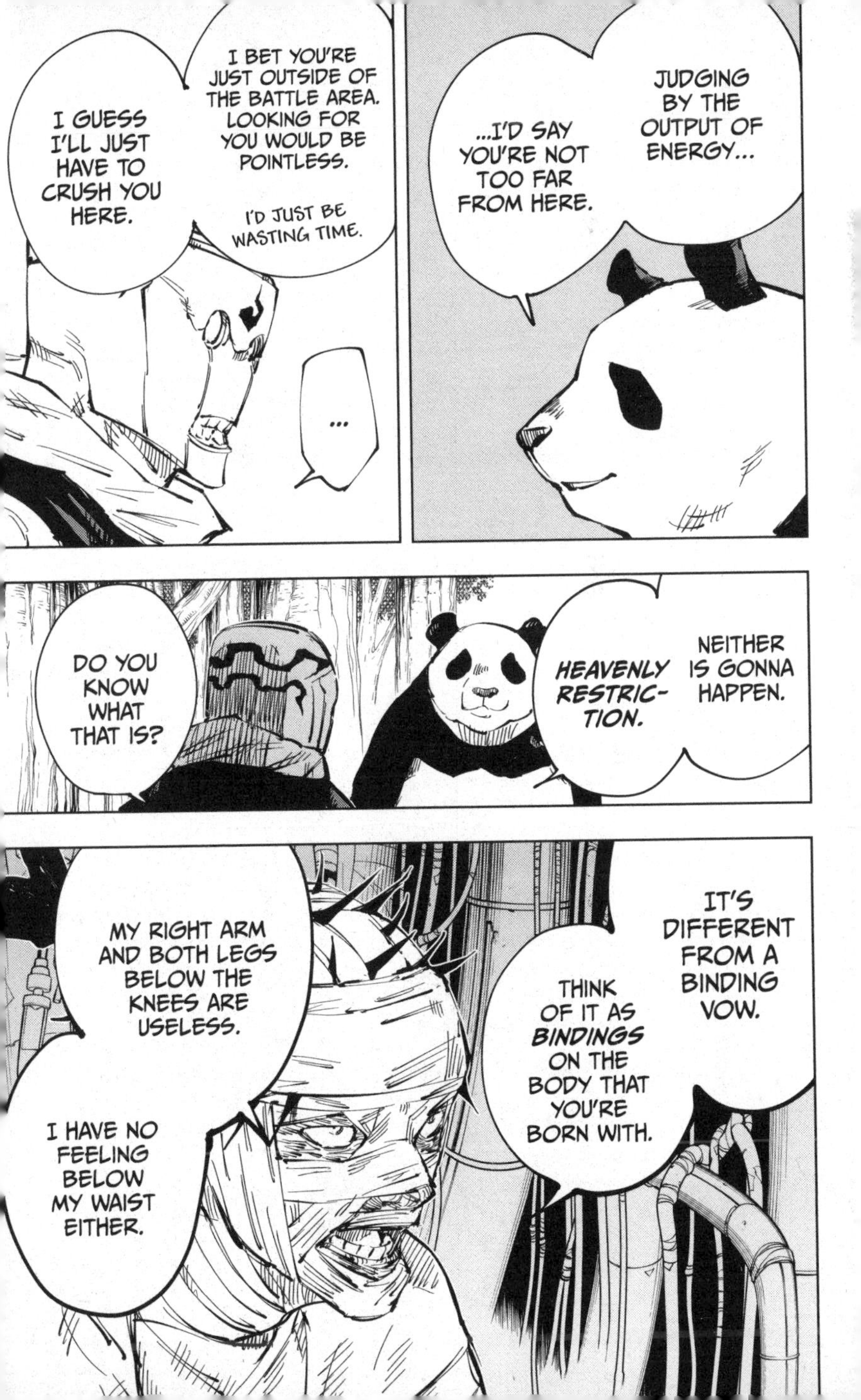
JUDGING BY THE OUTPUT OF ENERGY...
...I'D SAY YOU'RE NOT TOO FAR FROM HERE.
I BET YOU'RE JUST OUTSIDE OF THE BATTLE AREA. LOOKING FOR YOU WOULD BE POINTLESS.
I'D JUST BE WASTING TIME.
I GUESS I'LL JUST HAVE TO CRUSH YOU HERE.
...
NEITHER IS GONNA HAPPEN.
HEAVENLY RESTRICTION.
DO YOU KNOW WHAT THAT IS?
IT'S DIFFERENT FROM A BINDING VOW.
THINK OF IT AS *BINDINGS* ON THE BODY THAT YOU'RE BORN WITH.
MY RIGHT ARM AND BOTH LEGS BELOW THE KNEES ARE USELESS.
I HAVE NO FEELING BELOW MY WAIST EITHER.

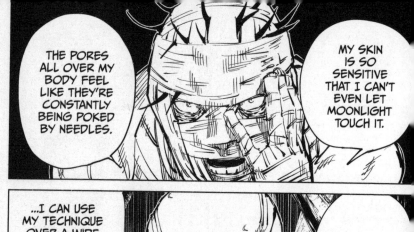

MY SKIN IS SO SENSITIVE THAT I CAN'T EVEN LET MOONLIGHT TOUCH IT.
THE PORES ALL OVER MY BODY FEEL LIKE THEY'RE CONSTANTLY BEING POKED BY NEEDLES.
BUT IN EXCHANGE...
...I CAN USE MY TECHNIQUE OVER A WIDE RANGE. I CAN ALSO EXCEED THE LIMITS OF MY CURSED ENERGY OUTPUT.
I DIDN'T ASK FOR THIS POWER.
IF I COULD EXCHANGE THIS BODY FOR A HEALTHY ONE, I'D DO IT IN A HEARTBEAT, EVEN IF IT MEANT LEAVING THE JUJUTSU WORLD BEHIND.
THE FACT THAT A DOLL LIKE YOU...
...AND NOT A HUMAN LIKE ME...
...GETS TO LIVE SO CAREFREE IN THE SUN...

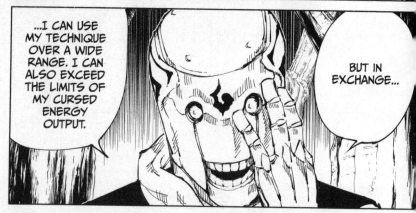

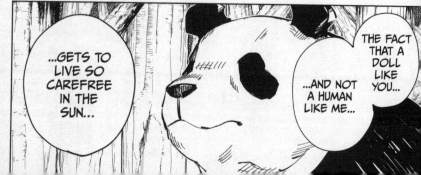

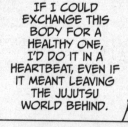

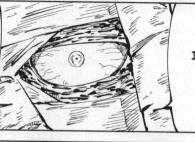

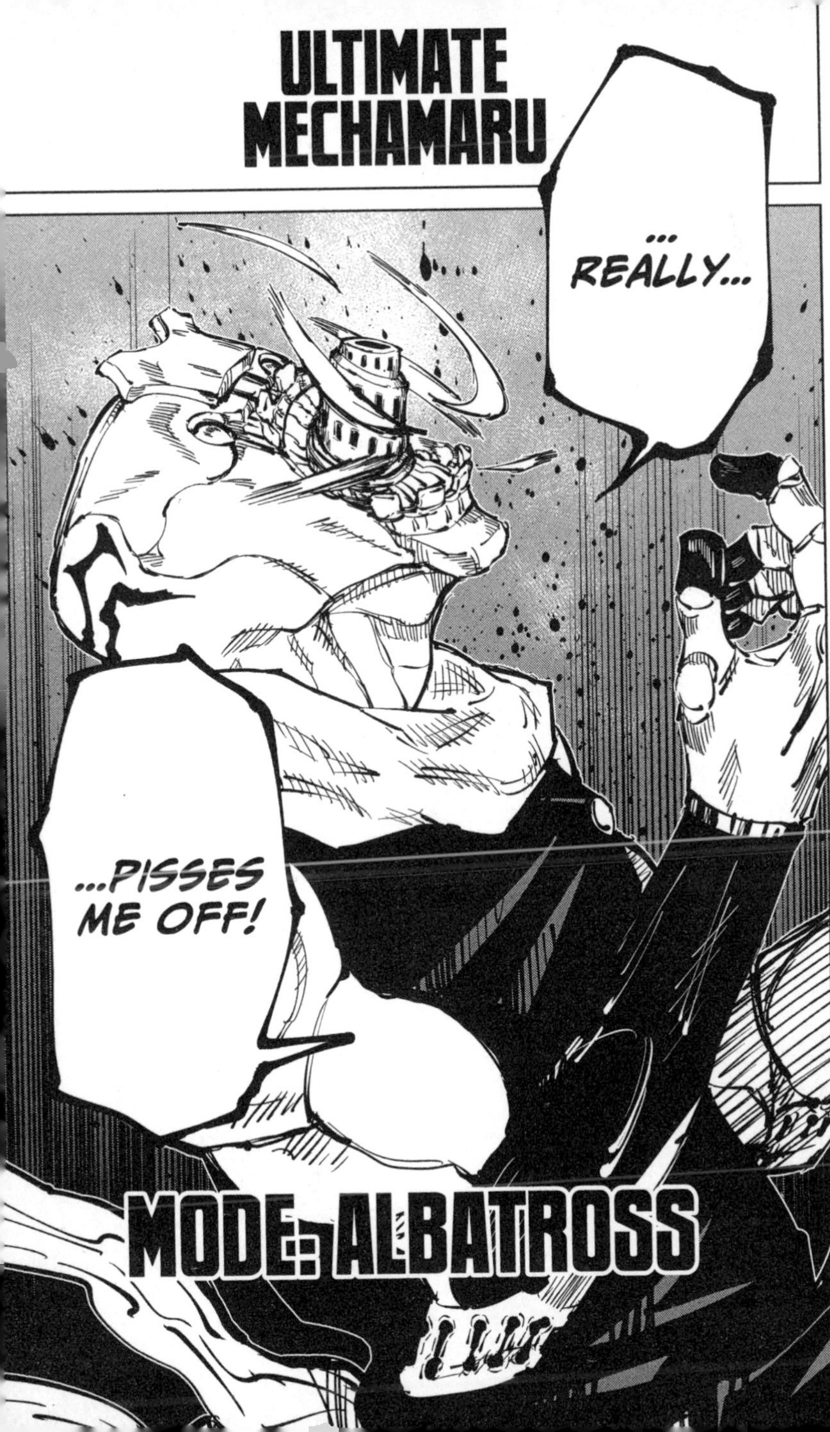
ULTIMATE MECHAMARU
... REALLY...
...PISSES ME OFF!
MODE: ALBATROSS

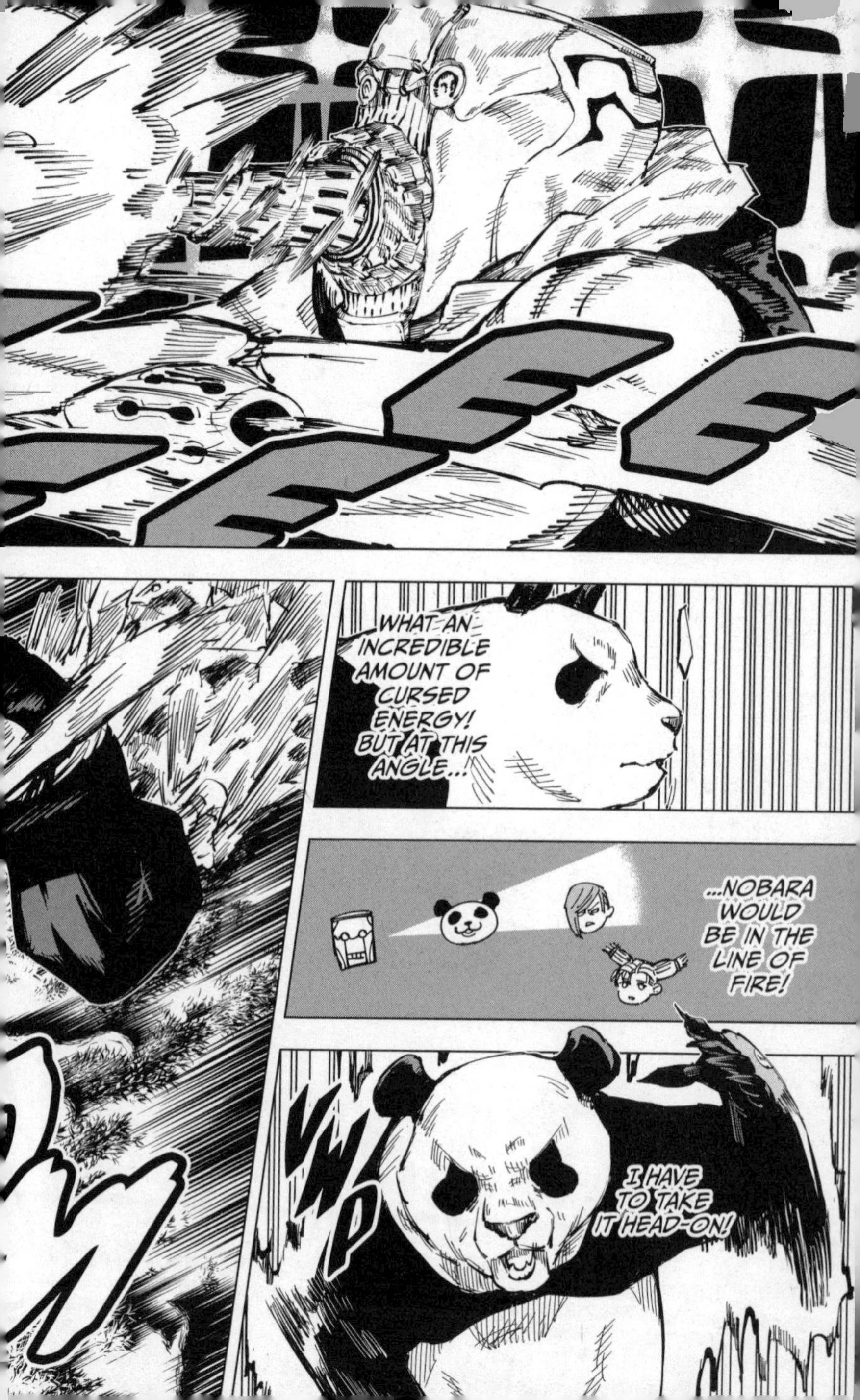
WHAT AN INCREDIBLE AMOUNT OF CURSED ENERGY! BUT AT THIS ANGLE...!
...NOBARA WOULD BE IN THE LINE OF FIRE!
I HAVE TO TAKE IT HEAD-ON!

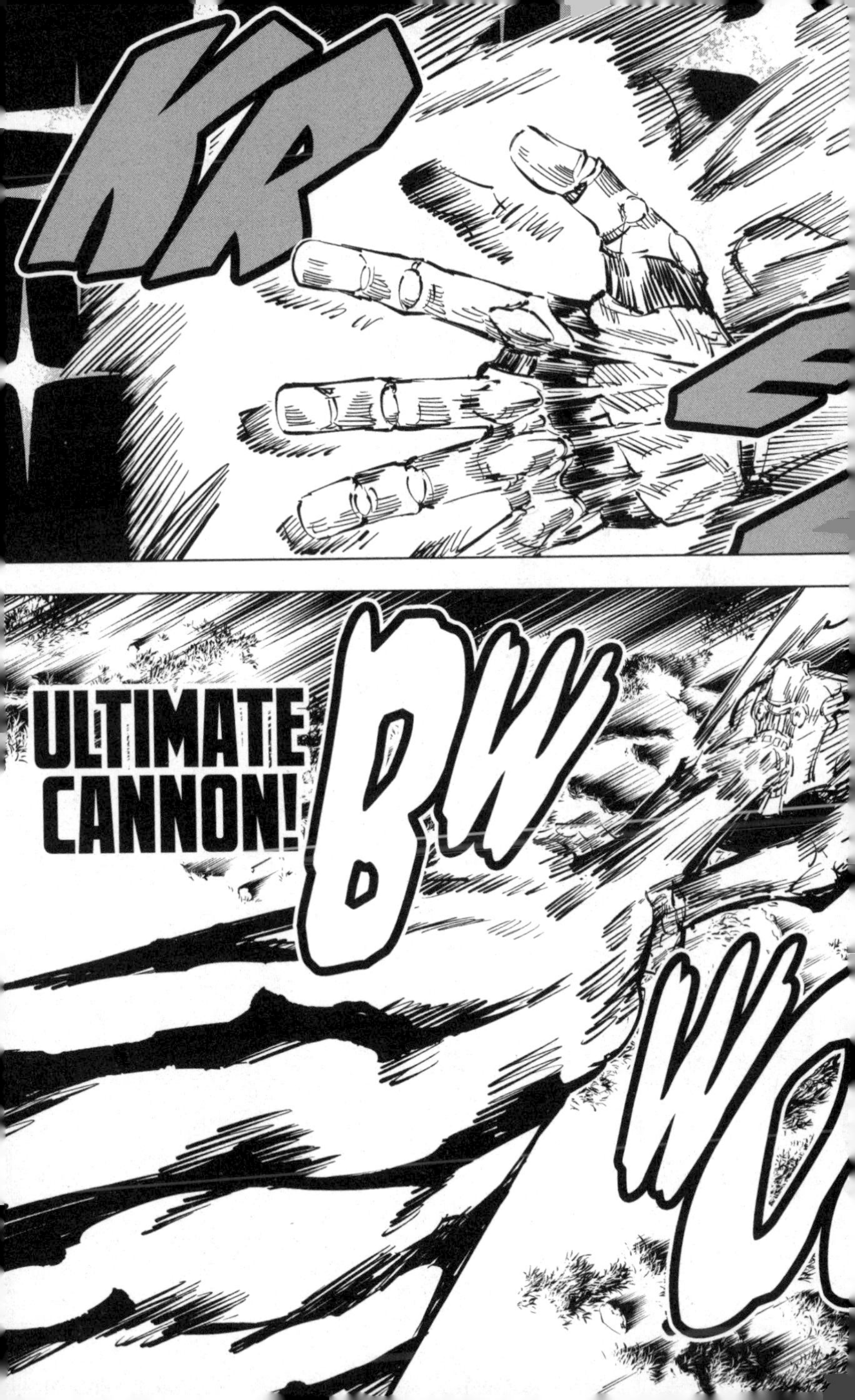
KR
ULTIMATE CANNON!
BW

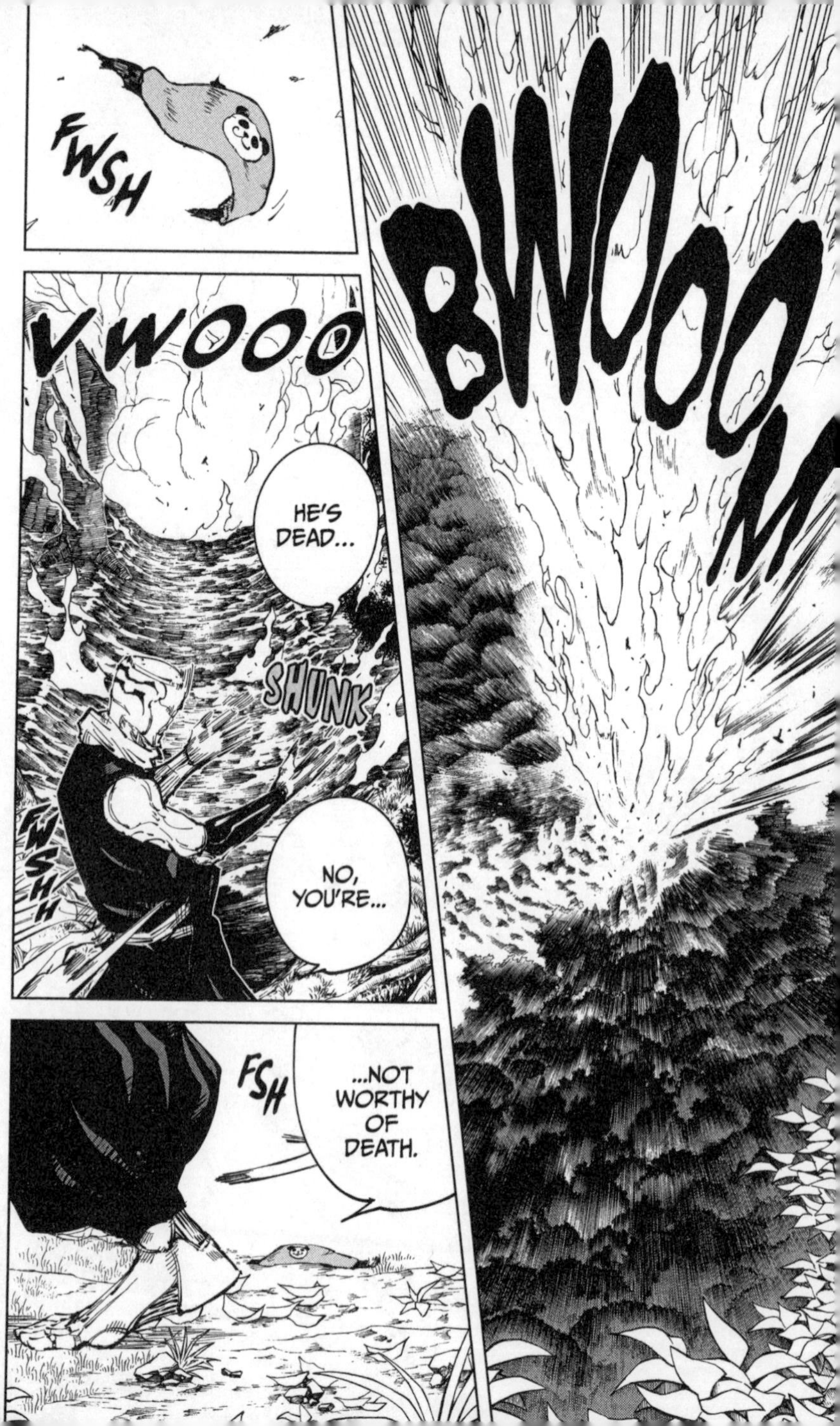
BWOOOM
FWSH
VWOOO
HE'S DEAD...
SHUNK
NO, YOU'RE...
FWSHH
FSH
...NOT WORTHY OF DEATH.

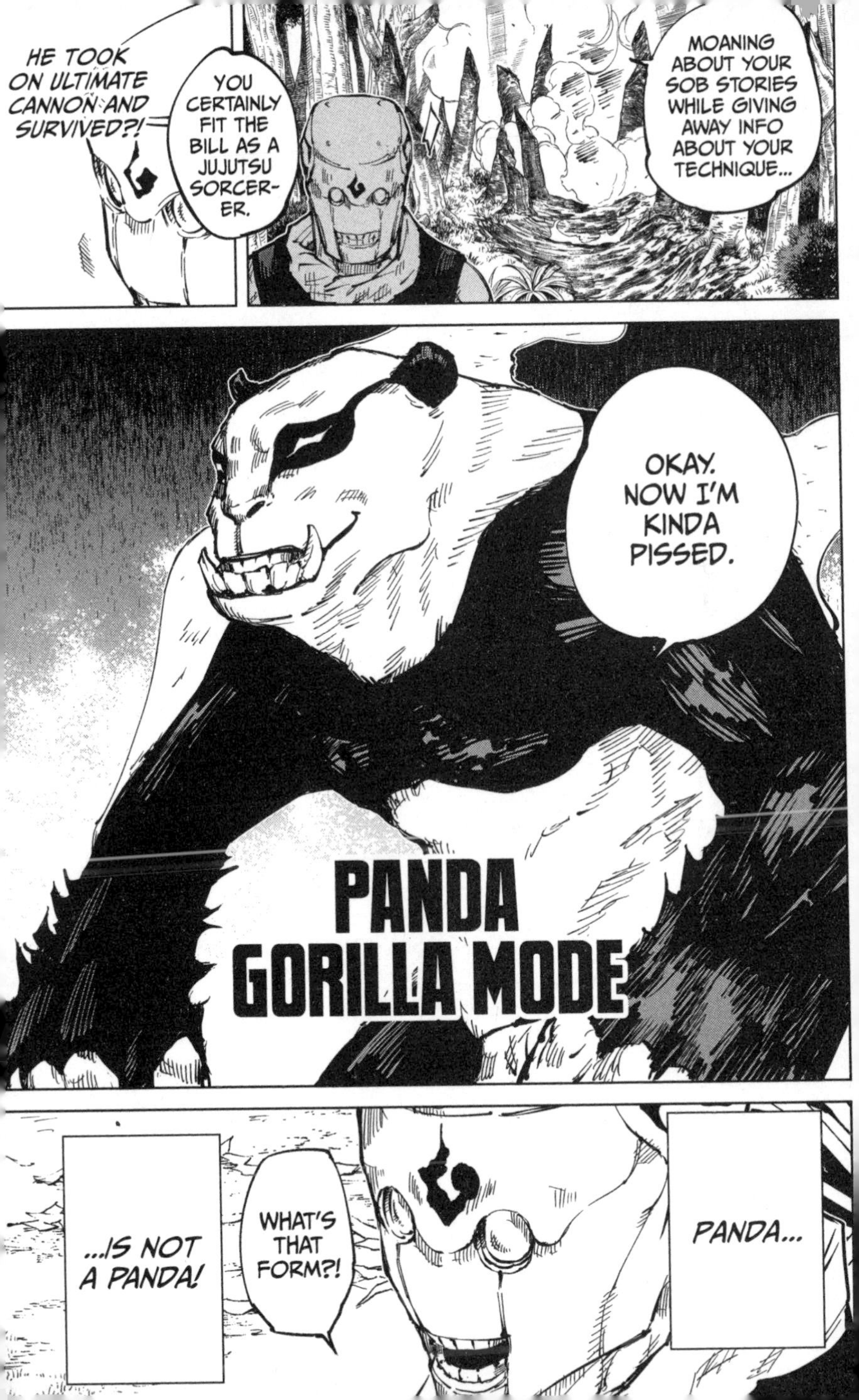
MOANING ABOUT YOUR SOB STORIES WHILE GIVING AWAY INFO ABOUT YOUR TECHNIQUE...
YOU CERTAINLY FIT THE BILL AS A JUJUTSU SORCERER.
HE TOOK ON ULTIMATE CANNON AND SURVIVED?!
OKAY. NOW I'M KINDA PISSED.
PANDA GORILLA MODE
PANDA...
WHAT'S THAT FORM?!
...IS NOT A PANDA!

KASUMI MIWA

• Miwa was scouted to become a jujutsu sorcerer while in her first year in middle school at her part-time job by the foremost figure of the New Shadow Style. She got swept up and here she is!

• She thinks of herself as reliable, normal and nothing special. She's right, but the fact that someone can think that and also be a jujutsu sorcerer is a bit crazy.

• She loves trendy things. That's why her name is Miwa. (Note: Miwa's name in Japanese is a homonym for a word that means "someone who follows trends.")

ULTIMATE MECHAMARU

• I had decided from the beginning that I would wrap his whole body in bandages for his character design. But no matter how I approached it, he ended up looking like Shishio! So, I gave up.

• Mechamaru is not his real name. He named himself after a robot in a robot anime he was introduced to a long time ago. He likes the anime very much and has been using that name for some time now.

CHAPTER 39: KYOTO SISTER-SCHOOL
GOODWILL EVENT—TEAM BATTLE, PART 6

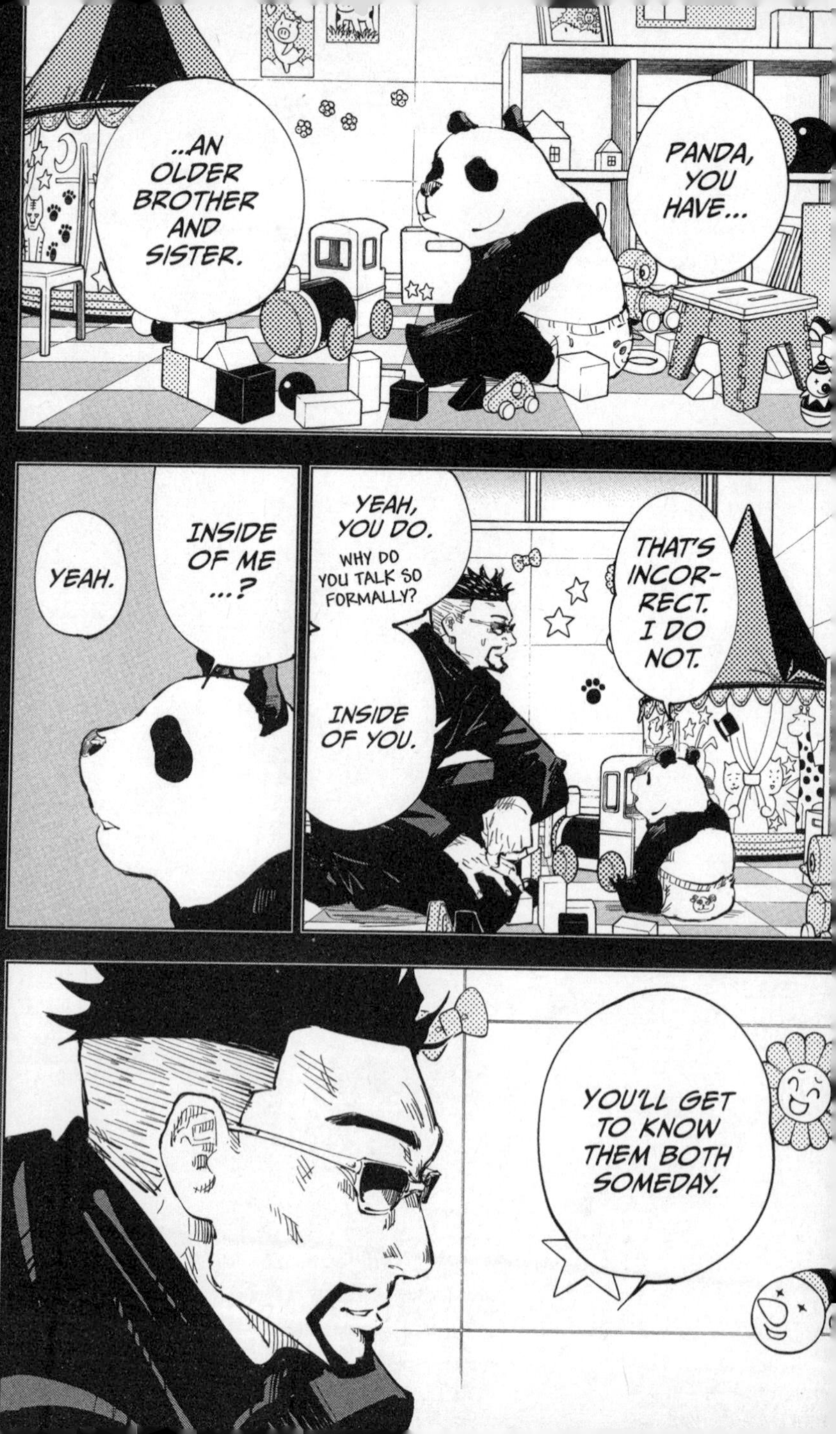
PANDA, YOU HAVE...
...AN OLDER BROTHER AND SISTER.
THAT'S INCOR-RECT. I DO NOT.
YEAH, YOU DO.
WHY DO YOU TALK SO FORMALLY?
INSIDE OF YOU.
INSIDE OF ME ...?
YEAH.
YOU'LL GET TO KNOW THEM BOTH SOMEDAY.

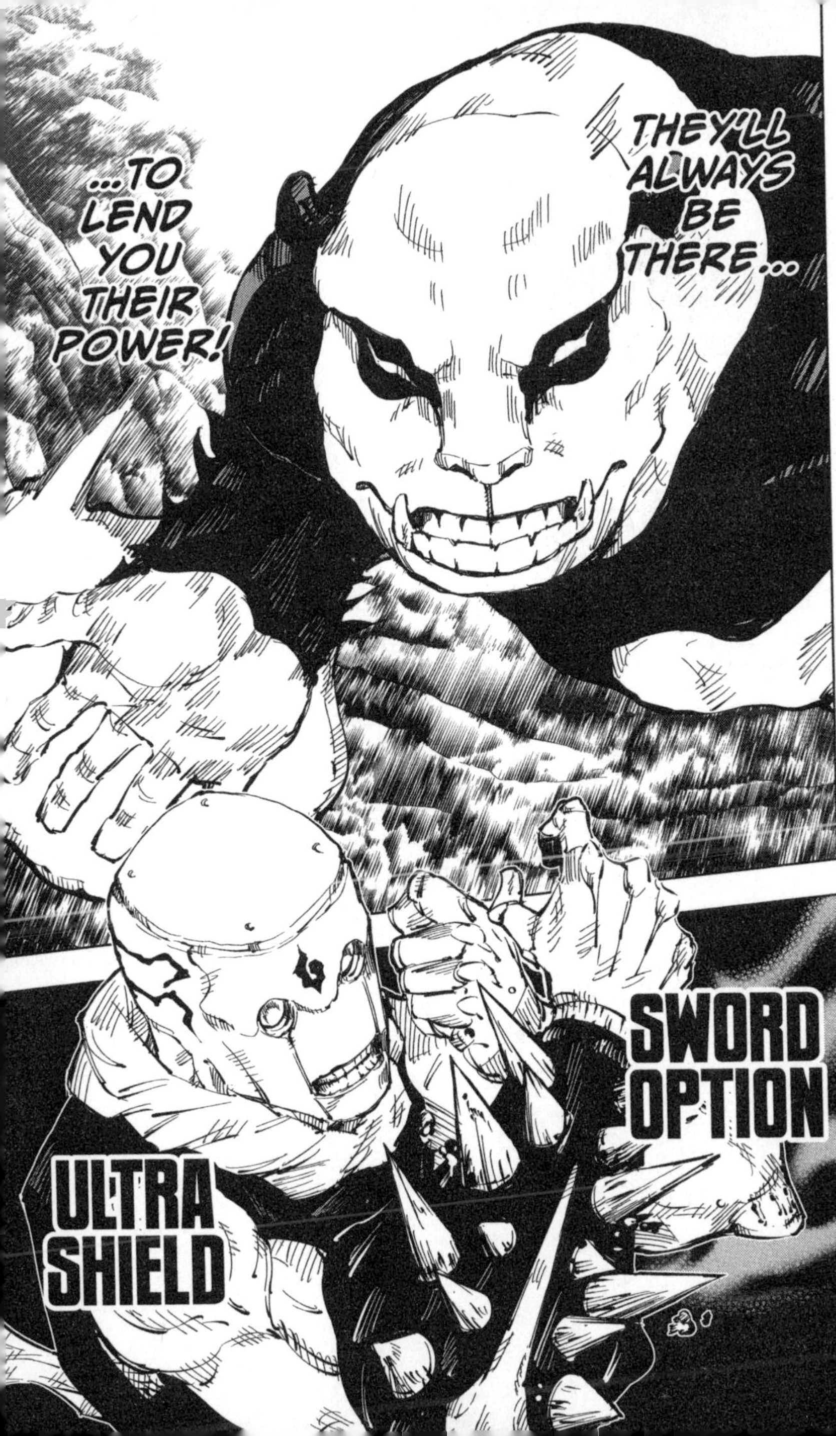
THEY'LL ALWAYS BE THERE...
...TO LEND YOU THEIR POWER!
SWORD OPTION
ULTRA SHIELD

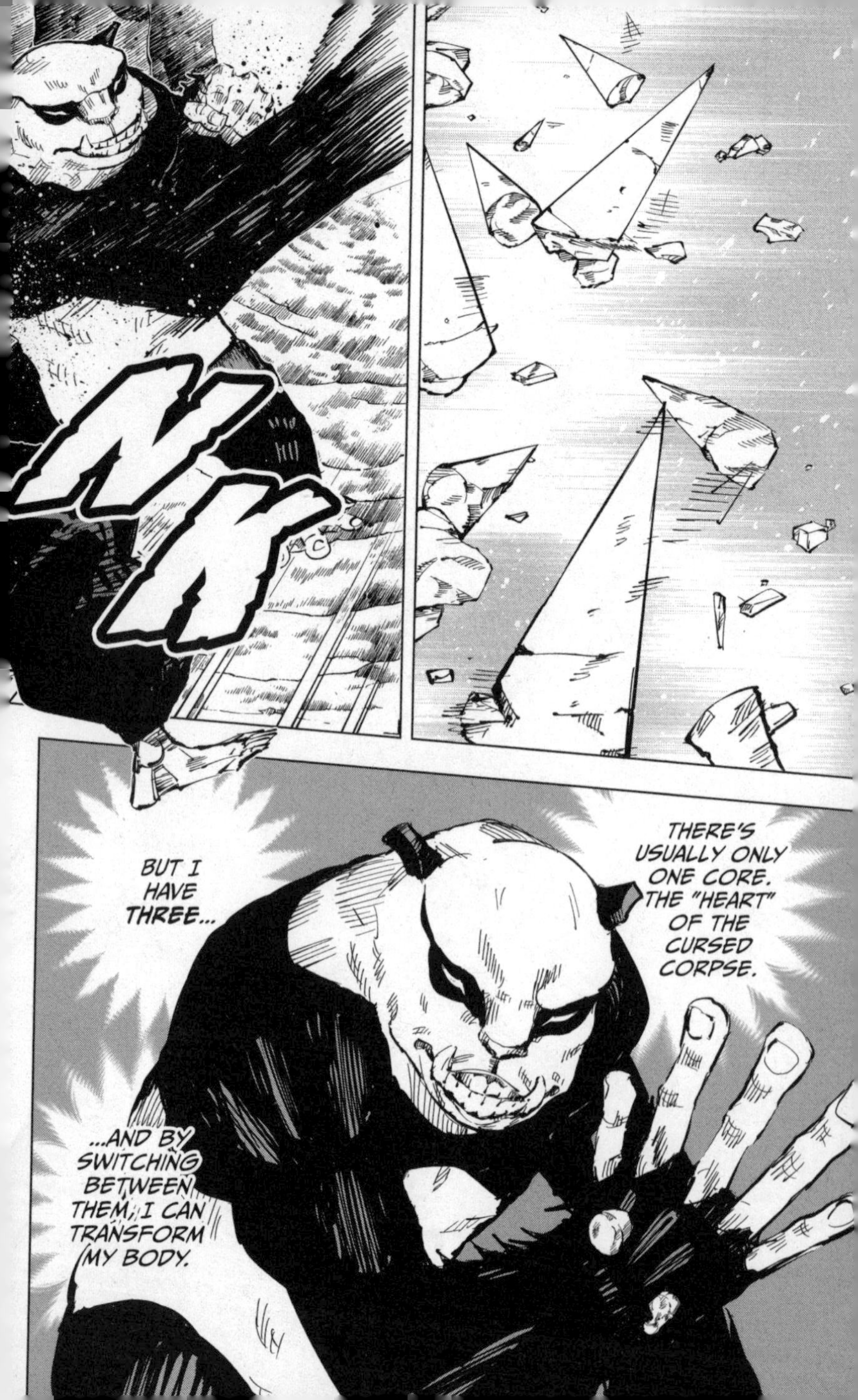
THERE'S USUALLY ONLY ONE CORE. THE "HEART" OF THE CURSED CORPSE.
BUT I HAVE THREE...
...AND BY SWITCHING BETWEEN THEM, I CAN TRANSFORM MY BODY.

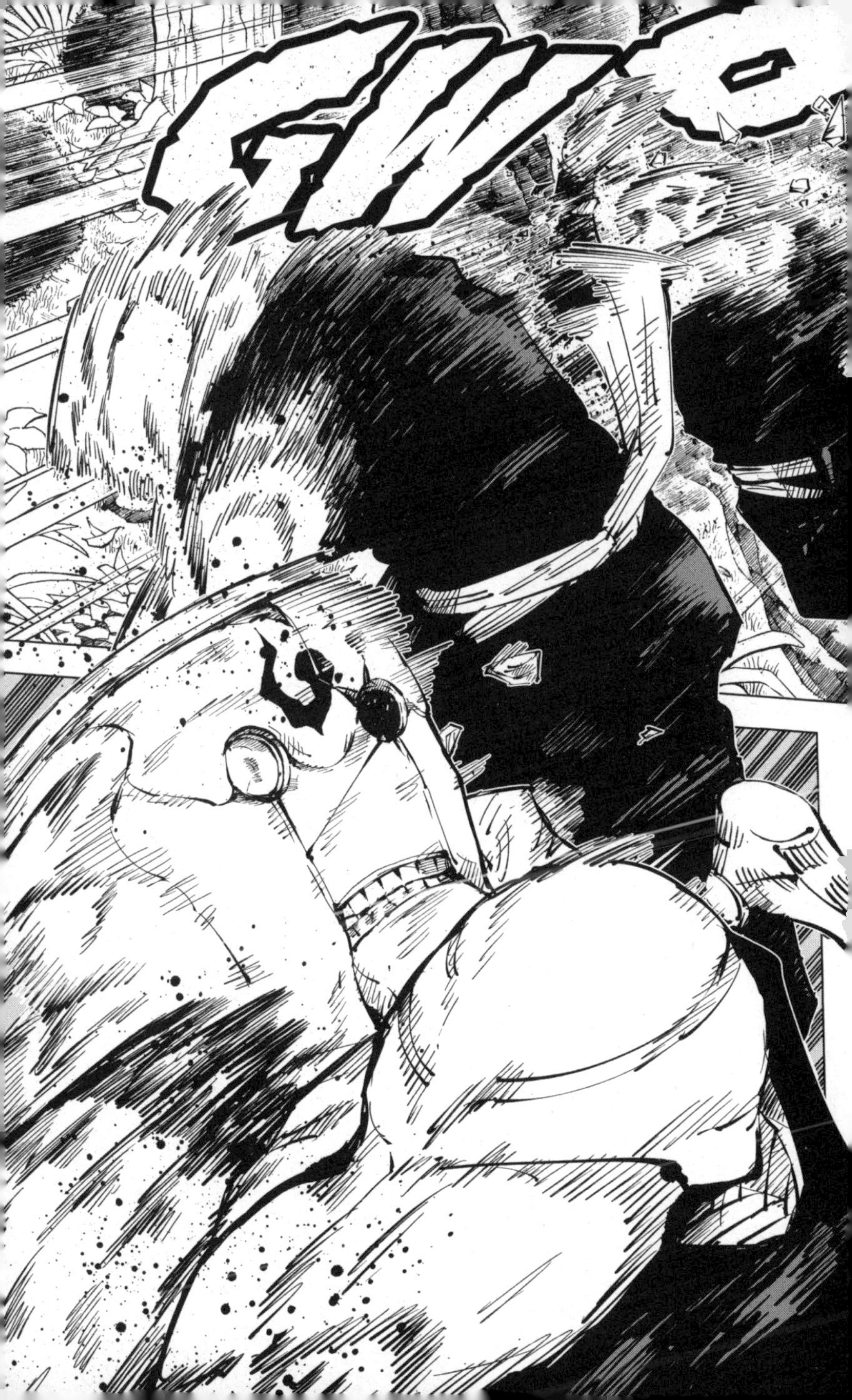

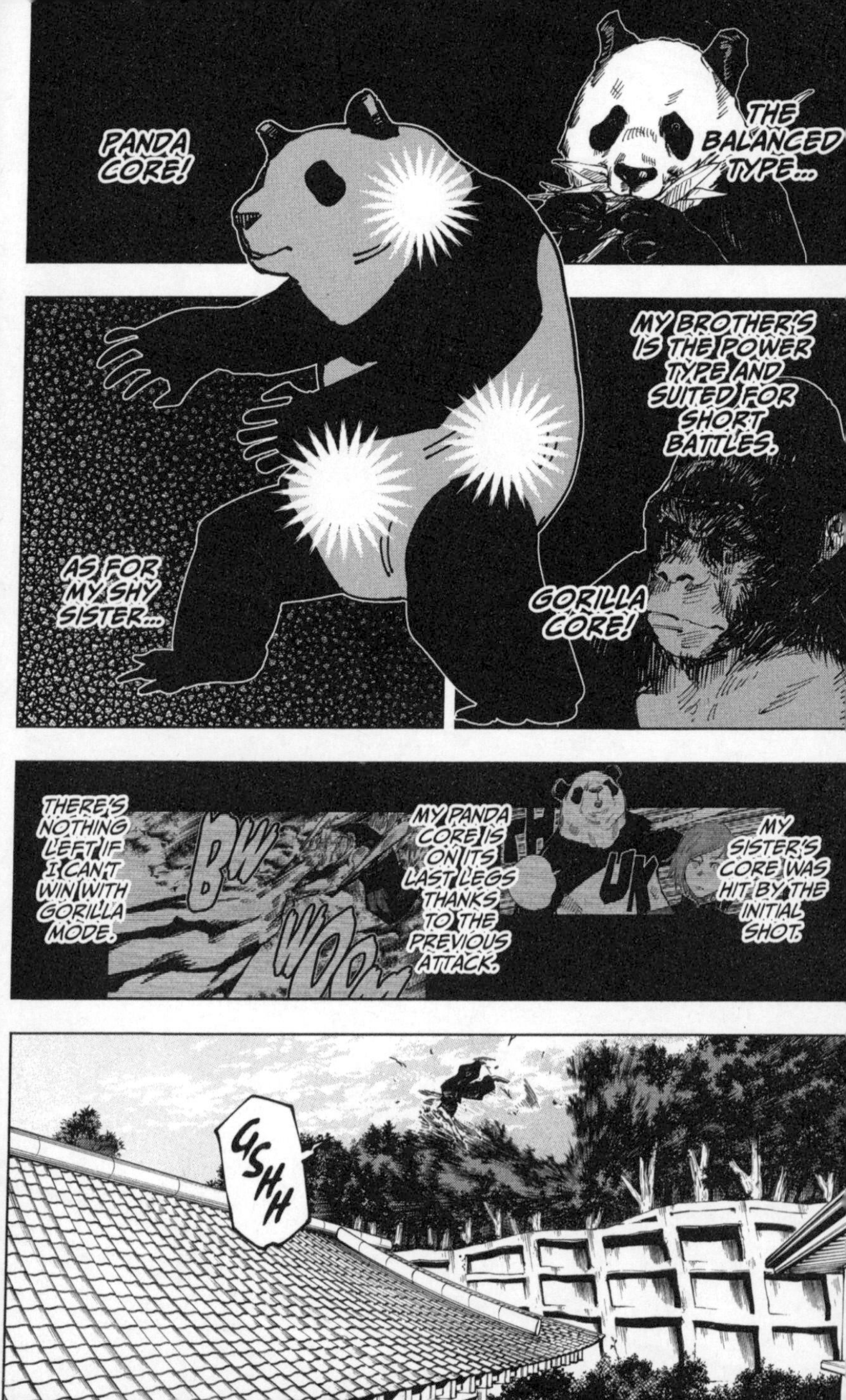
THE BALANCED TYPE...
PANDA CORE!
MY BROTHER'S IS THE POWER TYPE AND SUITED FOR SHORT BATTLES.
GORILLA CORE!
AS FOR MY SHY SISTER...
MY SISTER'S CORE WAS HIT BY THE INITIAL SHOT.
MY PANDA CORE IS ON ITS LAST LEGS THANKS TO THE PREVIOUS ATTACK.
THERE'S NOTHING LEFT IF I CAN'T WIN WITH GORILLA MODE.
BWOOM
USHH

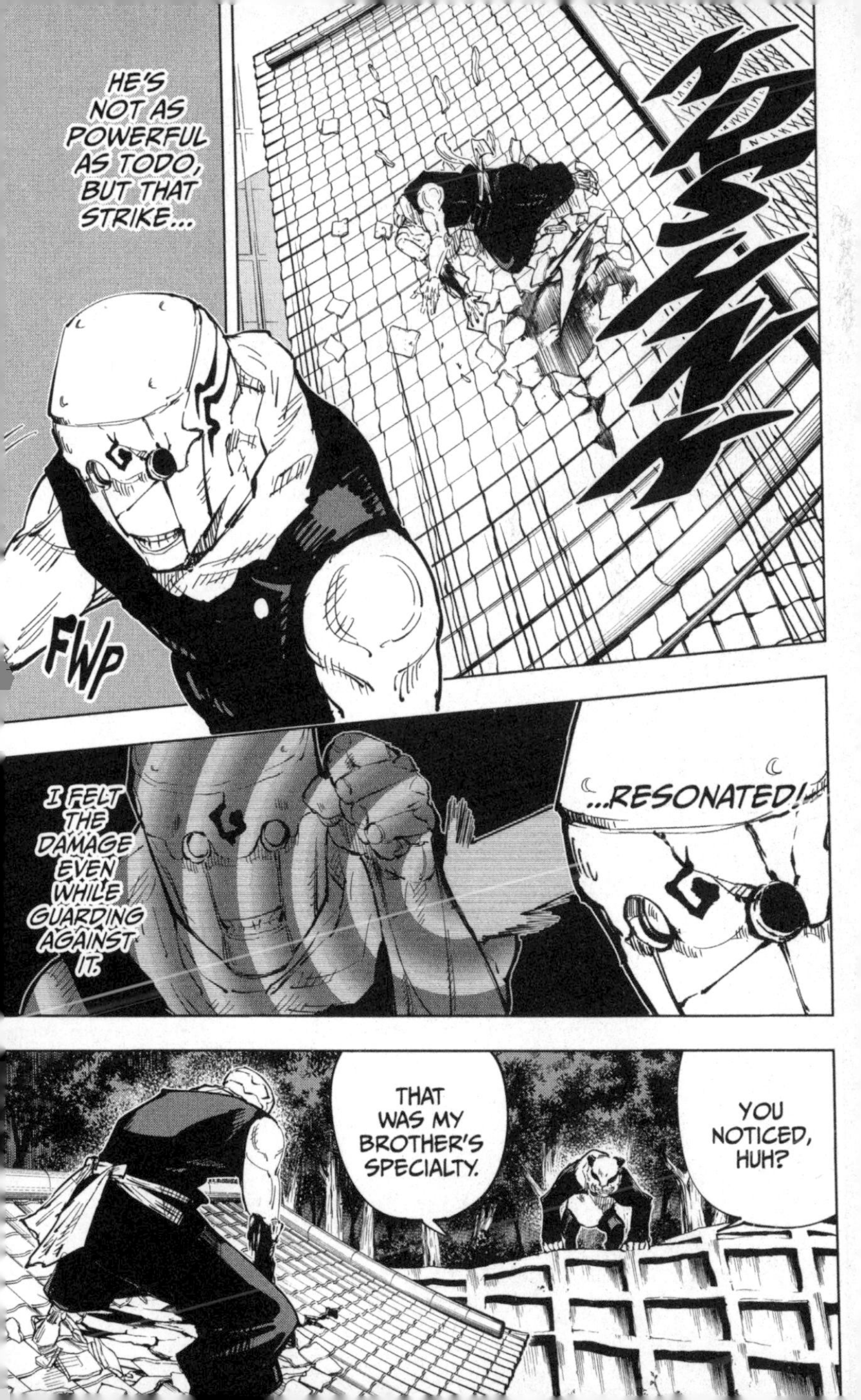
HE'S NOT AS POWERFUL AS TODO, BUT THAT STRIKE...
FWP
...RESONATED!
I FELT THE DAMAGE EVEN WHILE GUARDING AGAINST IT.
YOU NOTICED, HUH?
THAT WAS MY BROTHER'S SPECIALTY.

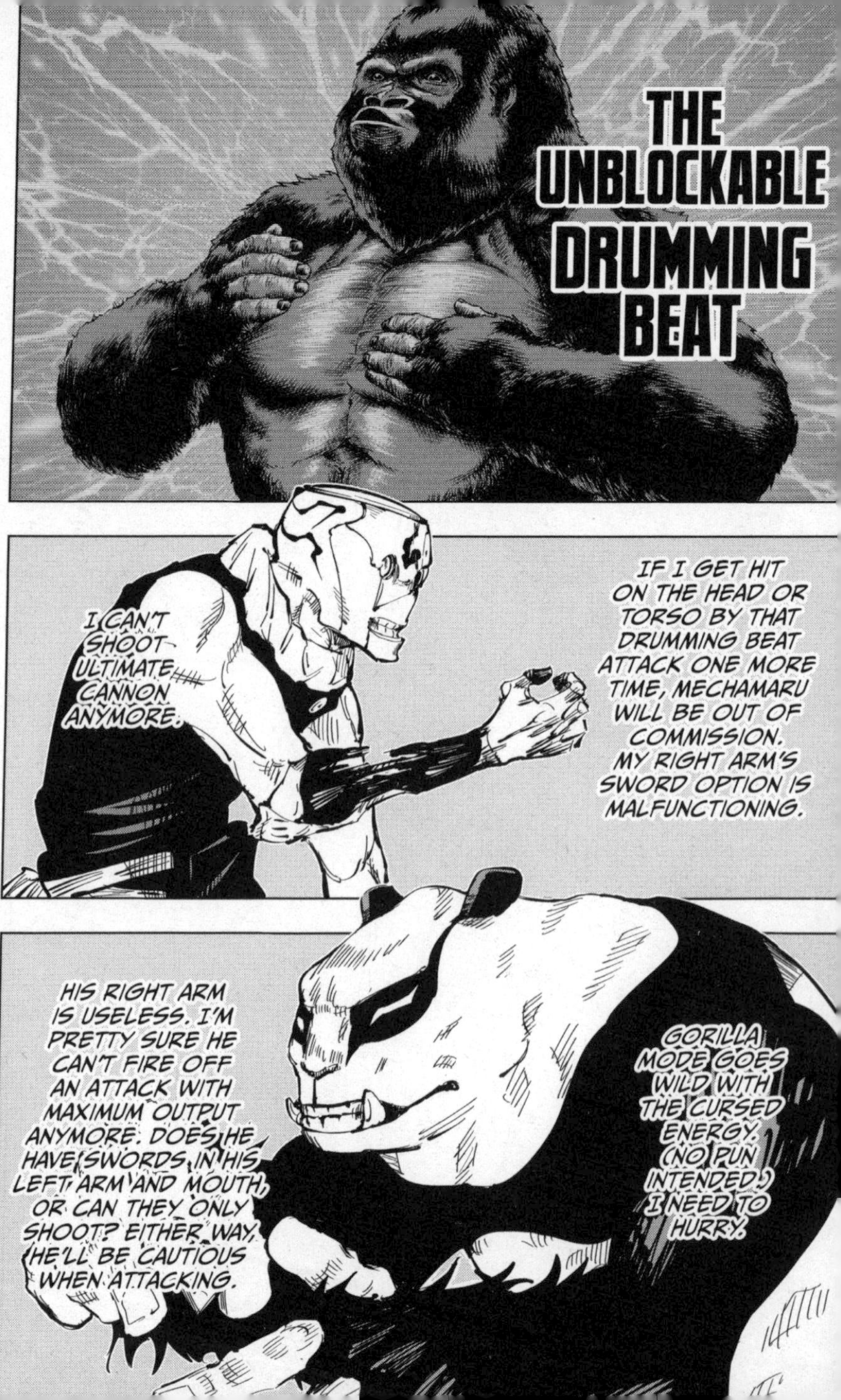
THE UNBLOCKABLE DRUMMING BEAT
IF I GET HIT ON THE HEAD OR TORSO BY THAT DRUMMING BEAT ATTACK ONE MORE TIME, MECHAMARU WILL BE OUT OF COMMISSION. MY RIGHT ARM'S SWORD OPTION IS MALFUNCTIONING.
I CAN'T SHOOT ULTIMATE CANNON ANYMORE.
GORILLA MODE GOES WILD WITH THE CURSED ENERGY. (NO PUN INTENDED.) I NEED TO HURRY.
HIS RIGHT ARM IS USELESS. I'M PRETTY SURE HE CAN'T FIRE OFF AN ATTACK WITH MAXIMUM OUTPUT ANYMORE. DOES HE HAVE SWORDS IN HIS LEFT ARM AND MOUTH, OR CAN THEY ONLY SHOOT? EITHER WAY, HE'LL BE CAUTIOUS WHEN ATTACKING.

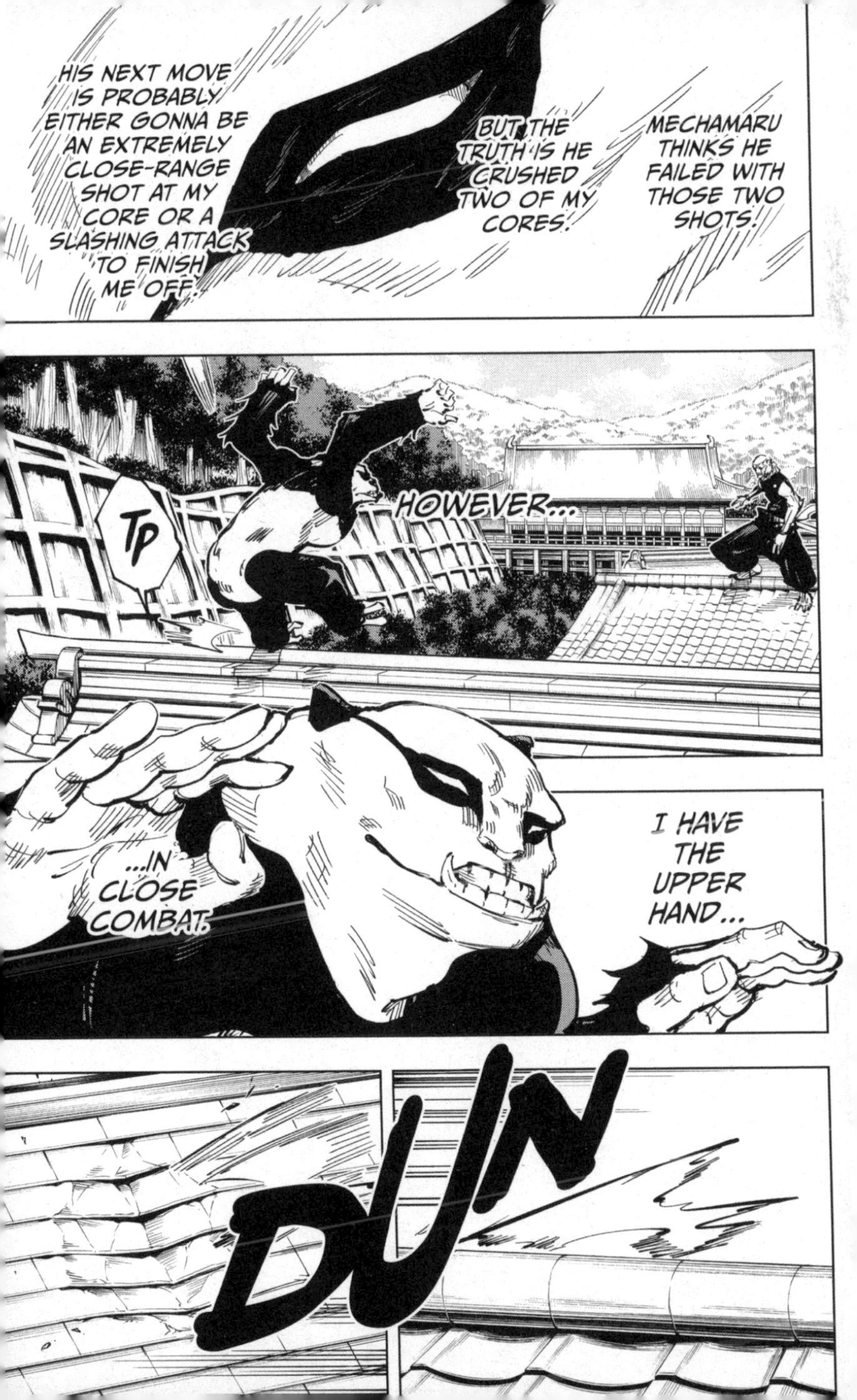
MECHAMARU THINKS HE FAILED WITH THOSE TWO SHOTS.
BUT THE TRUTH IS HE CRUSHED TWO OF MY CORES.
HIS NEXT MOVE IS PROBABLY EITHER GONNA BE AN EXTREMELY CLOSE-RANGE SHOT AT MY CORE OR A SLASHING ATTACK TO FINISH ME OFF.
HOWEVER...
TP
I HAVE THE UPPER HAND...
...IN CLOSE COMBAT.
DUN

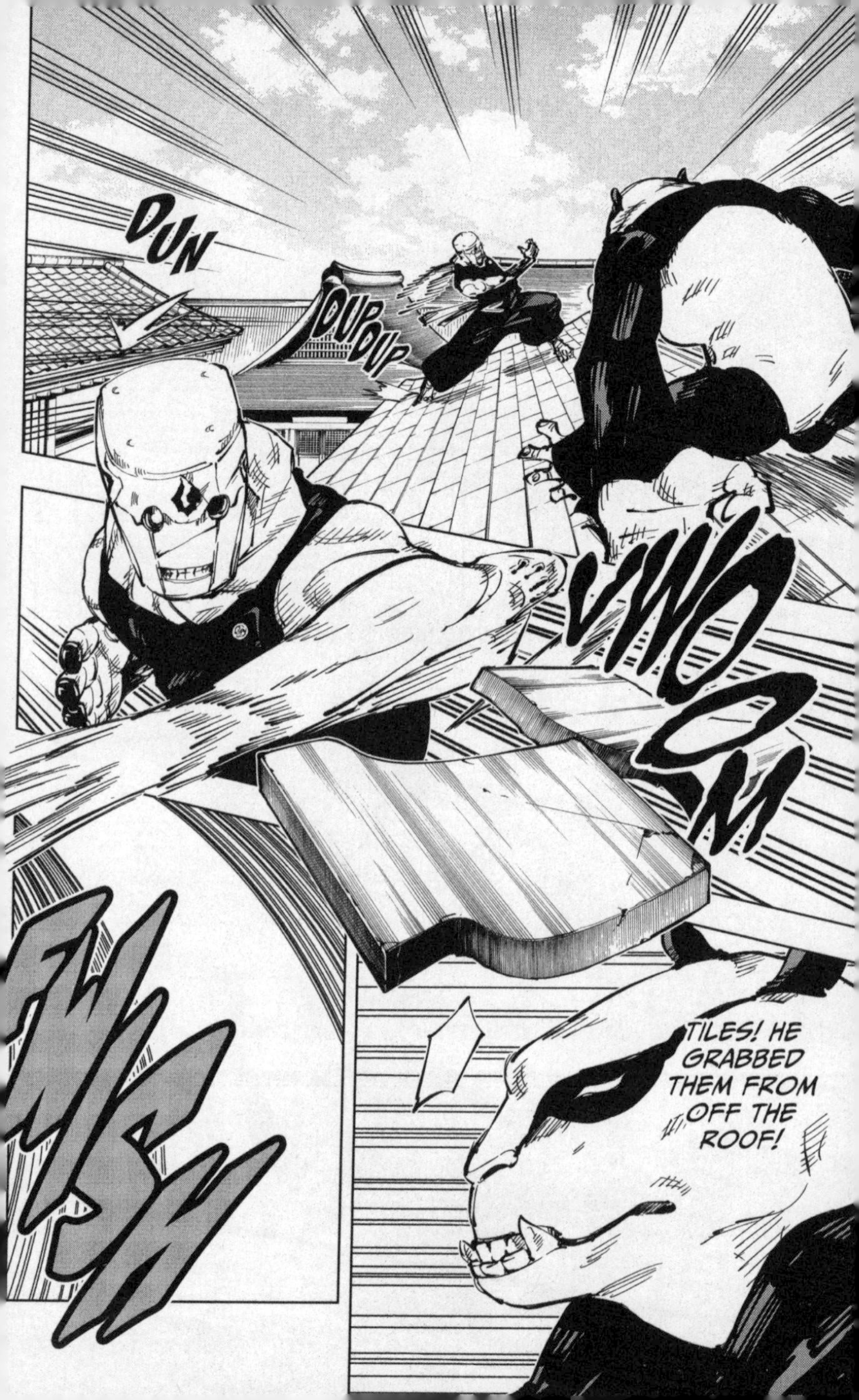
DUN
DUPDUPDUP
VWOOM
TILES! HE GRABBED THEM FROM OFF THE ROOF!
FWISH

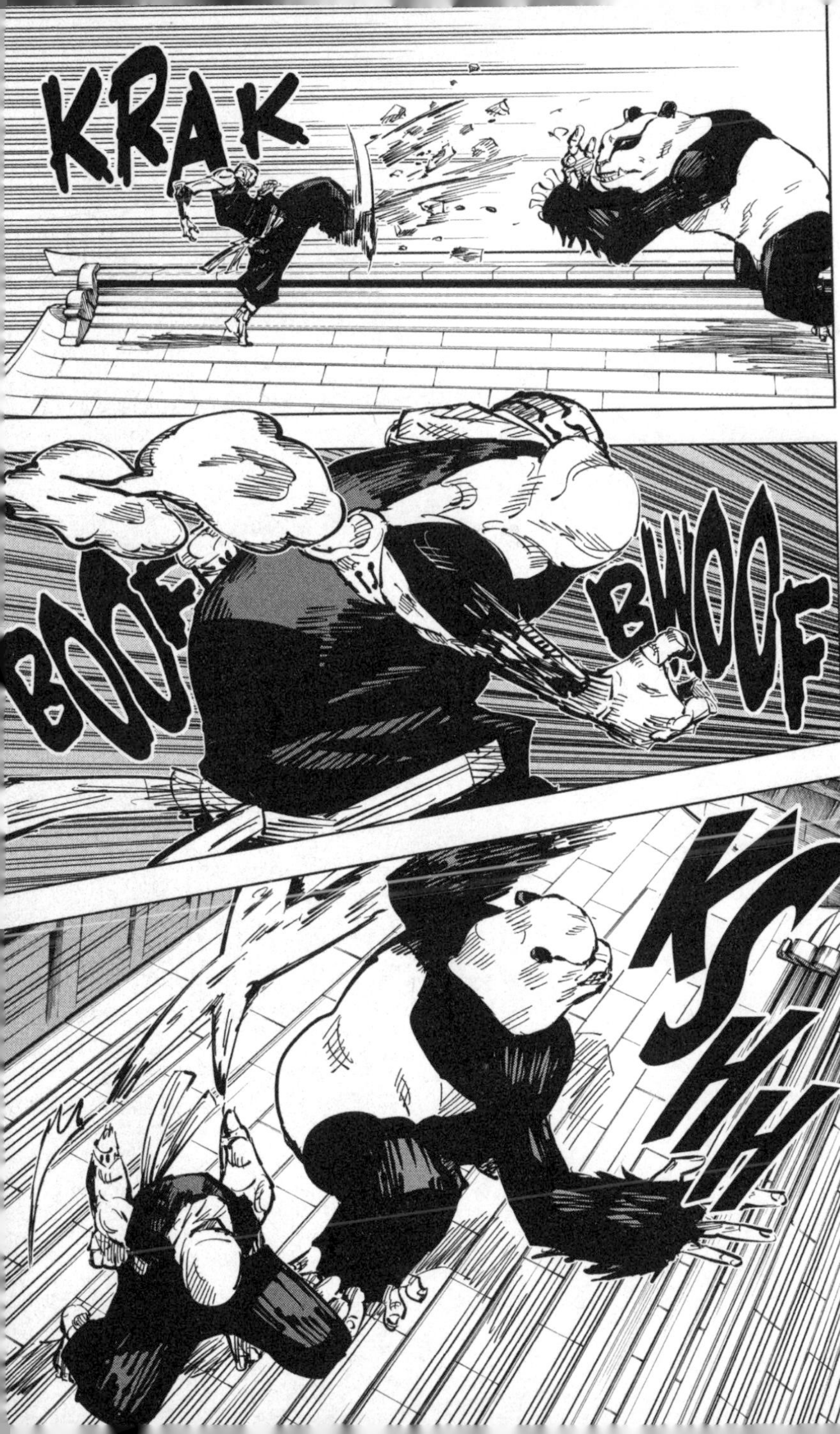
KRAK
BWOOF
BOOF
KSHH

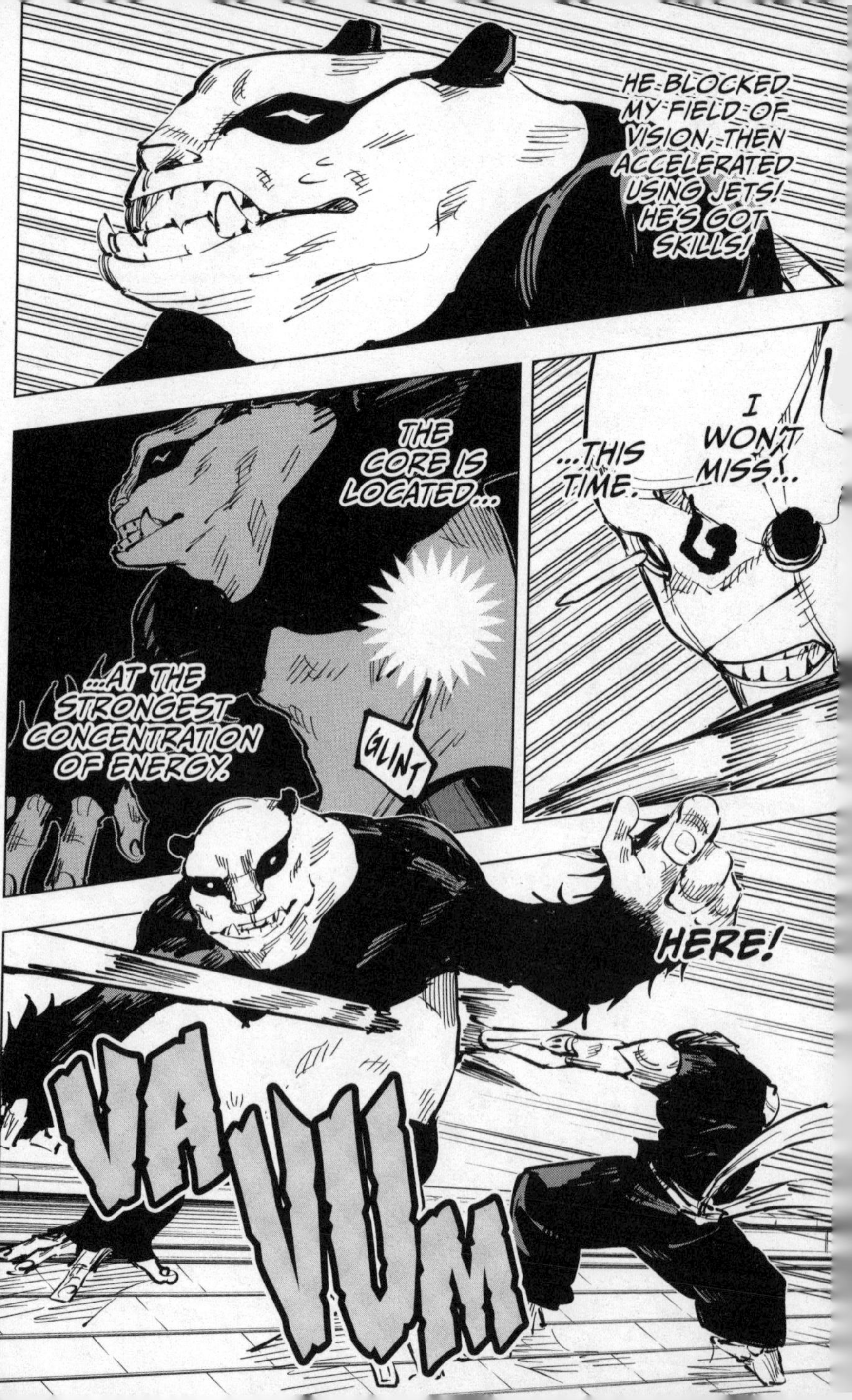
HE BLOCKED MY FIELD OF VISION, THEN ACCELERATED USING JETS! HE'S GOT SKILLS!
I WON'T MISS...
...THIS TIME.
THE CORE IS LOCATED...
...AT THE STRONGEST CONCENTRATION OF ENERGY.
GLINT
HERE!
VA VUM

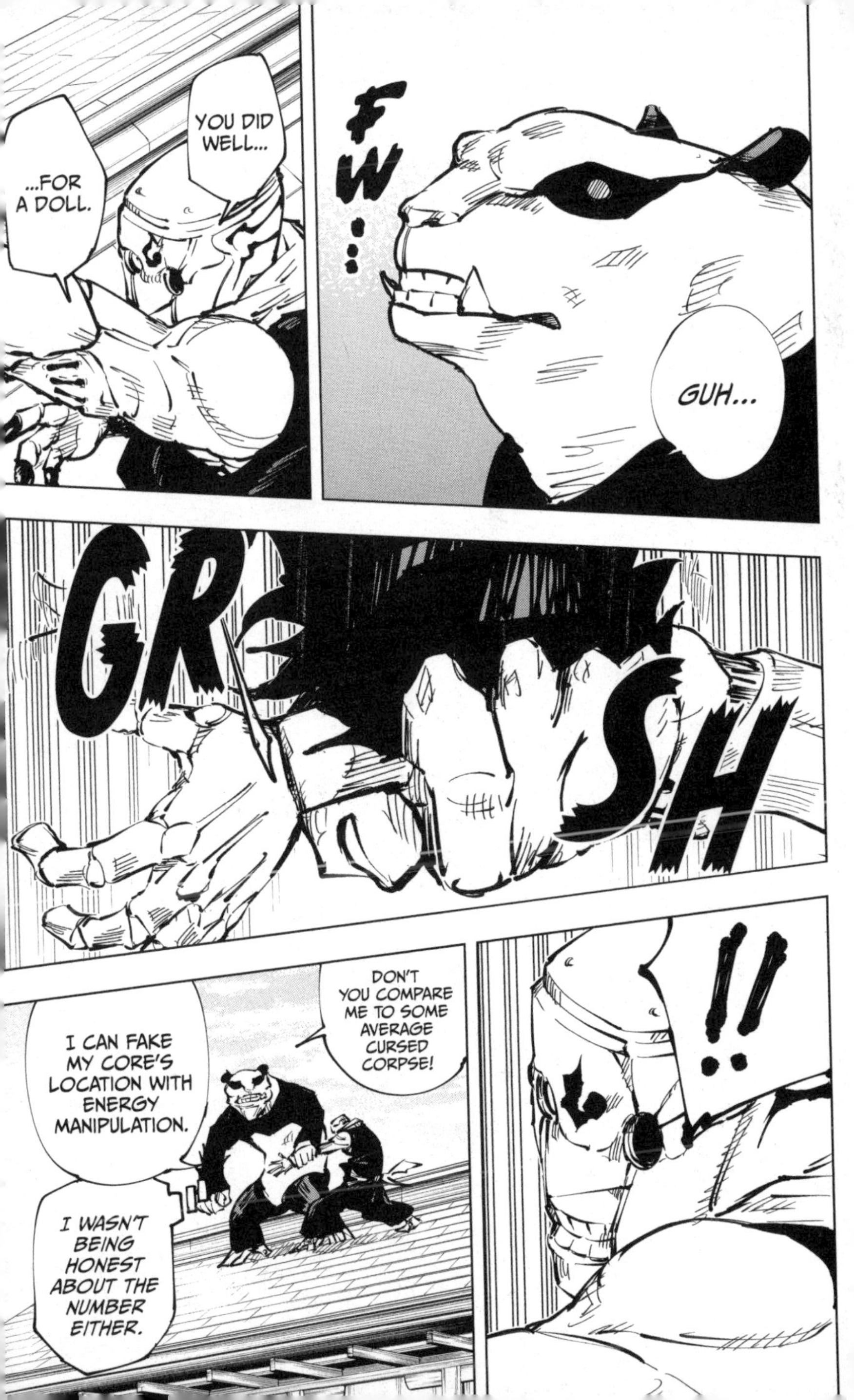
FW...
GUH...
YOU DID WELL...
...FOR A DOLL.
GRSH
!!
DON'T YOU COMPARE ME TO SOME AVERAGE CURSED CORPSE!
I CAN FAKE MY CORE'S LOCATION WITH ENERGY MANIPULATION.
I WASN'T BEING HONEST ABOUT THE NUMBER EITHER.

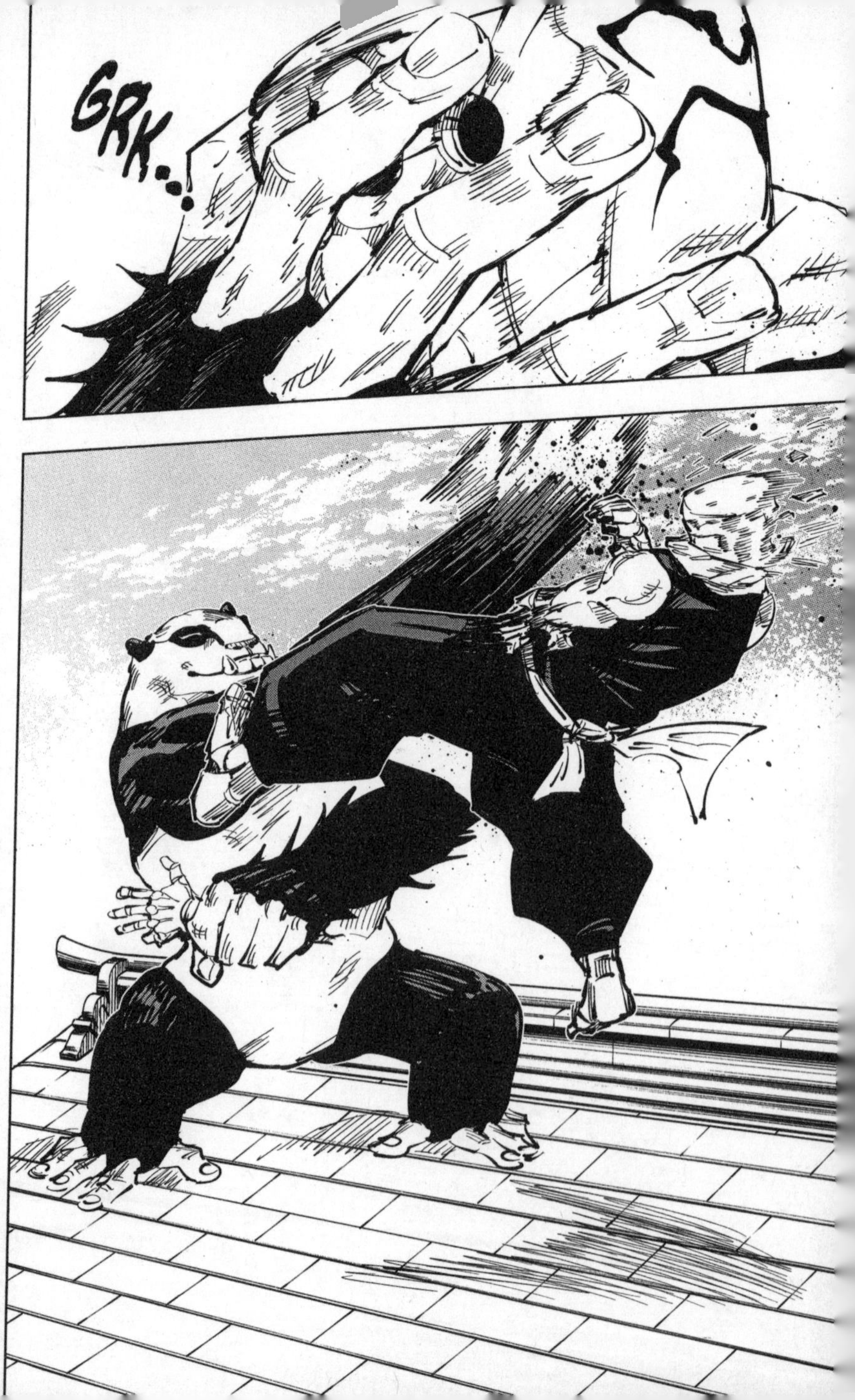
GRK...

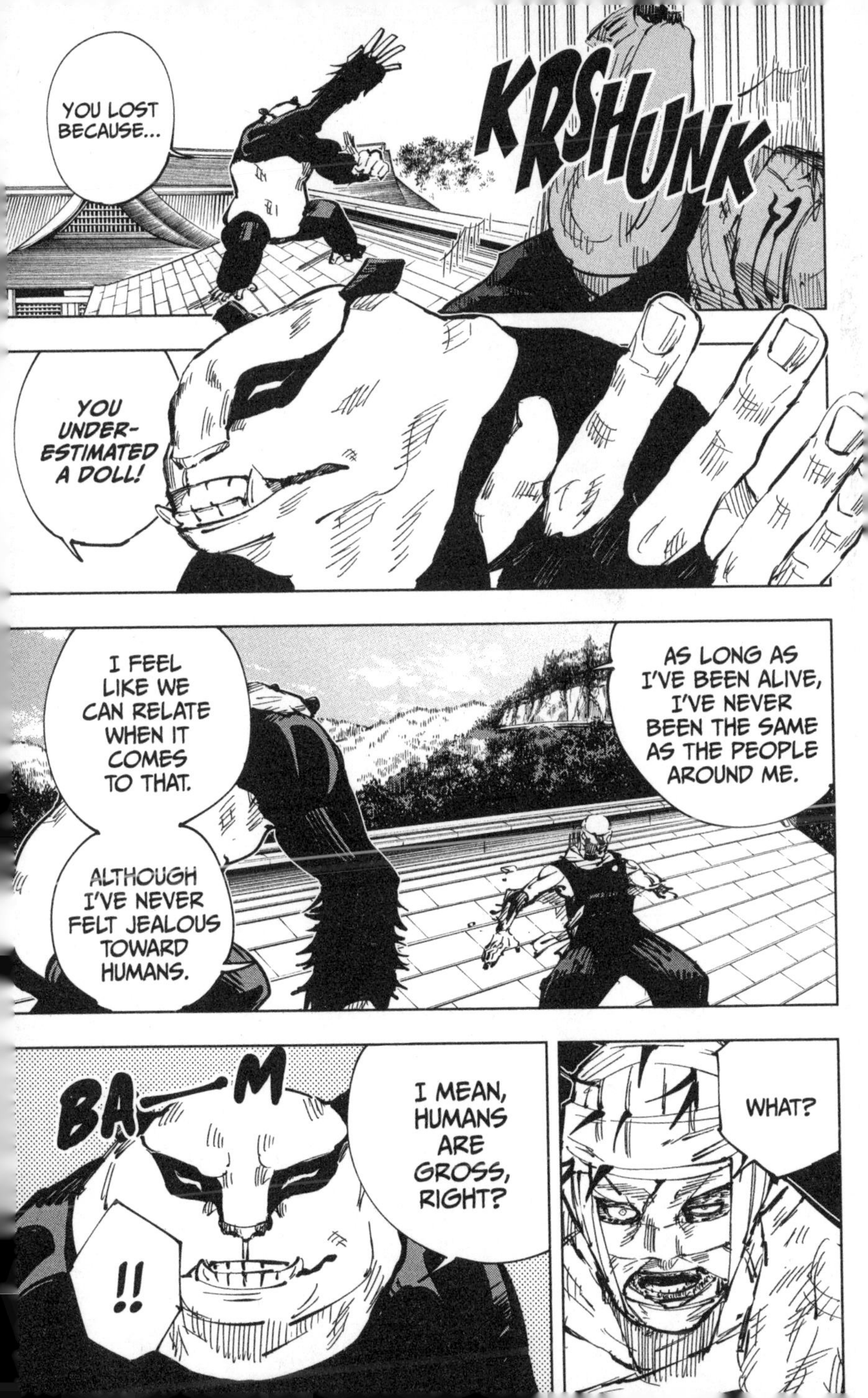
KRSHUNK
YOU LOST BECAUSE...
YOU UNDER-ESTIMATED A DOLL!
AS LONG AS I'VE BEEN ALIVE, I'VE NEVER BEEN THE SAME AS THE PEOPLE AROUND ME.
I FEEL LIKE WE CAN RELATE WHEN IT COMES TO THAT.
ALTHOUGH I'VE NEVER FELT JEALOUS TOWARD HUMANS.
WHAT?
I MEAN, HUMANS ARE GROSS, RIGHT?
BA-M
!!

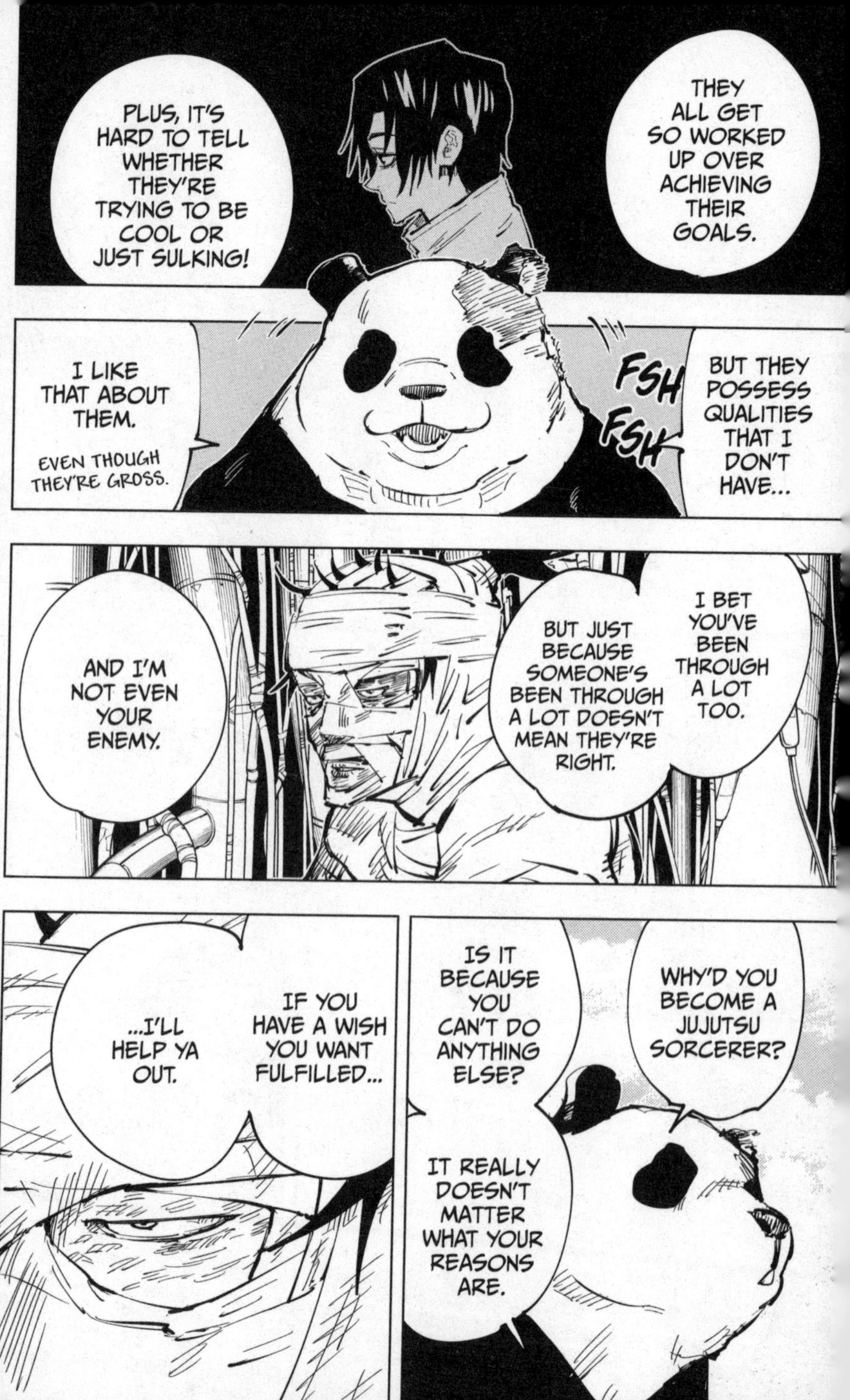
THEY ALL GET SO WORKED UP OVER ACHIEVING THEIR GOALS.
PLUS, IT'S HARD TO TELL WHETHER THEY'RE TRYING TO BE COOL OR JUST SULKING!
BUT THEY POSSESS QUALITIES THAT I DON'T HAVE...
FSH FSH
I LIKE THAT ABOUT THEM.
EVEN THOUGH THEY'RE GROSS.
I BET YOU'VE BEEN THROUGH A LOT TOO.
BUT JUST BECAUSE SOMEONE'S BEEN THROUGH A LOT DOESN'T MEAN THEY'RE RIGHT.
AND I'M NOT EVEN YOUR ENEMY.
WHY'D YOU BECOME A JUJUTSU SORCERER?
IS IT BECAUSE YOU CAN'T DO ANYTHING ELSE?
IT REALLY DOESN'T MATTER WHAT YOUR REASONS ARE.
IF YOU HAVE A WISH YOU WANT FULFILLED...
...I'LL HELP YA OUT.

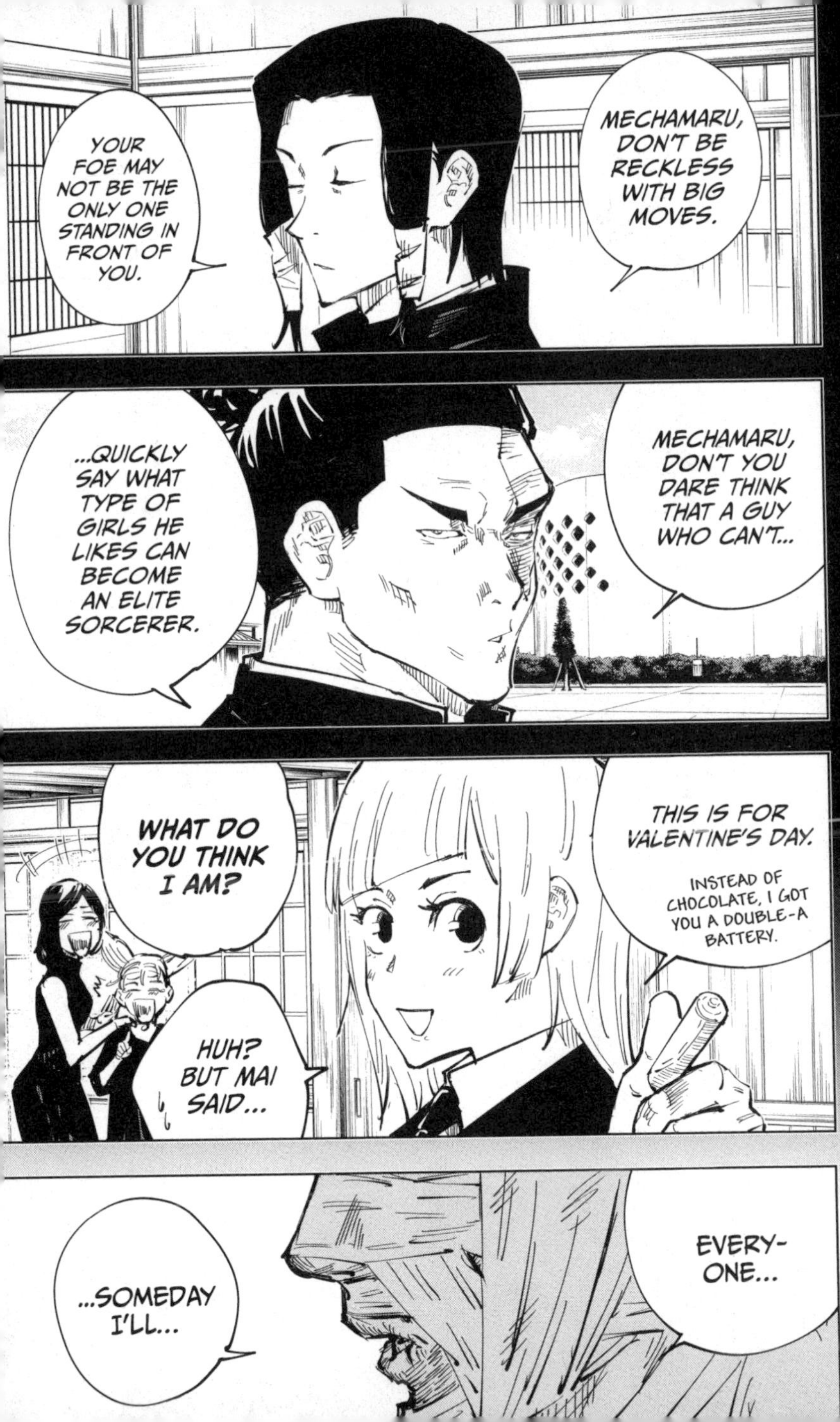
MECHAMARU, DON'T BE RECKLESS WITH BIG MOVES.
YOUR FOE MAY NOT BE THE ONLY ONE STANDING IN FRONT OF YOU.
MECHAMARU, DON'T YOU DARE THINK THAT A GUY WHO CAN'T...
...QUICKLY SAY WHAT TYPE OF GIRLS HE LIKES CAN BECOME AN ELITE SORCERER.
THIS IS FOR VALENTINE'S DAY.
INSTEAD OF CHOCOLATE, I GOT YOU A DOUBLE-A BATTERY.
WHAT DO YOU THINK I AM?
HUH? BUT MAI SAID...
EVERY-ONE...
...SOMEDAY I'LL...

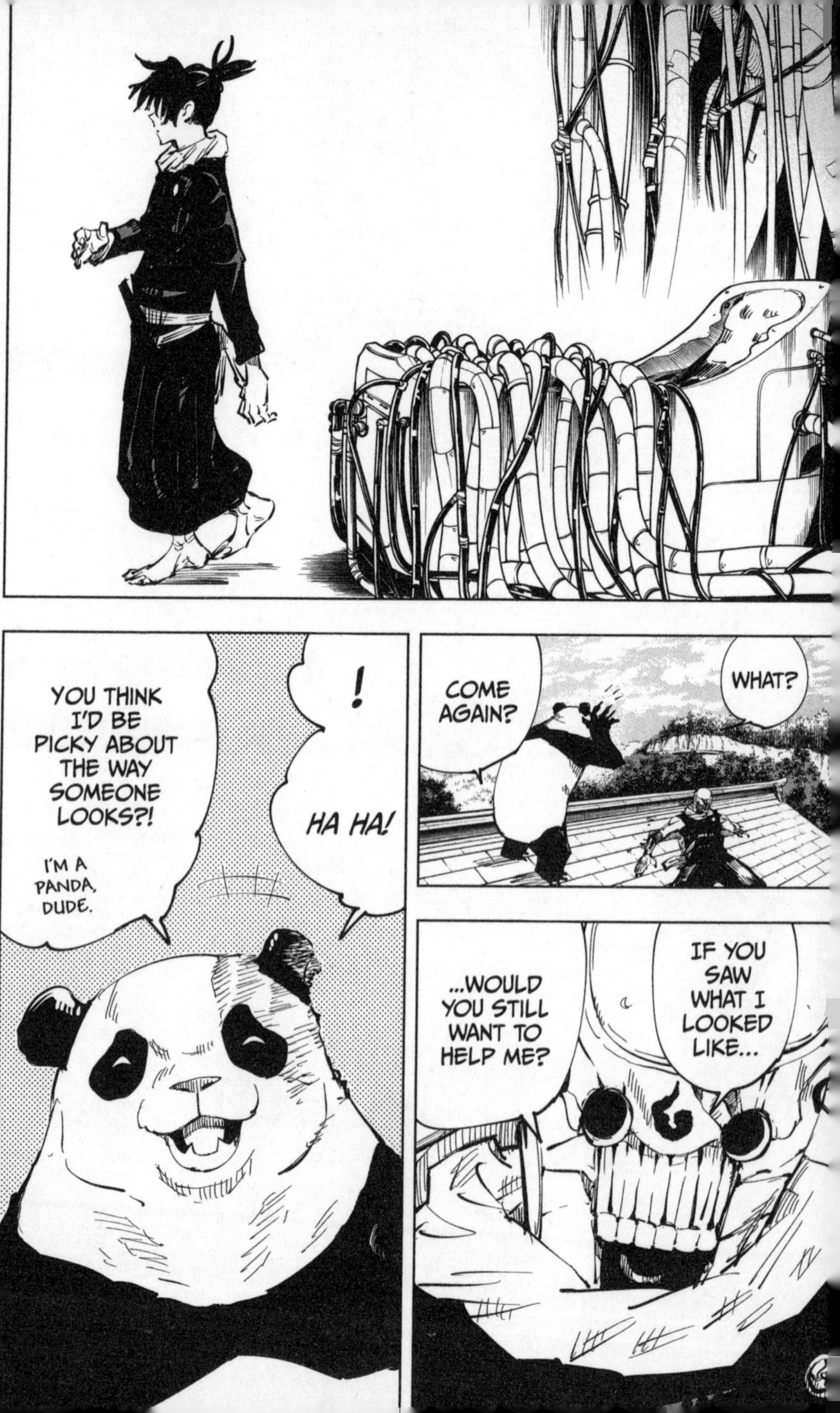
WHAT?
COME AGAIN?
IF YOU SAW WHAT I LOOKED LIKE...
...WOULD YOU STILL WANT TO HELP ME?
!
HA HA!
YOU THINK I'D BE PICKY ABOUT THE WAY SOMEONE LOOKS?!
I'M A PANDA, DUDE.

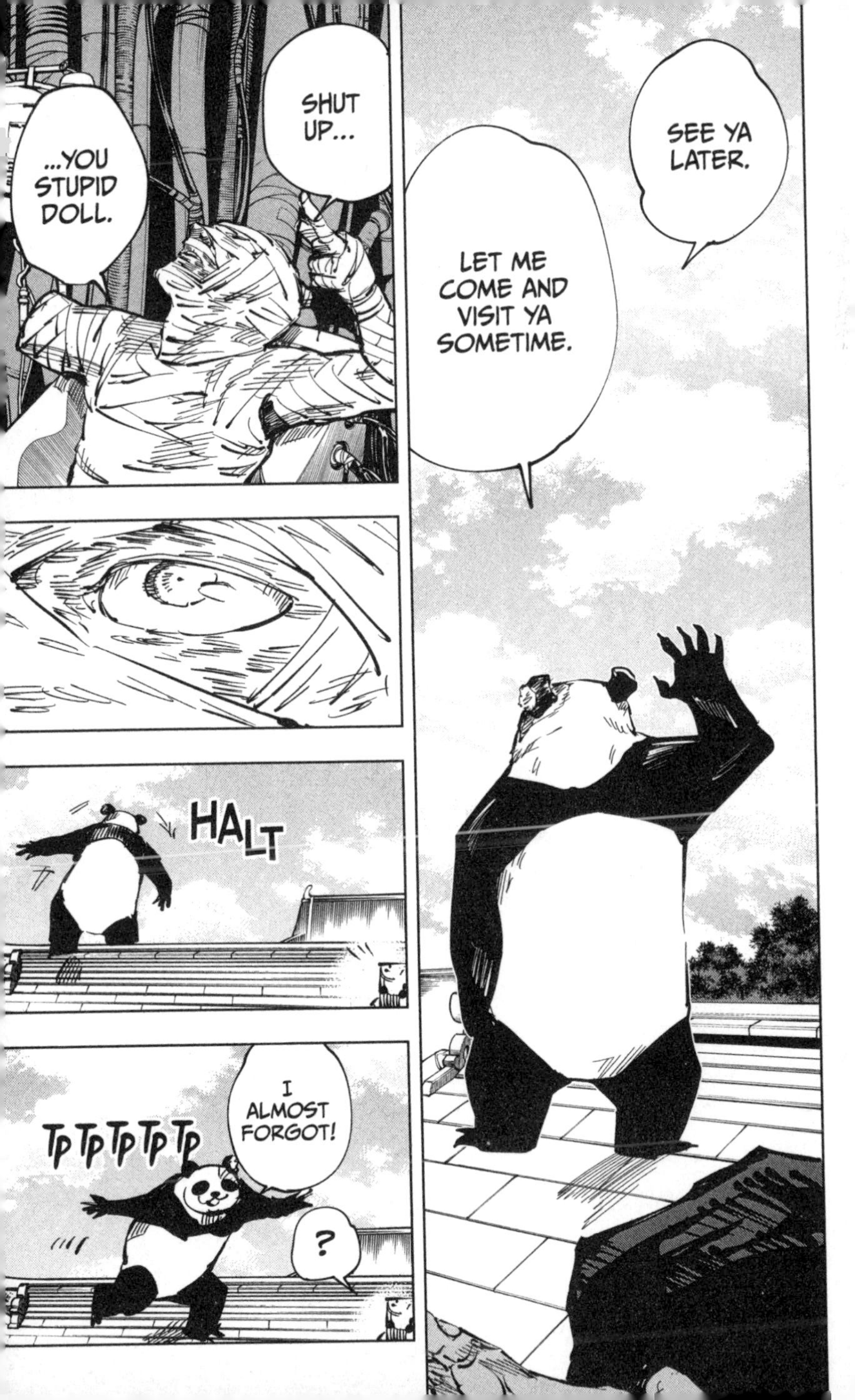
SEE YA LATER.
LET ME COME AND VISIT YA SOMETIME.
SHUT UP...
...YOU STUPID DOLL.
HALT
I ALMOST FORGOT!
TP TP TP TP TP
?

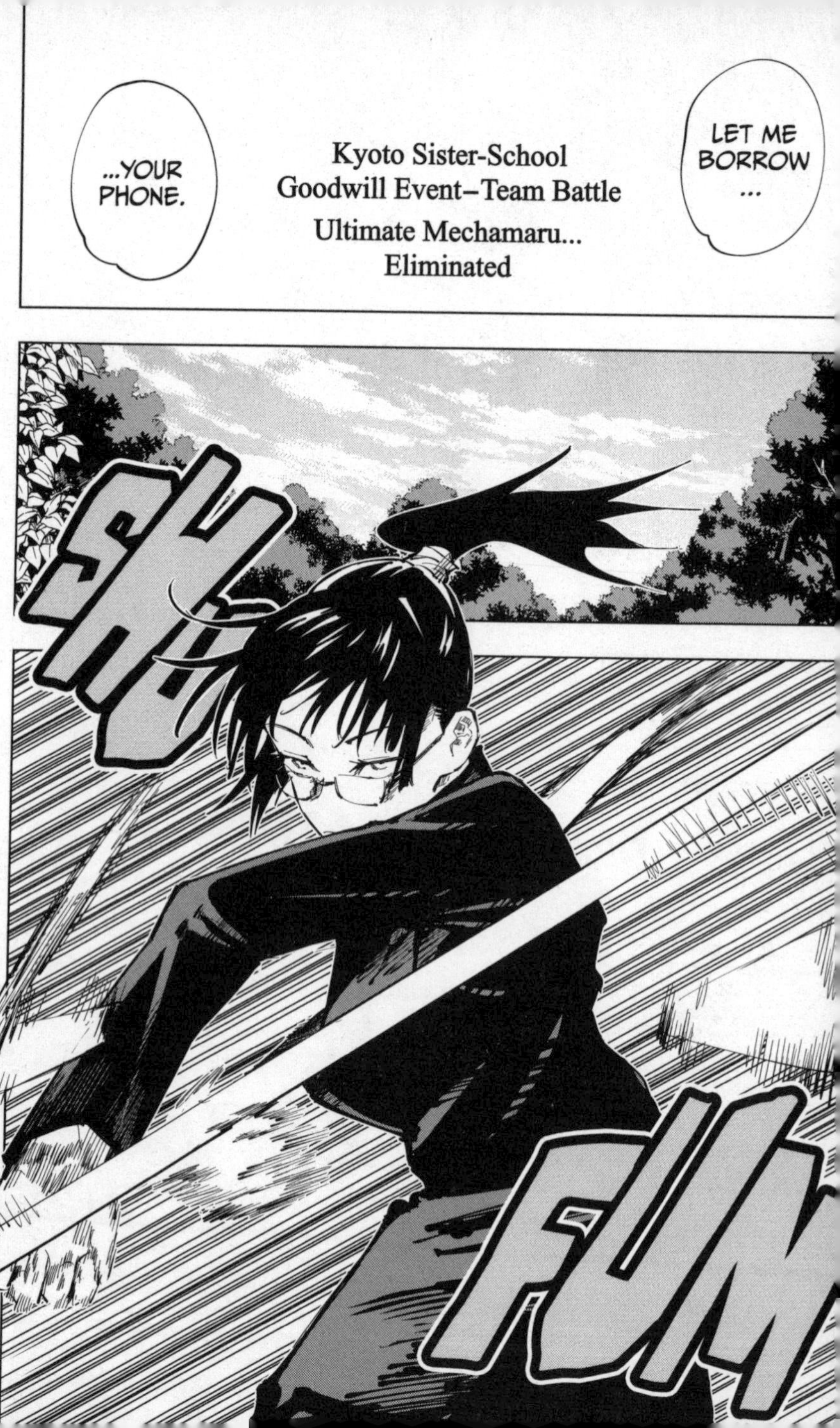
LET ME BORROW ...
Kyoto Sister-School Goodwill Event–Team Battle
Ultimate Mechamaru... Eliminated
...YOUR PHONE.
SHU
FUM

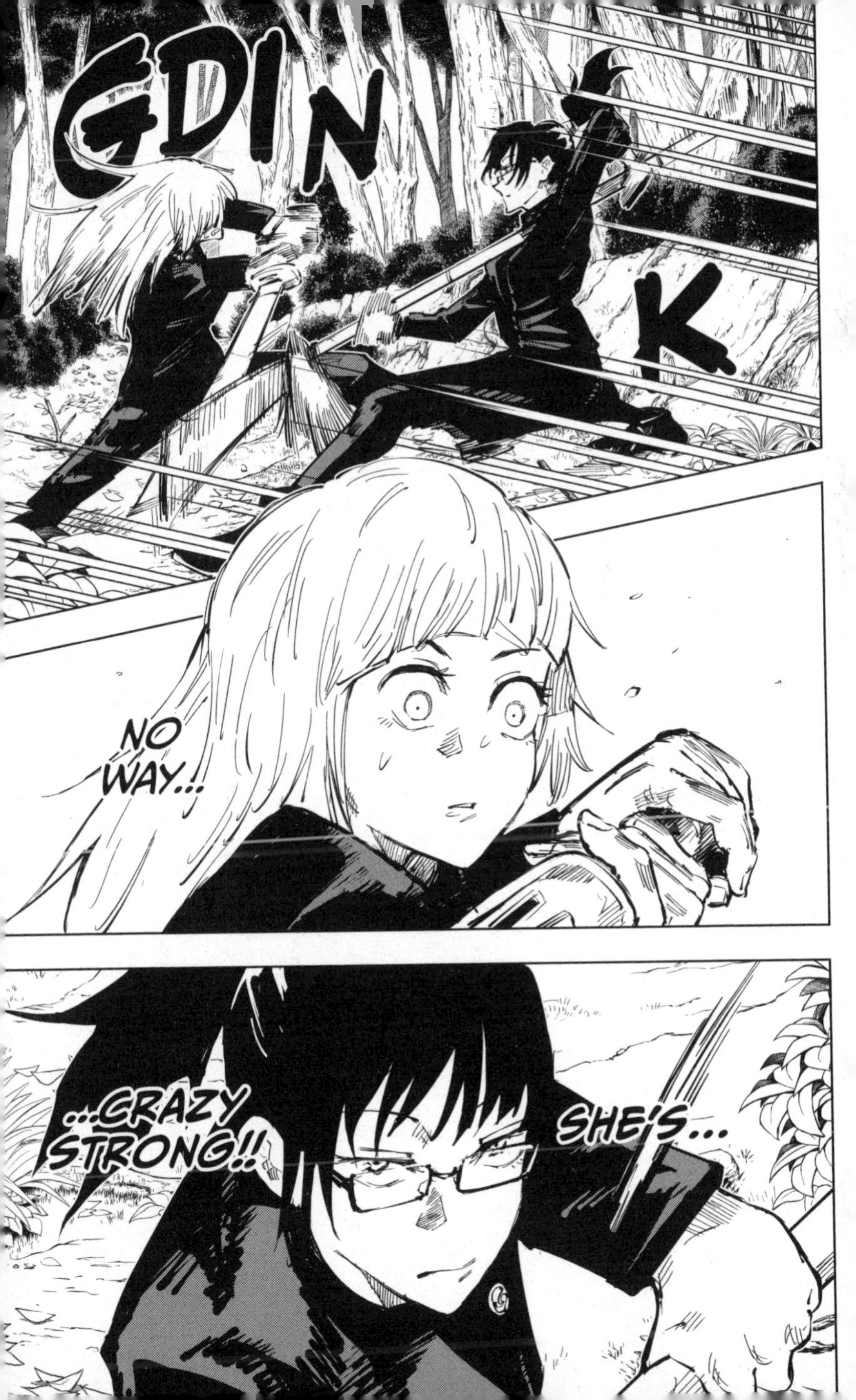
GDINK
NO WAY...
SHE'S...
...CRAZY STRONG!!

THE SURPRISE

• For *Jujutsu Kaisen* volume 5, Kohei Horikoshi Sensei, creator of *My Hero Academia*, wrote a note on the cover belt.

• Daisuke Ashihara Sensei did the same for volume 3. I was so honored and humbled that I spent the entire day with a smile on my face. I'm really lucky to have this experience more than once.

• And it's not just these two creators. I'm incredibly humbled to be supported by all the amazing creators who have come before me in *Weekly Shonen Jump*. Thank you, always. I'll do my best to be deemed worthy.

• So, what's the surprise you ask?
Horikoshi Sensei and I traded bonus pages.
Horikoshi Sensei and I traded bonus pages.
It's so important to me that I wrote it twice.

• Since this is a trade, I'll have a page in *My Hero Academia* volume 23. When I think about it, I break into a cold sweat, but that's neither here nor there!

• So, everyone, brace yourselves and check out page 150...

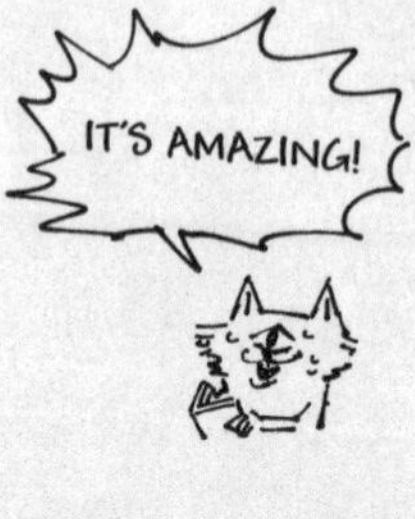
IT'S AMAZING!

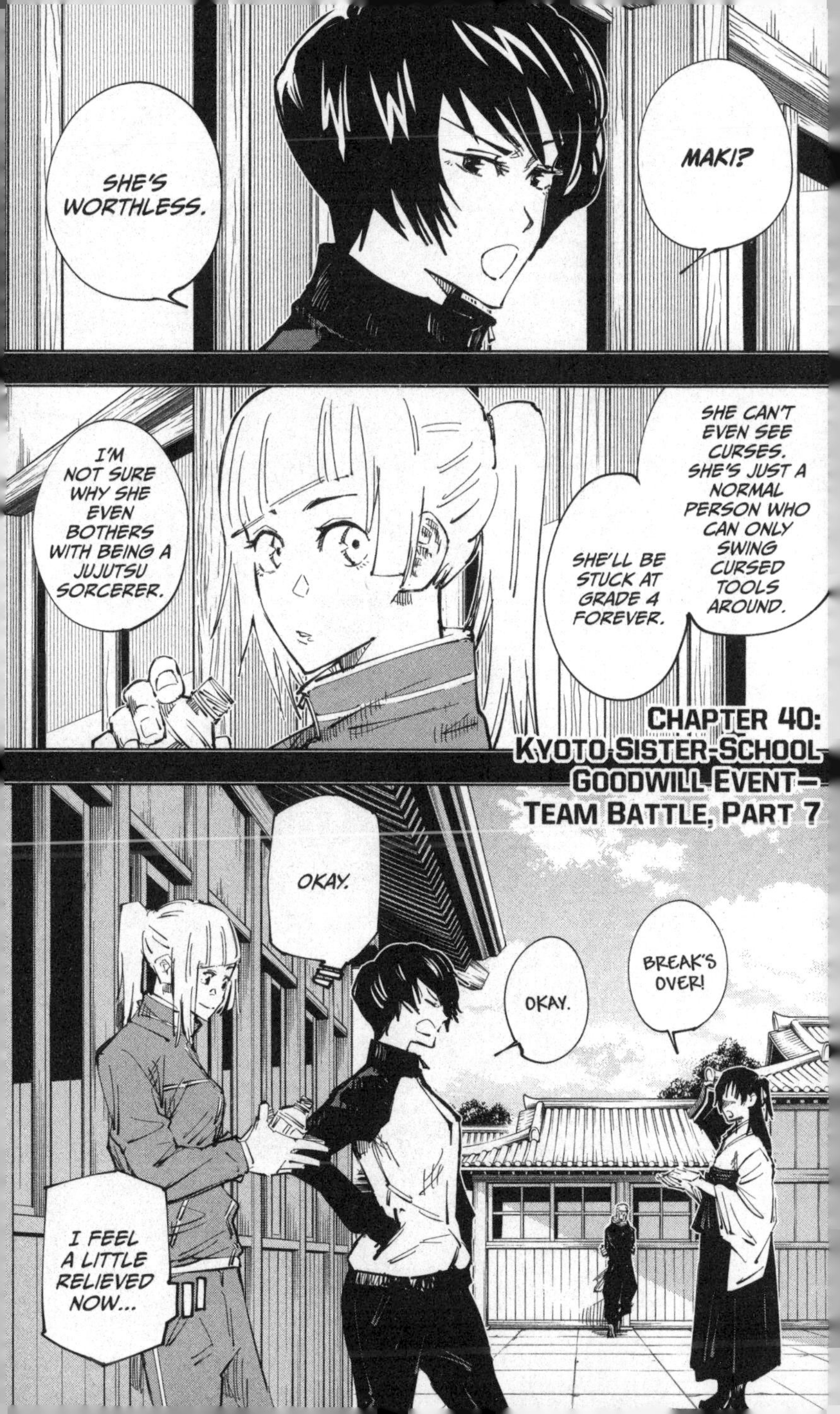
MAKI?
SHE'S WORTHLESS.
SHE CAN'T EVEN SEE CURSES. SHE'S JUST A NORMAL PERSON WHO CAN ONLY SWING CURSED TOOLS AROUND.
SHE'LL BE STUCK AT GRADE 4 FOREVER.
I'M NOT SURE WHY SHE EVEN BOTHERS WITH BEING A JUJUTSU SORCERER.
CHAPTER 40: KYOTO SISTER-SCHOOL GOODWILL EVENT—TEAM BATTLE, PART 7
BREAK'S OVER!
OKAY.
OKAY.
I FEEL A LITTLE RELIEVED NOW...

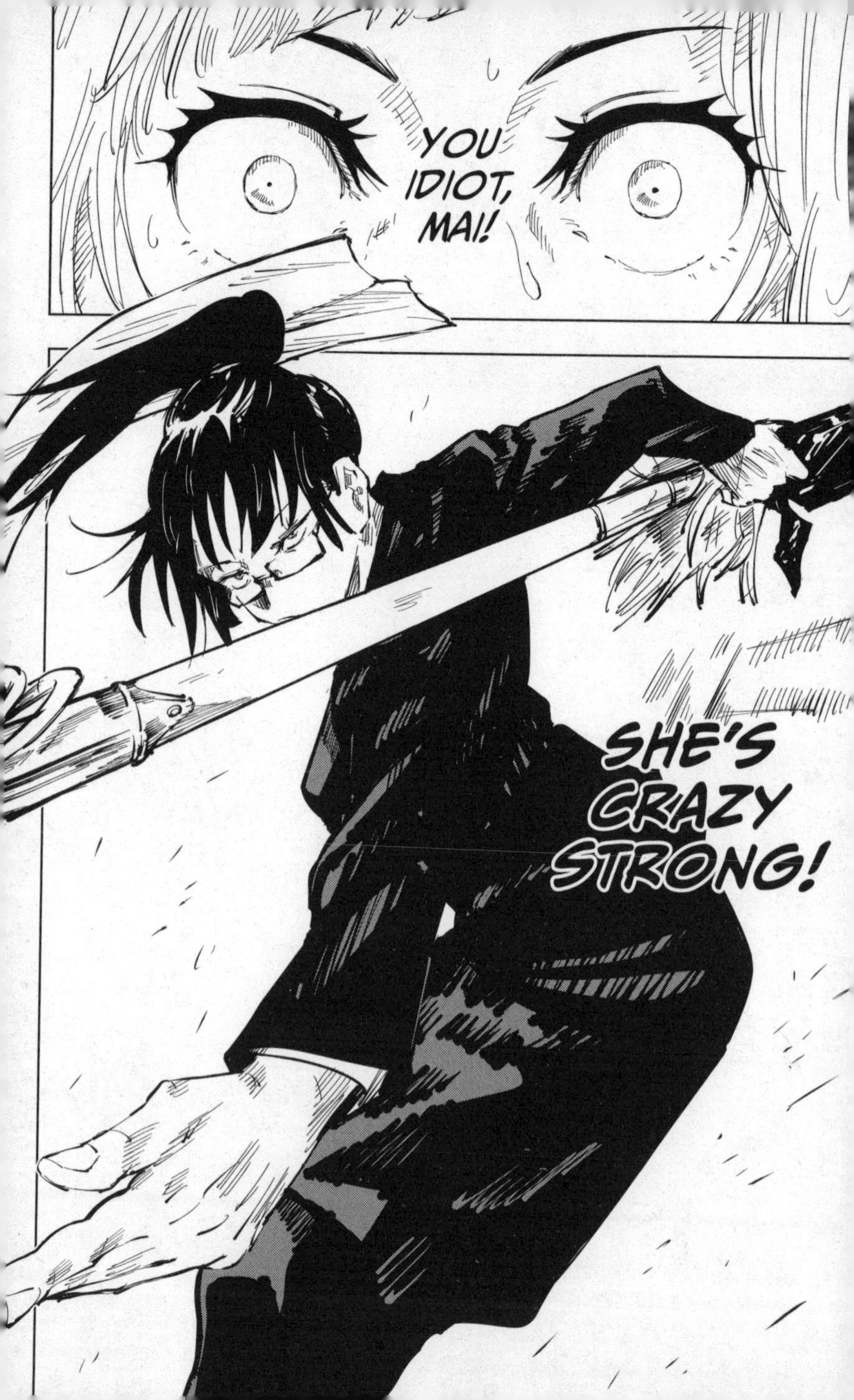
YOU IDIOT, MAI!
SHE'S CRAZY STRONG!

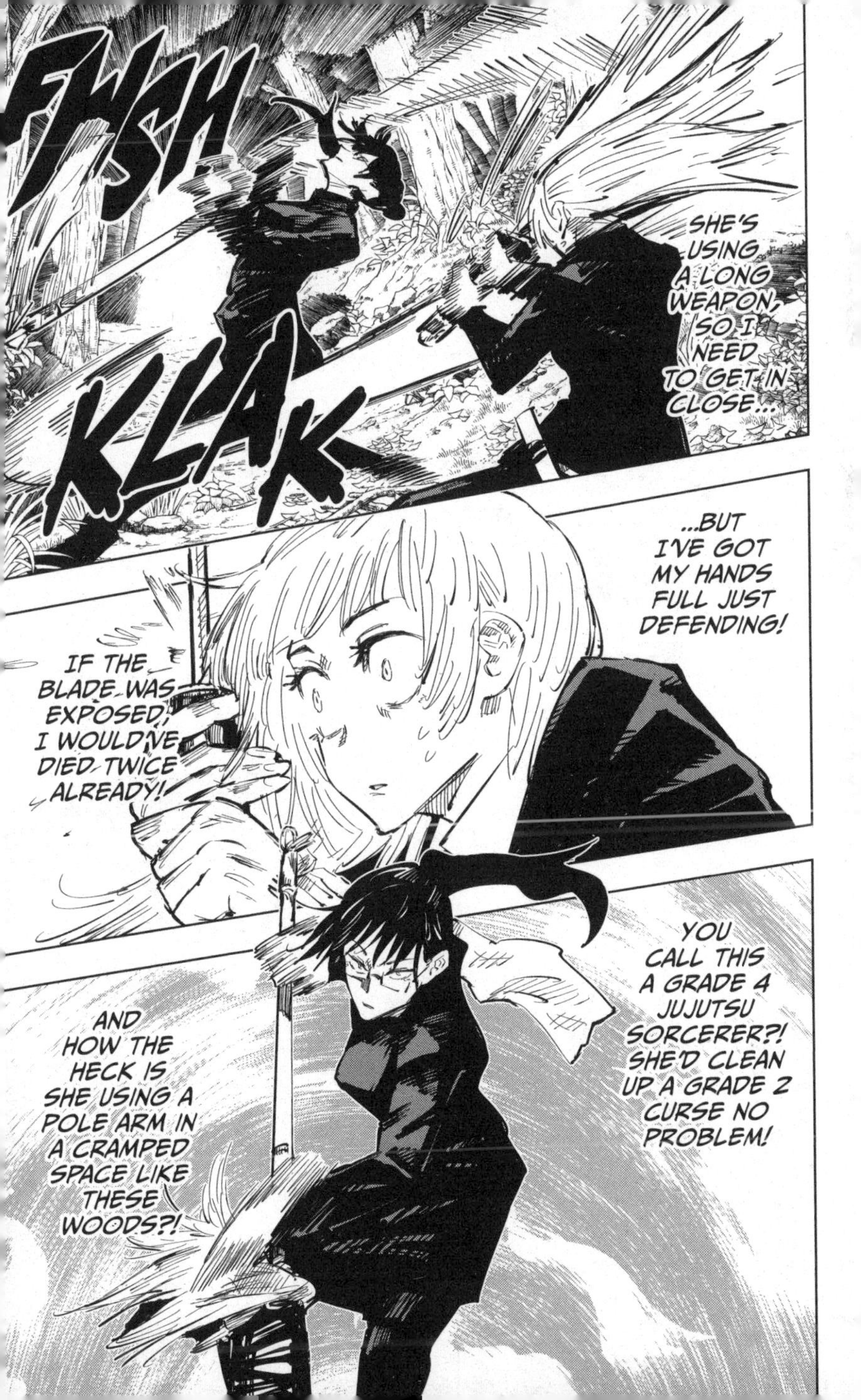
FWSH
KLAK
SHE'S USING A LONG WEAPON, SO I NEED TO GET IN CLOSE...
...BUT I'VE GOT MY HANDS FULL JUST DEFENDING!
IF THE BLADE WAS EXPOSED, I WOULD'VE DIED TWICE ALREADY!
YOU CALL THIS A GRADE 4 JUJUTSU SORCERER?! SHE'D CLEAN UP A GRADE 2 CURSE NO PROBLEM!
AND HOW THE HECK IS SHE USING A POLE ARM IN A CRAMPED SPACE LIKE THESE WOODS?!

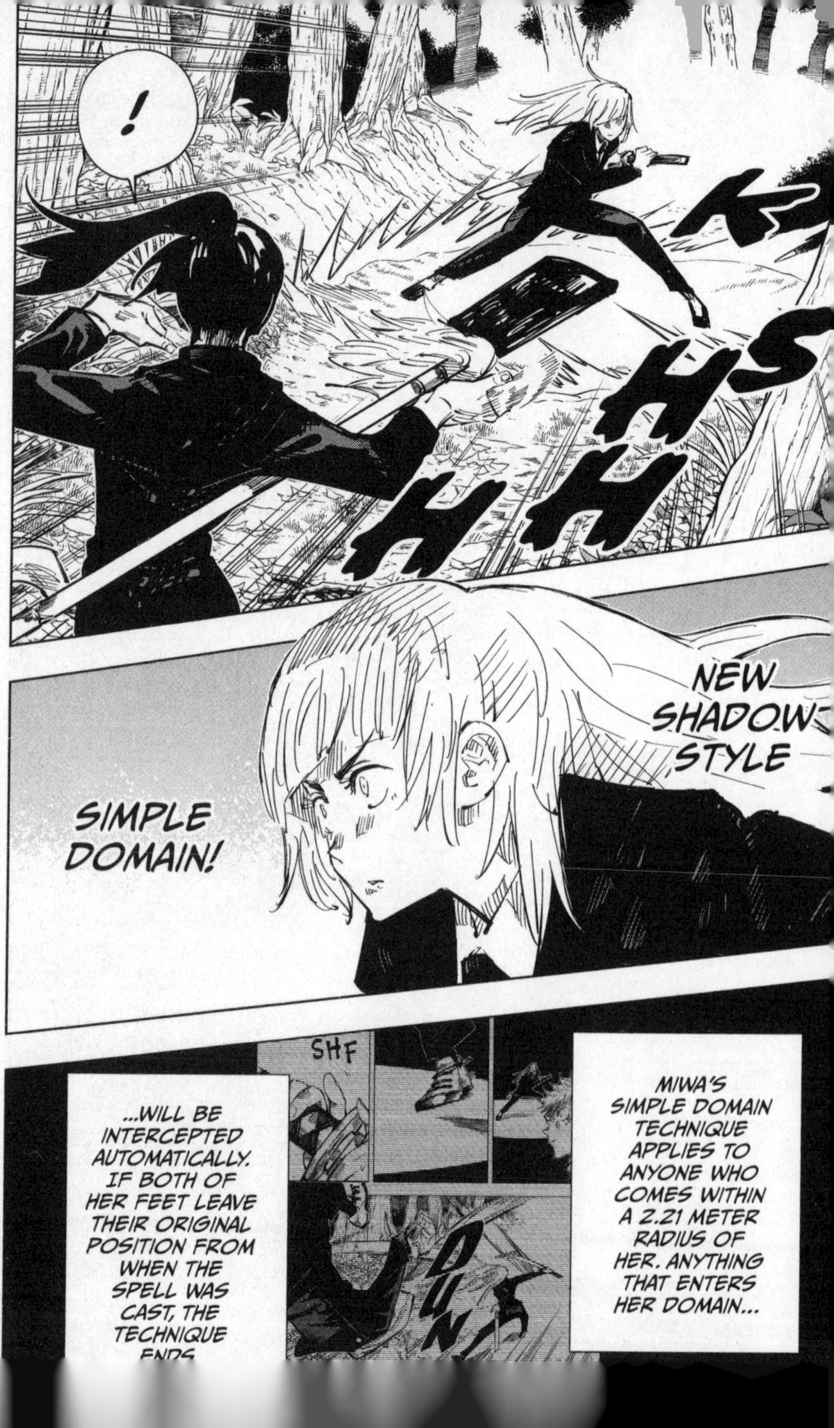
!
KSHHHH
NEW SHADOW STYLE
SIMPLE DOMAIN!
MIWA'S SIMPLE DOMAIN TECHNIQUE APPLIES TO ANYONE WHO COMES WITHIN A 2.21 METER RADIUS OF HER. ANYTHING THAT ENTERS HER DOMAIN...
SHF
DUN
...WILL BE INTERCEPTED AUTOMATICALLY. IF BOTH OF HER FEET LEAVE THEIR ORIGINAL POSITION FROM WHEN THE SPELL WAS CAST, THE TECHNIQUE ENDS

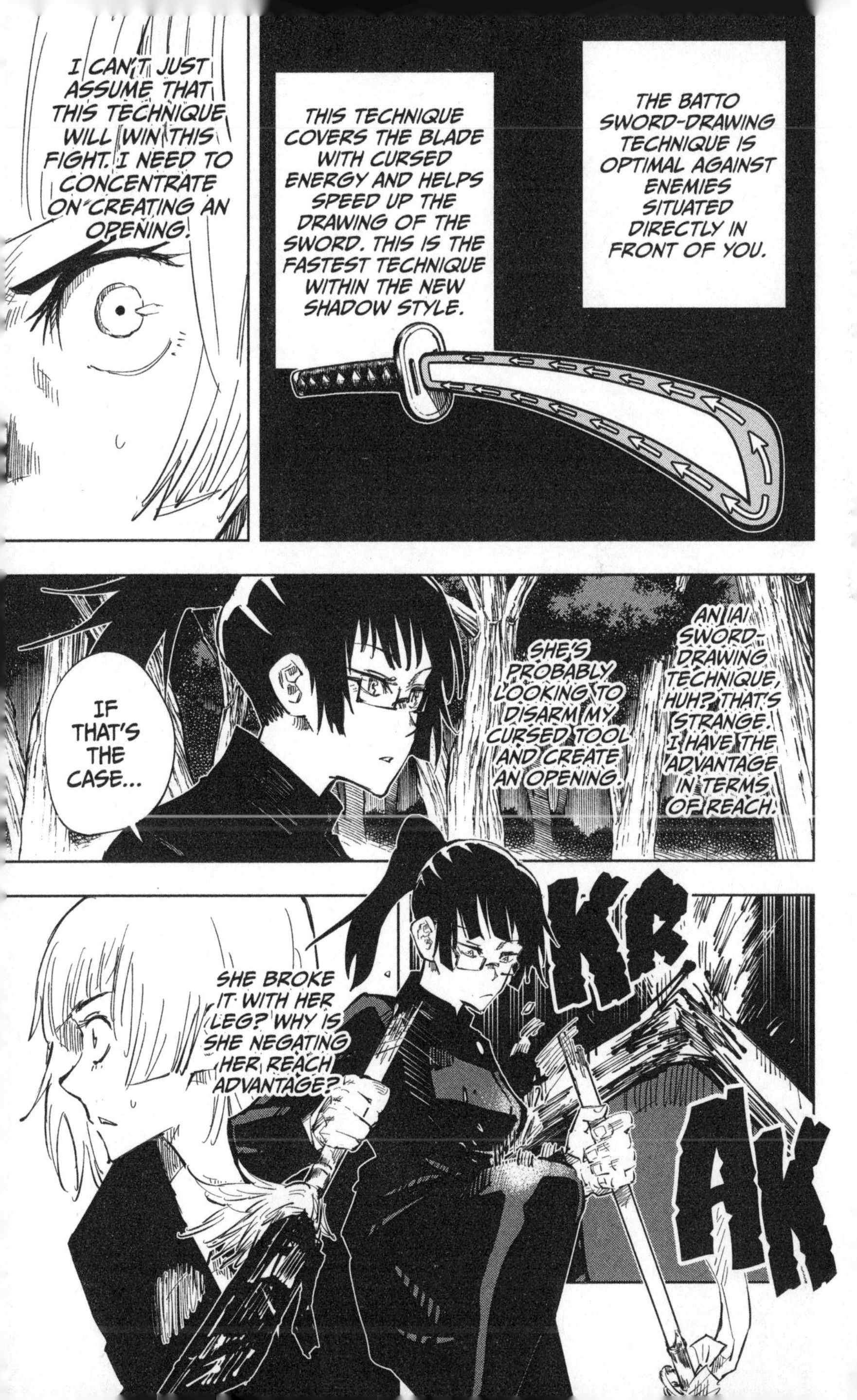
THE BATTO SWORD-DRAWING TECHNIQUE IS OPTIMAL AGAINST ENEMIES SITUATED DIRECTLY IN FRONT OF YOU.
THIS TECHNIQUE COVERS THE BLADE WITH CURSED ENERGY AND HELPS SPEED UP THE DRAWING OF THE SWORD. THIS IS THE FASTEST TECHNIQUE WITHIN THE NEW SHADOW STYLE.
I CAN'T JUST ASSUME THAT THIS TECHNIQUE WILL WIN THIS FIGHT. I NEED TO CONCENTRATE ON CREATING AN OPENING.
AN IAI SWORD-DRAWING TECHNIQUE, HUH? THAT'S STRANGE. I HAVE THE ADVANTAGE IN TERMS OF REACH.
SHE'S PROBABLY LOOKING TO DISARM MY CURSED TOOL AND CREATE AN OPENING.
IF THAT'S THE CASE...
KRAK
SHE BROKE IT WITH HER LEG? WHY IS SHE NEGATING HER REACH ADVANTAGE?

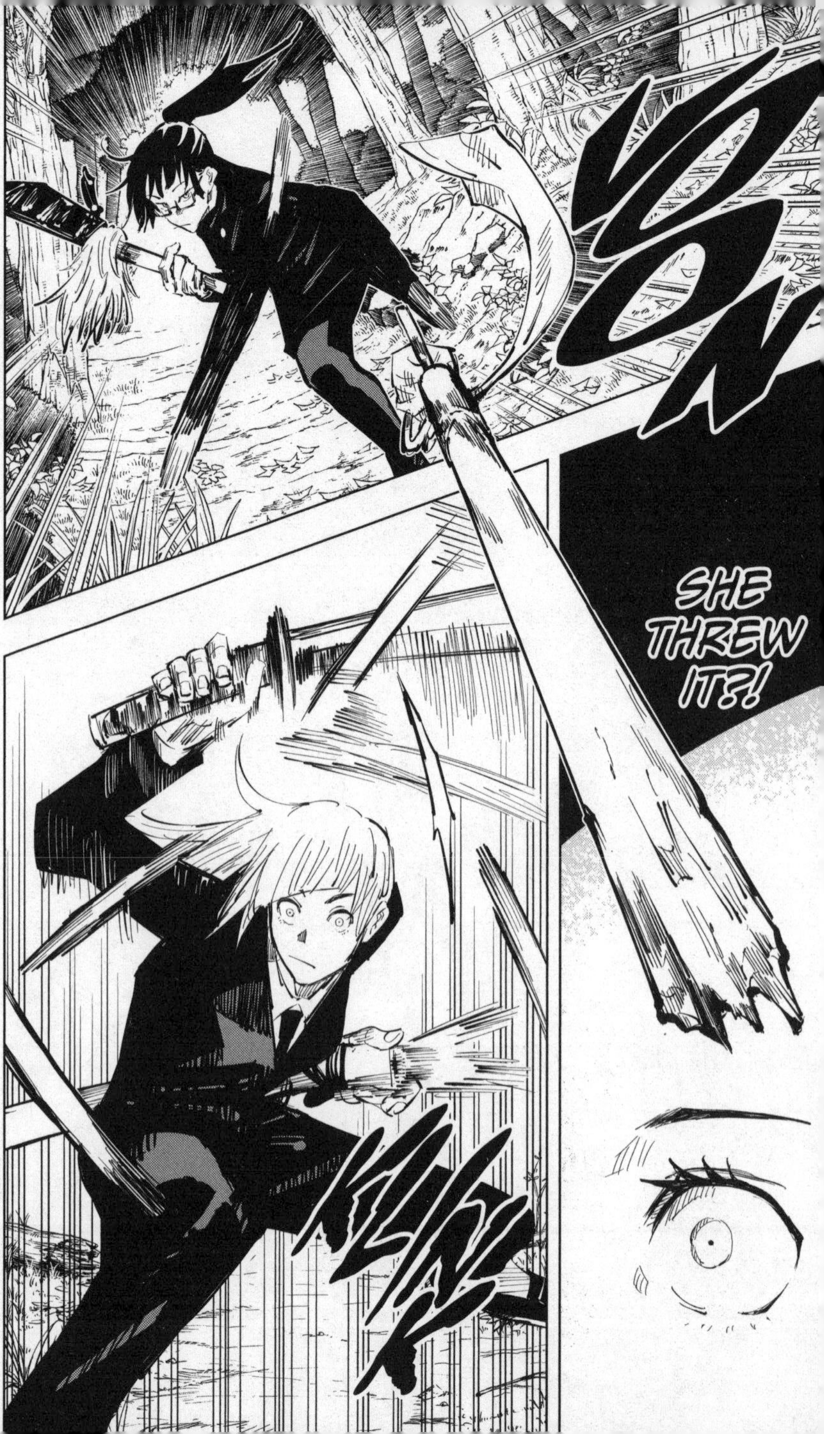
SHE THREW IT?!

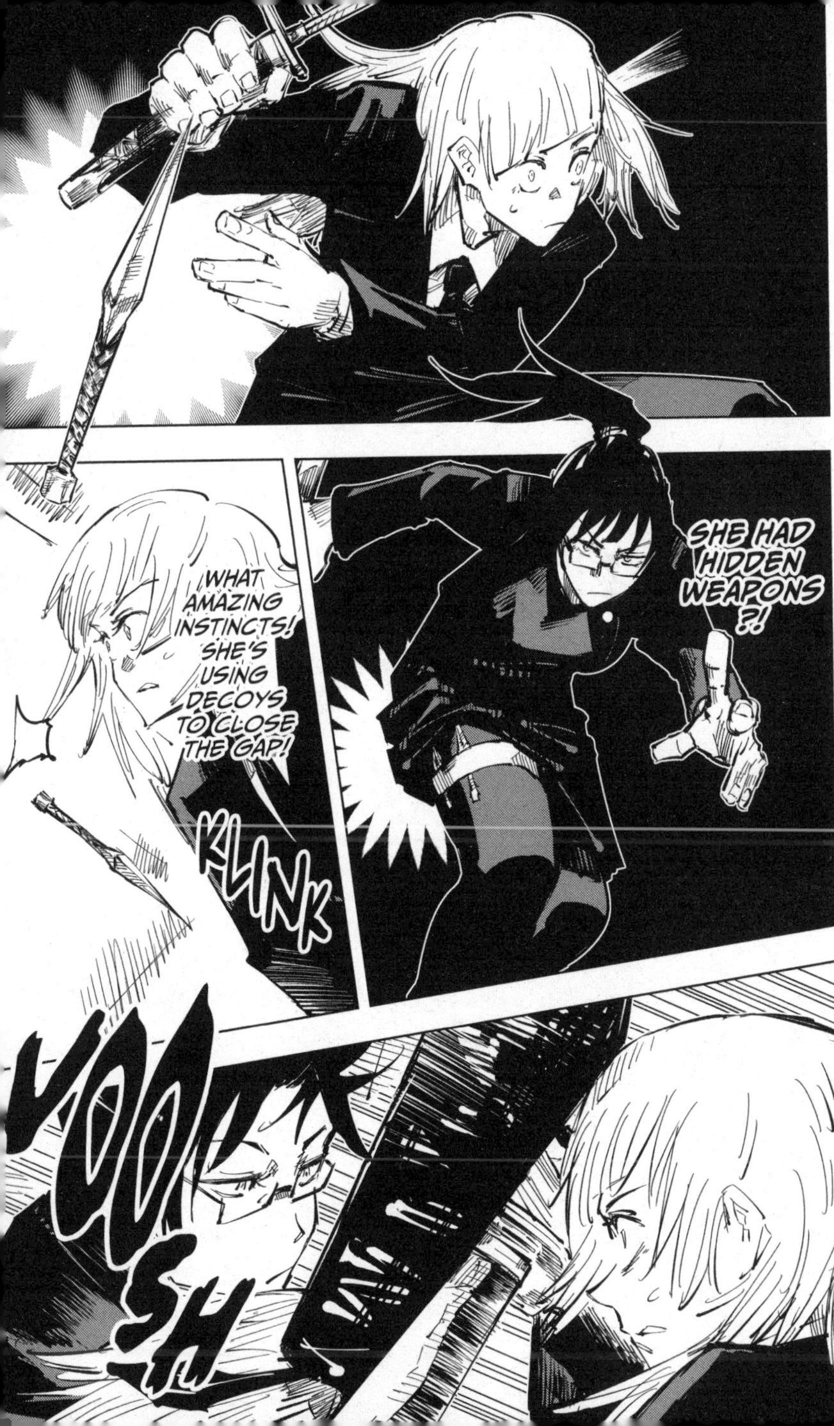
SHE HAD HIDDEN WEAPONS?!
WHAT AMAZING INSTINCTS! SHE'S USING DECOYS TO CLOSE THE GAP!
KLINK
VOOOSH

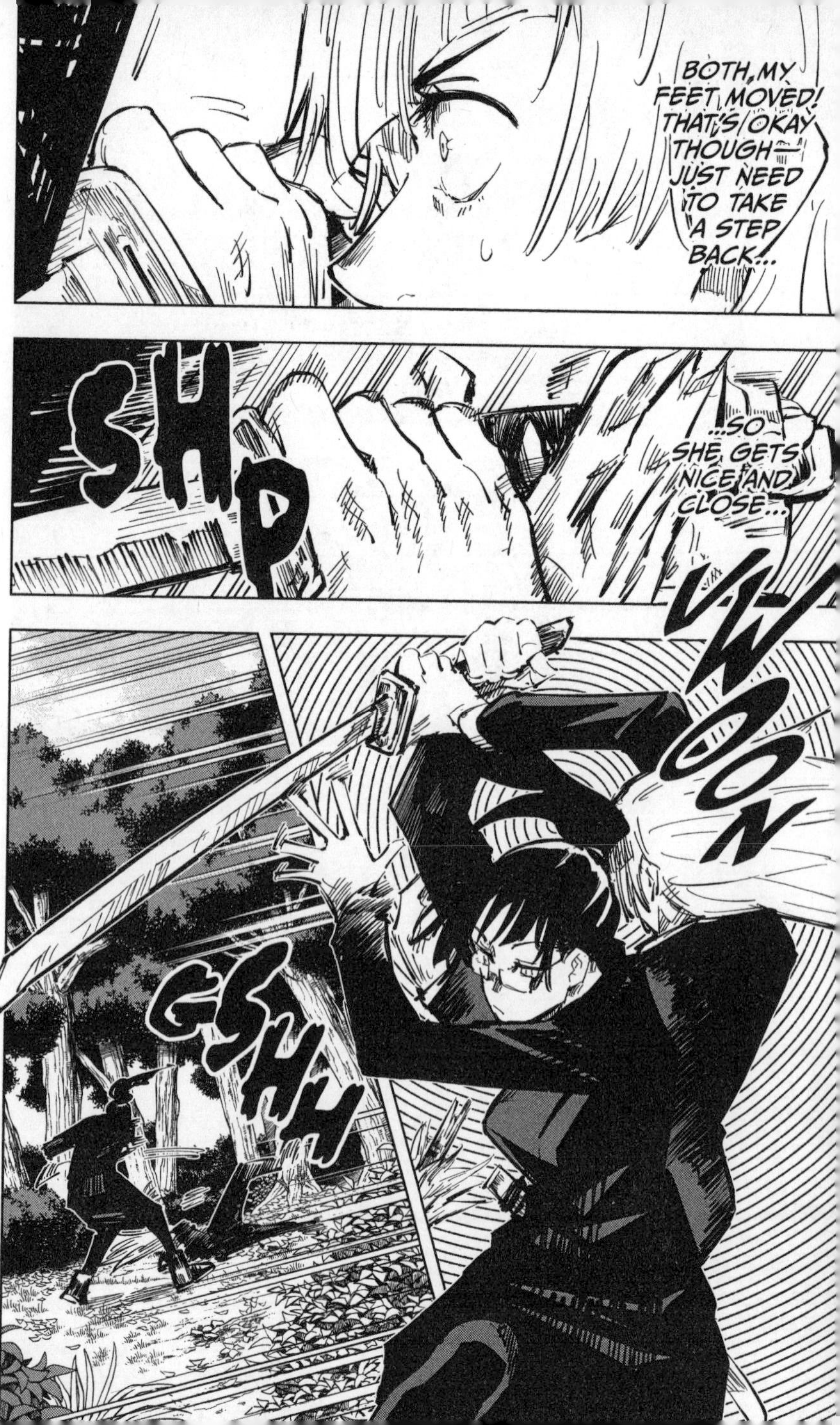
BOTH, MY FEET MOVED! THAT'S OKAY THOUGH— JUST NEED TO TAKE A STEP BACK...
...SO SHE GETS NICE AND CLOSE...
SHP
VWOOON
GSHH

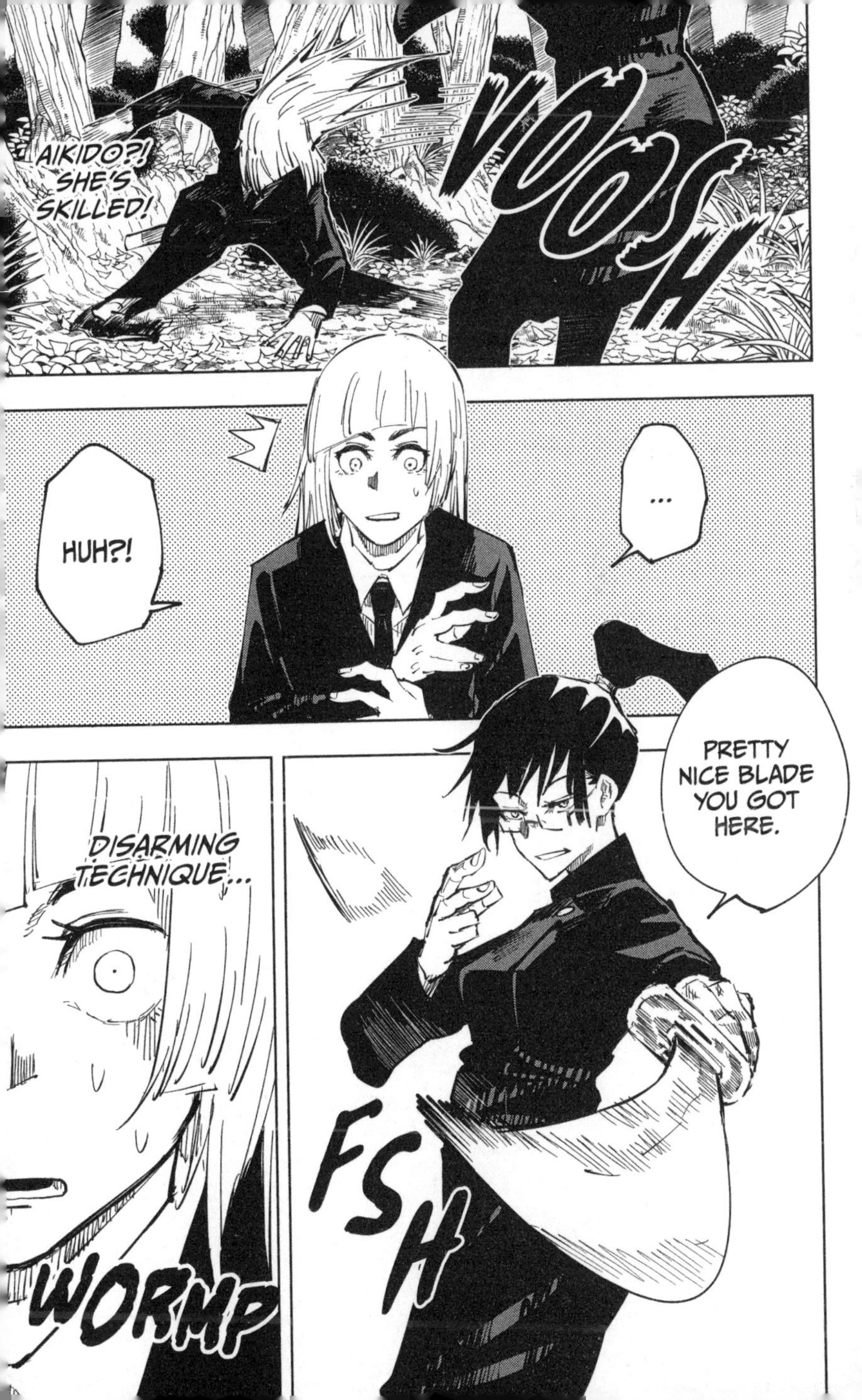
VOOSH
AIKIDO?! SHE'S SKILLED!
...
HUH?!
PRETTY NICE BLADE YOU GOT HERE.
FSH
DISARMING TECHNIQUE...
WORMP

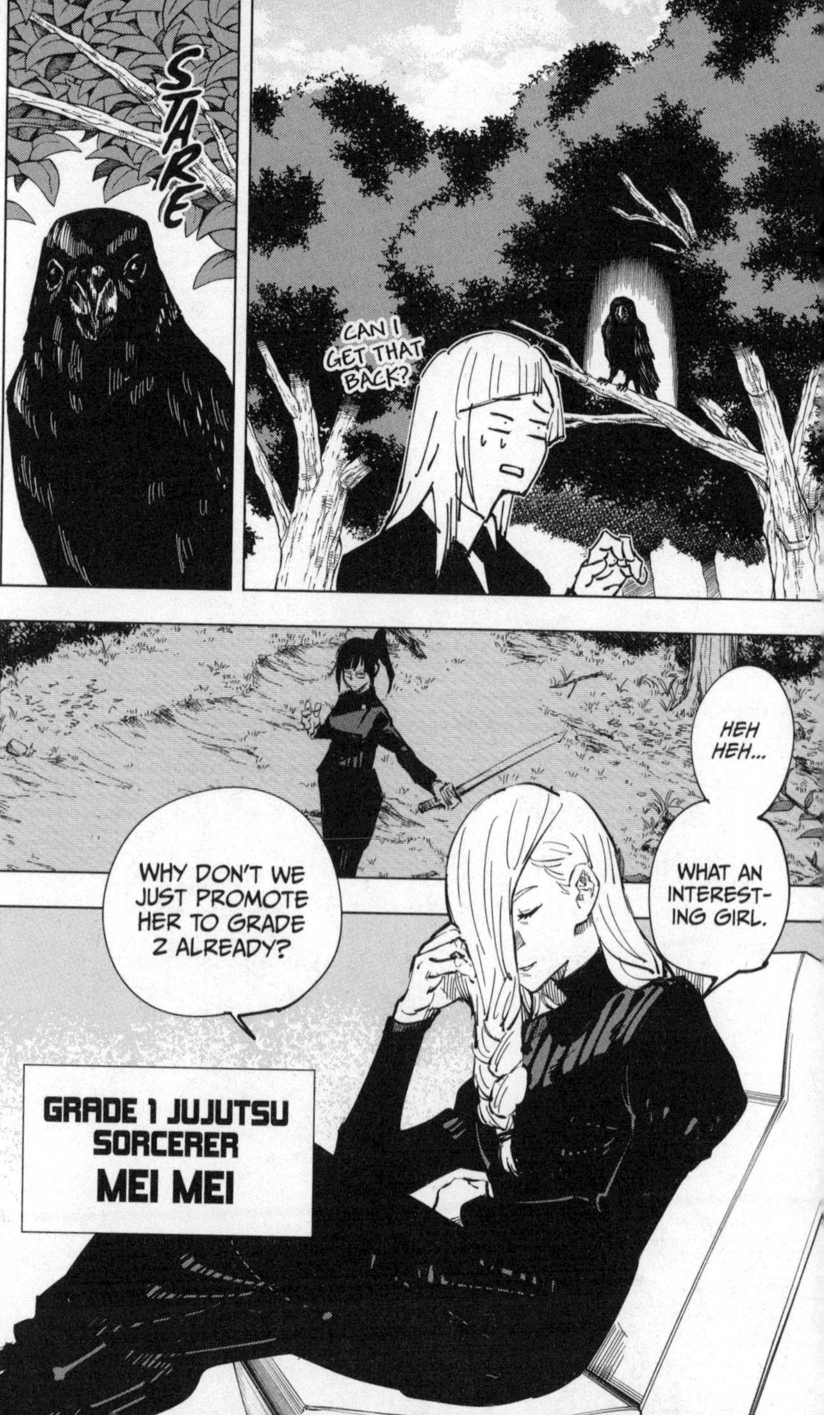
CAN I GET THAT BACK?
STARE
HEH HEH...
WHAT AN INTEREST-ING GIRL.
WHY DON'T WE JUST PROMOTE HER TO GRADE 2 ALREADY?
GRADE 1 JUJUTSU SORCERER
MEI MEI

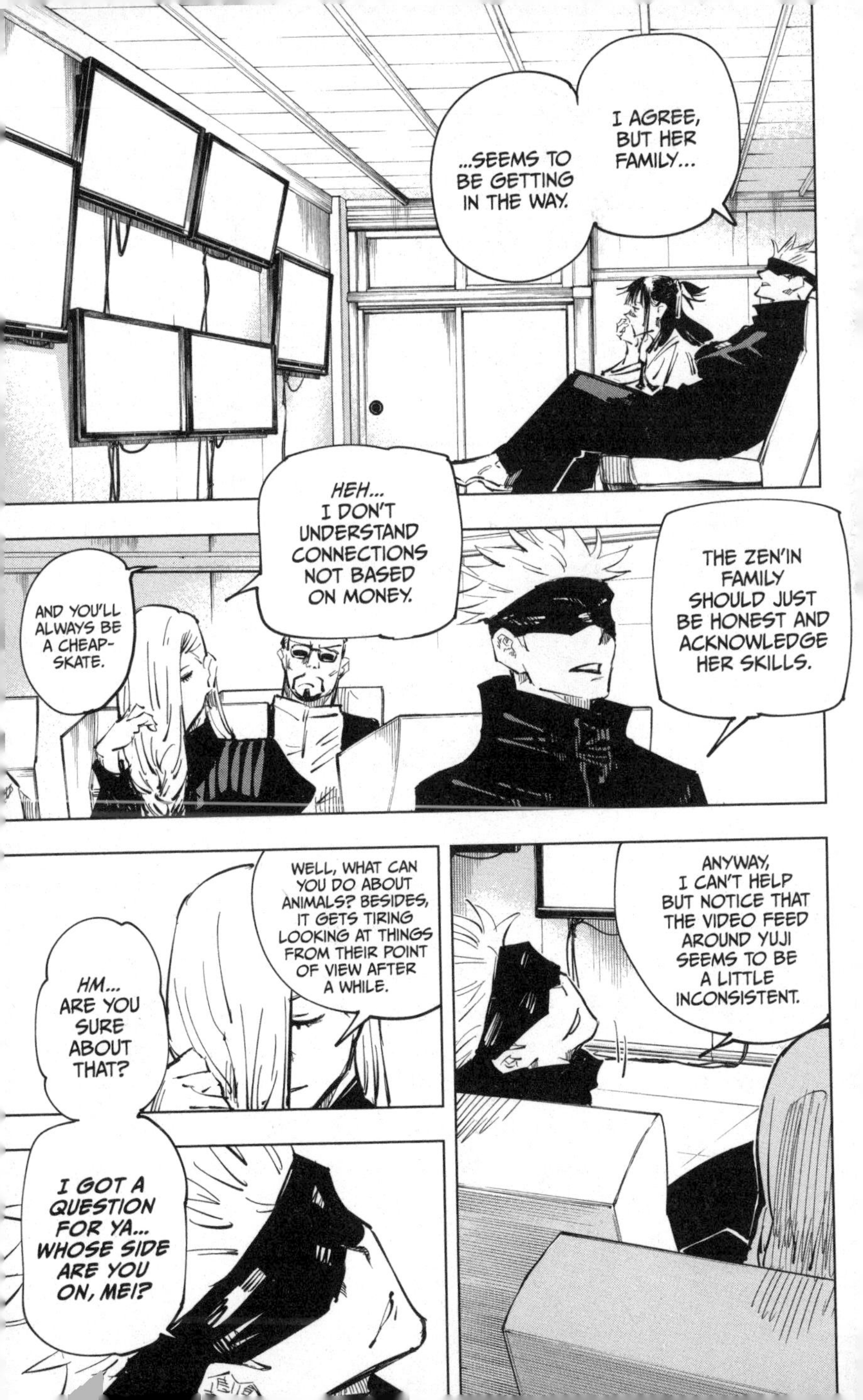
I AGREE, BUT HER FAMILY...
...SEEMS TO BE GETTING IN THE WAY.
THE ZEN'IN FAMILY SHOULD JUST BE HONEST AND ACKNOWLEDGE HER SKILLS.
HEH... I DON'T UNDERSTAND CONNECTIONS NOT BASED ON MONEY.
AND YOU'LL ALWAYS BE A CHEAP-SKATE.
ANYWAY, I CAN'T HELP BUT NOTICE THAT THE VIDEO FEED AROUND YUJI SEEMS TO BE A LITTLE INCONSISTENT.
WELL, WHAT CAN YOU DO ABOUT ANIMALS? BESIDES, IT GETS TIRING LOOKING AT THINGS FROM THEIR POINT OF VIEW AFTER A WHILE.
HM... ARE YOU SURE ABOUT THAT?
I GOT A QUESTION FOR YA... WHOSE SIDE ARE YOU ON, MEI?

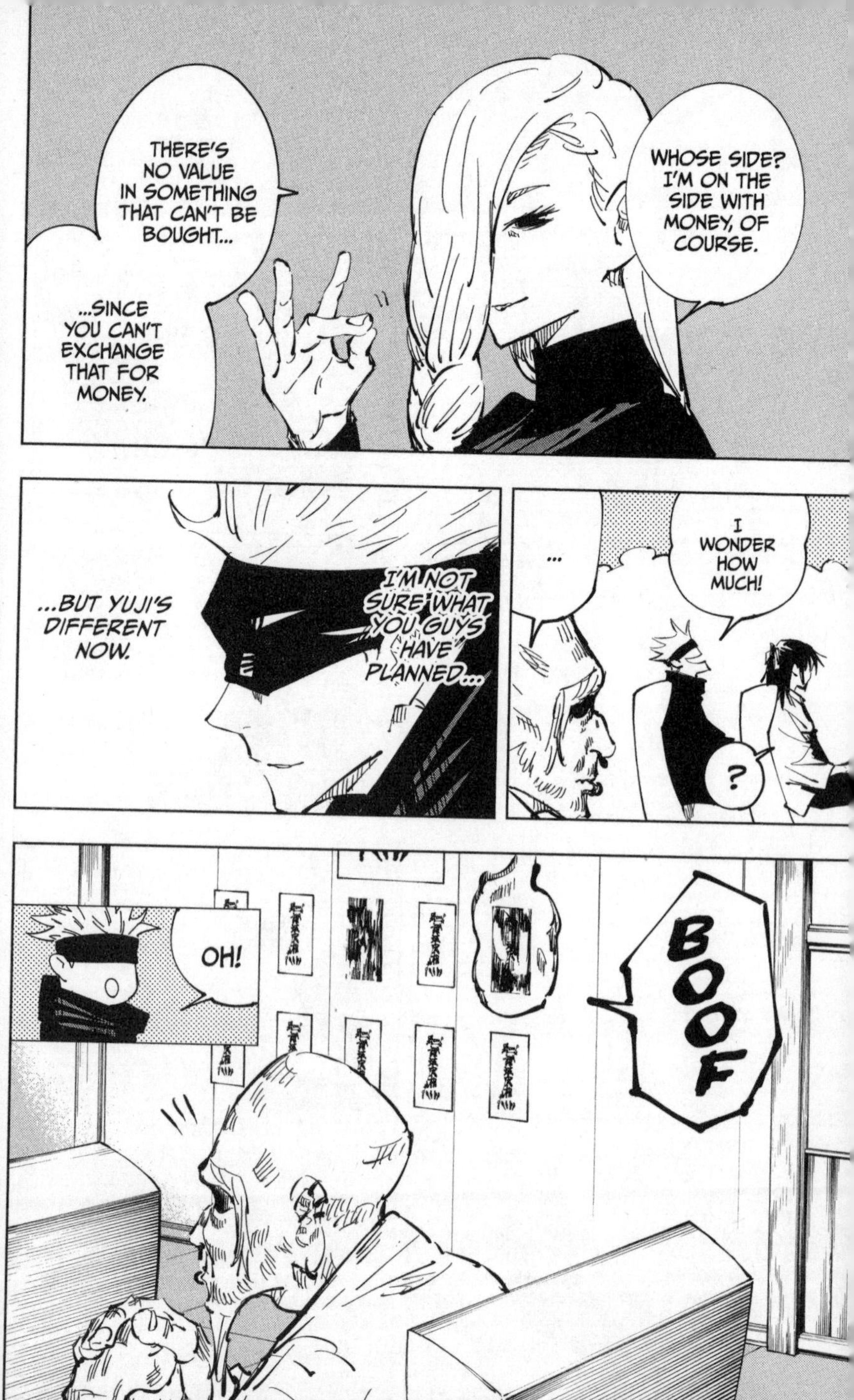
WHOSE SIDE? I'M ON THE SIDE WITH MONEY, OF COURSE.
THERE'S NO VALUE IN SOMETHING THAT CAN'T BE BOUGHT...
...SINCE YOU CAN'T EXCHANGE THAT FOR MONEY.
I WONDER HOW MUCH!
...
?
I'M NOT SURE WHAT YOU GUYS HAVE PLANNED...
...BUT YUJI'S DIFFERENT NOW.
BOOF
OH!

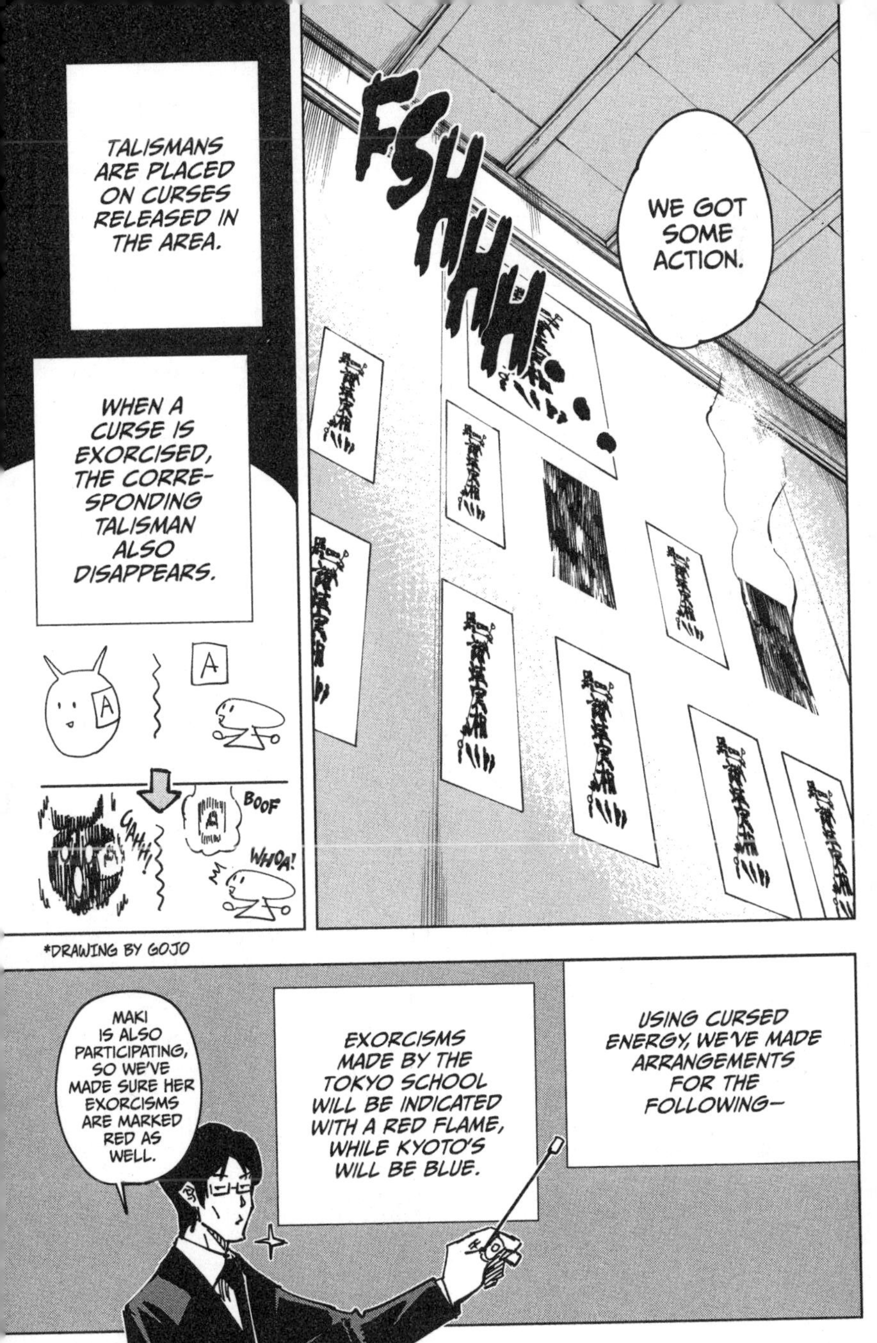
FSHHH...
WE GOT SOME ACTION.
TALISMANS ARE PLACED ON CURSES RELEASED IN THE AREA.
WHEN A CURSE IS EXORCISED, THE CORRESPONDING TALISMAN ALSO DISAPPEARS.
A
A
GYAHH!
BOOF
WHOA!
*DRAWING BY GOJO
USING CURSED ENERGY, WE'VE MADE ARRANGEMENTS FOR THE FOLLOWING—
EXORCISMS MADE BY THE TOKYO SCHOOL WILL BE INDICATED WITH A RED FLAME, WHILE KYOTO'S WILL BE BLUE.
MAKI IS ALSO PARTICIPATING, SO WE'VE MADE SURE HER EXORCISMS ARE MARKED RED AS WELL.

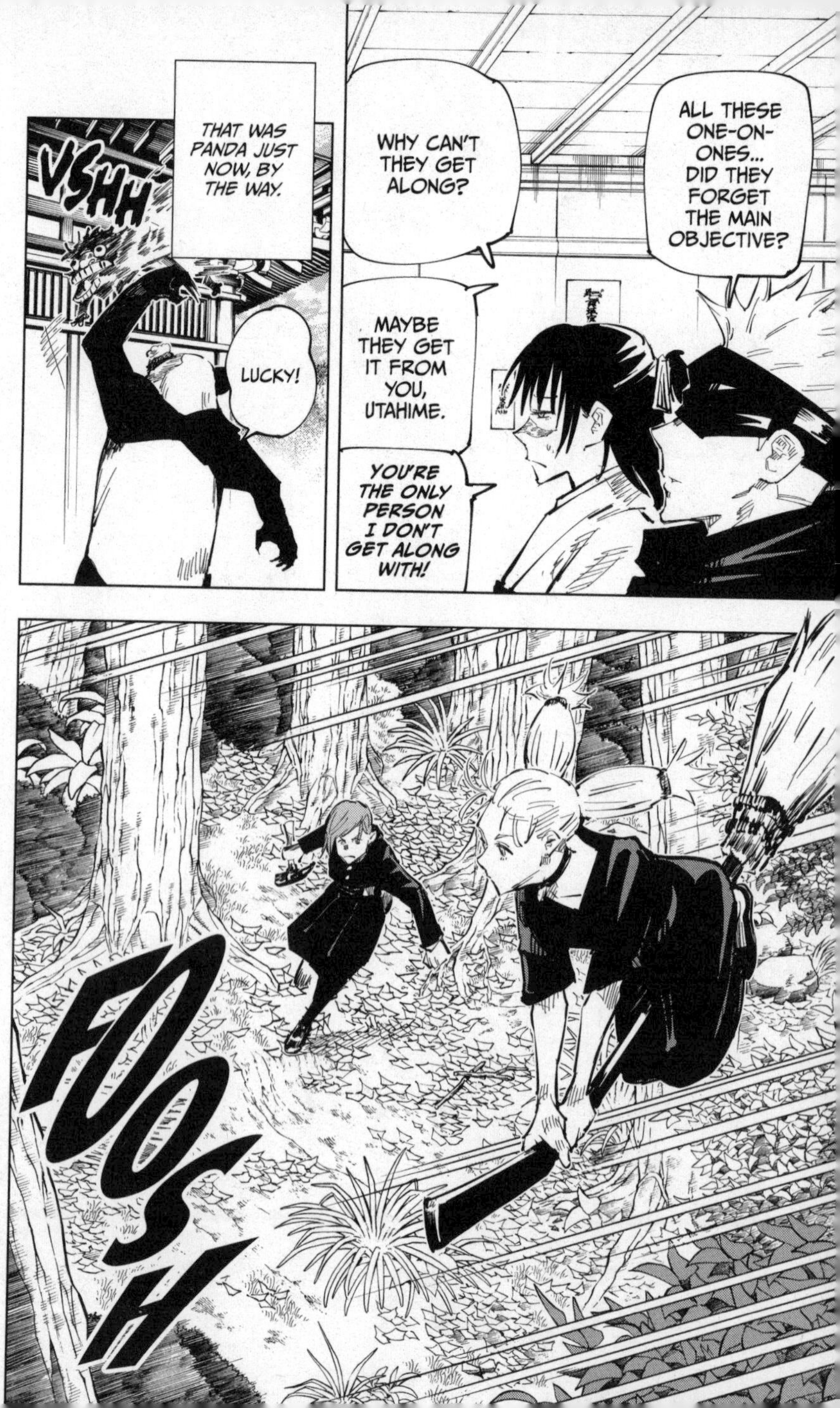
ALL THESE ONE-ON-ONES... DID THEY FORGET THE MAIN OBJECTIVE?
WHY CAN'T THEY GET ALONG?
MAYBE THEY GET IT FROM YOU, UTAHIME.
YOU'RE THE ONLY PERSON I DON'T GET ALONG WITH!
THAT WAS PANDA JUST NOW, BY THE WAY.
VSHH
LUCKY!
FOOSH

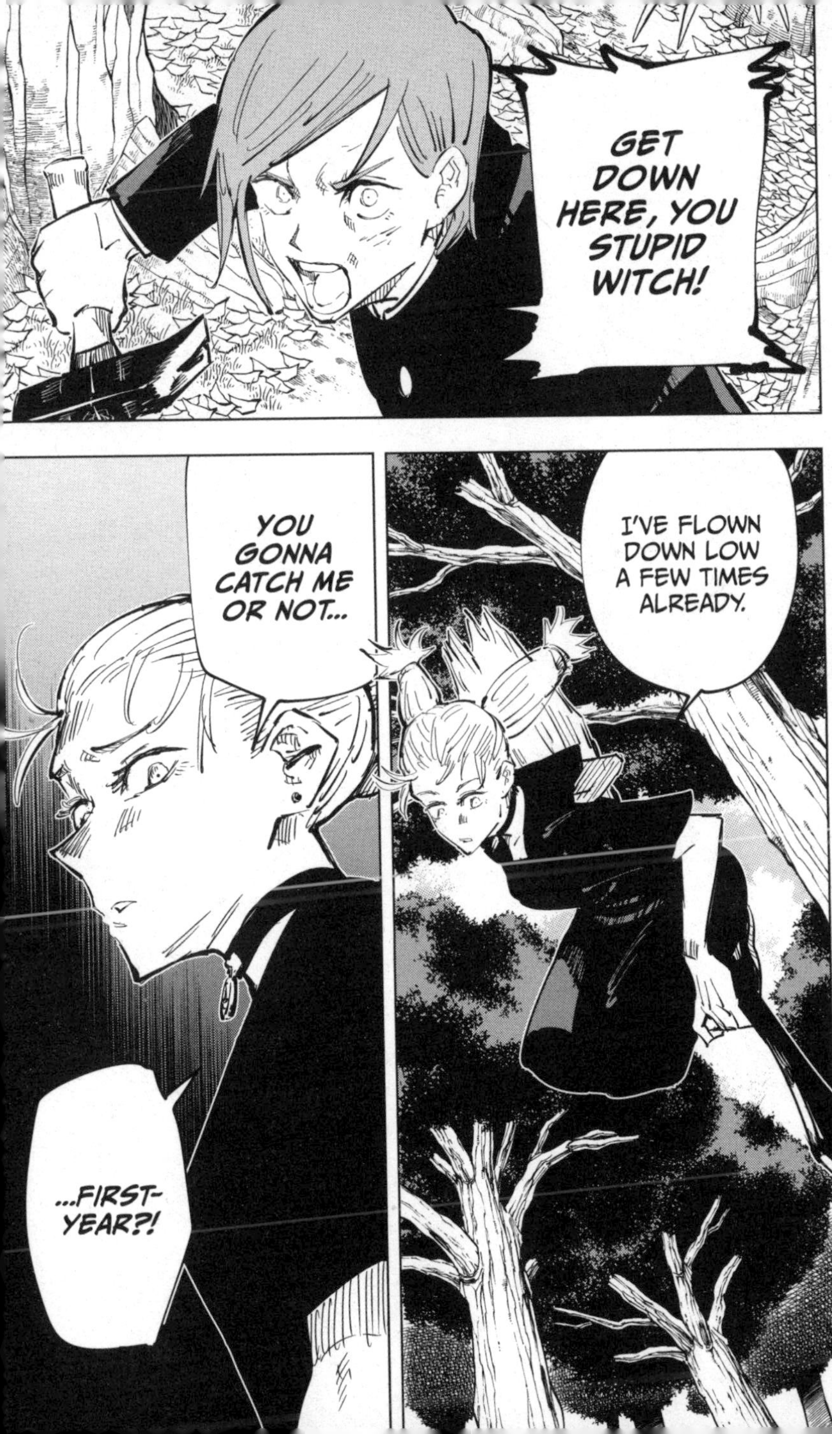
GET DOWN HERE, YOU STUPID WITCH!
I'VE FLOWN DOWN LOW A FEW TIMES ALREADY.
YOU GONNA CATCH ME OR NOT...
...FIRST-YEAR?!

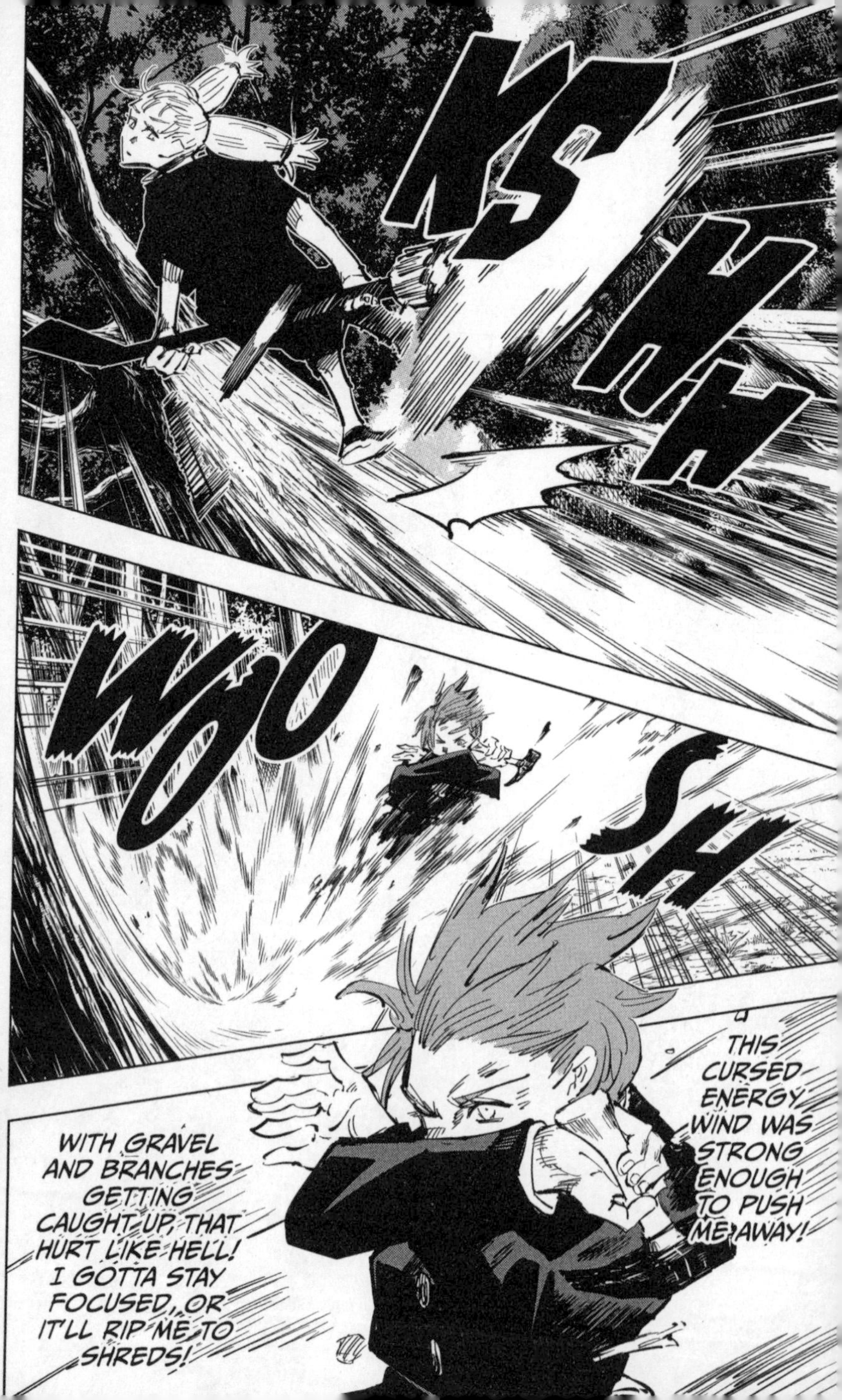
KSHHH
WOOSH
THIS CURSED ENERGY WIND WAS STRONG ENOUGH TO PUSH ME AWAY!
WITH GRAVEL AND BRANCHES GETTING CAUGHT UP, THAT HURT LIKE HELL! I GOTTA STAY FOCUSED, OR IT'LL RIP ME TO SHREDS!

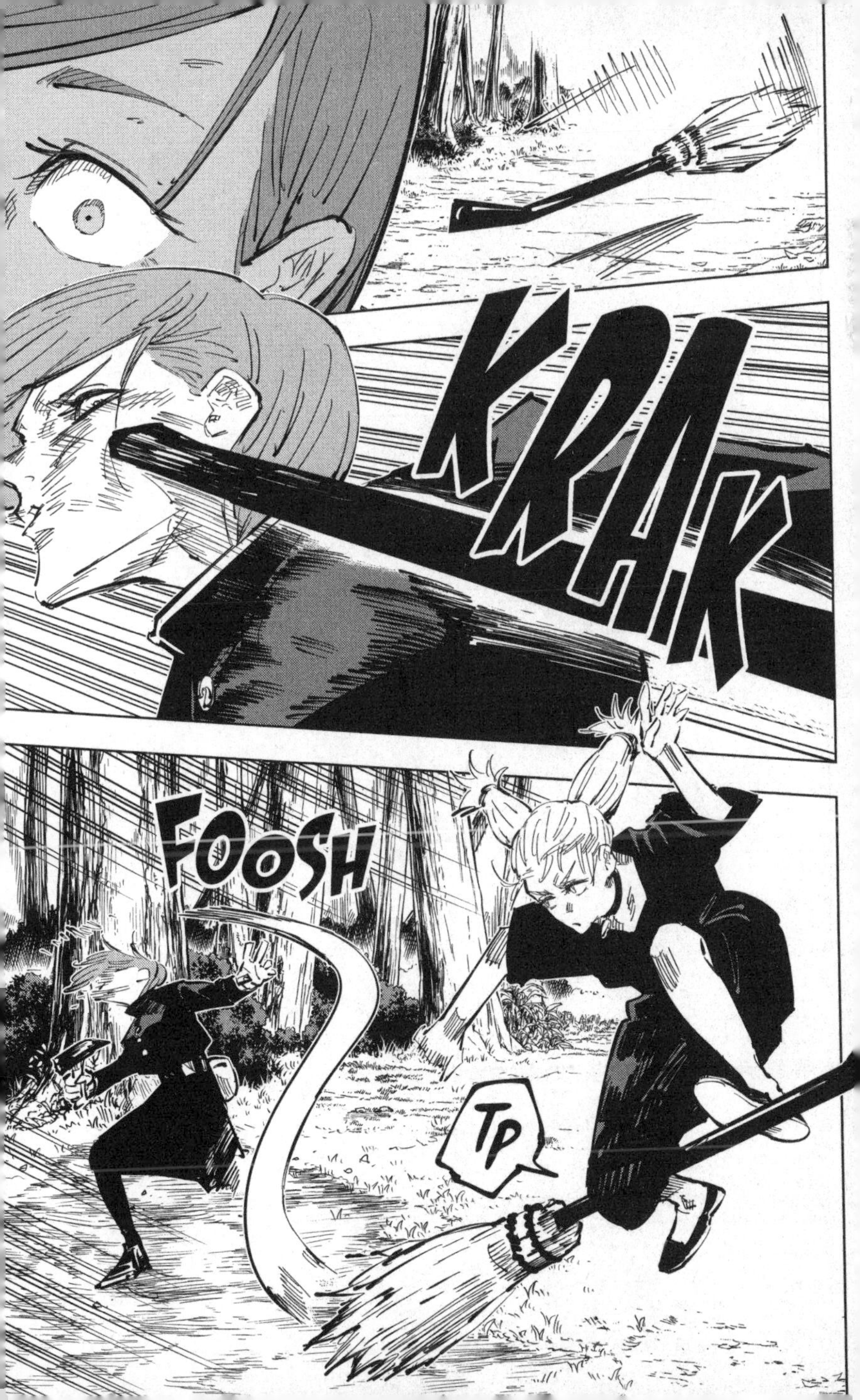
KRAK
FOOSH
TP

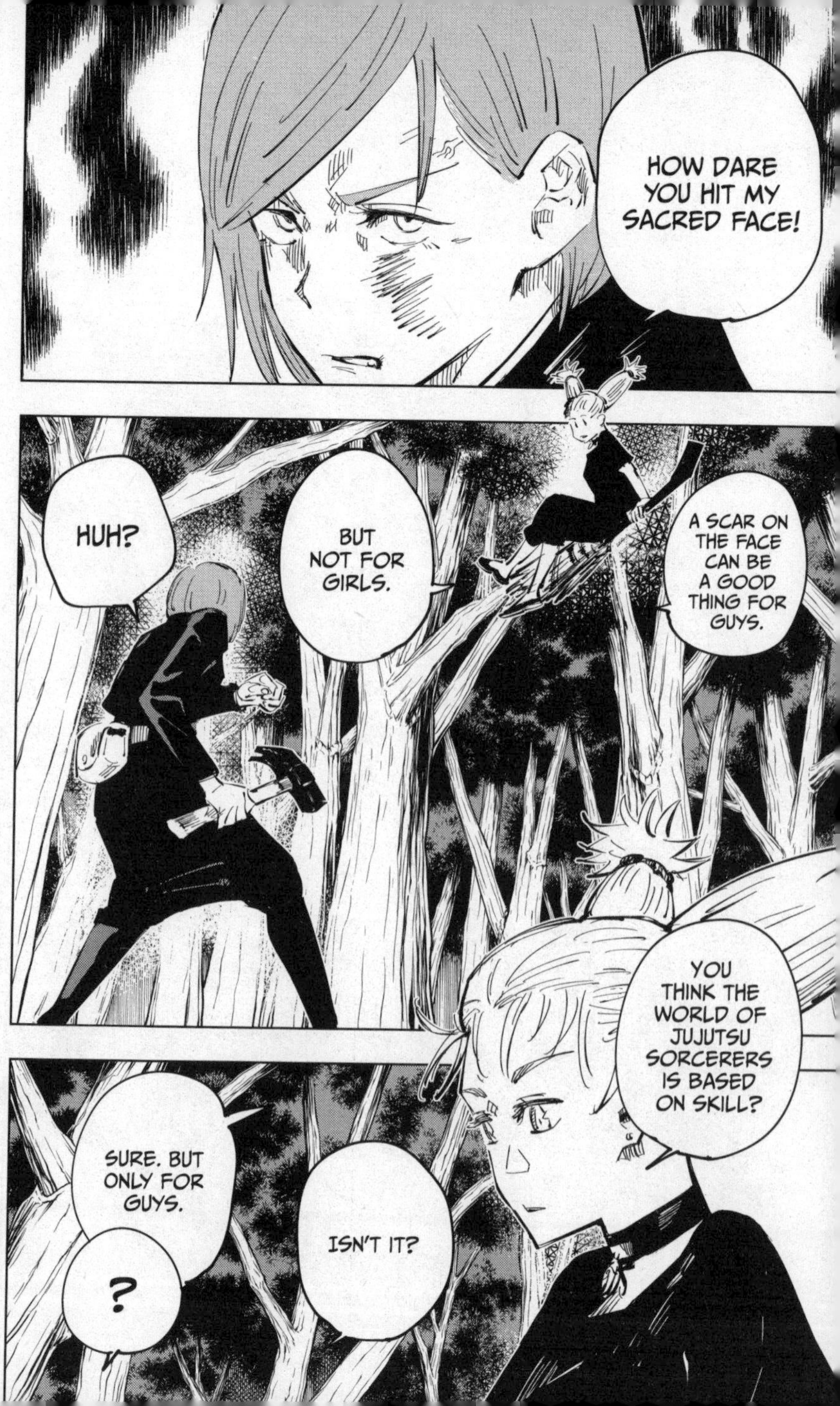
HOW DARE YOU HIT MY SACRED FACE!
A SCAR ON THE FACE CAN BE A GOOD THING FOR GUYS.
BUT NOT FOR GIRLS.
HUH?
YOU THINK THE WORLD OF JUJUTSU SORCERERS IS BASED ON SKILL?
ISN'T IT?
SURE. BUT ONLY FOR GUYS.
?

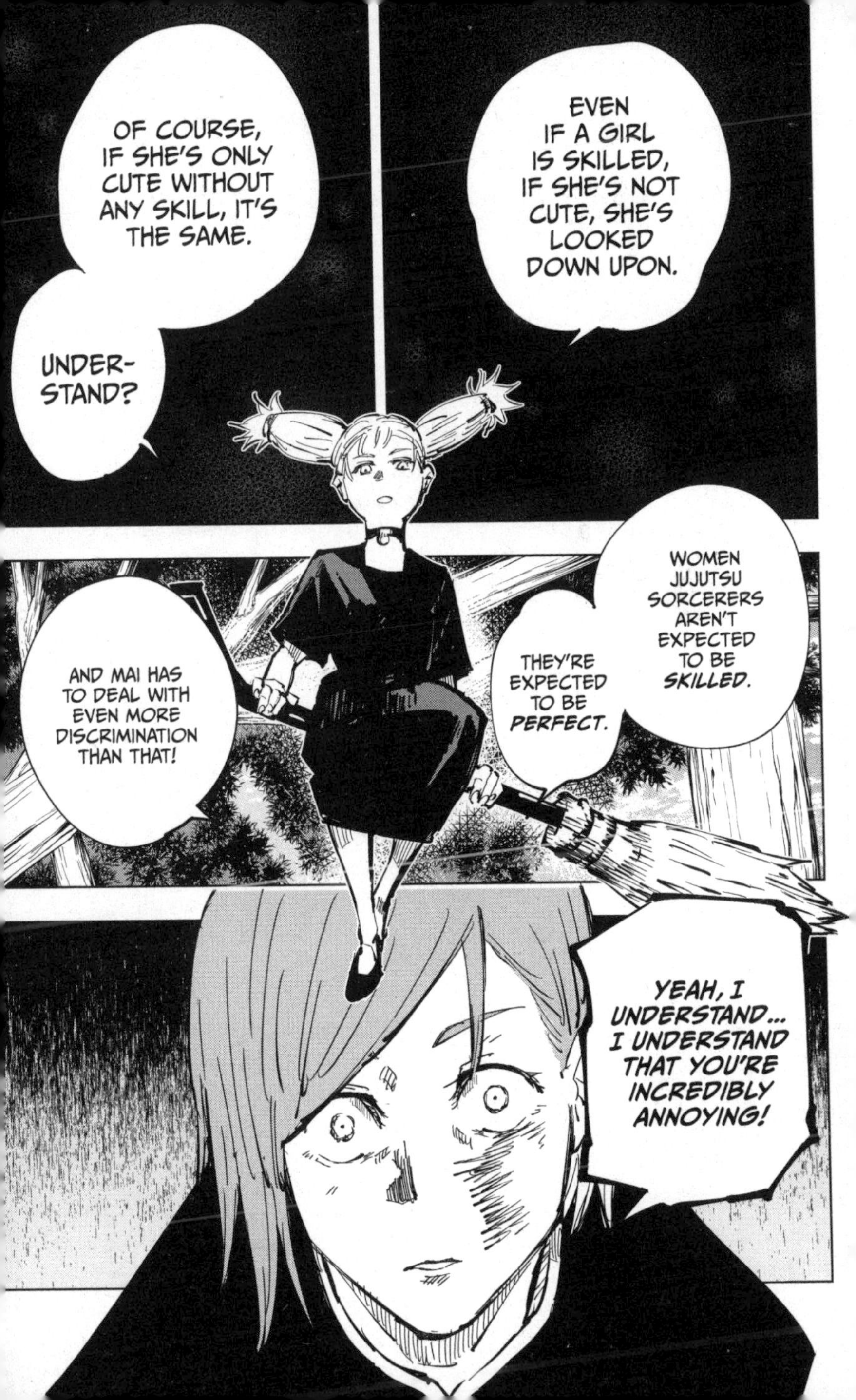
EVEN IF A GIRL IS SKILLED, IF SHE'S NOT CUTE, SHE'S LOOKED DOWN UPON.
OF COURSE, IF SHE'S ONLY CUTE WITHOUT ANY SKILL, IT'S THE SAME.
UNDER-STAND?
WOMEN JUJUTSU SORCERERS AREN'T EXPECTED TO BE *SKILLED.*
THEY'RE EXPECTED TO BE *PERFECT.*
AND MAI HAS TO DEAL WITH EVEN MORE DISCRIMINATION THAN THAT!
YEAH, I UNDERSTAND... I UNDERSTAND THAT YOU'RE INCREDIBLY ANNOYING!

"Wait a Moment -Playback"

← The reader's interest might have been piqued by this scene.

← Maki uses her brute strength to split a cursed tool in half! But...

CURSED TOOL

NOT A CURSED TOOL

← The pole arm's blade is a cursed tool, but the handle is just a regular handle. With that said, normally your thigh would be the one to break, so don't try it at home.

NOT A CURSED TOOL

← Fushiguro imbues these tonfas with cursed energy while using them, but the weapons aren't actually cursed tools.

SORT OF A CURSED TOOL

← Miwa's sword was originally a regular sword, but since she's been imbuing it with cursed energy for so long, it has sort of become a cursed tool.

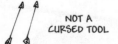

NOT A CURSED TOOL

← Kamo's arrows are not cursed tools. They are disposable.

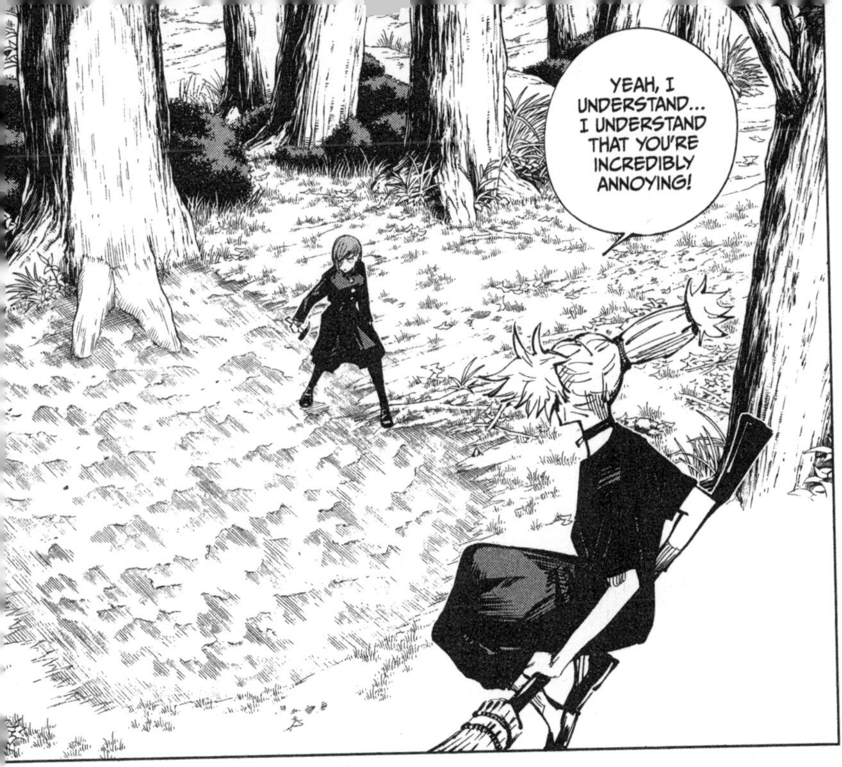
YEAH, I UNDERSTAND... I UNDERSTAND THAT YOU'RE INCREDIBLY ANNOYING!

Chapter 41: Kyoto Sister-School Goodwill Event—Team Battle, Part 8

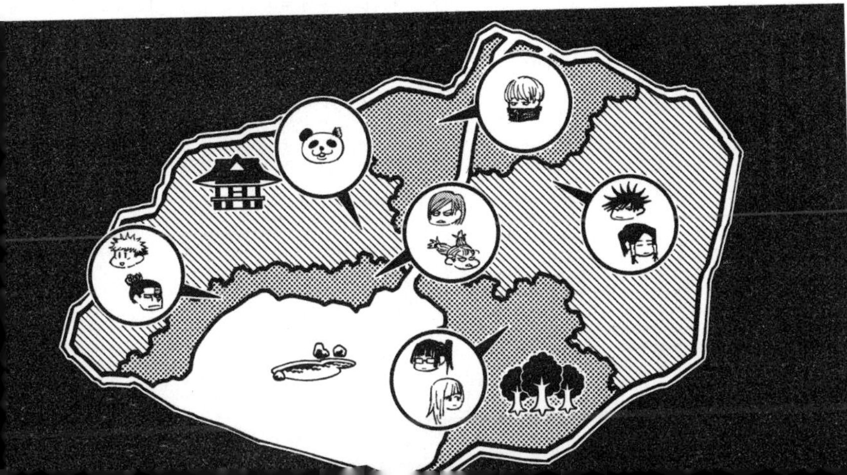

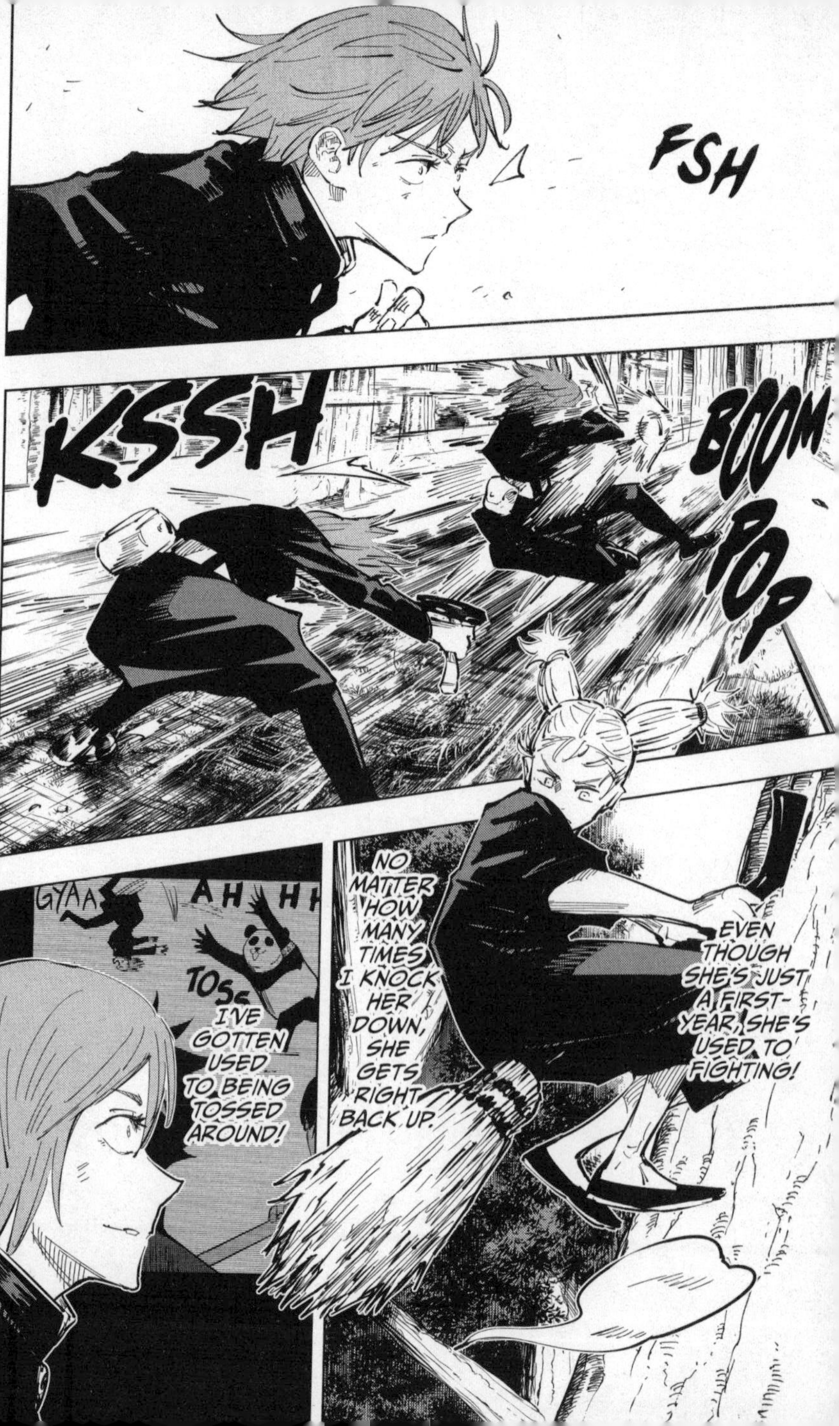
FSH
BOOM
POP
KSSH
EVEN THOUGH SHE'S JUST A FIRST-YEAR, SHE'S USED TO FIGHTING!
NO MATTER HOW MANY TIMES I KNOCK HER DOWN, SHE GETS RIGHT BACK UP.
GYAA AH HH
TOSS
I'VE GOTTEN USED TO BEING TOSSED AROUND!

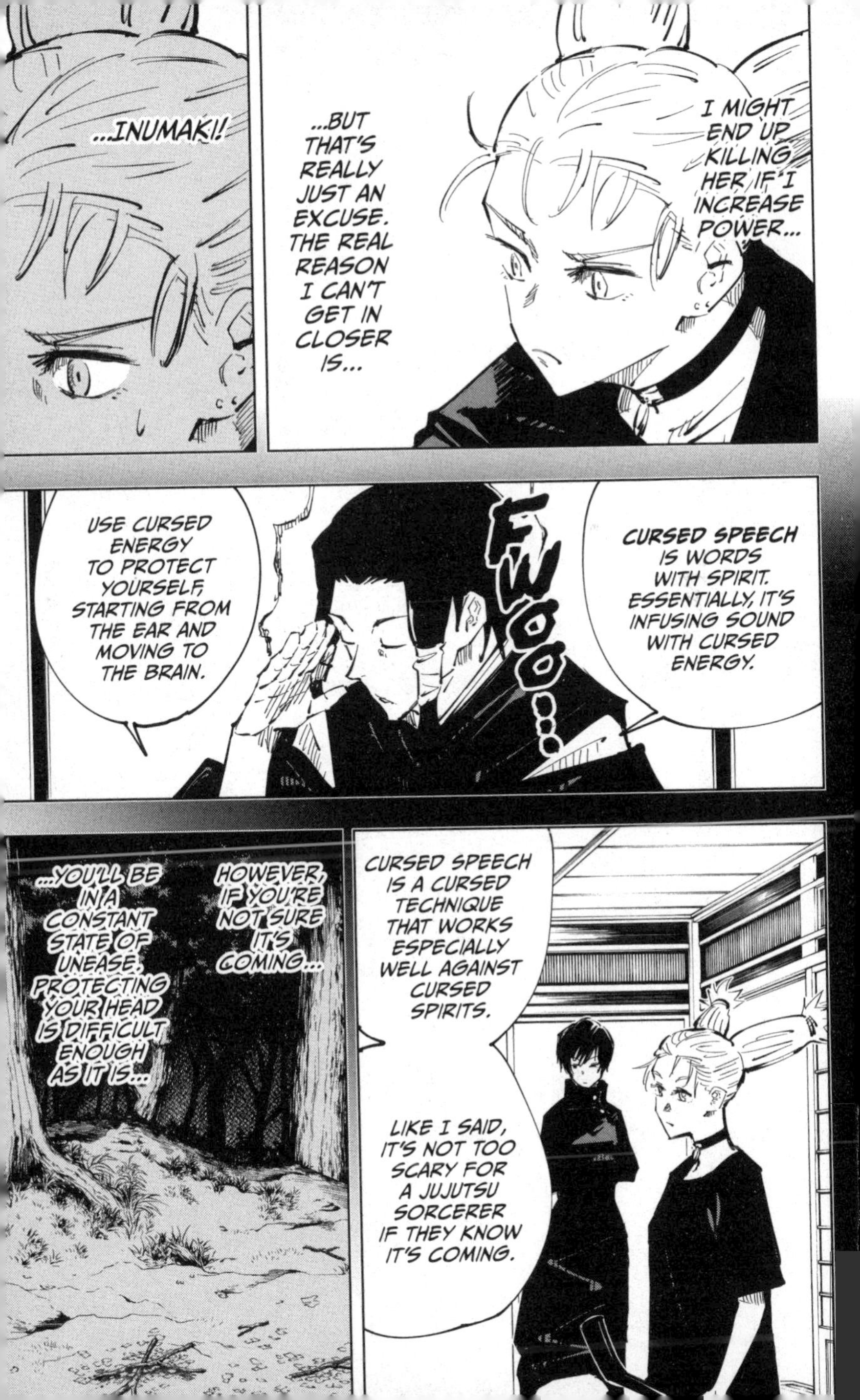
I MIGHT END UP KILLING HER IF I INCREASE POWER...
...BUT THAT'S REALLY JUST AN EXCUSE. THE REAL REASON I CAN'T GET IN CLOSER IS...
...INUMAKI!
CURSED SPEECH IS WORDS WITH SPIRIT. ESSENTIALLY, IT'S INFUSING SOUND WITH CURSED ENERGY.
FWOOO...
USE CURSED ENERGY TO PROTECT YOURSELF, STARTING FROM THE EAR AND MOVING TO THE BRAIN.
CURSED SPEECH IS A CURSED TECHNIQUE THAT WORKS ESPECIALLY WELL AGAINST CURSED SPIRITS.
LIKE I SAID, IT'S NOT TOO SCARY FOR A JUJUTSU SORCERER IF THEY KNOW IT'S COMING.
HOWEVER, IF YOU'RE NOT SURE IT'S COMING...
...YOU'LL BE IN A CONSTANT STATE OF UNEASE. PROTECTING YOUR HEAD IS DIFFICULT ENOUGH AS IT IS...

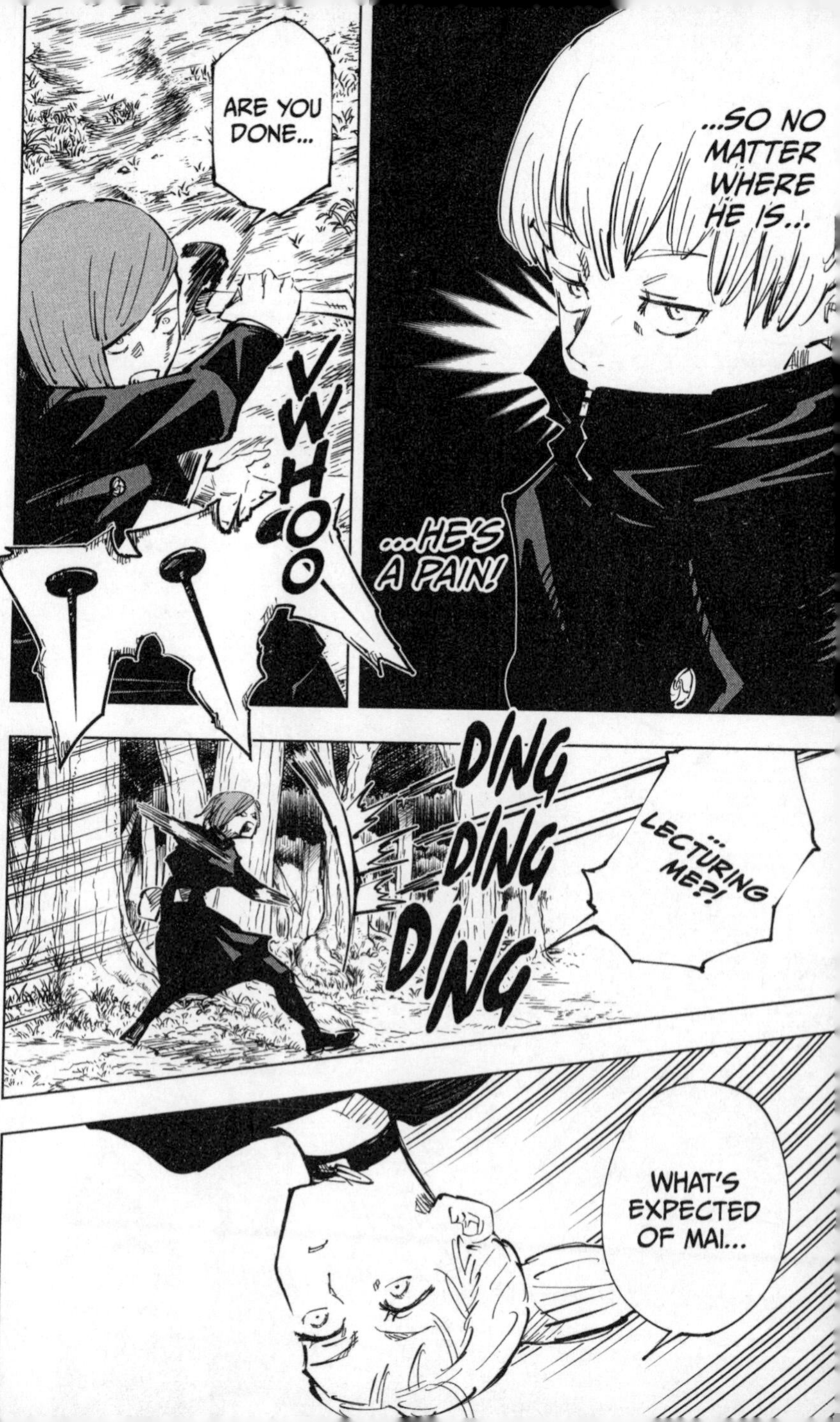
...SO NO MATTER WHERE HE IS...
...HE'S A PAIN!
ARE YOU DONE...
VWHOOO
...LECTURING ME?!
DING DING DING
WHAT'S EXPECTED OF MAI...

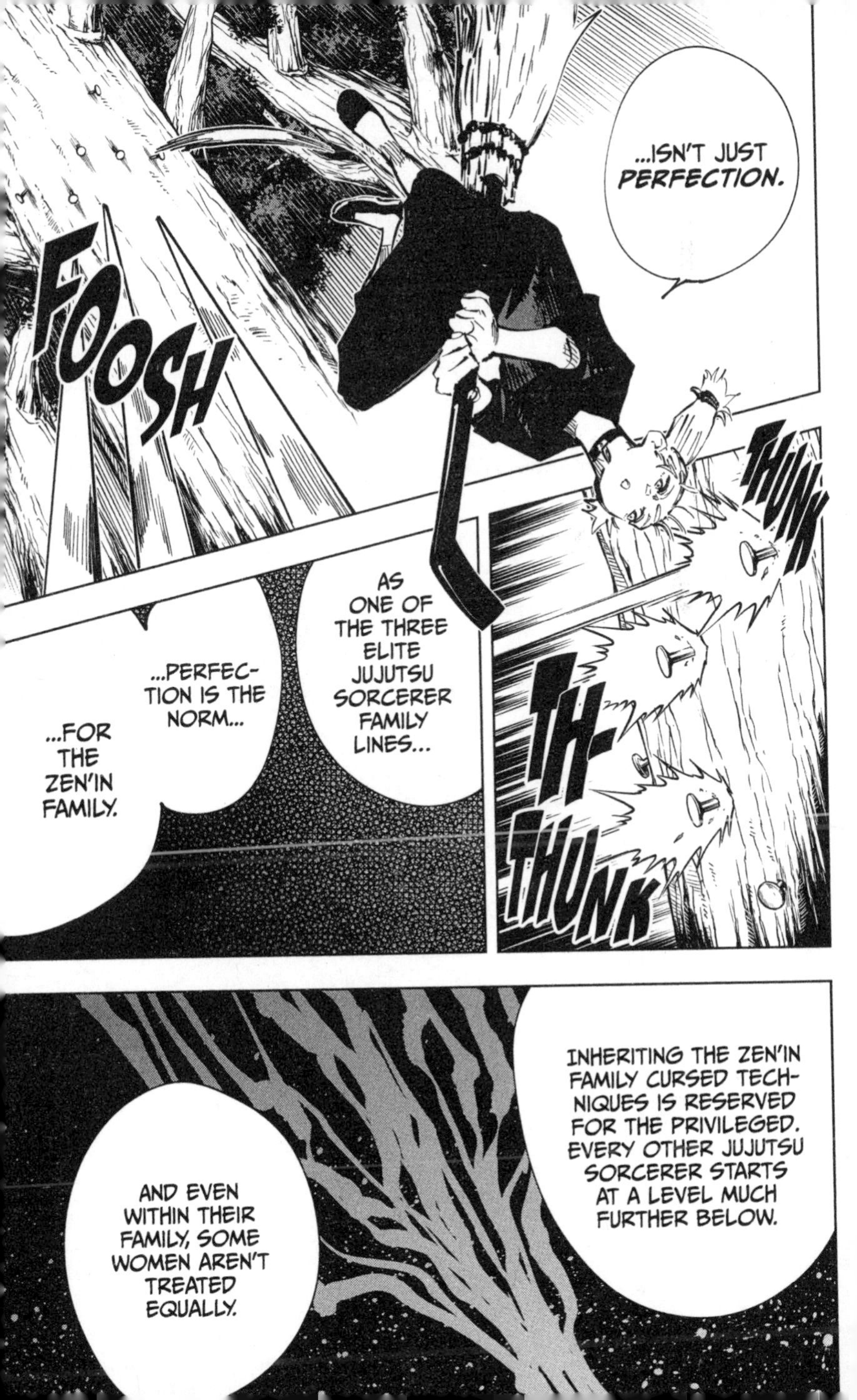
...ISN'T JUST PERFECTION.
FOOSH
THUNK
TH-THUNK
AS ONE OF THE THREE ELITE JUJUTSU SORCERER FAMILY LINES...
...PERFECTION IS THE NORM...
...FOR THE ZEN'IN FAMILY.
INHERITING THE ZEN'IN FAMILY CURSED TECHNIQUES IS RESERVED FOR THE PRIVILEGED. EVERY OTHER JUJUTSU SORCERER STARTS AT A LEVEL MUCH FURTHER BELOW.
AND EVEN WITHIN THEIR FAMILY, SOME WOMEN AREN'T TREATED EQUALLY.

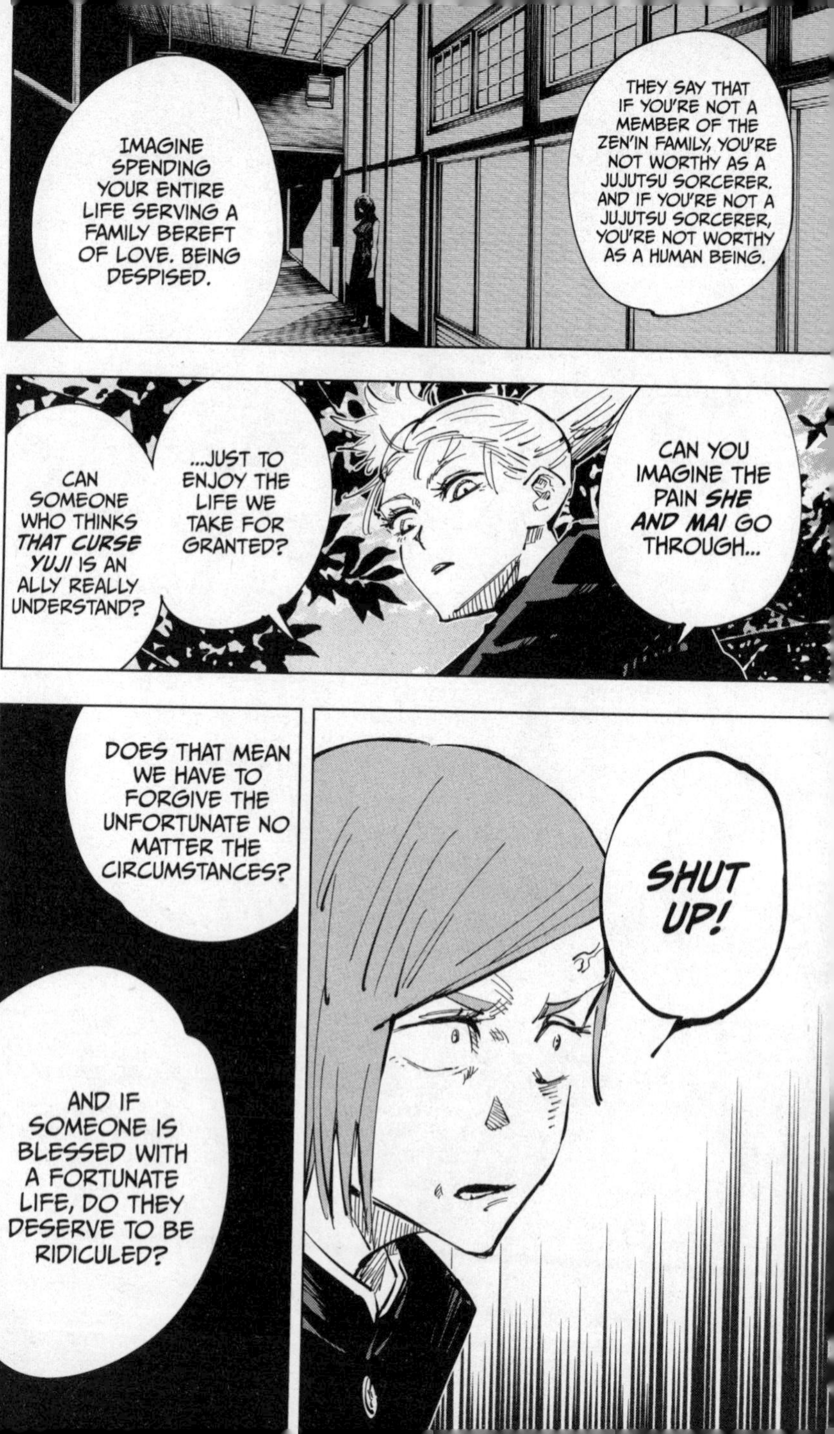
THEY SAY THAT IF YOU'RE NOT A MEMBER OF THE ZEN'IN FAMILY, YOU'RE NOT WORTHY AS A JUJUTSU SORCERER. AND IF YOU'RE NOT A JUJUTSU SORCERER, YOU'RE NOT WORTHY AS A HUMAN BEING.
IMAGINE SPENDING YOUR ENTIRE LIFE SERVING A FAMILY BEREFT OF LOVE. BEING DESPISED.
CAN YOU IMAGINE THE PAIN *SHE AND MAI* GO THROUGH...
...JUST TO ENJOY THE LIFE WE TAKE FOR GRANTED?
CAN SOMEONE WHO THINKS *THAT CURSE YUJI* IS AN ALLY REALLY UNDERSTAND?
SHUT UP!
DOES THAT MEAN WE HAVE TO FORGIVE THE UNFORTUNATE NO MATTER THE CIRCUMSTANCES?
AND IF SOMEONE IS BLESSED WITH A FORTUNATE LIFE, DO THEY DESERVE TO BE RIDICULED?

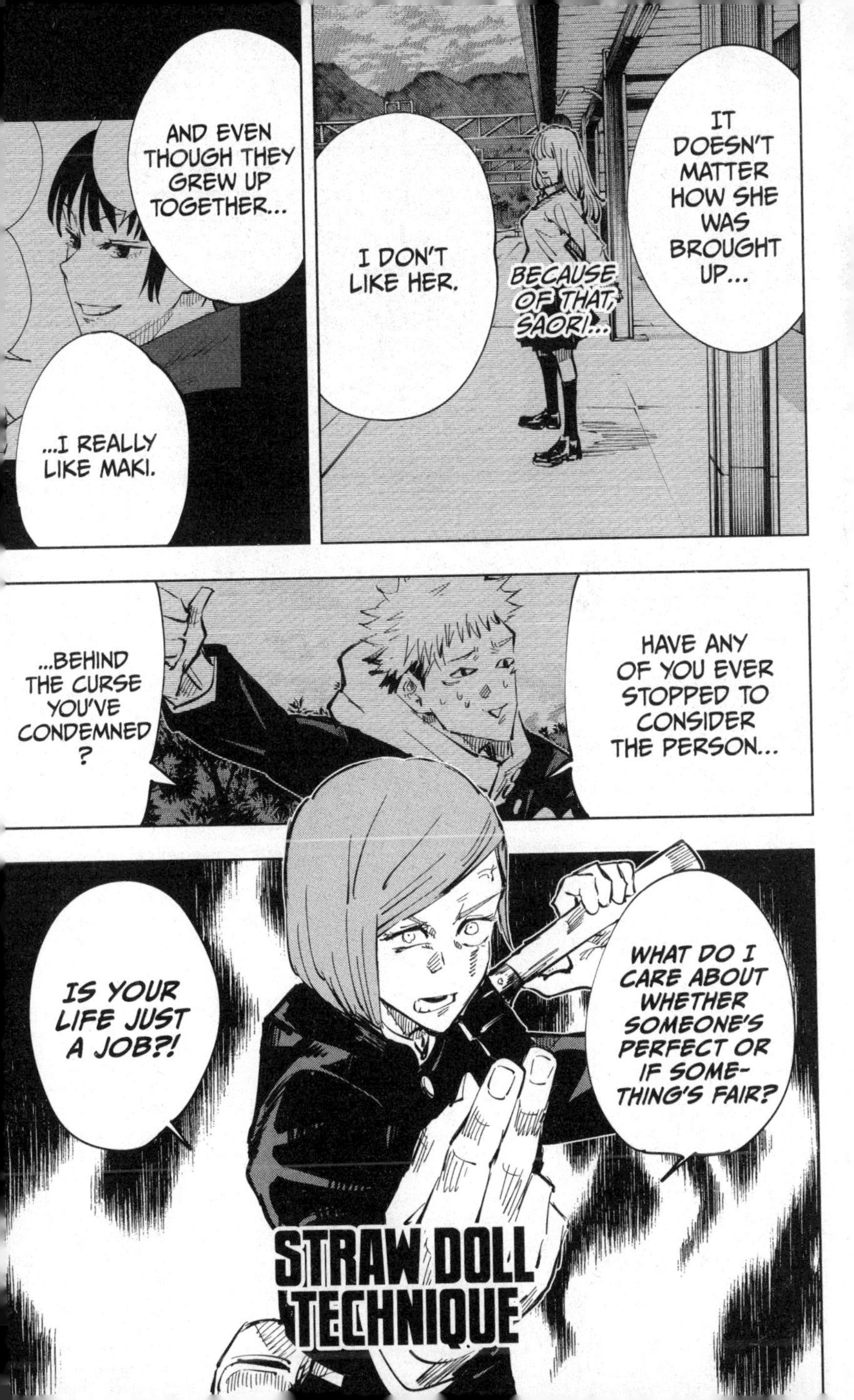
IT DOESN'T MATTER HOW SHE WAS BROUGHT UP...
BECAUSE OF THAT, SAORI...
I DON'T LIKE HER.
AND EVEN THOUGH THEY GREW UP TOGETHER...
...I REALLY LIKE MAKI.
HAVE ANY OF YOU EVER STOPPED TO CONSIDER THE PERSON...
...BEHIND THE CURSE YOU'VE CONDEMNED?
WHAT DO I CARE ABOUT WHETHER SOMEONE'S PERFECT OR IF SOME-THING'S FAIR?
IS YOUR LIFE JUST A JOB?!
STRAW DOLL TECHNIQUE

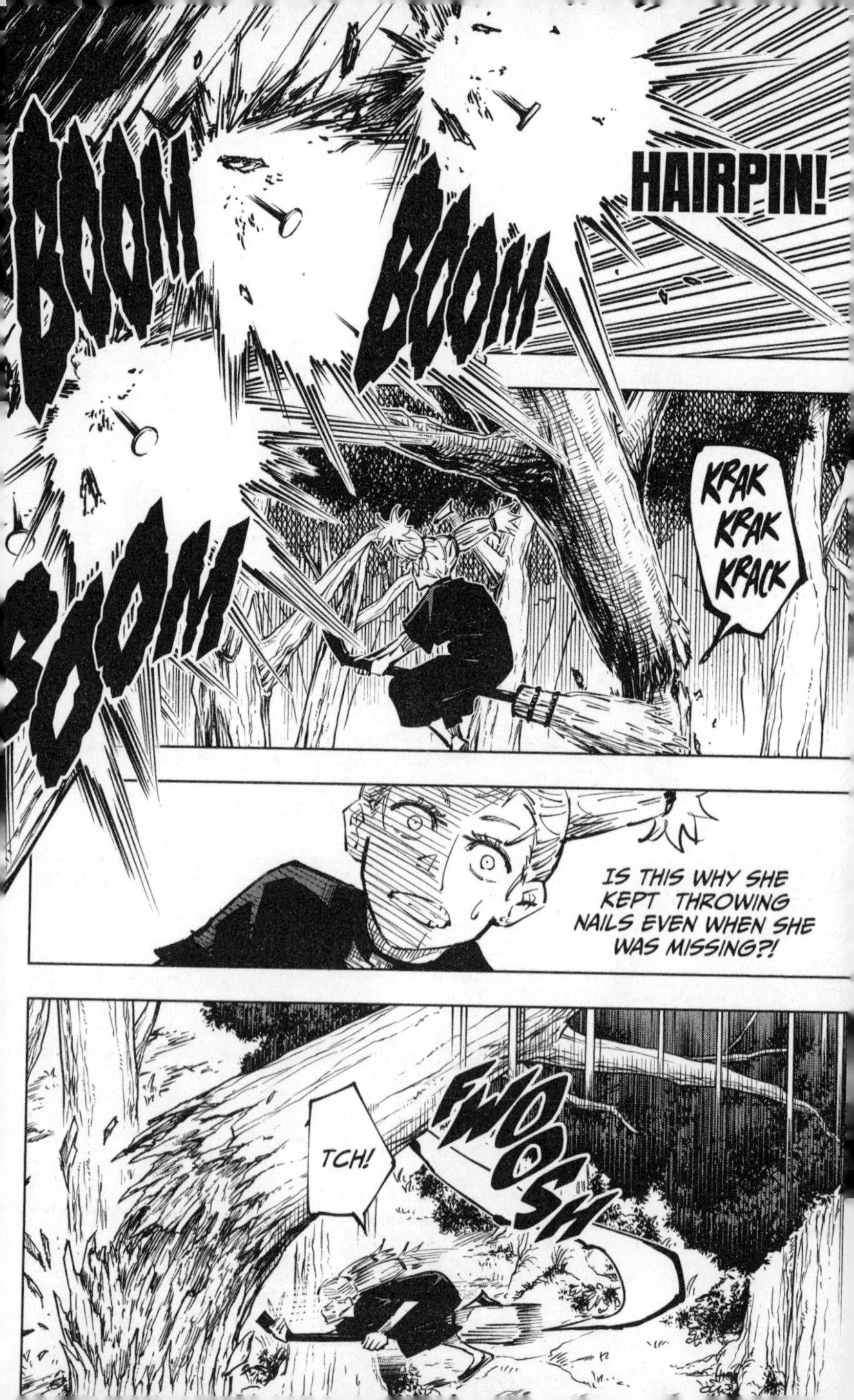
HAIRPIN!
BOOM
BOOM
BOOM
KRAK KRAK KRACK
IS THIS WHY SHE KEPT THROWING NAILS EVEN WHEN SHE WAS MISSING?!
FWOOSH
TCH!

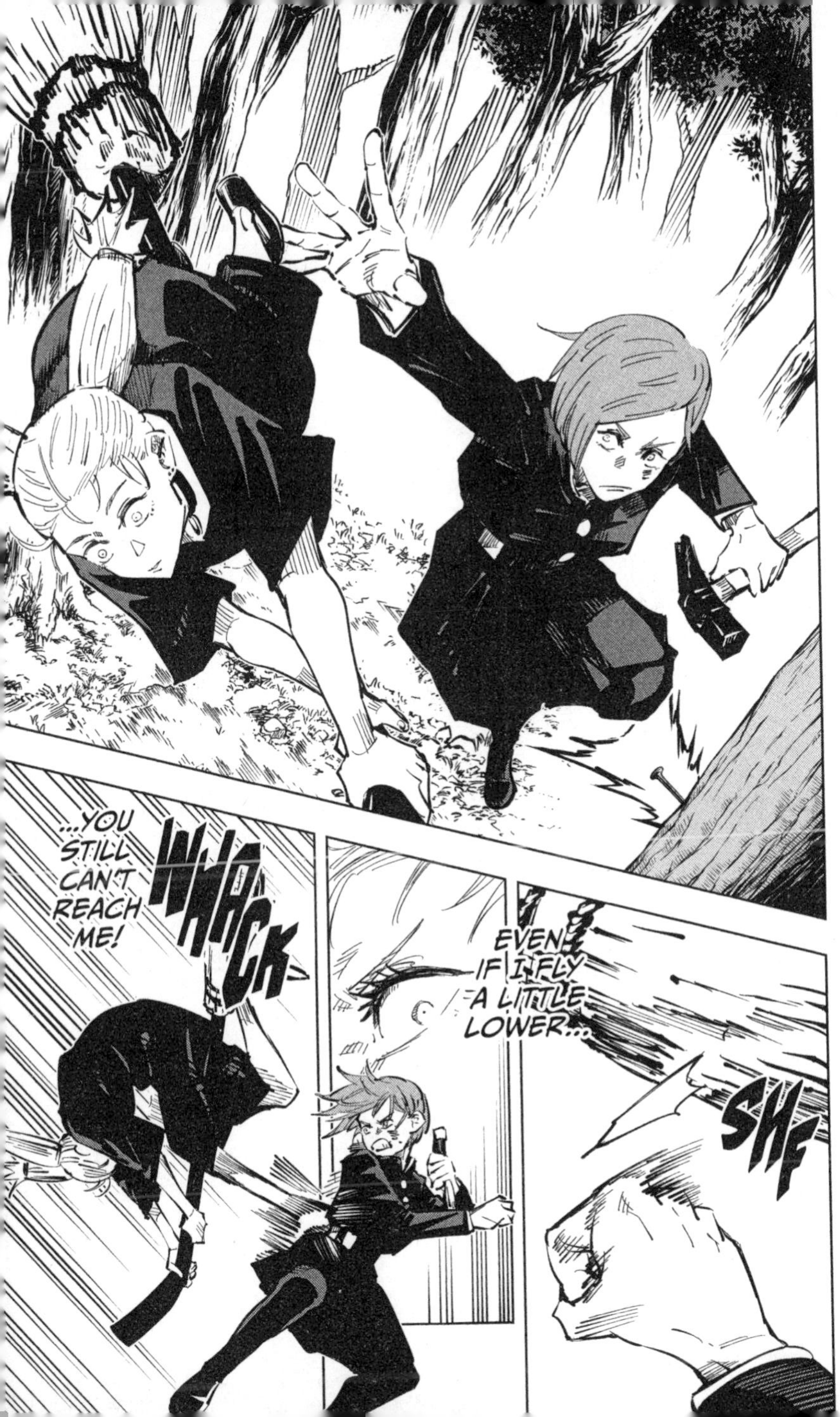
SHF
EVEN IF I FLY A LITTLE LOWER...
...YOU STILL CAN'T REACH ME!
WHACK

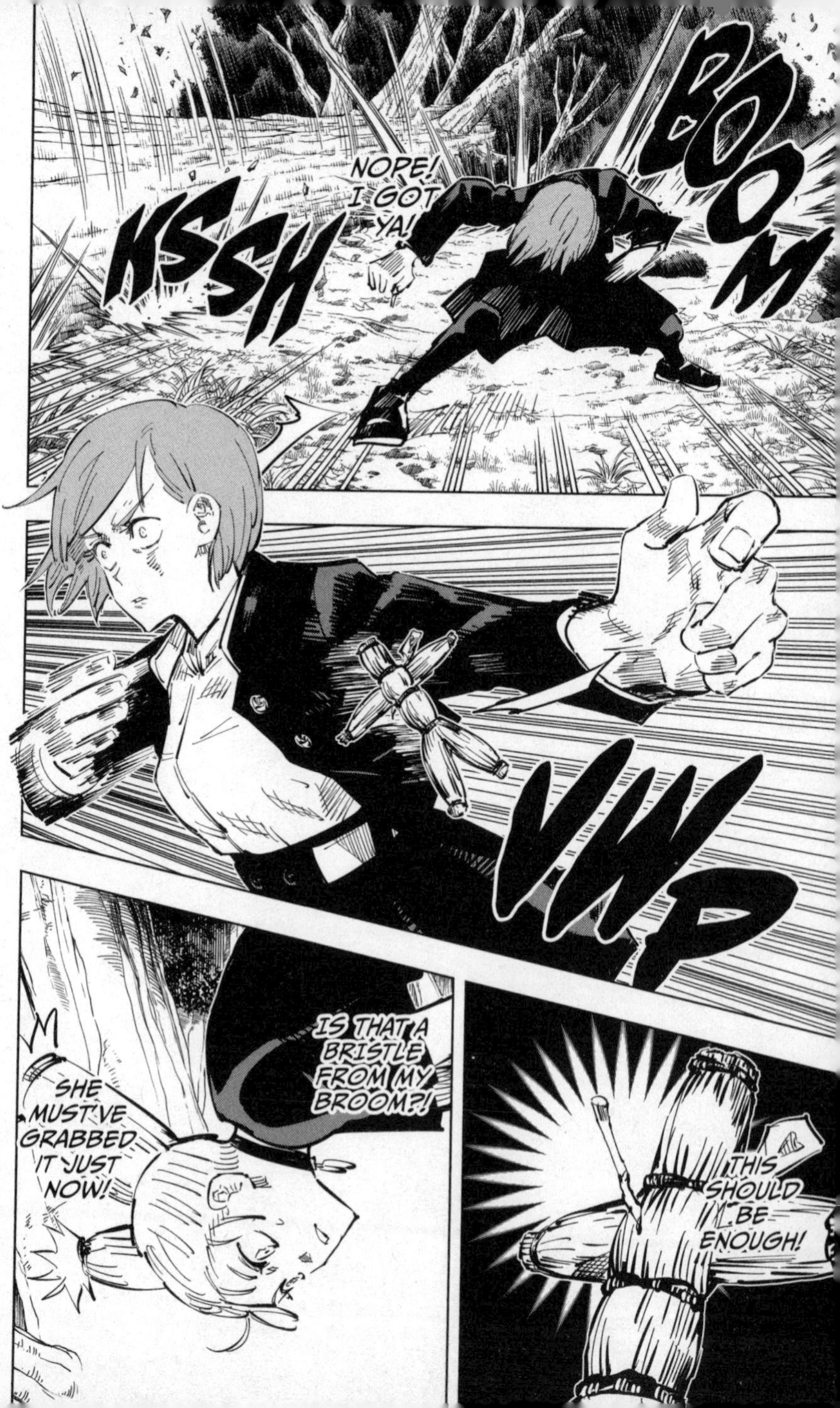
BOOM
NOPE! I GOT YA!
KSSH
VWP
THIS SHOULD BE ENOUGH!
IS THAT A BRISTLE FROM MY BROOM?!
SHE MUST'VE GRABBED IT JUST NOW!

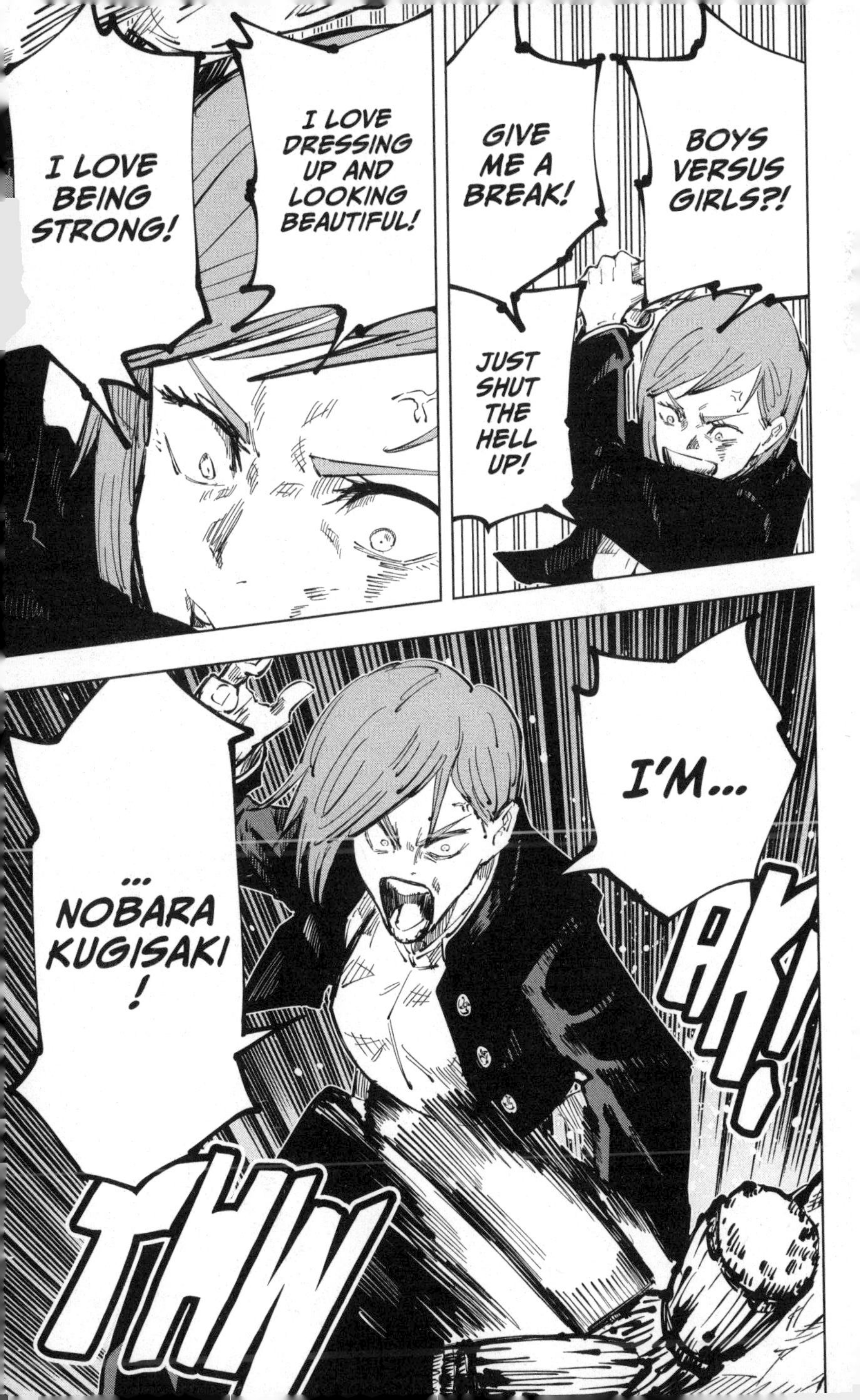
BOYS VERSUS GIRLS?!
GIVE ME A BREAK!
JUST SHUT THE HELL UP!
I LOVE DRESSING UP AND LOOKING BEAUTIFUL!
I LOVE BEING STRONG!
I'M...
...NOBARA KUGISAKI!

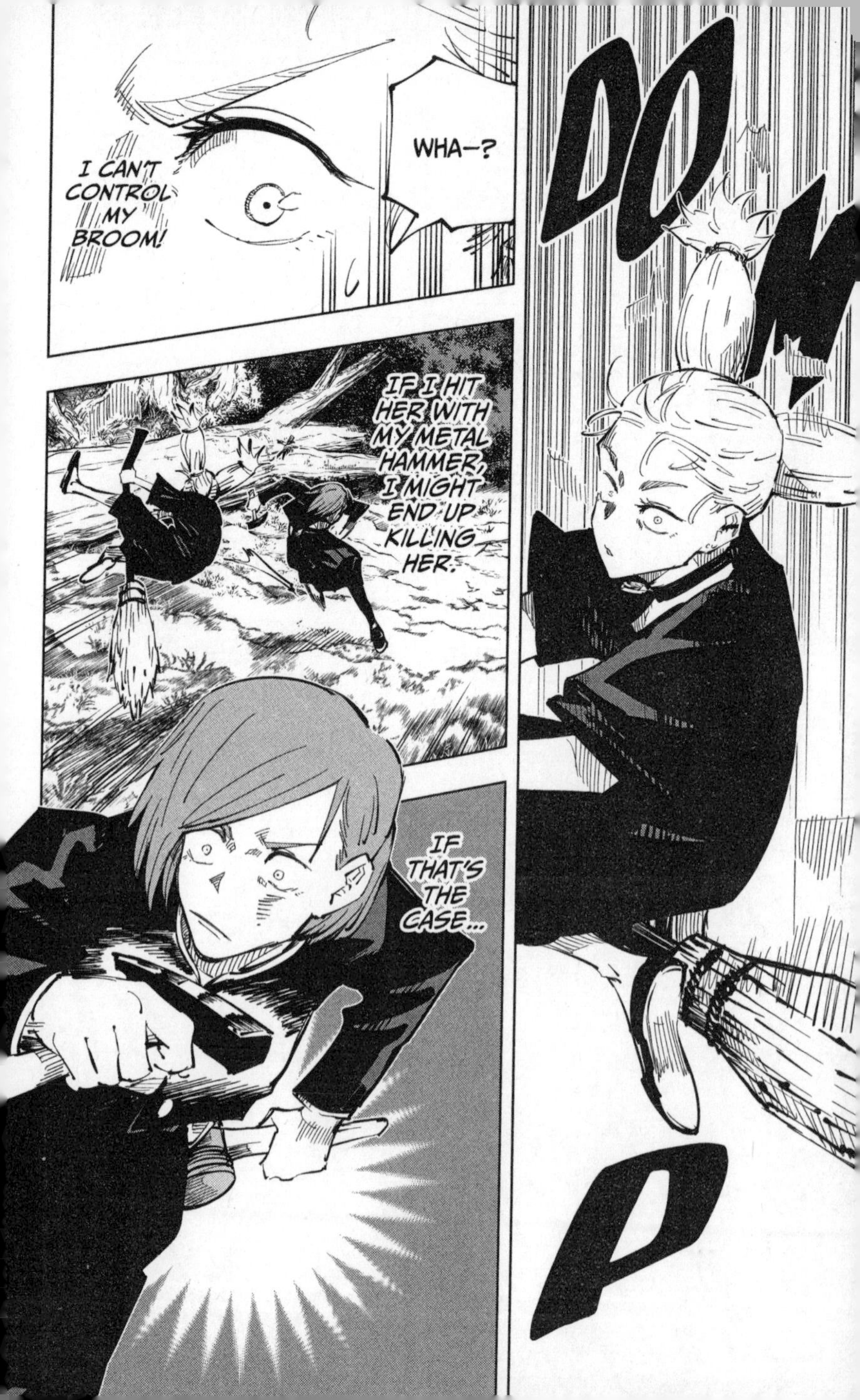
DOMP
WHA-?
I CAN'T CONTROL MY BROOM!
IF I HIT HER WITH MY METAL HAMMER, I MIGHT END UP KILLING HER.
IF THAT'S THE CASE...

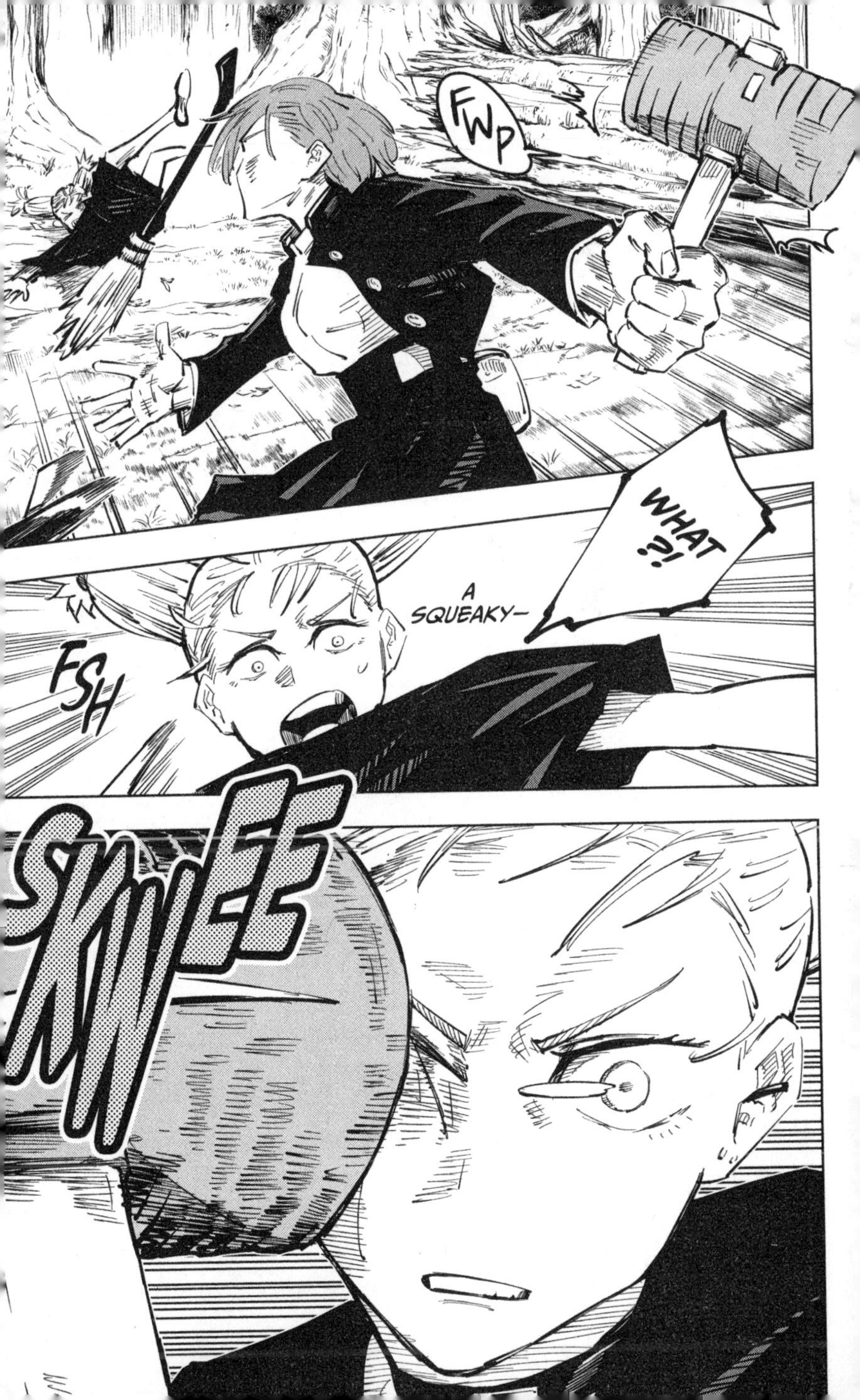
FWP
WHAT ?!
A SQUEAKY—
FSH
SKWEE

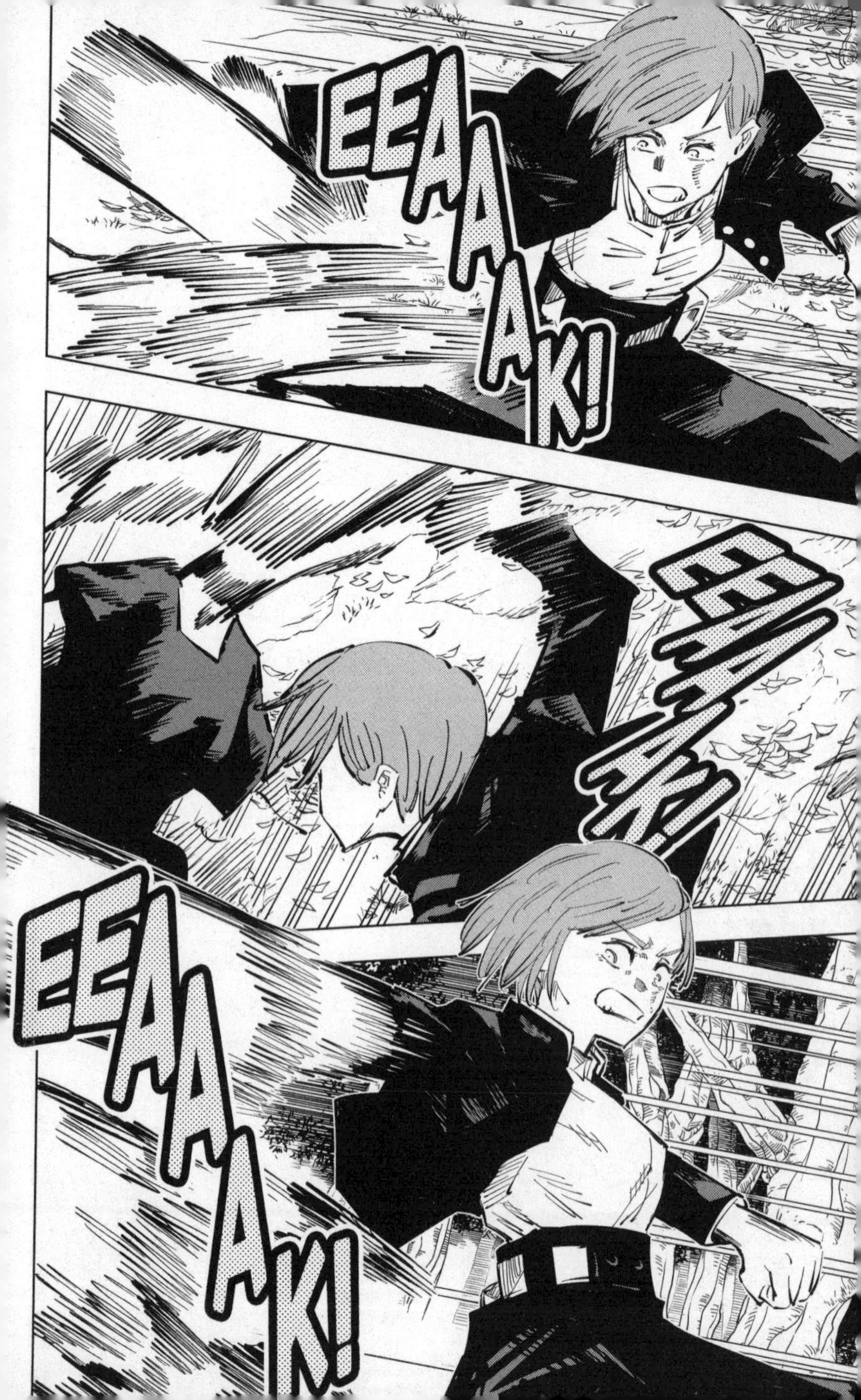
EEAAAK!
EEAAK!
EEAAAAK!

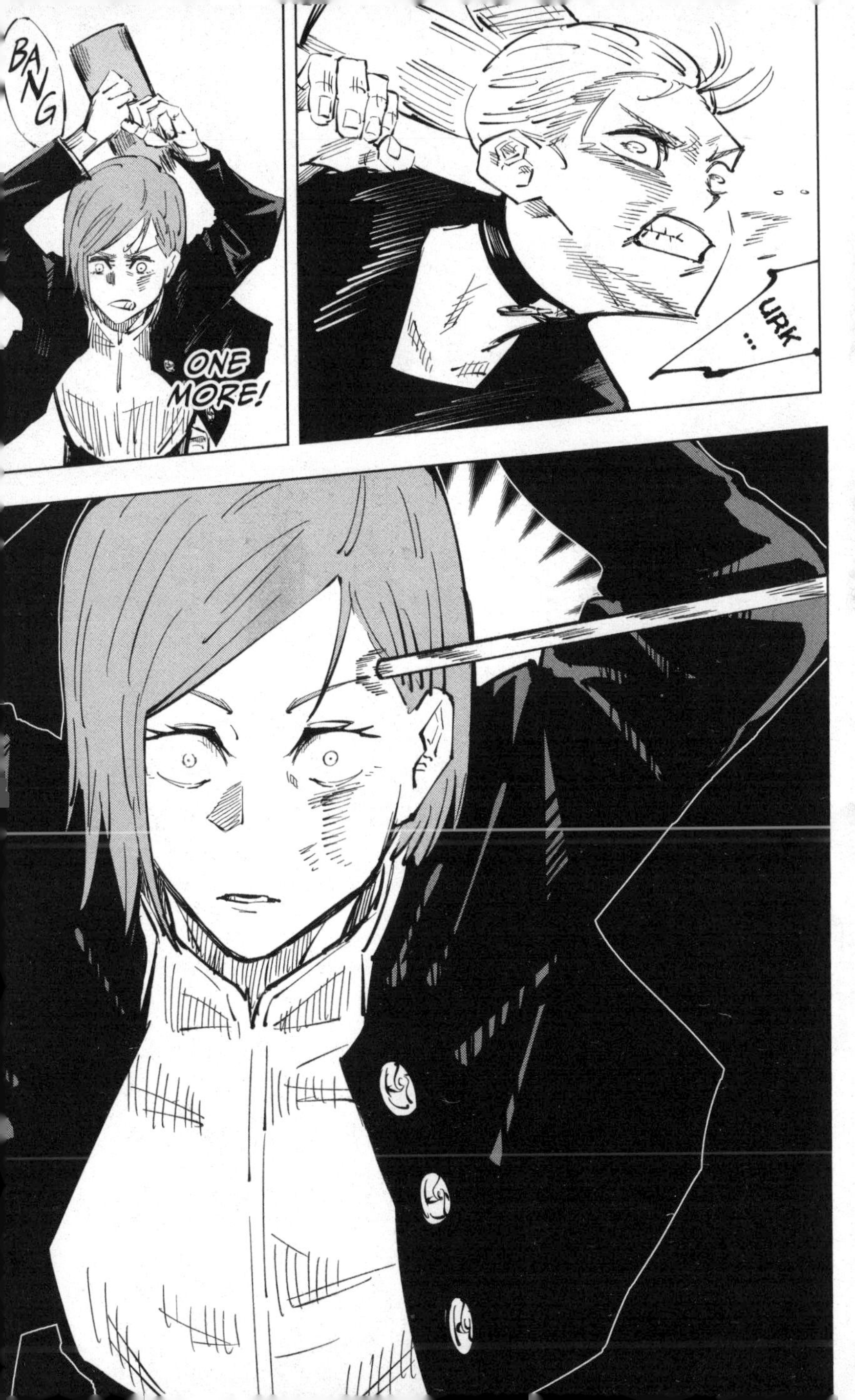
URK …
BANG
ONE MORE!

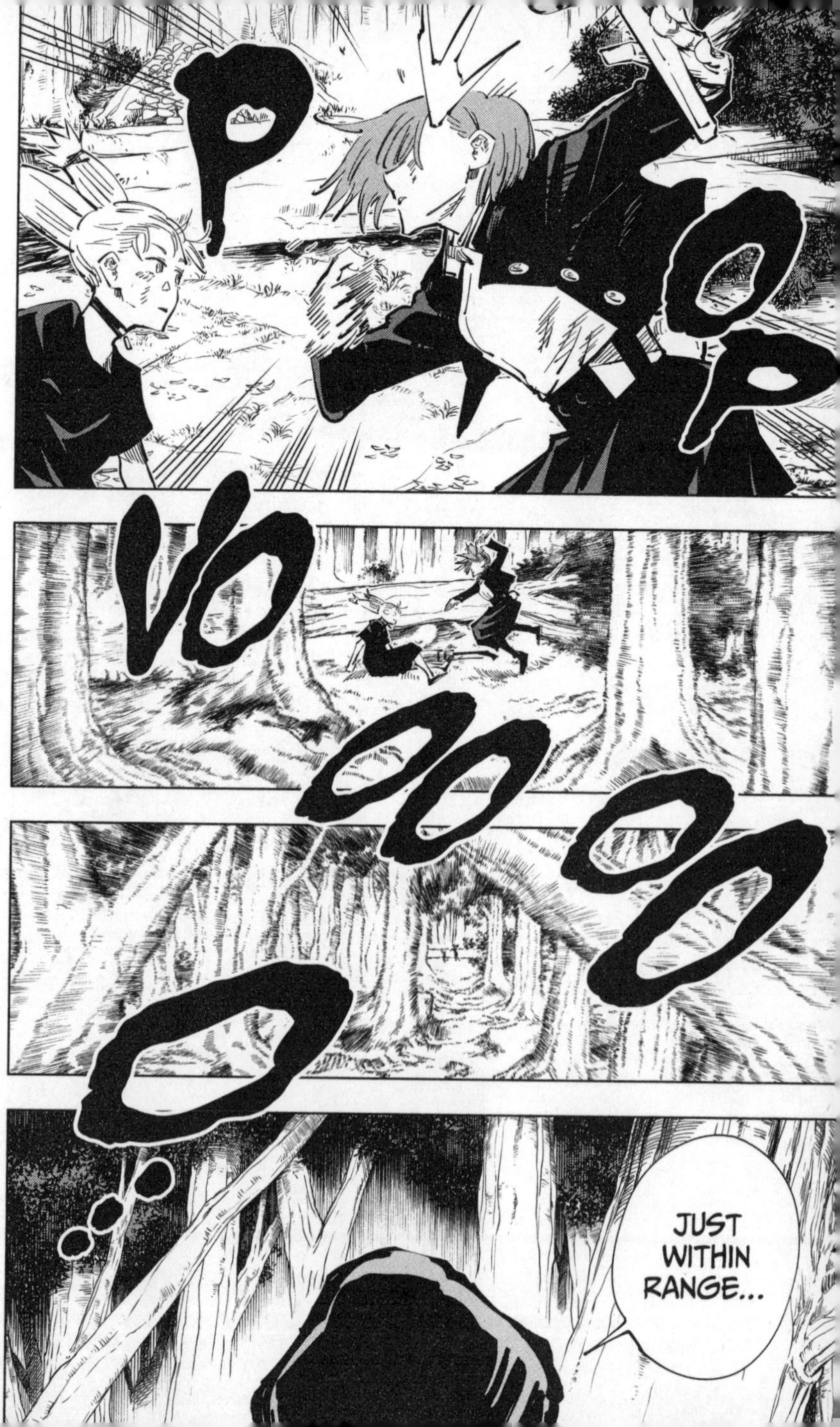
POP
VOOOOOO
JUST WITHIN RANGE...

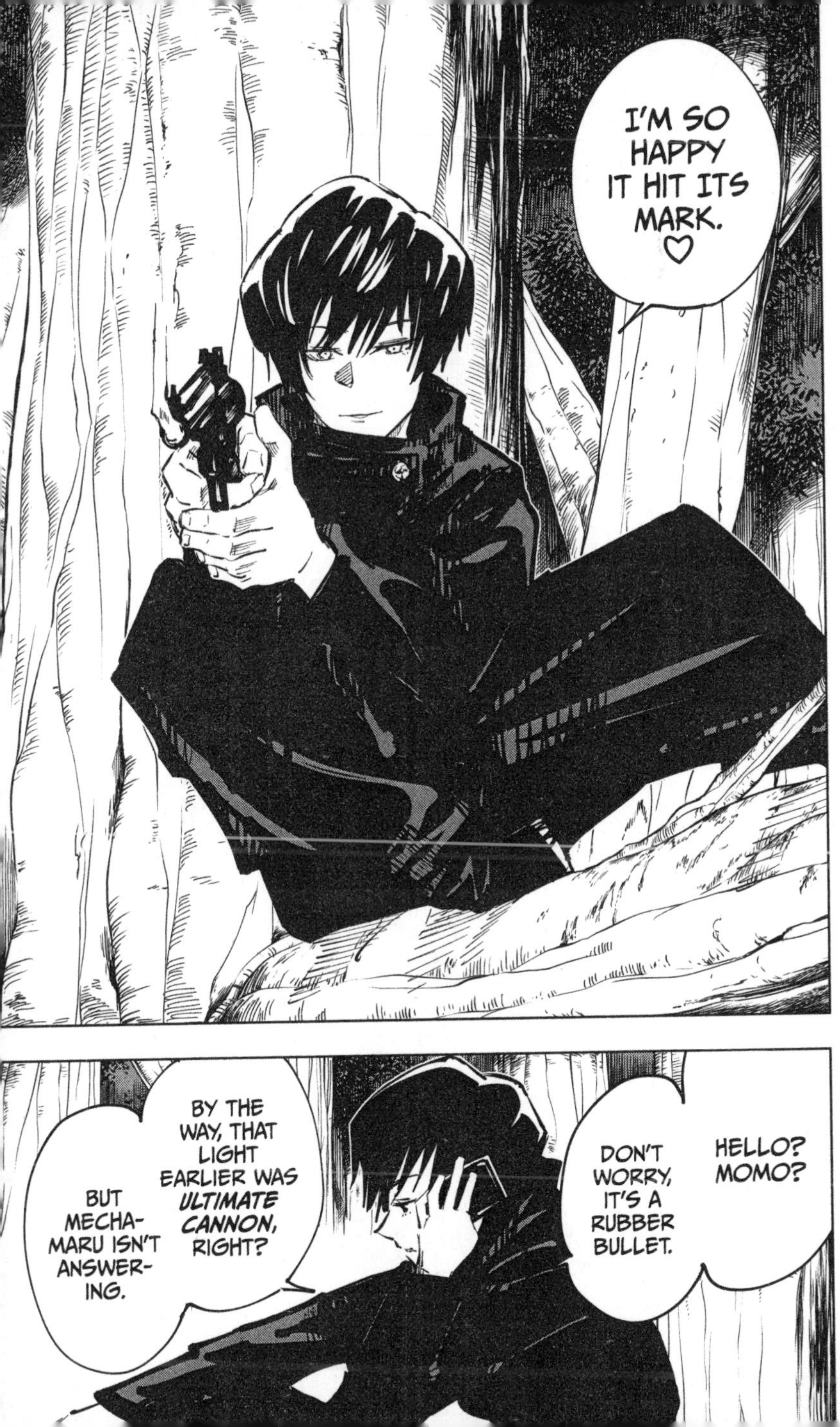
I'M SO HAPPY IT HIT ITS MARK. ♡
HELLO? MOMO?
DON'T WORRY, IT'S A RUBBER BULLET.
BY THE WAY, THAT LIGHT EARLIER WAS *ULTIMATE CANNON*, RIGHT?
BUT MECHA-MARU ISN'T ANSWER-ING.

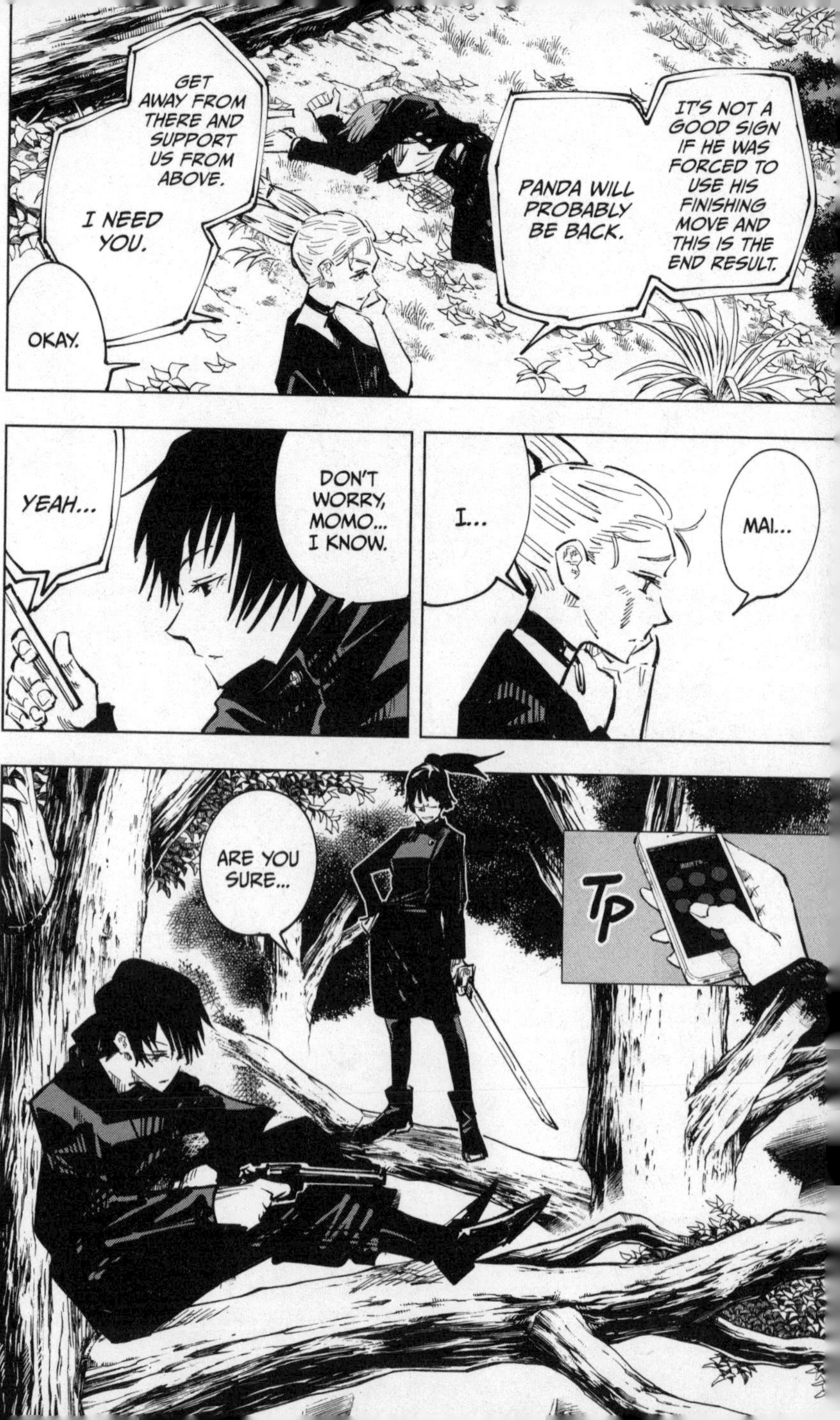
IT'S NOT A GOOD SIGN IF HE WAS FORCED TO USE HIS FINISHING MOVE AND THIS IS THE END RESULT.
PANDA WILL PROBABLY BE BACK.
GET AWAY FROM THERE AND SUPPORT US FROM ABOVE.
I NEED YOU.
OKAY.
MAI...
I...
DON'T WORRY, MOMO... I KNOW.
YEAH...
TP
ARE YOU SURE...

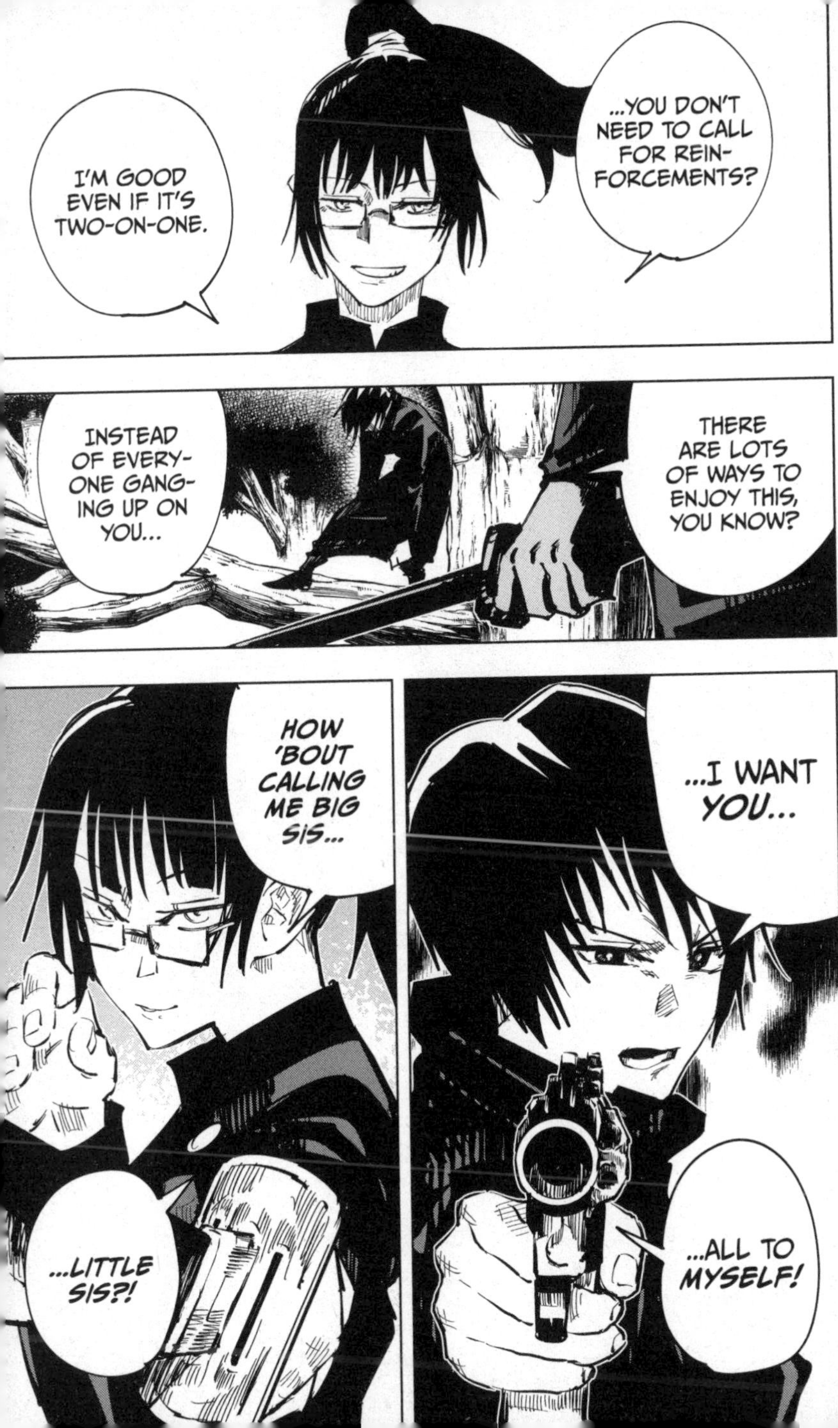
...YOU DON'T NEED TO CALL FOR REIN-FORCEMENTS?
I'M GOOD EVEN IF IT'S TWO-ON-ONE.
THERE ARE LOTS OF WAYS TO ENJOY THIS, YOU KNOW?
INSTEAD OF EVERY-ONE GANG-ING UP ON YOU...
...I WANT *YOU*...
...ALL TO *MYSELF!*
HOW 'BOUT CALLING ME BIG SIS...
...LITTLE SIS?!

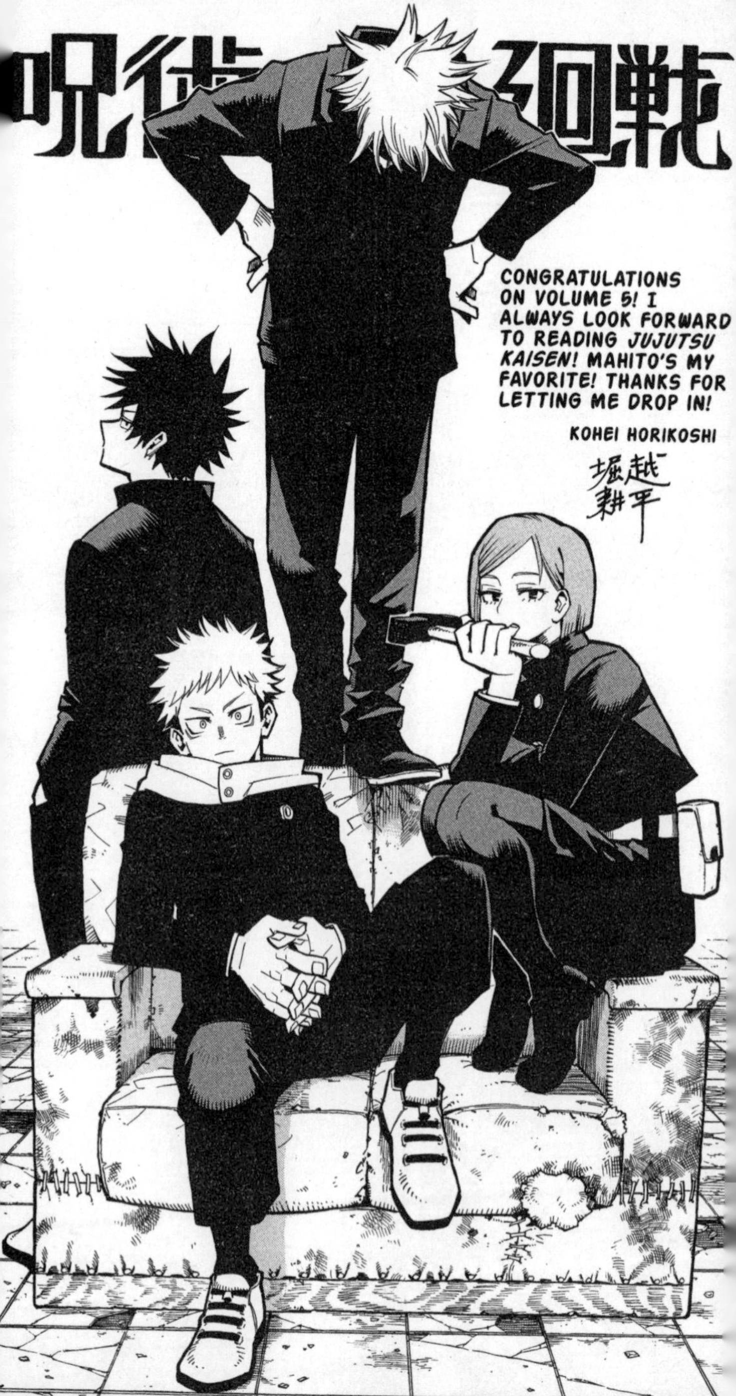
呪術廻戦
CONGRATULATIONS ON VOLUME 5! I ALWAYS LOOK FORWARD TO READING *JUJUTSU KAISEN*! MAHITO'S MY FAVORITE! THANKS FOR LETTING ME DROP IN!
KOHEI HORIKOSHI
堀越耕平

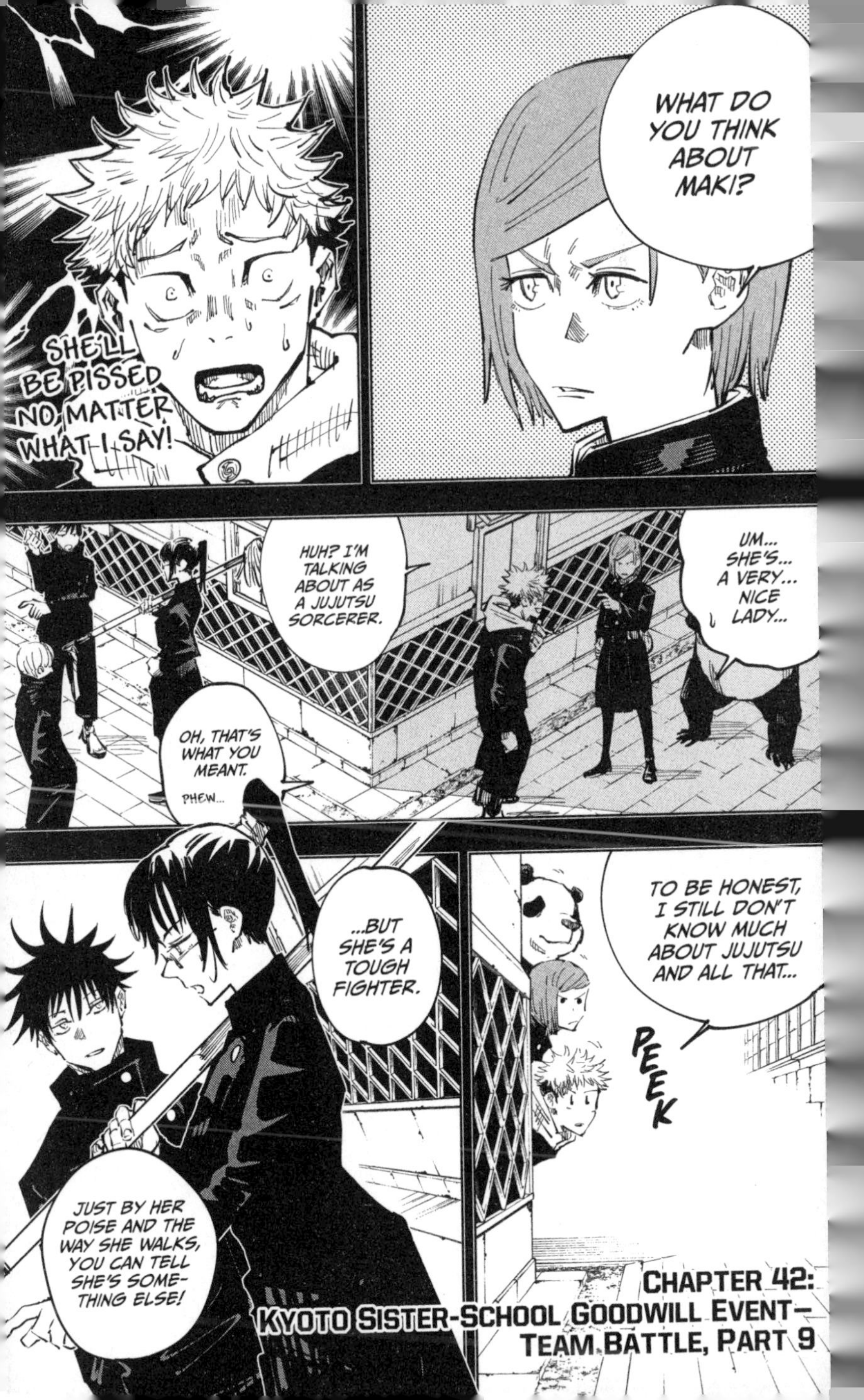
WHAT DO YOU THINK ABOUT MAKI?
SHE'LL BE PISSED NO MATTER WHAT I SAY!
UM... SHE'S... A VERY... NICE LADY...
HUH? I'M TALKING ABOUT AS A JUJUTSU SORCERER.
OH, THAT'S WHAT YOU MEANT.
PHEW...
TO BE HONEST, I STILL DON'T KNOW MUCH ABOUT JUJUTSU AND ALL THAT...
PEEK
...BUT SHE'S A TOUGH FIGHTER.
JUST BY HER POISE AND THE WAY SHE WALKS, YOU CAN TELL SHE'S SOME-THING ELSE!

Chapter 42: Kyoto Sister-School Goodwill Event—Team Battle, Part 9

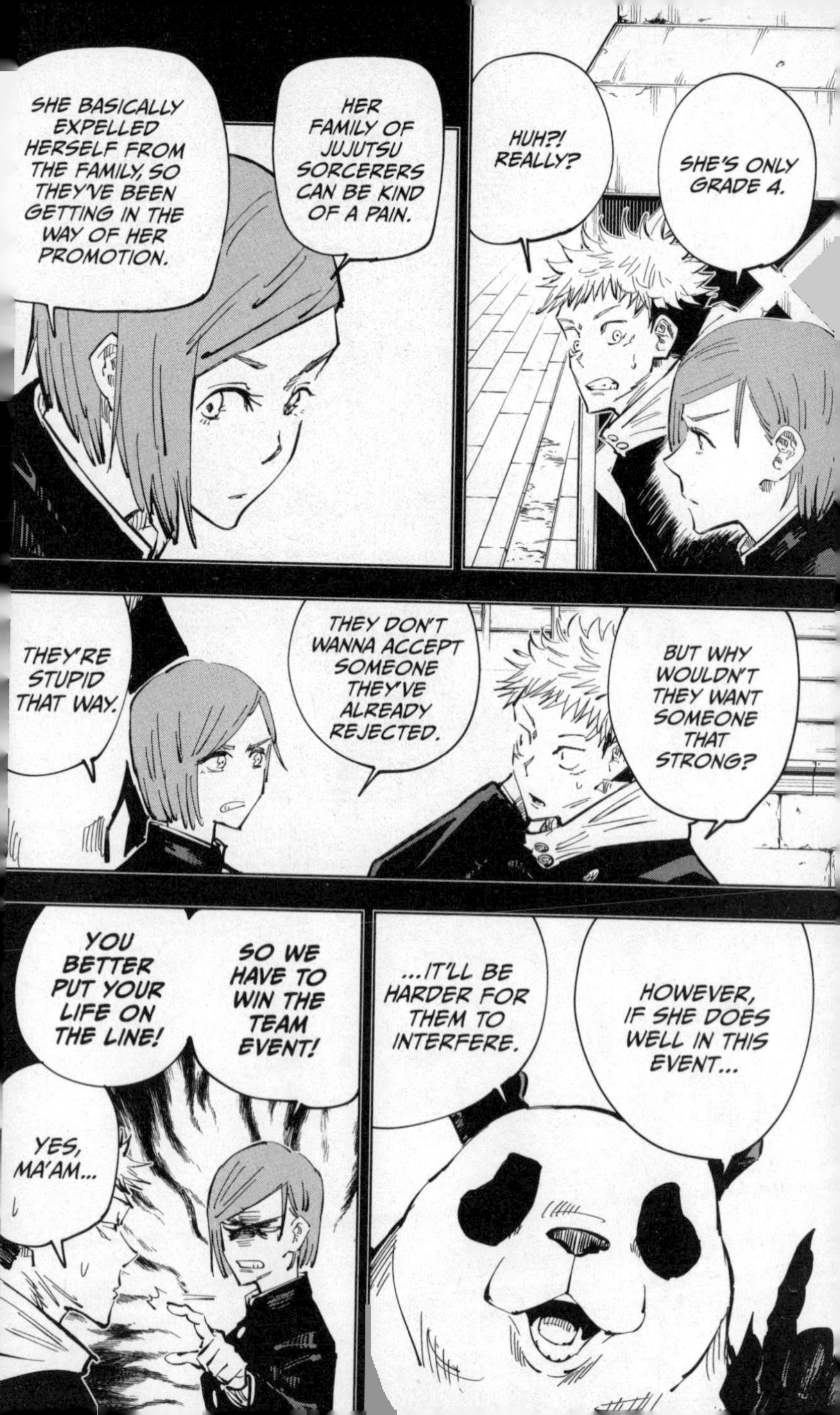
SHE'S ONLY GRADE 4.
HUH?! REALLY?
HER FAMILY OF JUJUTSU SORCERERS CAN BE KIND OF A PAIN.
SHE BASICALLY EXPELLED HERSELF FROM THE FAMILY, SO THEY'VE BEEN GETTING IN THE WAY OF HER PROMOTION.
BUT WHY WOULDN'T THEY WANT SOMEONE THAT STRONG?
THEY DON'T WANNA ACCEPT SOMEONE THEY'VE ALREADY REJECTED.
THEY'RE STUPID THAT WAY.
HOWEVER, IF SHE DOES WELL IN THIS EVENT...
...IT'LL BE HARDER FOR THEM TO INTERFERE.
SO WE HAVE TO WIN THE TEAM EVENT!
YOU BETTER PUT YOUR LIFE ON THE LINE!
YES, MA'AM...

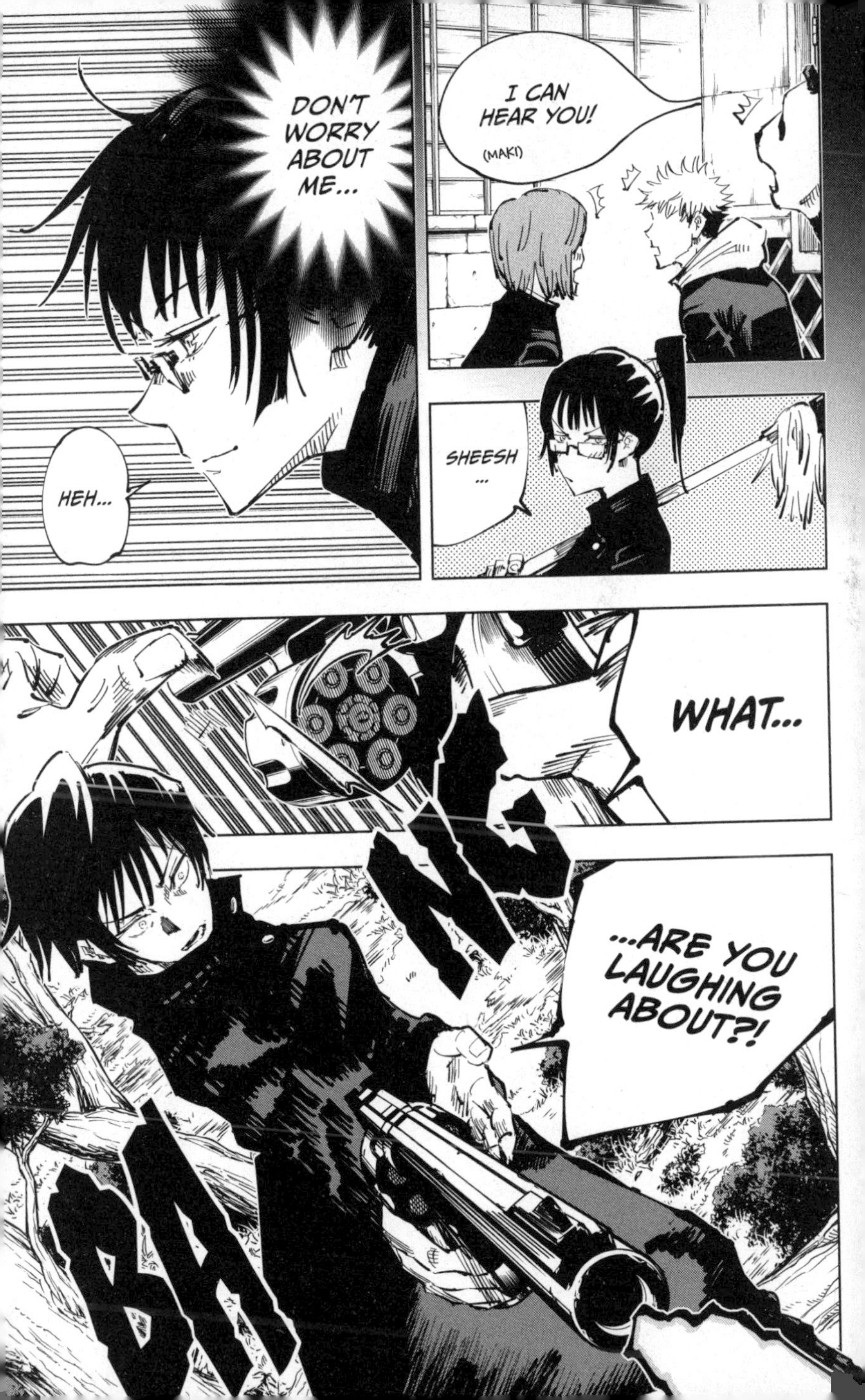
I CAN HEAR YOU!
(MAKI)
SHEESH ...
DON'T WORRY ABOUT ME...
HEH...
WHAT...
...ARE YOU LAUGHING ABOUT?!

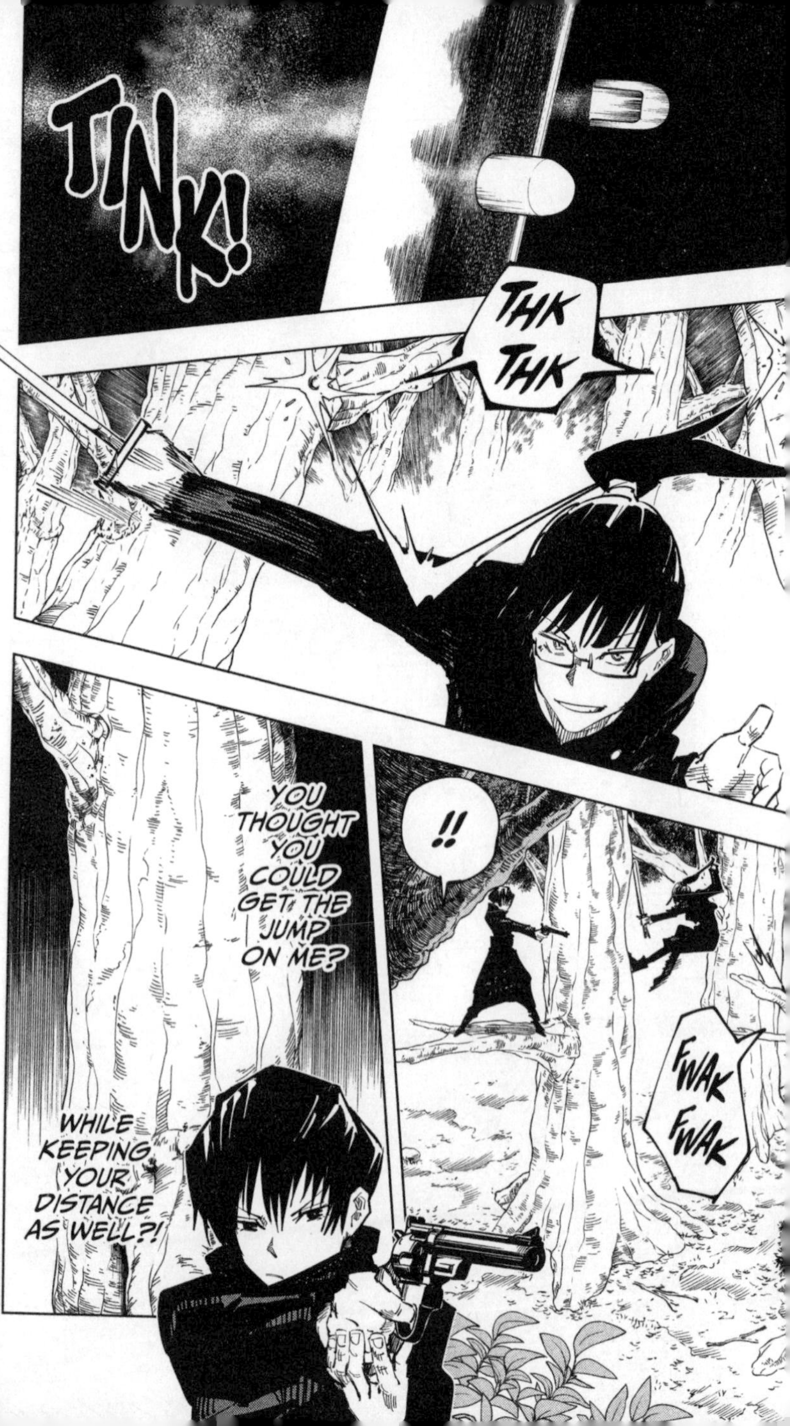
TINK!
THK THK
!!
FWAK FWAK
YOU THOUGHT YOU COULD GET THE JUMP ON ME?
WHILE KEEPING YOUR DISTANCE AS WELL?!

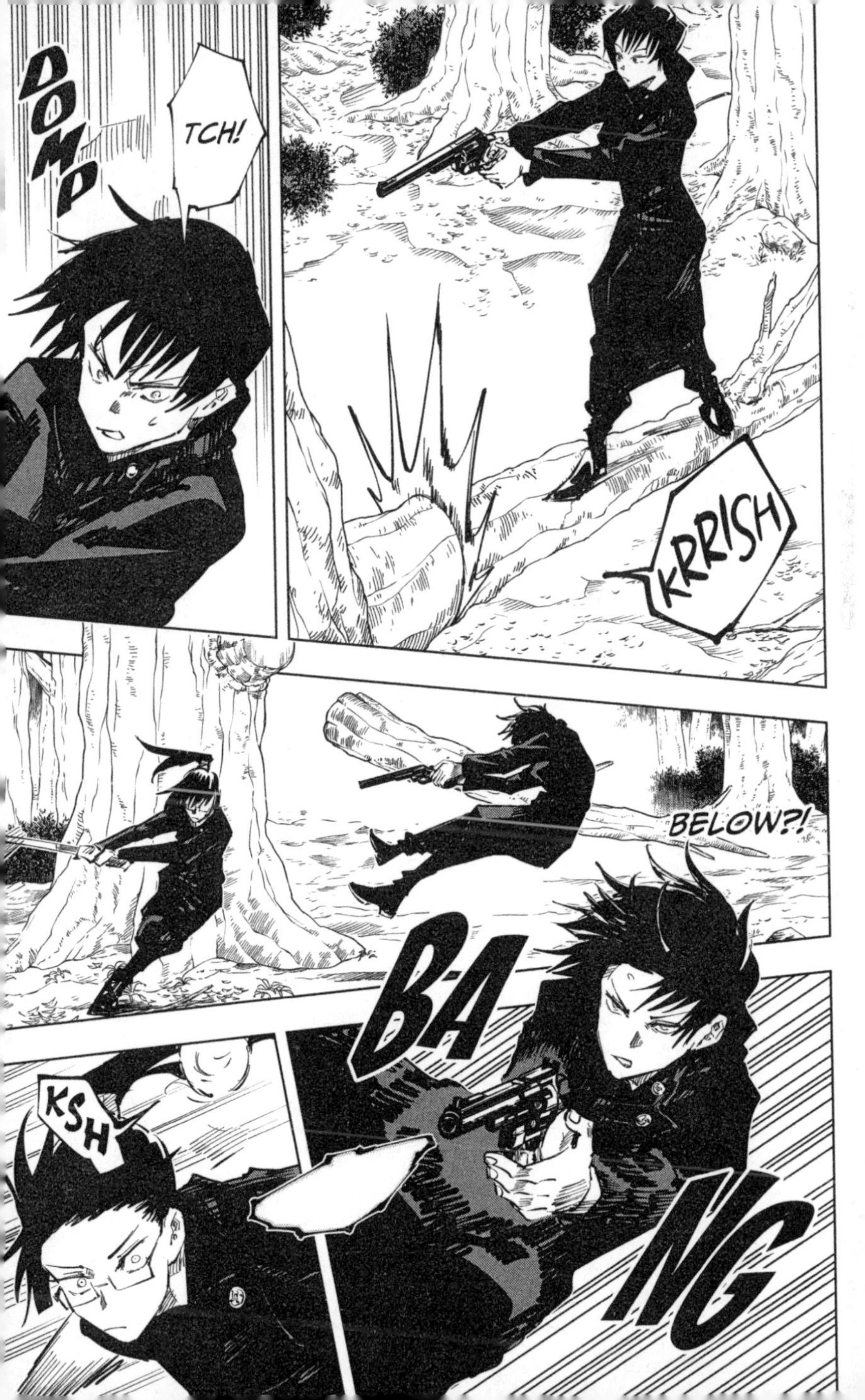
KRRISH
TCH!
DOMP
BELOW?!
BA-NG
KSH

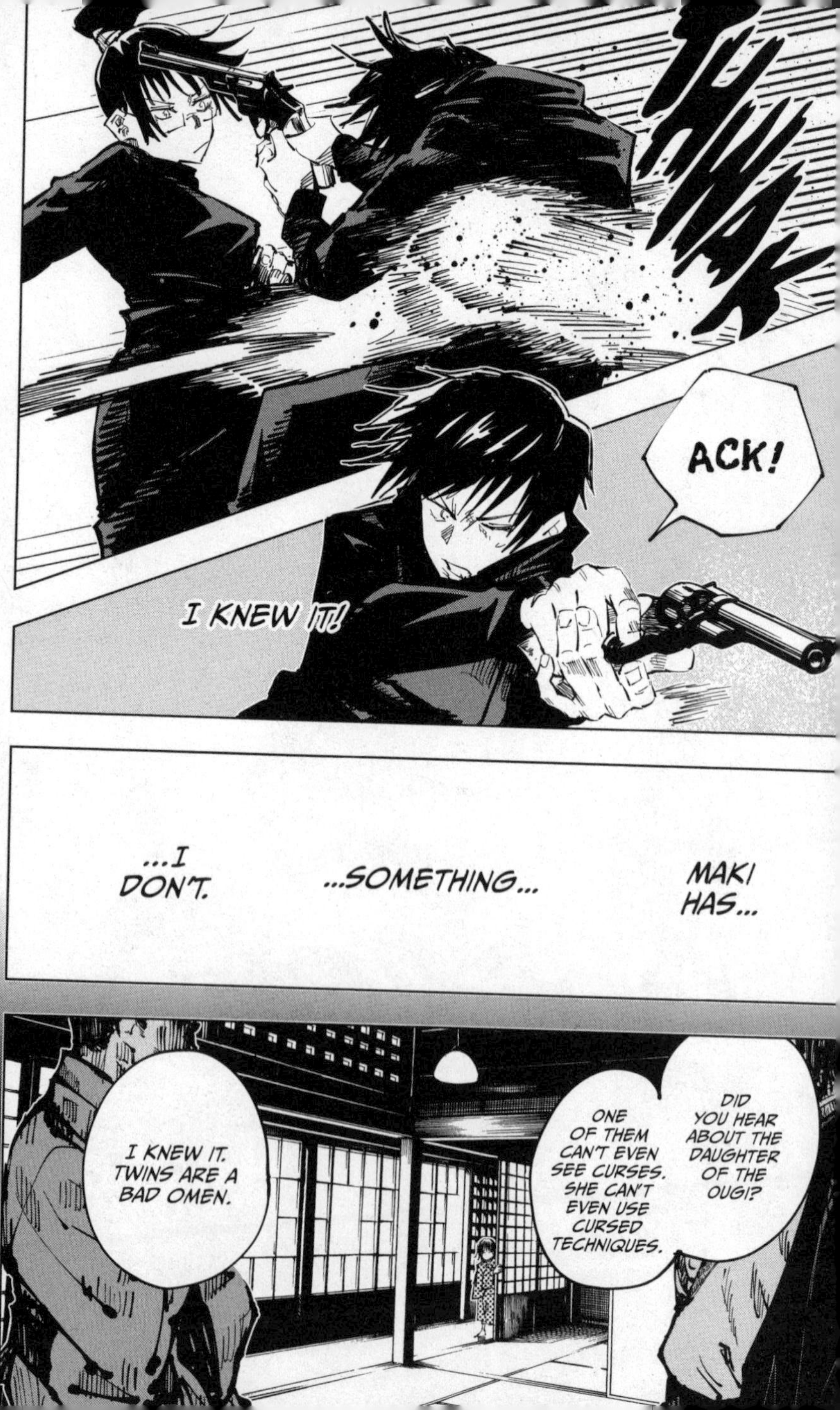
ACK!
I KNEW IT!
MAKI HAS...
...SOMETHING...
...I DON'T.
DID YOU HEAR ABOUT THE DAUGHTER OF THE OUGI?
ONE OF THEM CAN'T EVEN SEE CURSES. SHE CAN'T EVEN USE CURSED TECHNIQUES.
I KNEW IT. TWINS ARE A BAD OMEN.

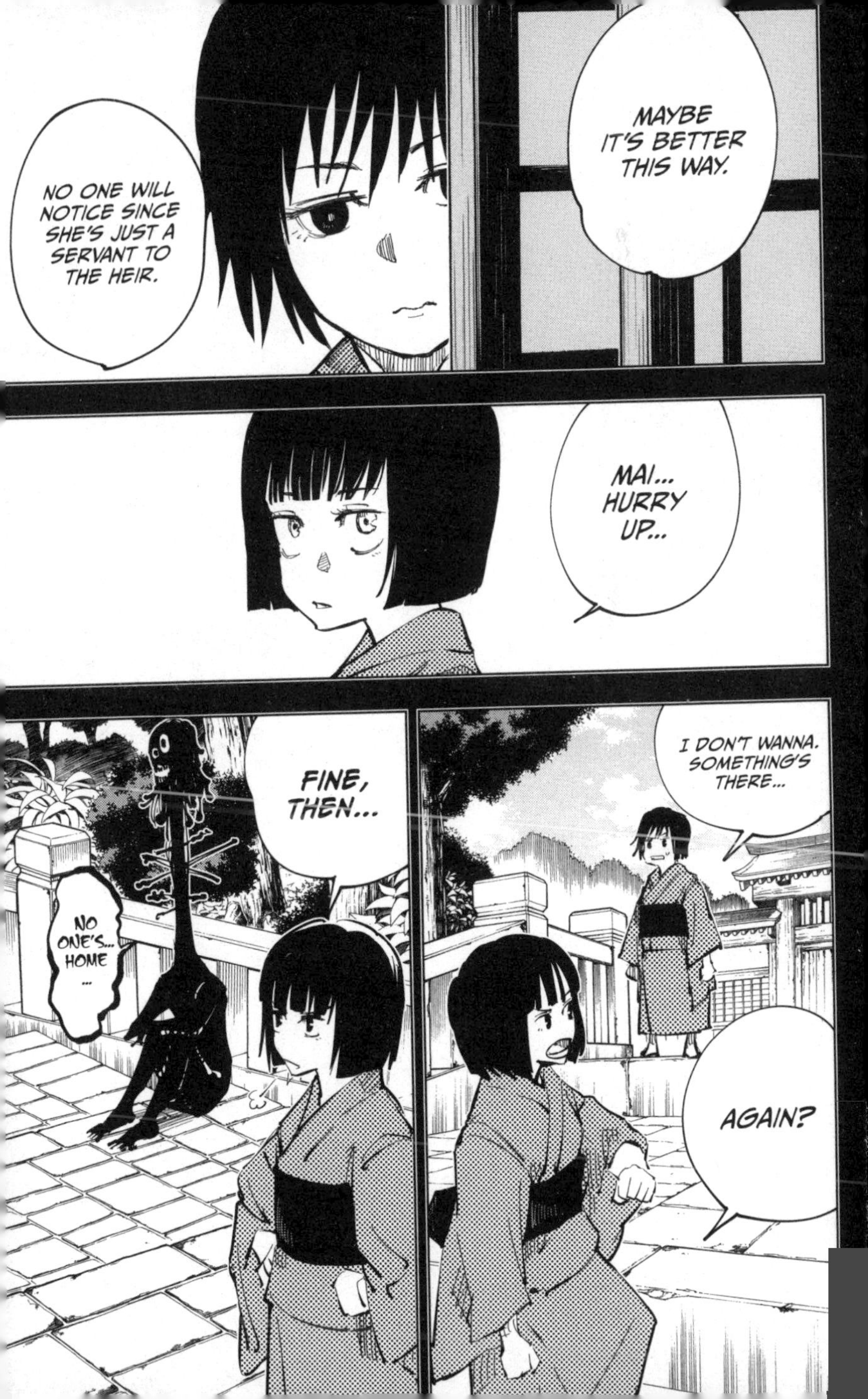
MAYBE IT'S BETTER THIS WAY.
NO ONE WILL NOTICE SINCE SHE'S JUST A SERVANT TO THE HEIR.
MAI... HURRY UP...
I DON'T WANNA. SOMETHING'S THERE...
AGAIN?
FINE, THEN...
NO ONE'S... HOME ...

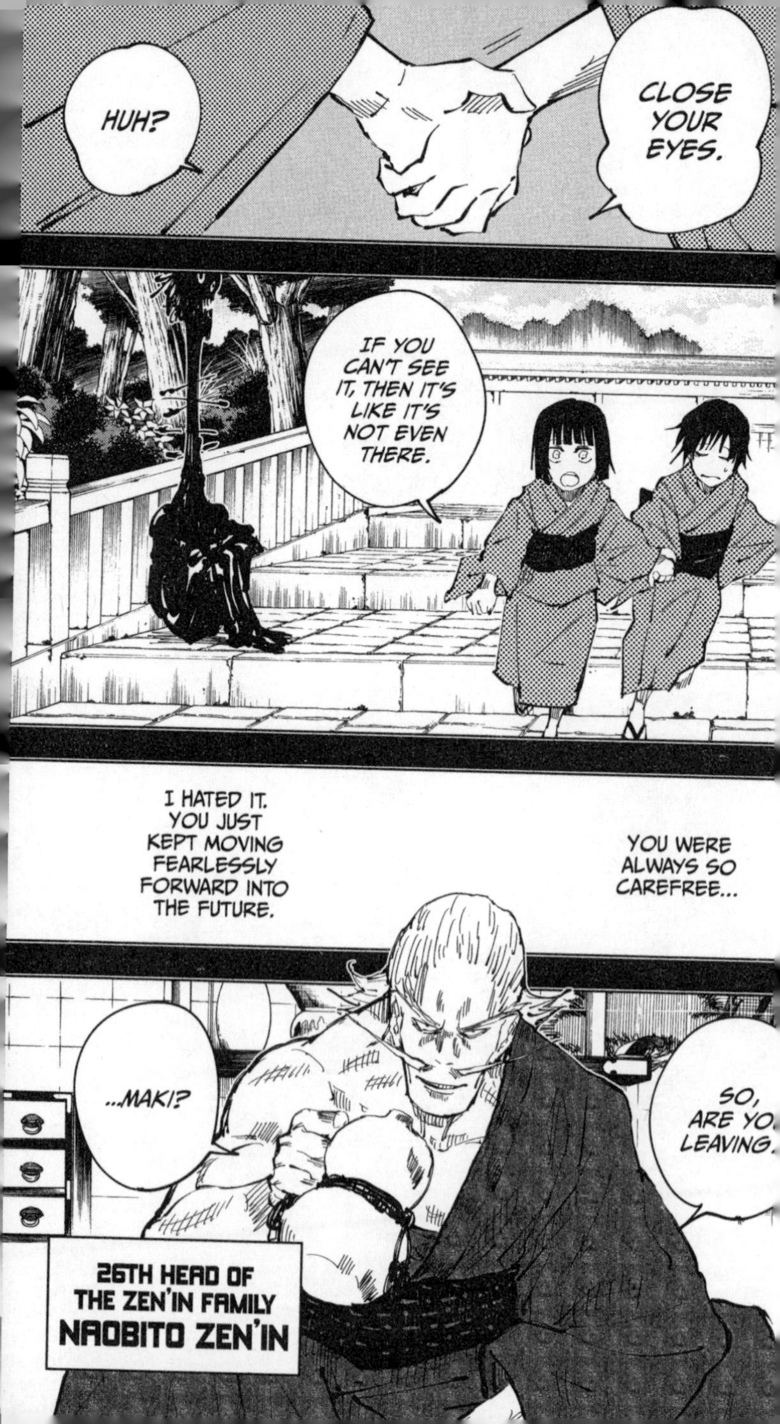

CLOSE YOUR EYES.
HUH?
IF YOU CAN'T SEE IT, THEN IT'S LIKE IT'S NOT EVEN THERE.
YOU WERE ALWAYS SO CAREFREE...
I HATED IT. YOU JUST KEPT MOVING FEARLESSLY FORWARD INTO THE FUTURE.
SO, ARE YO LEAVING
...MAKI?
26TH HEAD OF THE ZEN'IN FAMILY NAOBITO ZEN'IN

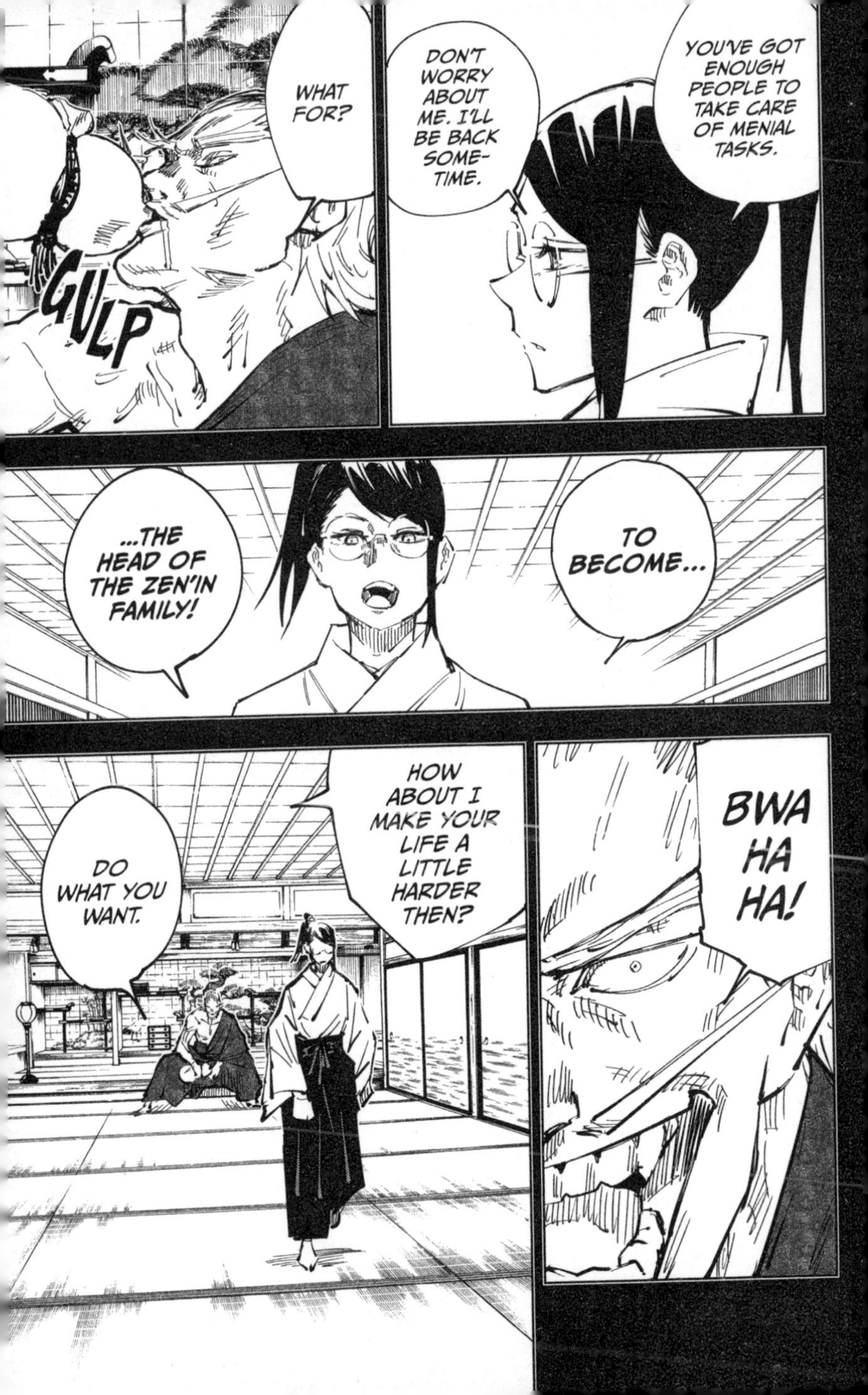
YOU'VE GOT ENOUGH PEOPLE TO TAKE CARE OF MENIAL TASKS.
DON'T WORRY ABOUT ME. I'LL BE BACK SOMETIME.
WHAT FOR?
GULP
TO BECOME...
...THE HEAD OF THE ZEN'IN FAMILY!
BWA HA HA!
HOW ABOUT I MAKE YOUR LIFE A LITTLE HARDER THEN?
DO WHAT YOU WANT.

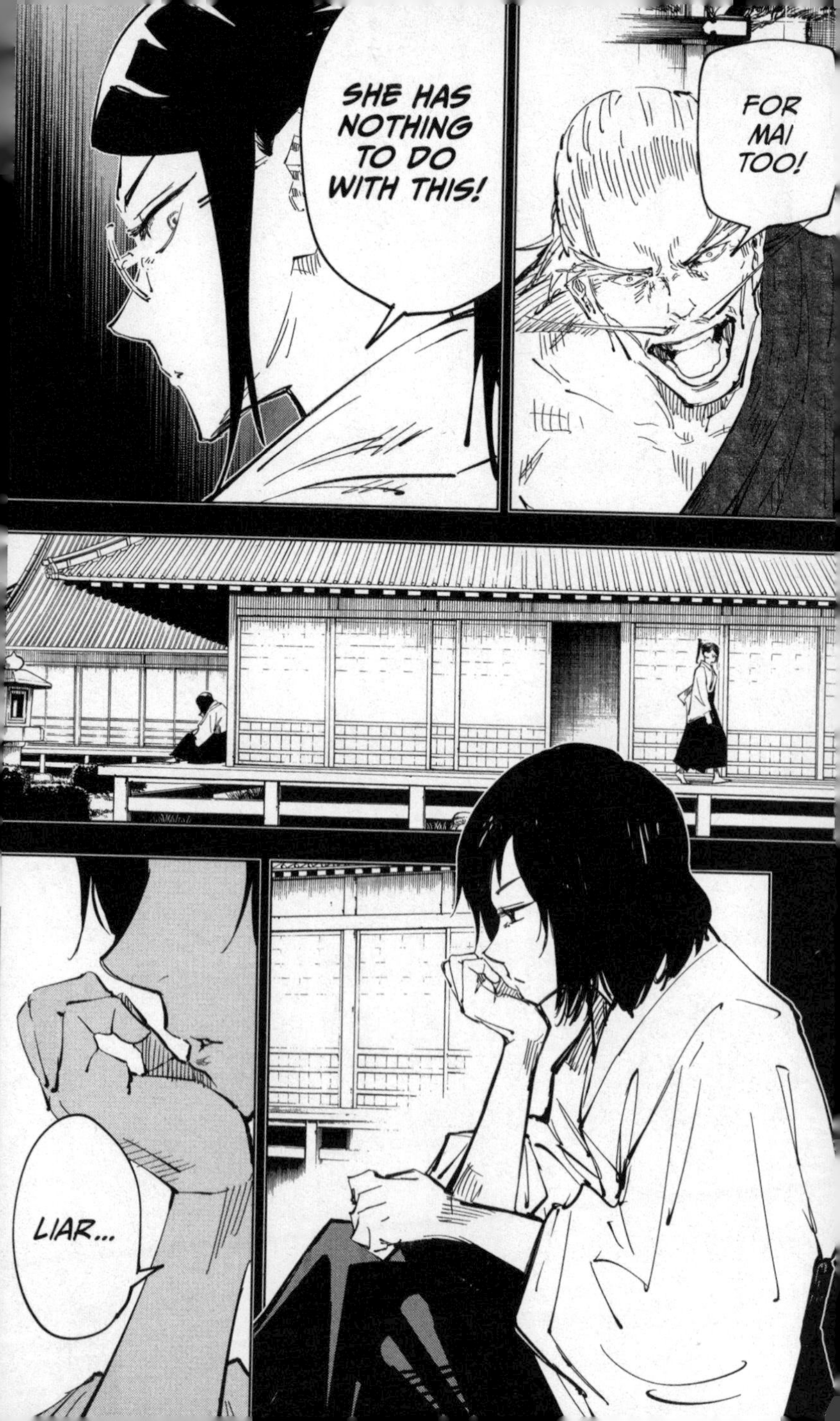
FOR MAI TOO!
SHE HAS NOTHING TO DO WITH THIS!
LIAR...

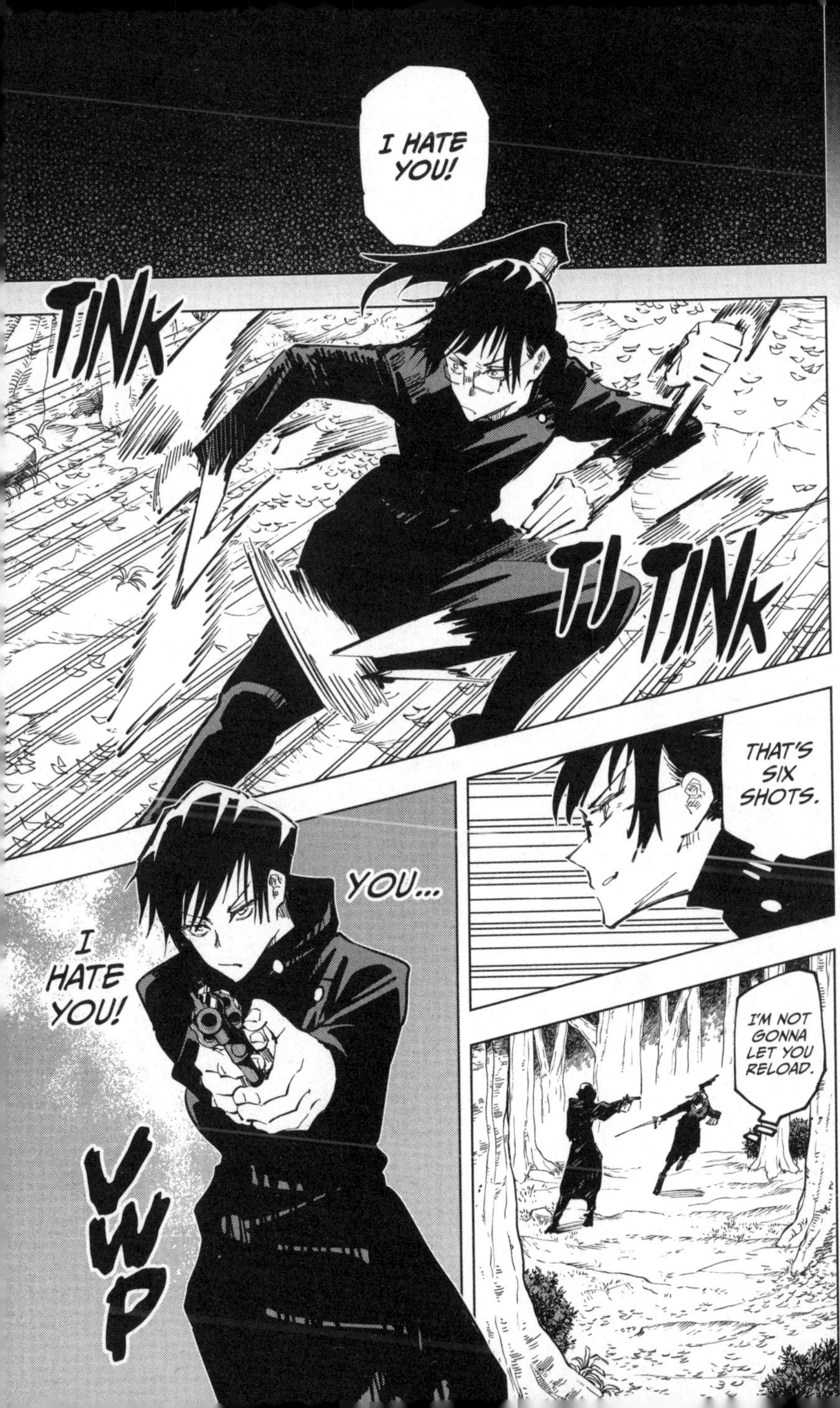

I HATE YOU!
TINK
TU TINK
THAT'S SIX SHOTS.
I'M NOT GONNA LET YOU RELOAD.
YOU...
I HATE YOU!
VWP

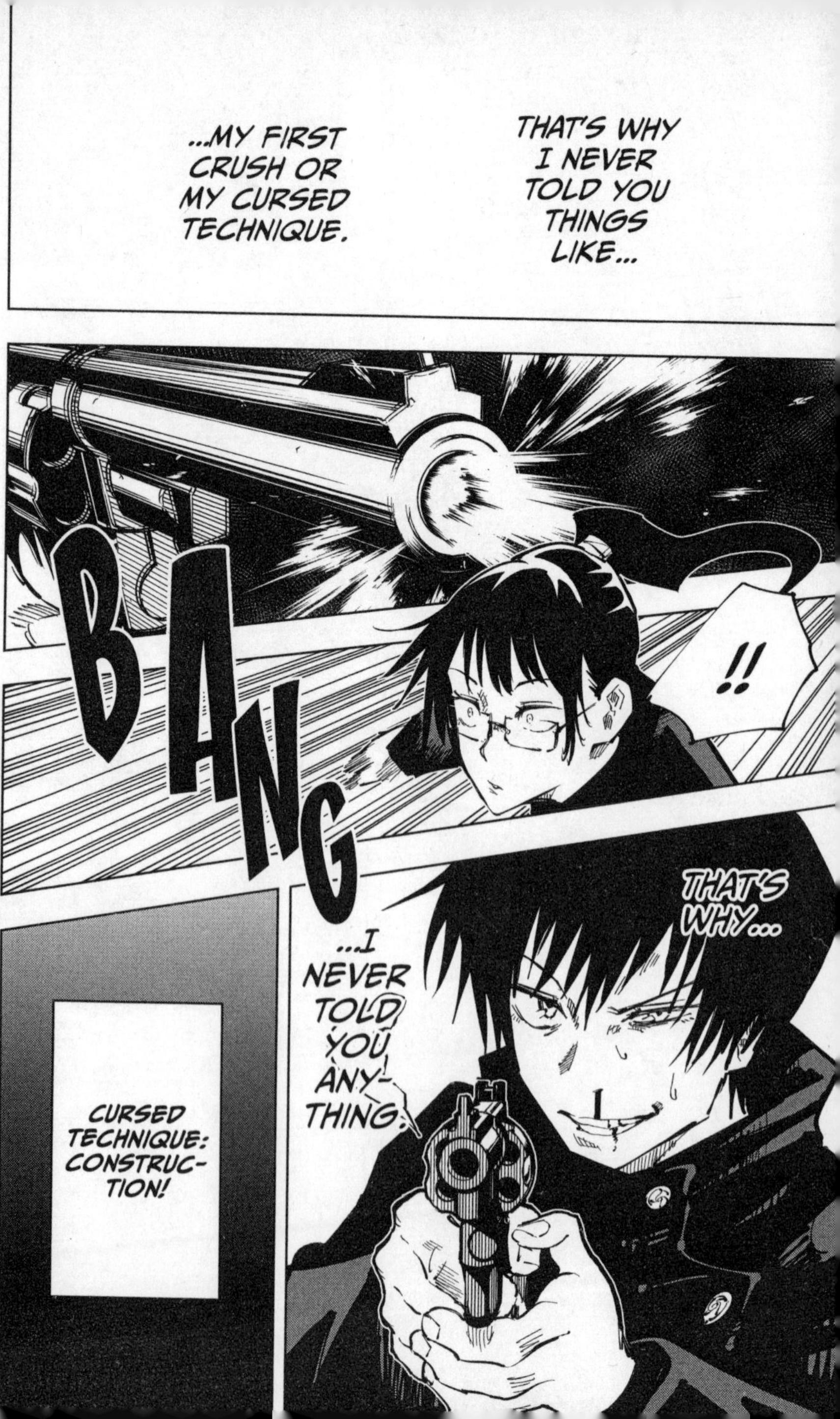
THAT'S WHY I NEVER TOLD YOU THINGS LIKE...
...MY FIRST CRUSH OR MY CURSED TECHNIQUE.
BANG
!!
THAT'S WHY...
...I NEVER TOLD YOU ANYTHING.
CURSED TECHNIQUE: CONSTRUCTION!

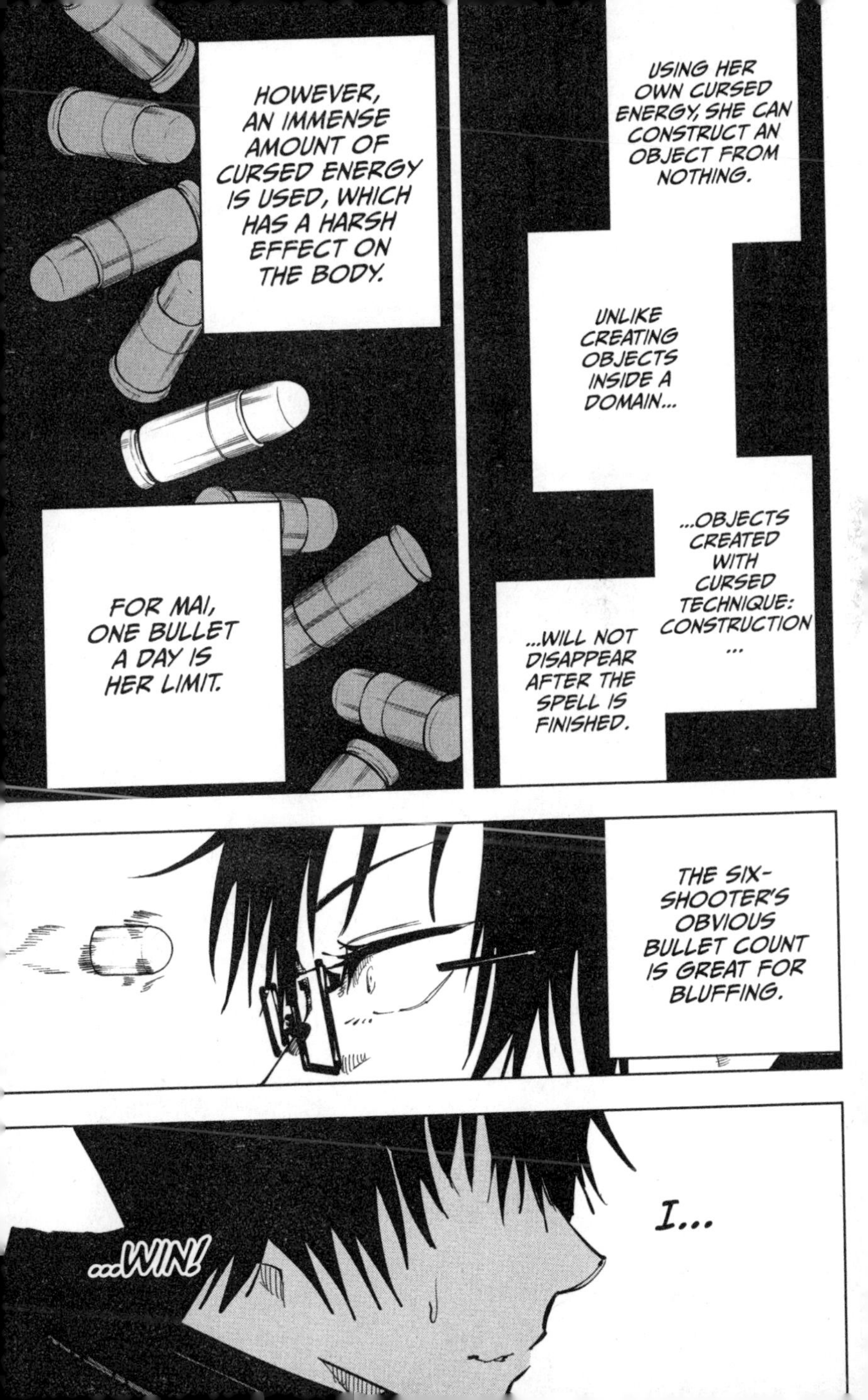
USING HER OWN CURSED ENERGY, SHE CAN CONSTRUCT AN OBJECT FROM NOTHING.
UNLIKE CREATING OBJECTS INSIDE A DOMAIN...
...OBJECTS CREATED WITH CURSED TECHNIQUE: CONSTRUCTION...
...WILL NOT DISAPPEAR AFTER THE SPELL IS FINISHED.
HOWEVER, AN IMMENSE AMOUNT OF CURSED ENERGY IS USED, WHICH HAS A HARSH EFFECT ON THE BODY.
FOR MAI, ONE BULLET A DAY IS HER LIMIT.
THE SIX-SHOOTER'S OBVIOUS BULLET COUNT IS GREAT FOR BLUFFING.
I...
...WIN!

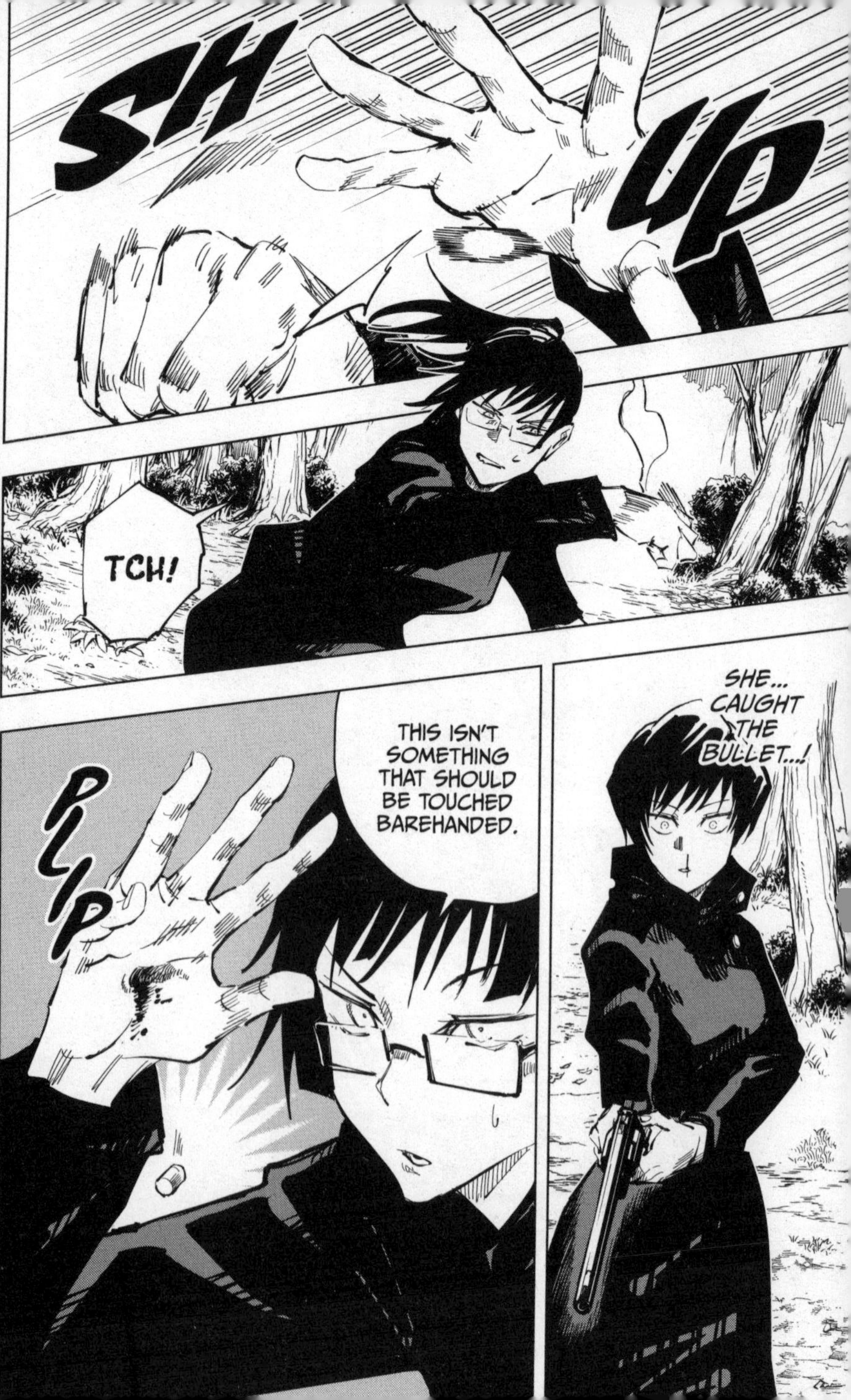
SHUP
TCH!
SHE... CAUGHT THE BULLET...!
THIS ISN'T SOMETHING THAT SHOULD BE TOUCHED BAREHANDED.
PLIP

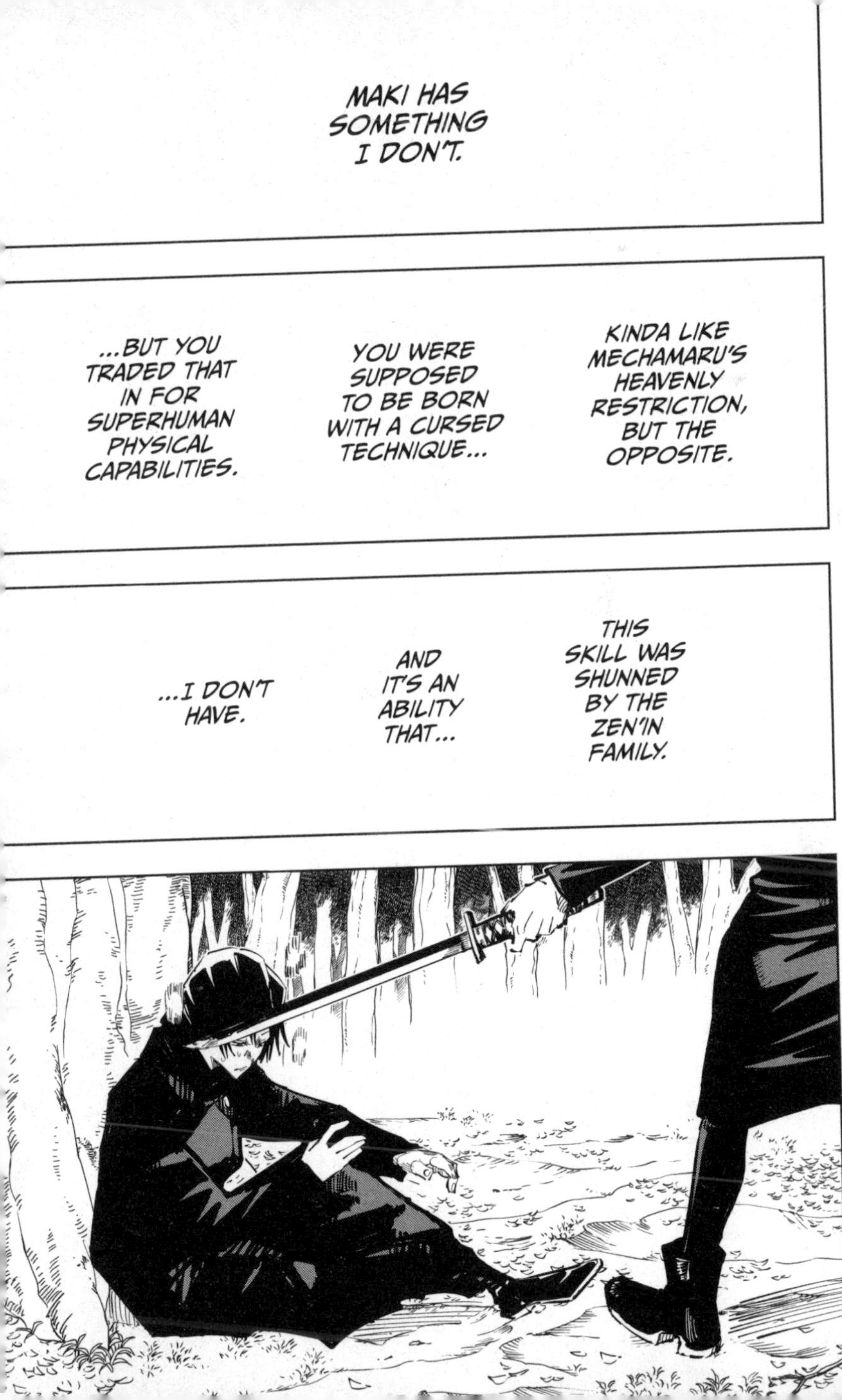
MAKI HAS SOMETHING I DON'T.
KINDA LIKE MECHAMARU'S HEAVENLY RESTRICTION, BUT THE OPPOSITE.
YOU WERE SUPPOSED TO BE BORN WITH A CURSED TECHNIQUE...
...BUT YOU TRADED THAT IN FOR SUPERHUMAN PHYSICAL CAPABILITIES.
THIS SKILL WAS SHUNNED BY THE ZEN'IN FAMILY.
AND IT'S AN ABILITY THAT...
...I DON'T HAVE.

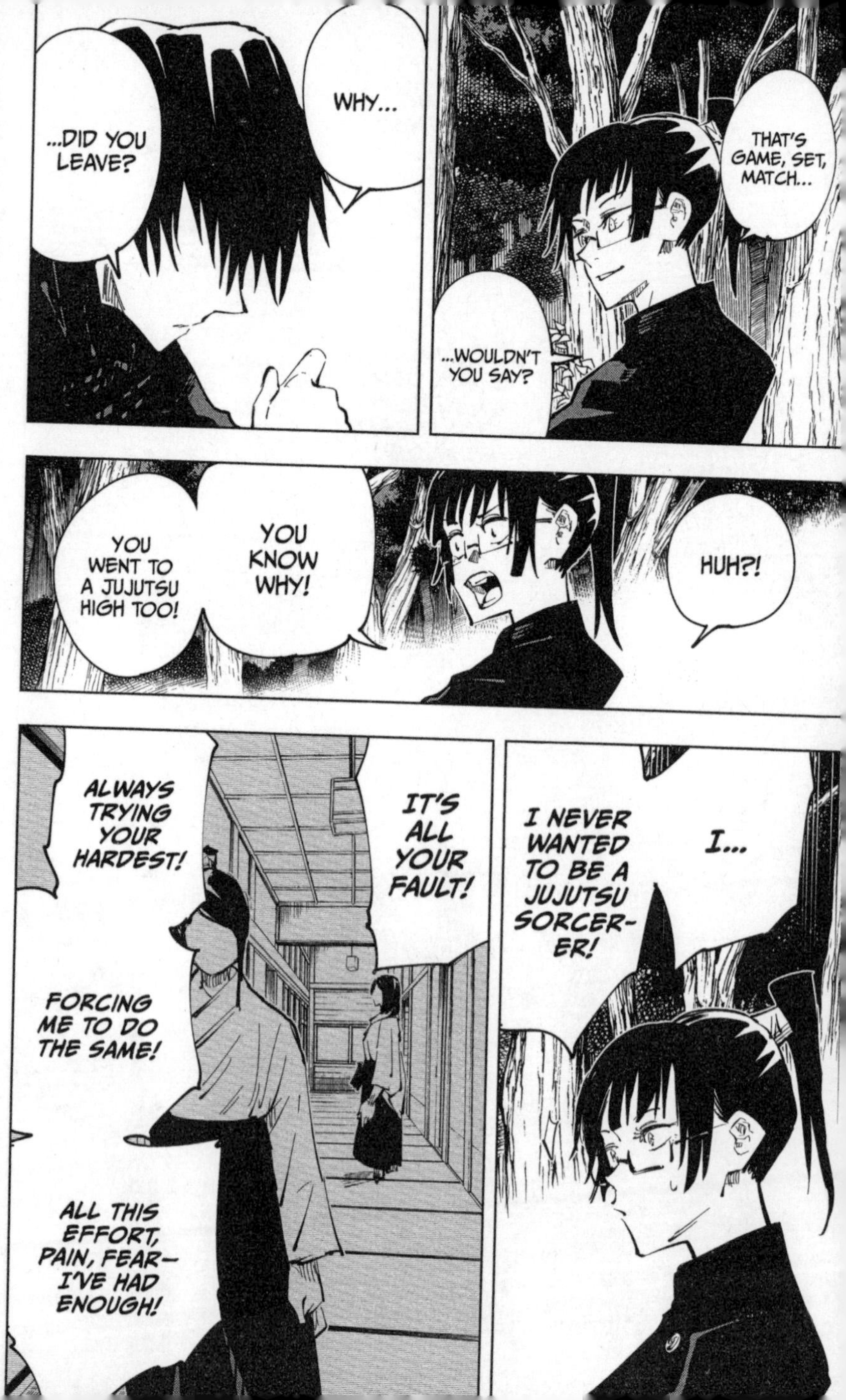
THAT'S GAME, SET, MATCH...
...WOULDN'T YOU SAY?
WHY...
...DID YOU LEAVE?
HUH?!
YOU KNOW WHY!
YOU WENT TO A JUJUTSU HIGH TOO!
I...
I NEVER WANTED TO BE A JUJUTSU SORCERER-ER!
IT'S ALL YOUR FAULT!
ALWAYS TRYING YOUR HARDEST!
FORCING ME TO DO THE SAME!
ALL THIS EFFORT, PAIN, FEAR— I'VE HAD ENOUGH!

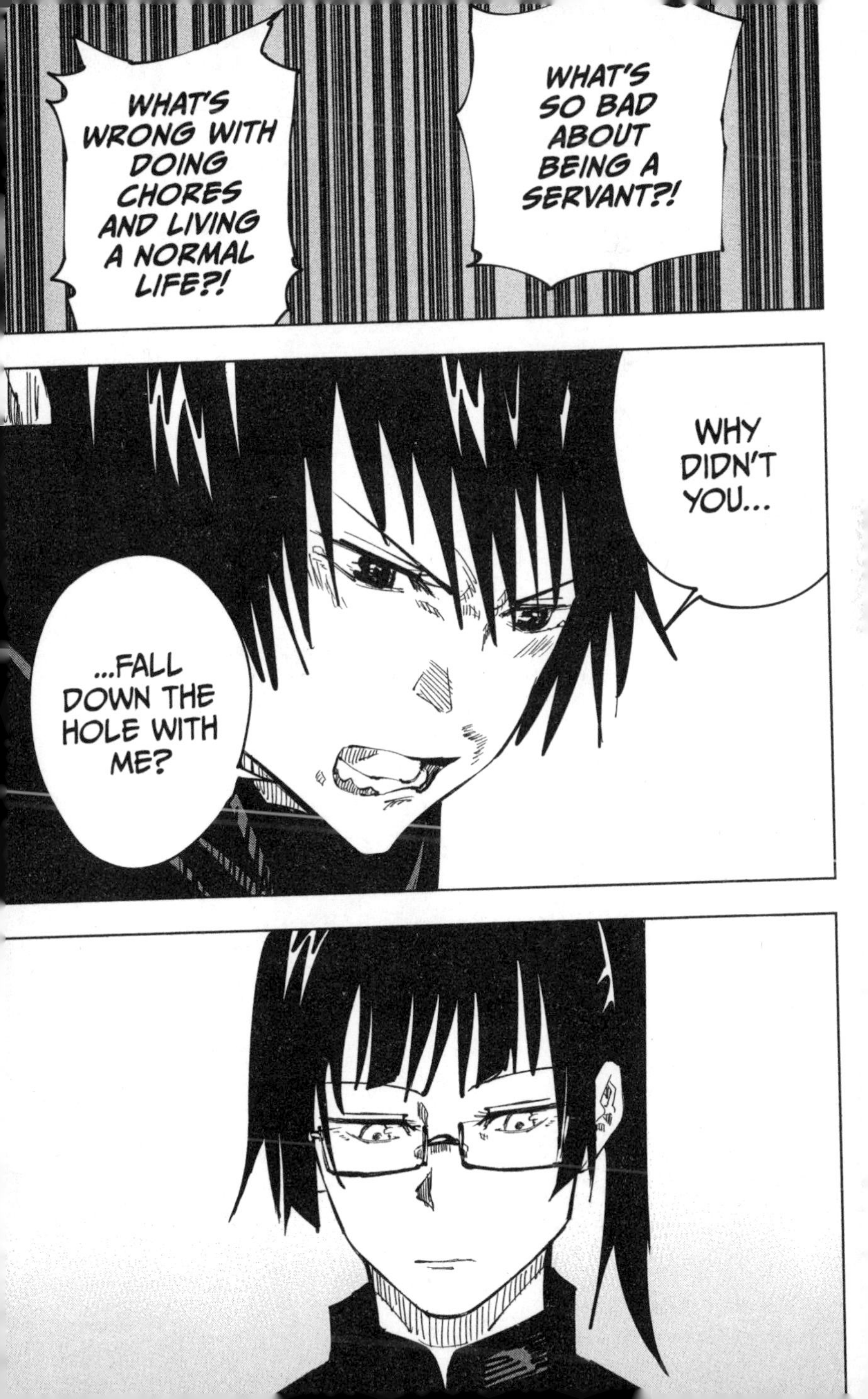
WHAT'S SO BAD ABOUT BEING A SERVANT?!
WHAT'S WRONG WITH DOING CHORES AND LIVING A NORMAL LIFE?!
WHY DIDN'T YOU...
...FALL DOWN THE HOLE WITH ME?

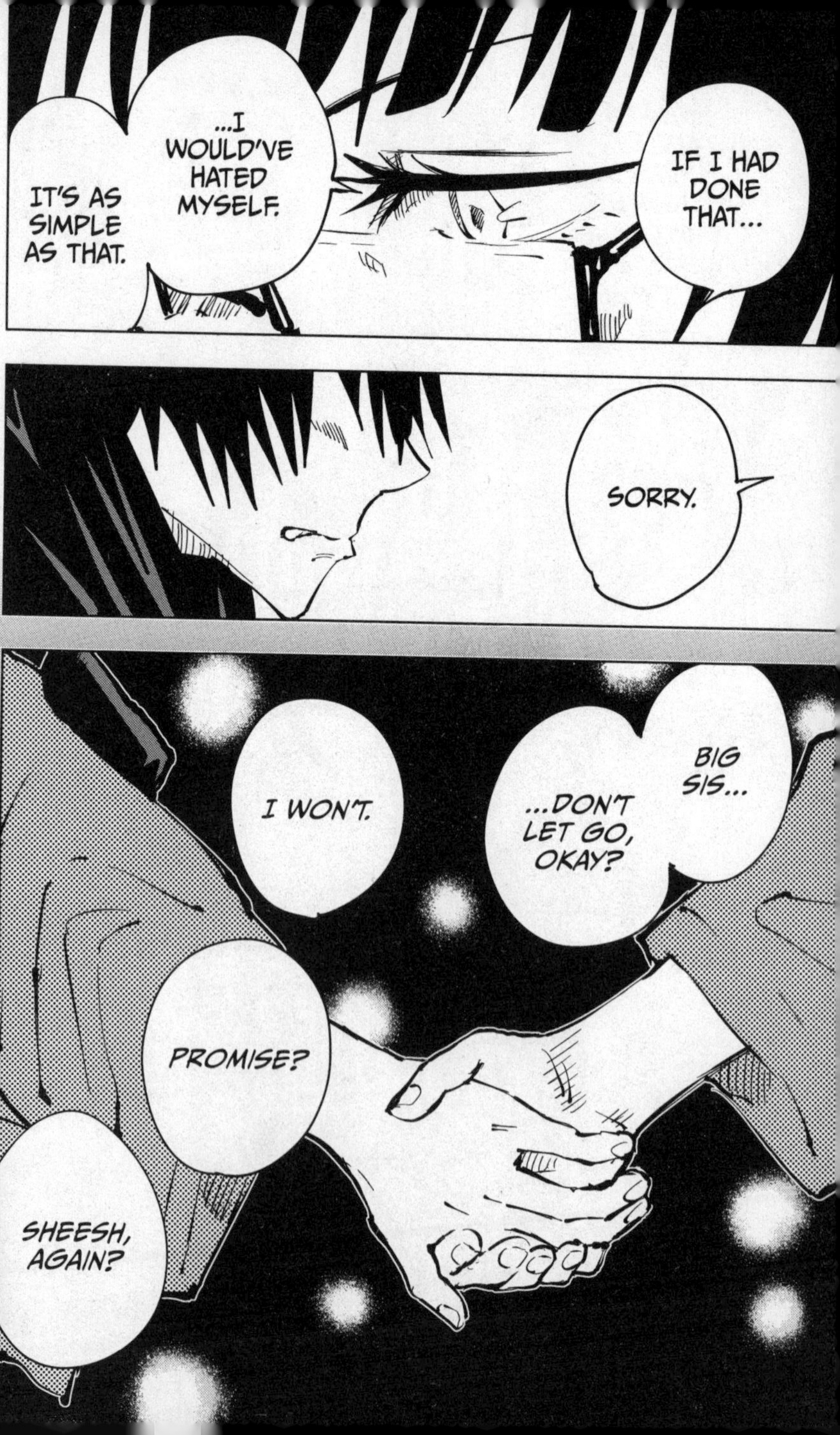
IF I HAD DONE THAT...
...I WOULD'VE HATED MYSELF.
IT'S AS SIMPLE AS THAT.
SORRY.
BIG SIS...
...DON'T LET GO, OKAY?
I WON'T.
PROMISE?
SHEESH, AGAIN?

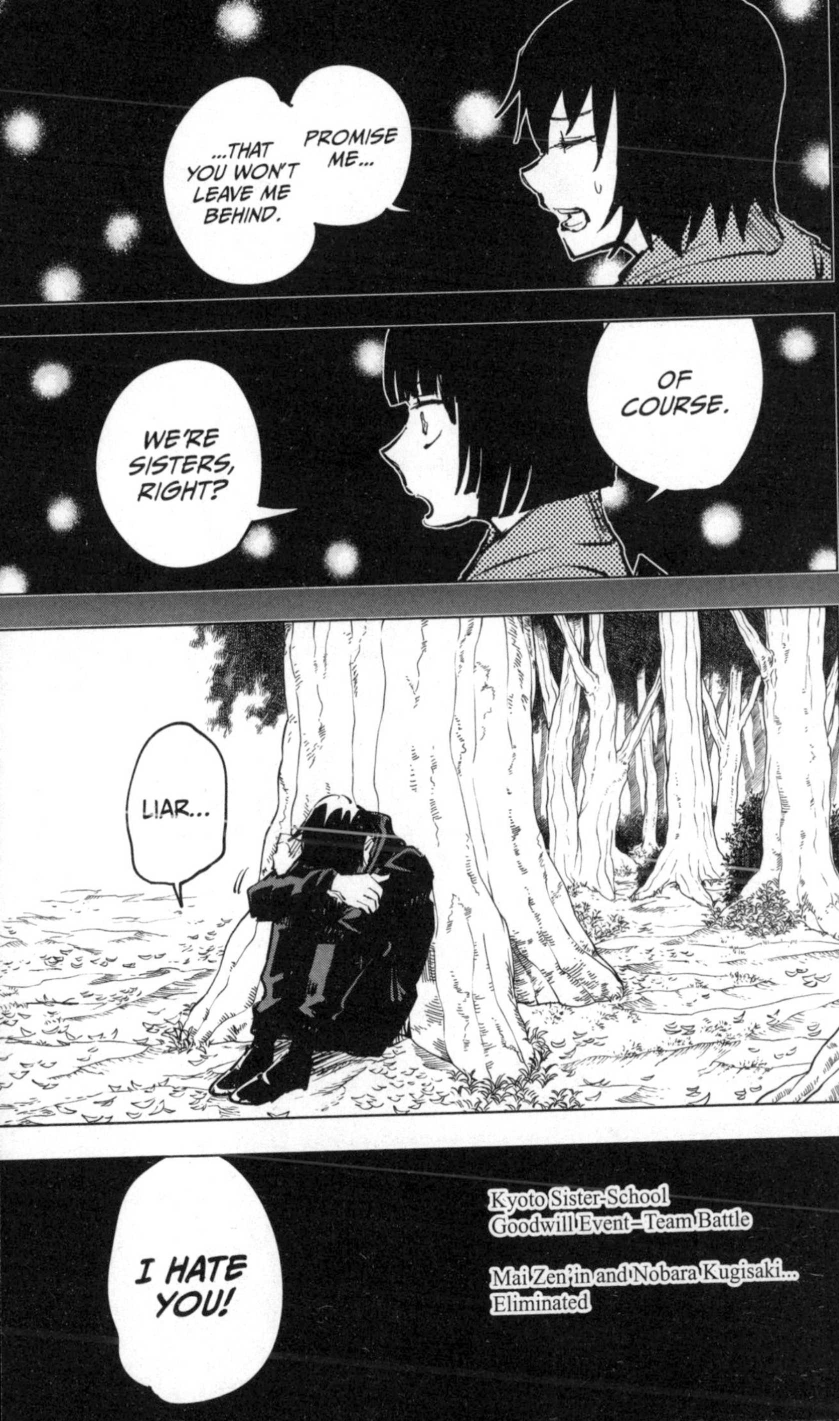
PROMISE ME...
...THAT YOU WON'T LEAVE ME BEHIND.
OF COURSE.
WE'RE SISTERS, RIGHT?
LIAR...
Kyoto Sister-School Goodwill Event–Team Battle
Mai Zen'in and Nobara Kugisaki... Eliminated
I HATE YOU!

THE SURPRISE ②

• I don't need to say anything more, but... Horikoshi Sensei, thank you so much!!

• Before *Jujutsu* was featured in *Jump GIGA* (which became volume 0) and confirmed for serialization, my previous work was turned down quite quickly. The reason I was always given was something like, "It's interesting, but it's not *Jump*." "What the—?! If it's interesting, shouldn't that be enough?!" I thought to my rotten self. (To be honest, it wasn't even really that interesting...I guess that's just a part of being young.)

• Around that time, Kawada Sensei (creator of *Hinomaru Sumo*) and Horikoshi Sensei were also getting their start (but not at the same time). I was really surprised and thought to myself, "This is so *Jump*! It's so much fun!"

• That was when I started to think deeply about what it means for a manga series to be considered mainstream. I experienced many things along the way and *Jujutsu Kaisen* was born. I, Akutami, can do nothing alone.

GEGE AKUTAMI

Quirk: - Excuse making
- Cutting finger-nails too deep

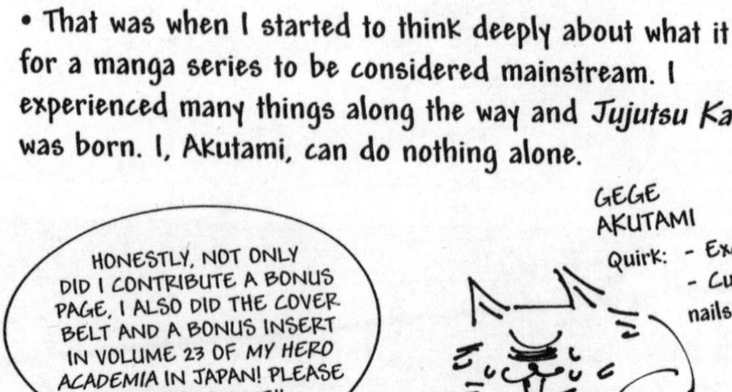
HONESTLY, NOT ONLY DID I CONTRIBUTE A BONUS PAGE, I ALSO DID THE COVER BELT AND A BONUS INSERT IN VOLUME 23 OF MY HERO ACADEMIA IN JAPAN! PLEASE GO EASY ON ME!!

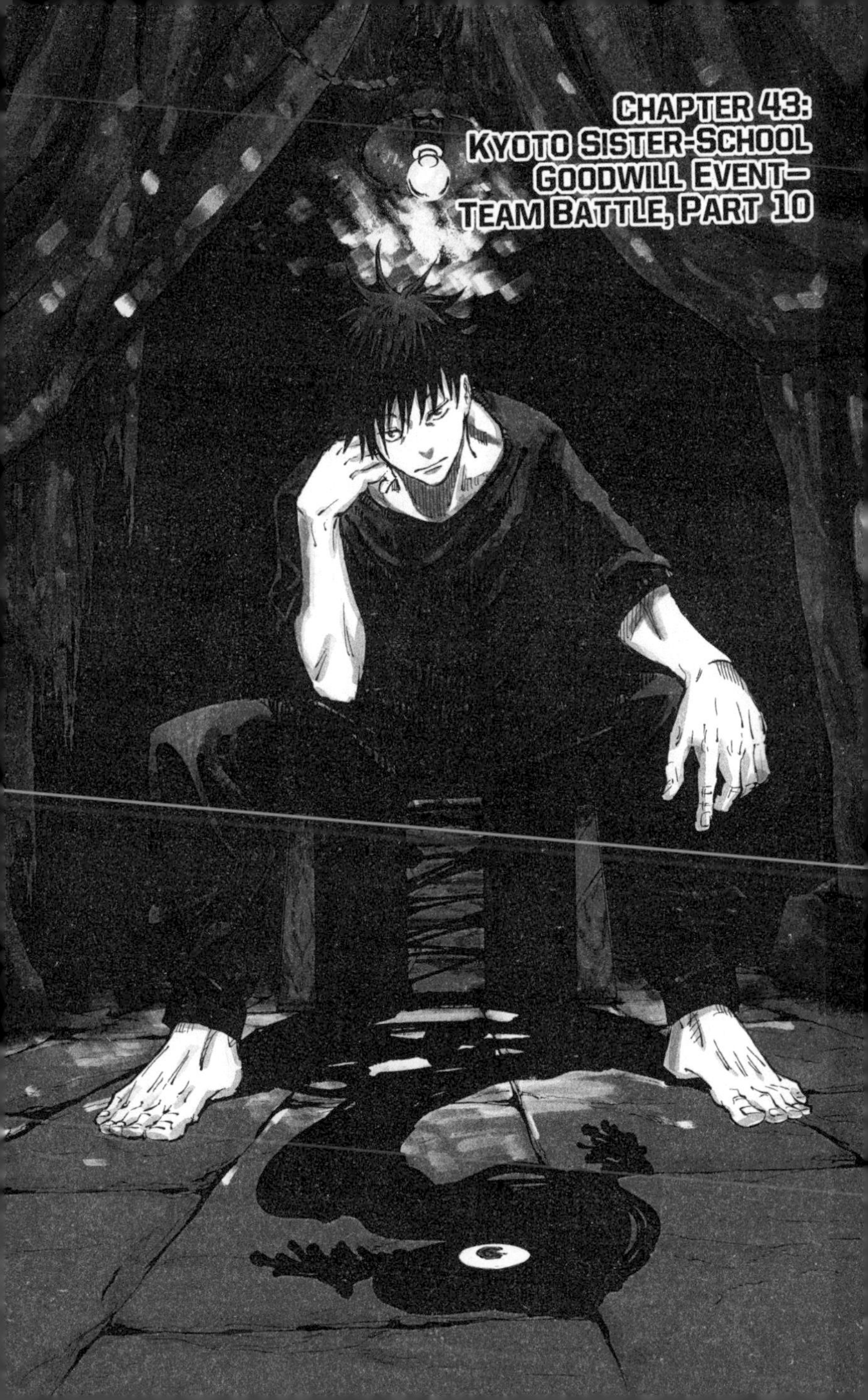
Chapter 43:
Kyoto Sister-School
Goodwill Event–
Team Battle, Part 10

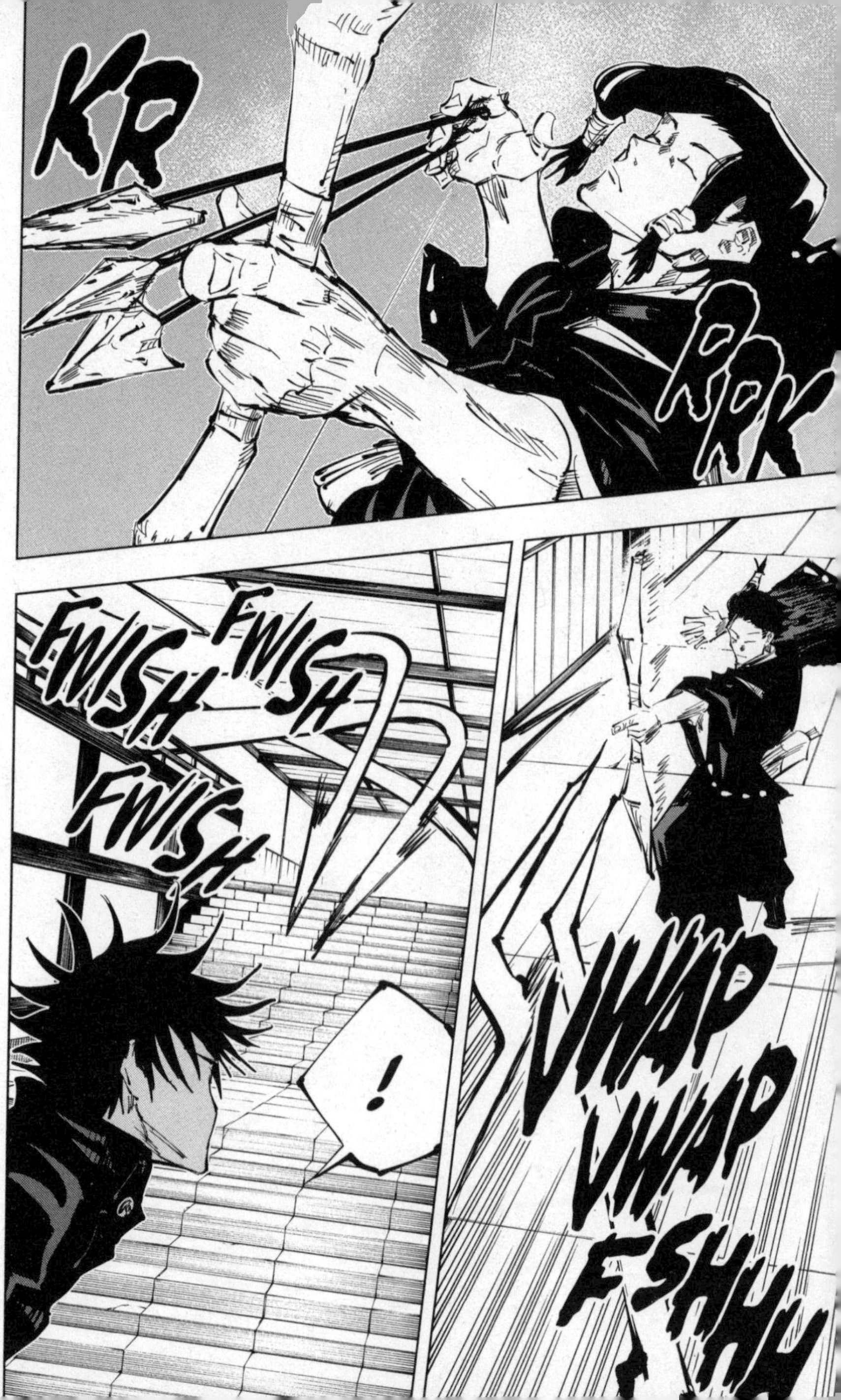
KR
RRK
VWAP
VWAP
FSHHH
FWISH
FWISH
FWISH
!

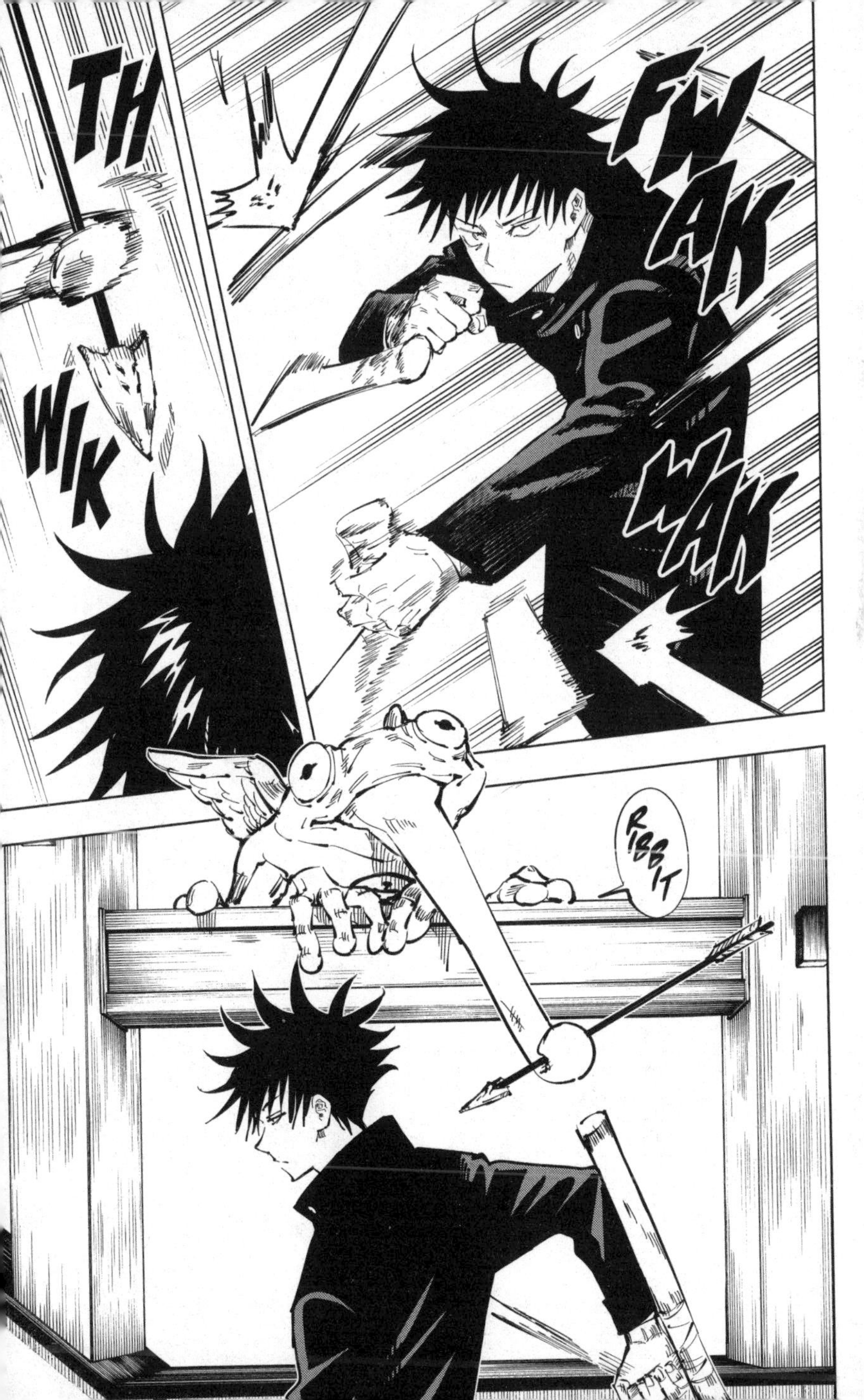
FWAK
WAK
THWIK
RIBBIT

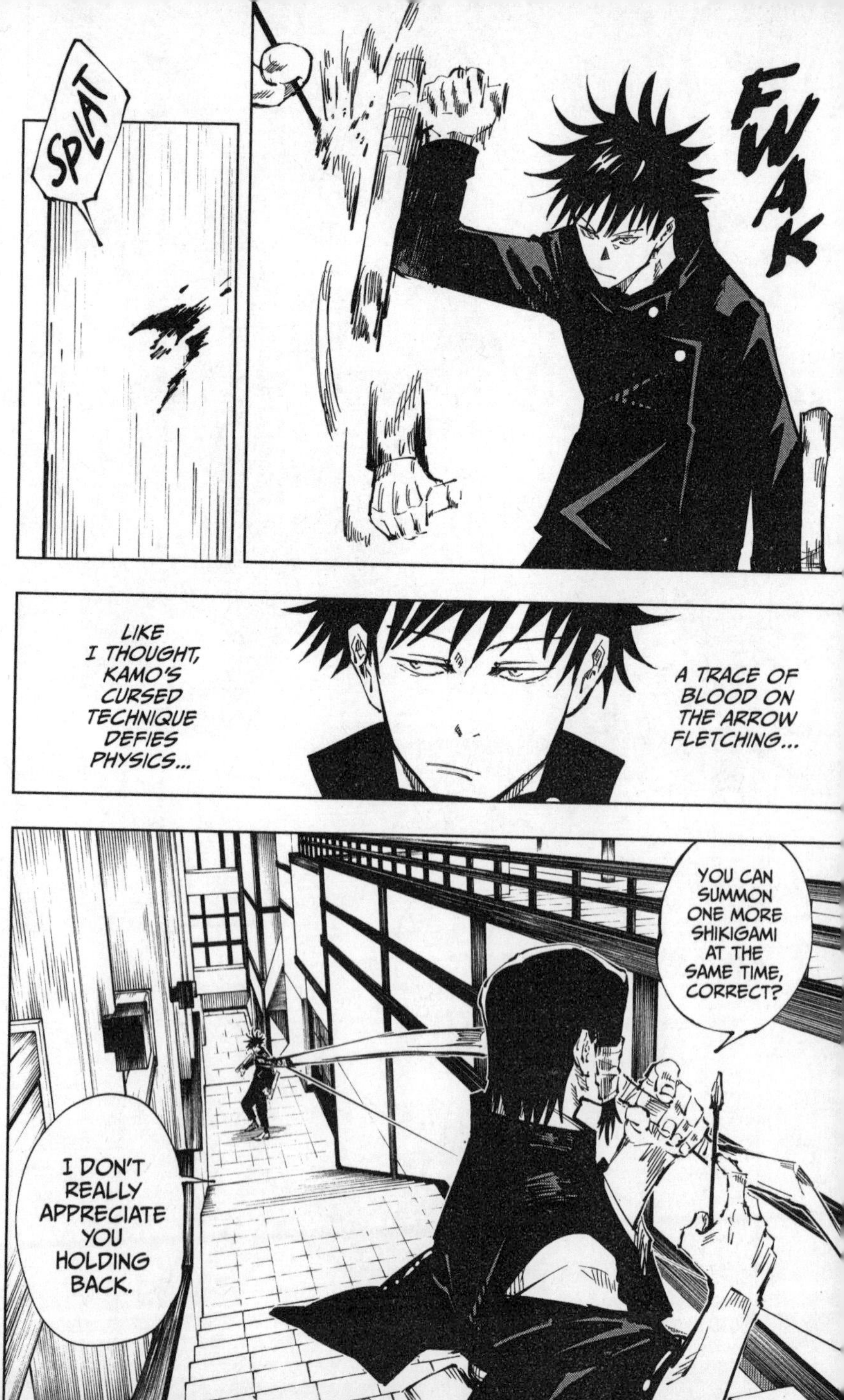
FWAK
SPLAT
A TRACE OF BLOOD ON THE ARROW FLETCHING...
LIKE I THOUGHT, KAMO'S CURSED TECHNIQUE DEFIES PHYSICS...
YOU CAN SUMMON ONE MORE SHIKIGAMI AT THE SAME TIME, CORRECT?
I DON'T REALLY APPRECIATE YOU HOLDING BACK.

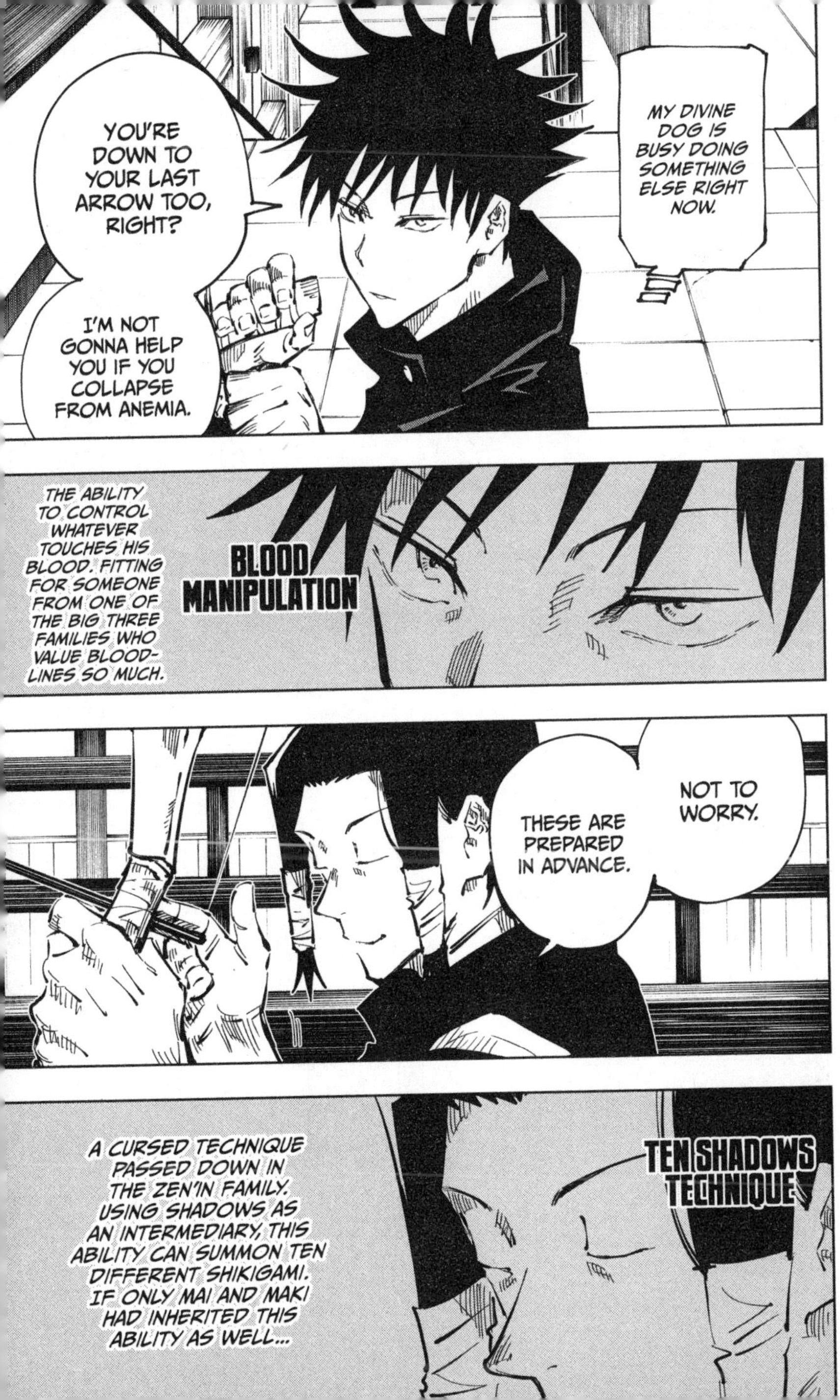
MY DIVINE DOG IS BUSY DOING SOMETHING ELSE RIGHT NOW.
YOU'RE DOWN TO YOUR LAST ARROW TOO, RIGHT?
I'M NOT GONNA HELP YOU IF YOU COLLAPSE FROM ANEMIA.
BLOOD MANIPULATION
THE ABILITY TO CONTROL WHATEVER TOUCHES HIS BLOOD. FITTING FOR SOMEONE FROM ONE OF THE BIG THREE FAMILIES WHO VALUE BLOOD-LINES SO MUCH.
NOT TO WORRY.
THESE ARE PREPARED IN ADVANCE.
TEN SHADOWS TECHNIQUE
A CURSED TECHNIQUE PASSED DOWN IN THE ZEN'IN FAMILY. USING SHADOWS AS AN INTERMEDIARY, THIS ABILITY CAN SUMMON TEN DIFFERENT SHIKIGAMI. IF ONLY MAI AND MAKI HAD INHERITED THIS ABILITY AS WELL...

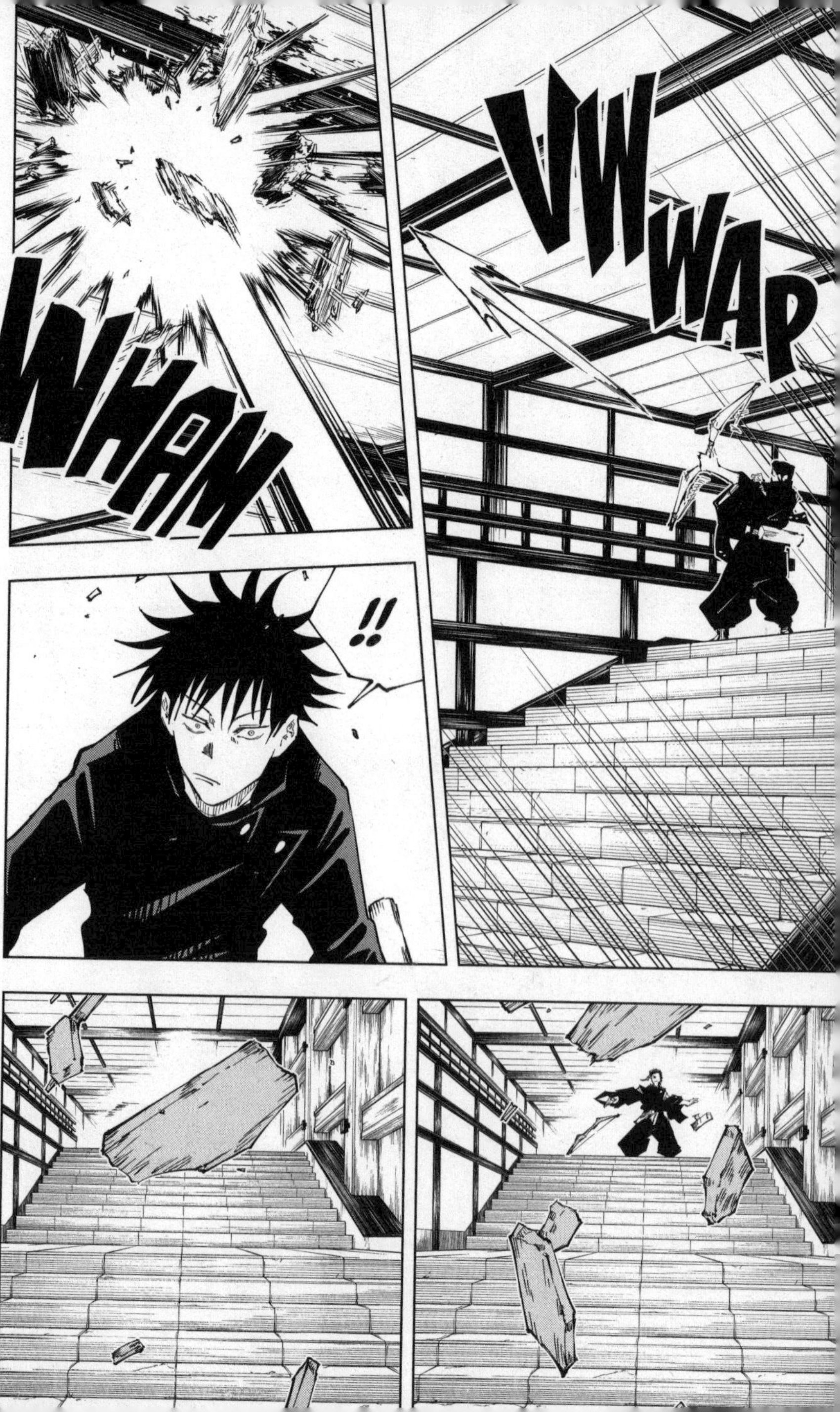
VWWAP
WHAM
!!

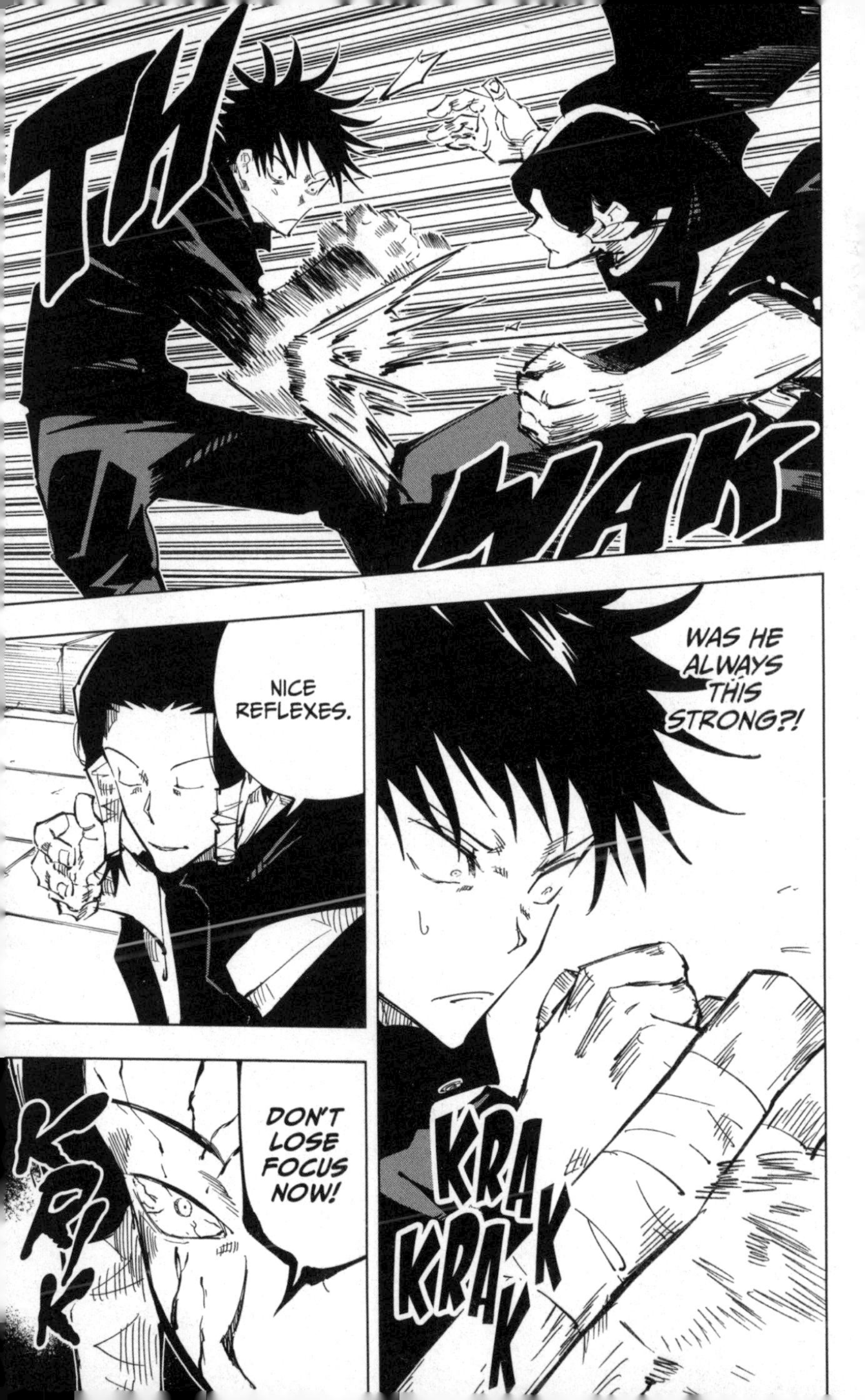
THWAK
WAS HE ALWAYS THIS STRONG?!
KRAK KRAK
NICE REFLEXES.
DON'T LOSE FOCUS NOW!
KRAK

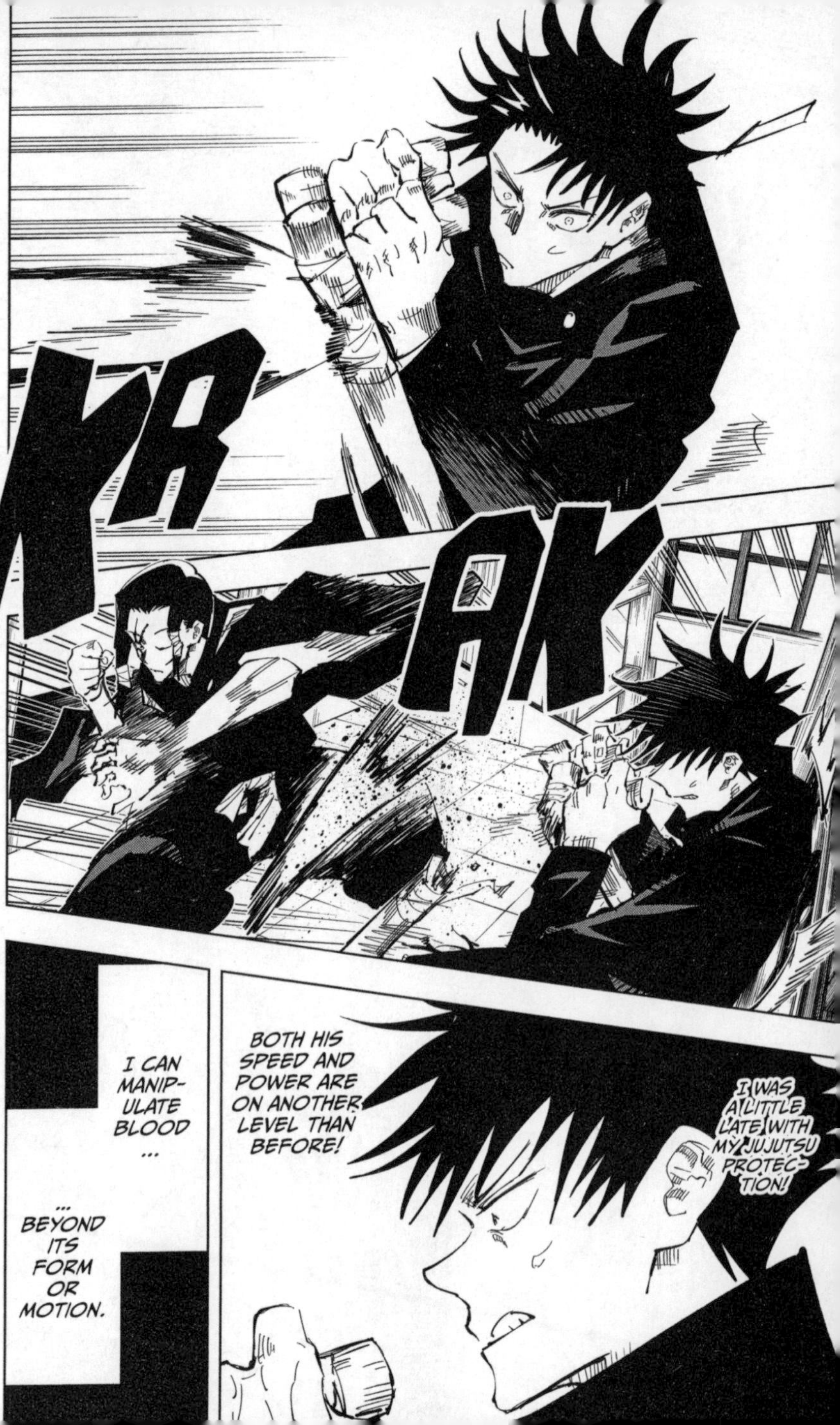
KRAK
I WAS A LITTLE LATE WITH MY JUJUTSU PROTEC-TION!
BOTH HIS SPEED AND POWER ARE ON ANOTHER LEVEL THAN BEFORE!
I CAN MANIP-ULATE BLOOD ...
... BEYOND ITS FORM OR MOTION.

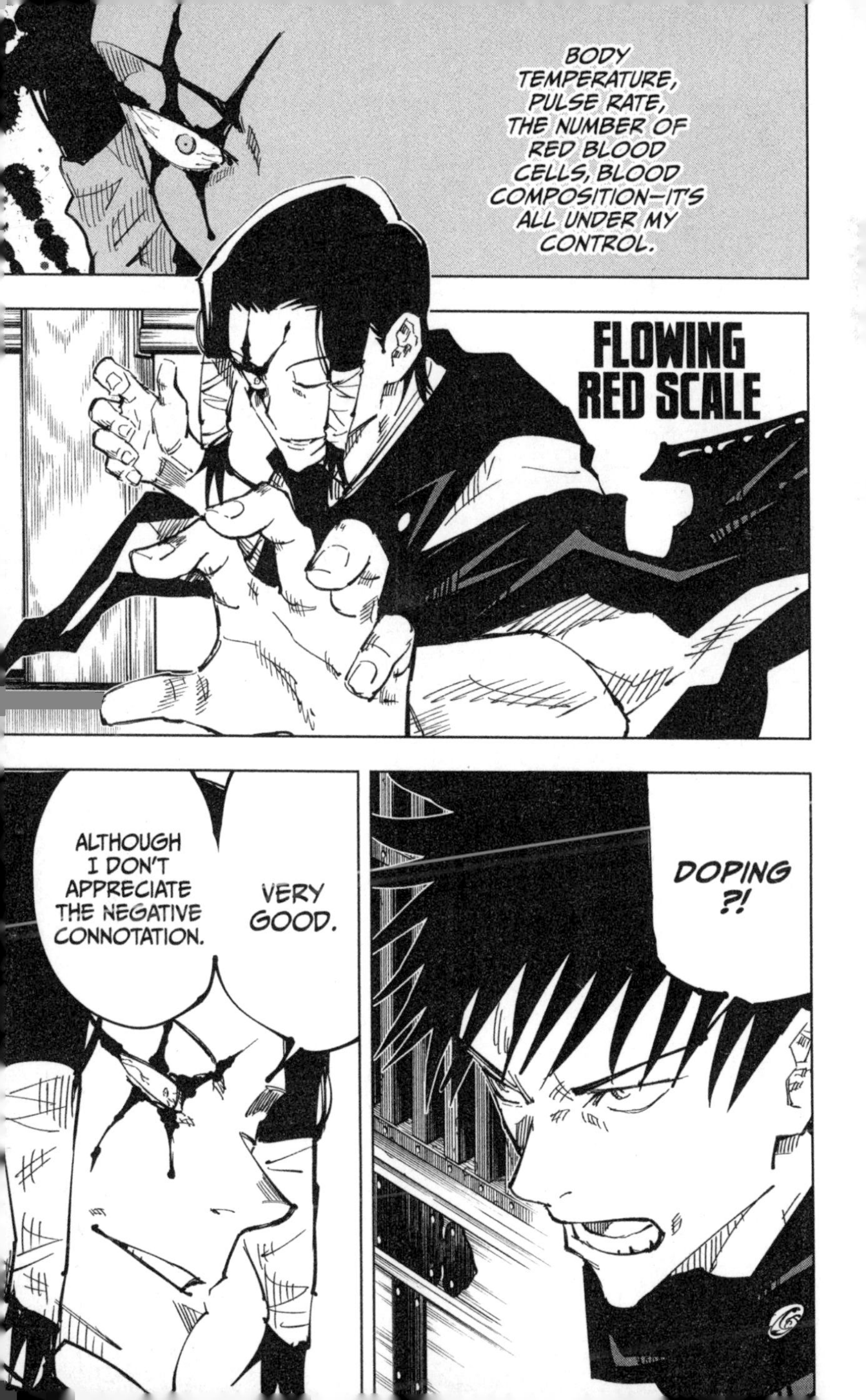
BODY TEMPERATURE, PULSE RATE, THE NUMBER OF RED BLOOD CELLS, BLOOD COMPOSITION—IT'S ALL UNDER MY CONTROL.
FLOWING RED SCALE
DOPING ?!
VERY GOOD.
ALTHOUGH I DON'T APPRECIATE THE NEGATIVE CONNOTATION.

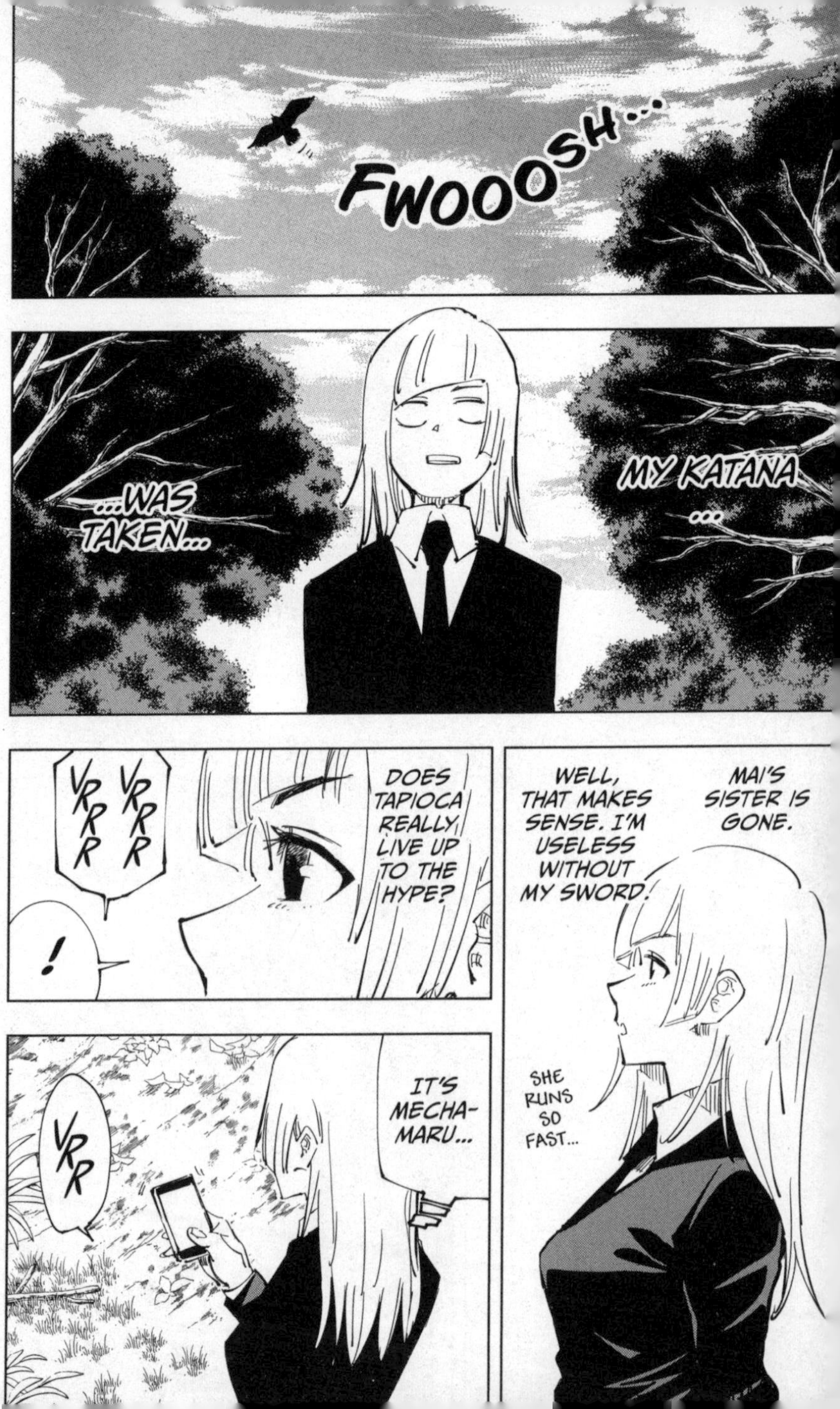
FWOOOSH...
MY KATANA...
...WAS TAKEN...
MAI'S SISTER IS GONE.
WELL, THAT MAKES SENSE. I'M USELESS WITHOUT MY SWORD.
SHE RUNS SO FAST...
DOES TAPIOCA REALLY LIVE UP TO THE HYPE?
VRRR VRRR
!
IT'S MECHA-MARU...
VRR

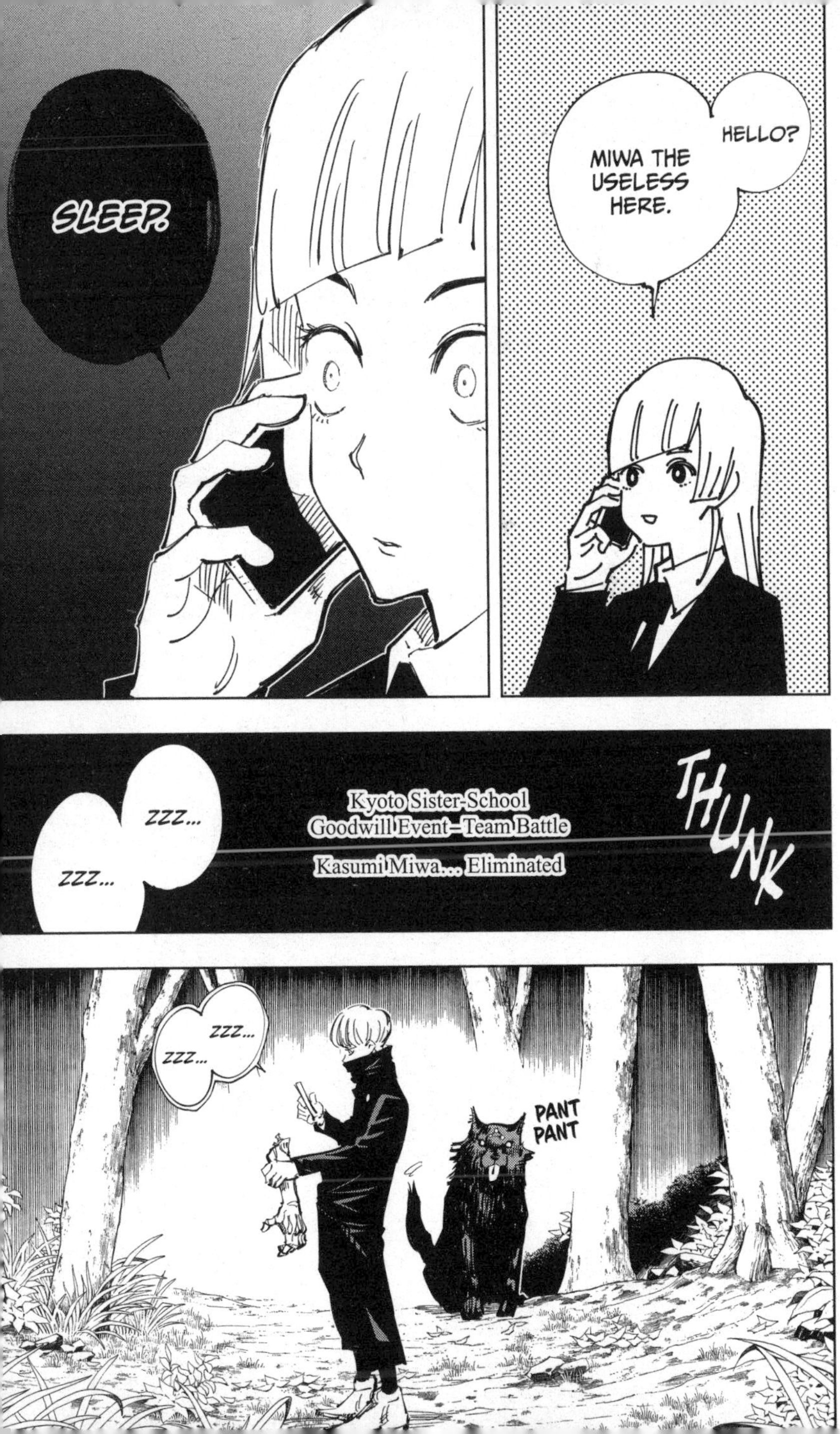
HELLO?
MIWA THE USELESS HERE.
SLEEP.
THUNK
Kyoto Sister-School Goodwill Event–Team Battle
Kasumi Miwa… Eliminated
ZZZ...
ZZZ...
PANT PANT
ZZZ...
ZZZ...

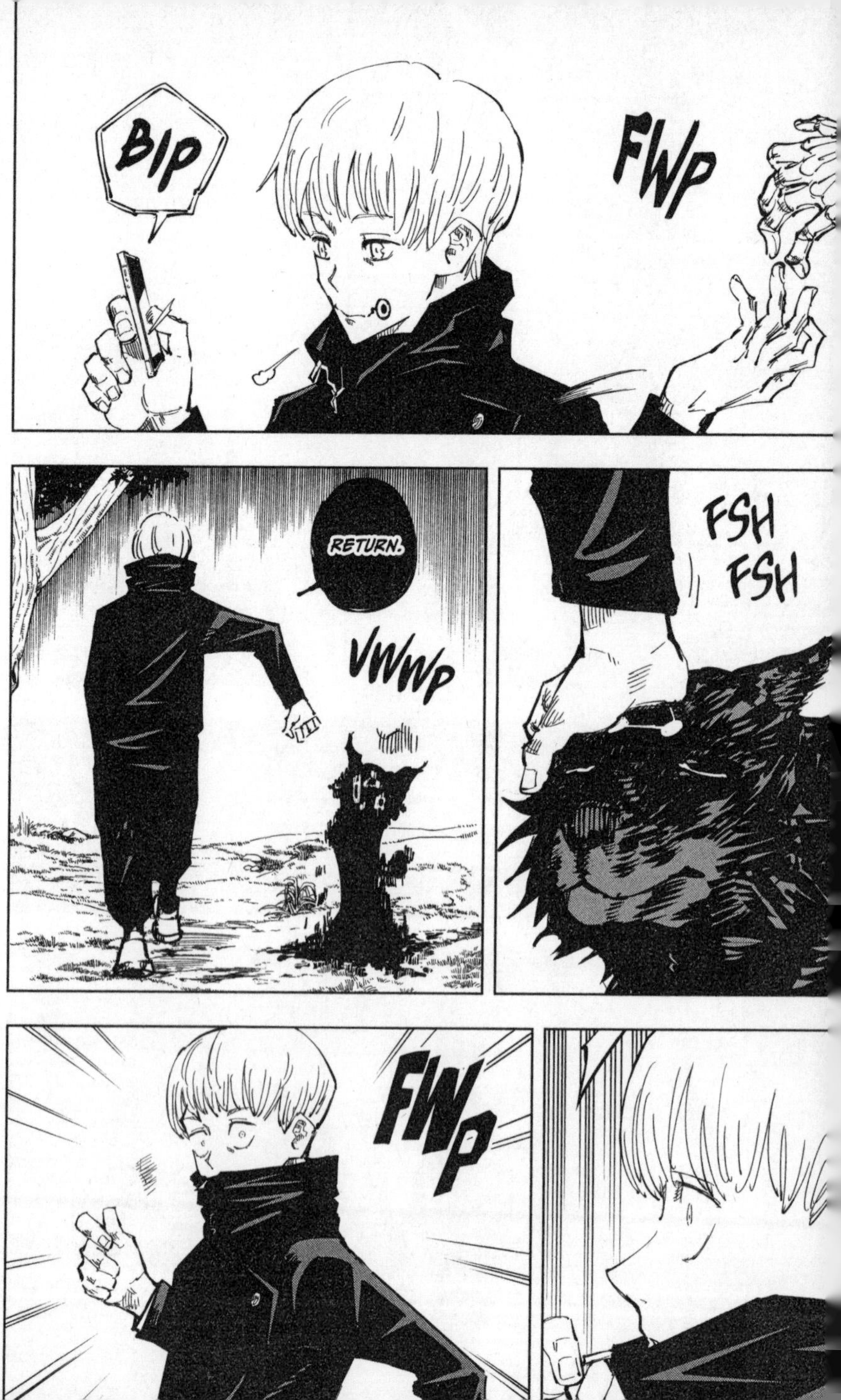
FWP
BIP
FSH FSH
RETURN.
VWWP
FWP

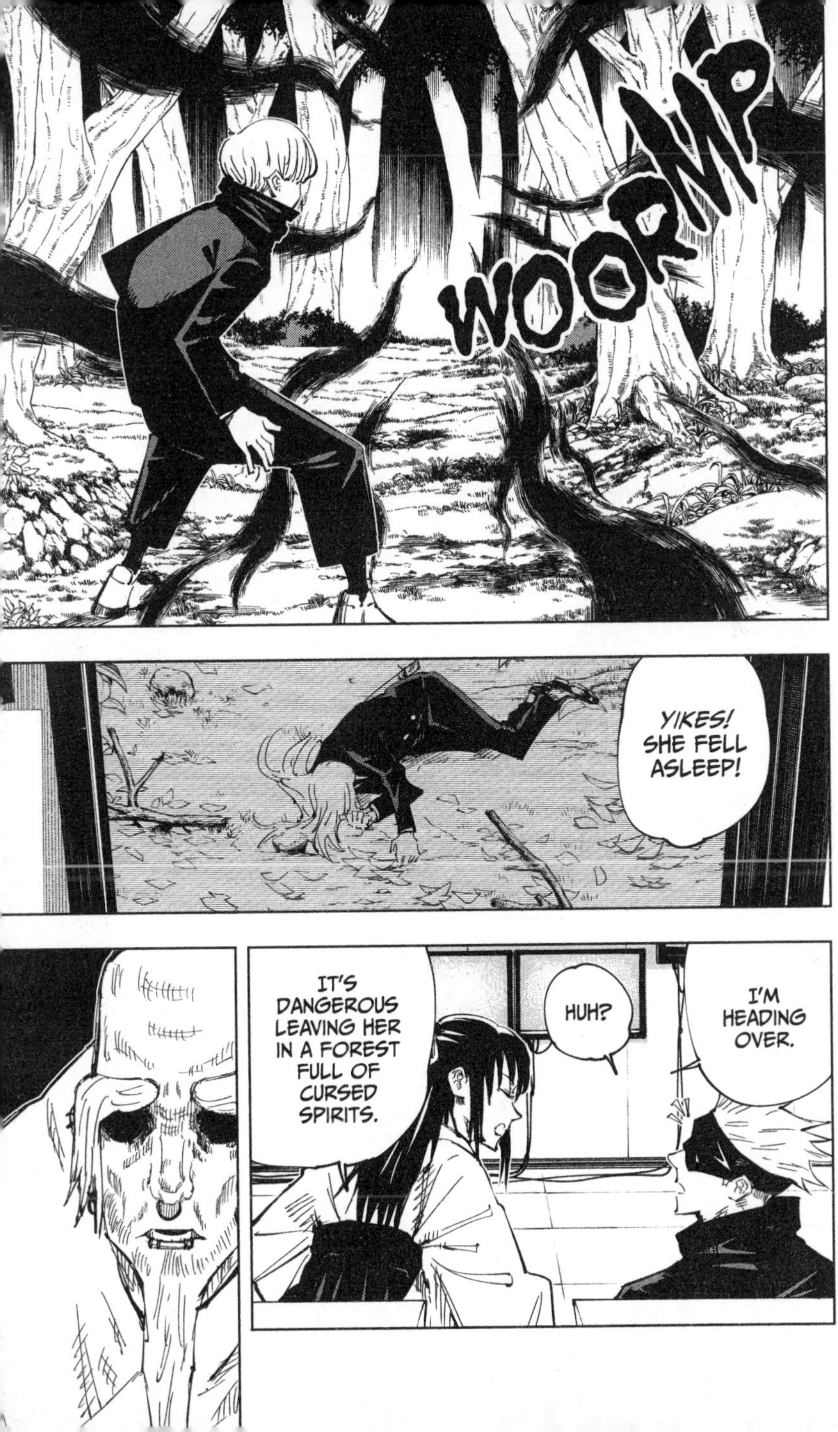
WOOMP
YIKES! SHE FELL ASLEEP!
I'M HEADING OVER.
HUH?
IT'S DANGEROUS LEAVING HER IN A FOREST FULL OF CURSED SPIRITS.

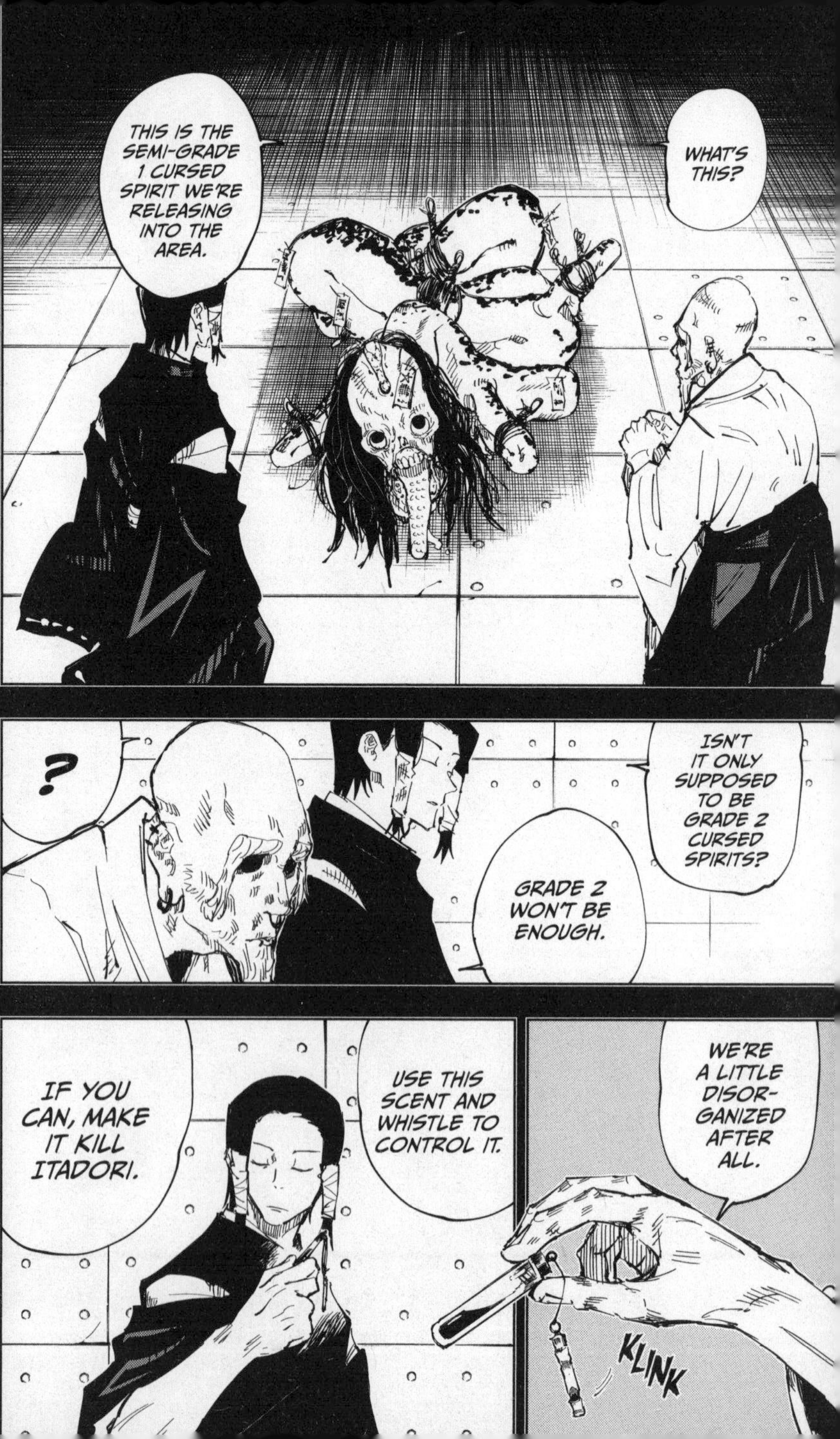
WHAT'S THIS?
THIS IS THE SEMI-GRADE 1 CURSED SPIRIT WE'RE RELEASING INTO THE AREA.
ISN'T IT ONLY SUPPOSED TO BE GRADE 2 CURSED SPIRITS?
GRADE 2 WON'T BE ENOUGH.
?
WE'RE A LITTLE DISOR-GANIZED AFTER ALL.
KLINK
USE THIS SCENT AND WHISTLE TO CONTROL IT.
IF YOU CAN, MAKE IT KILL ITADORI.

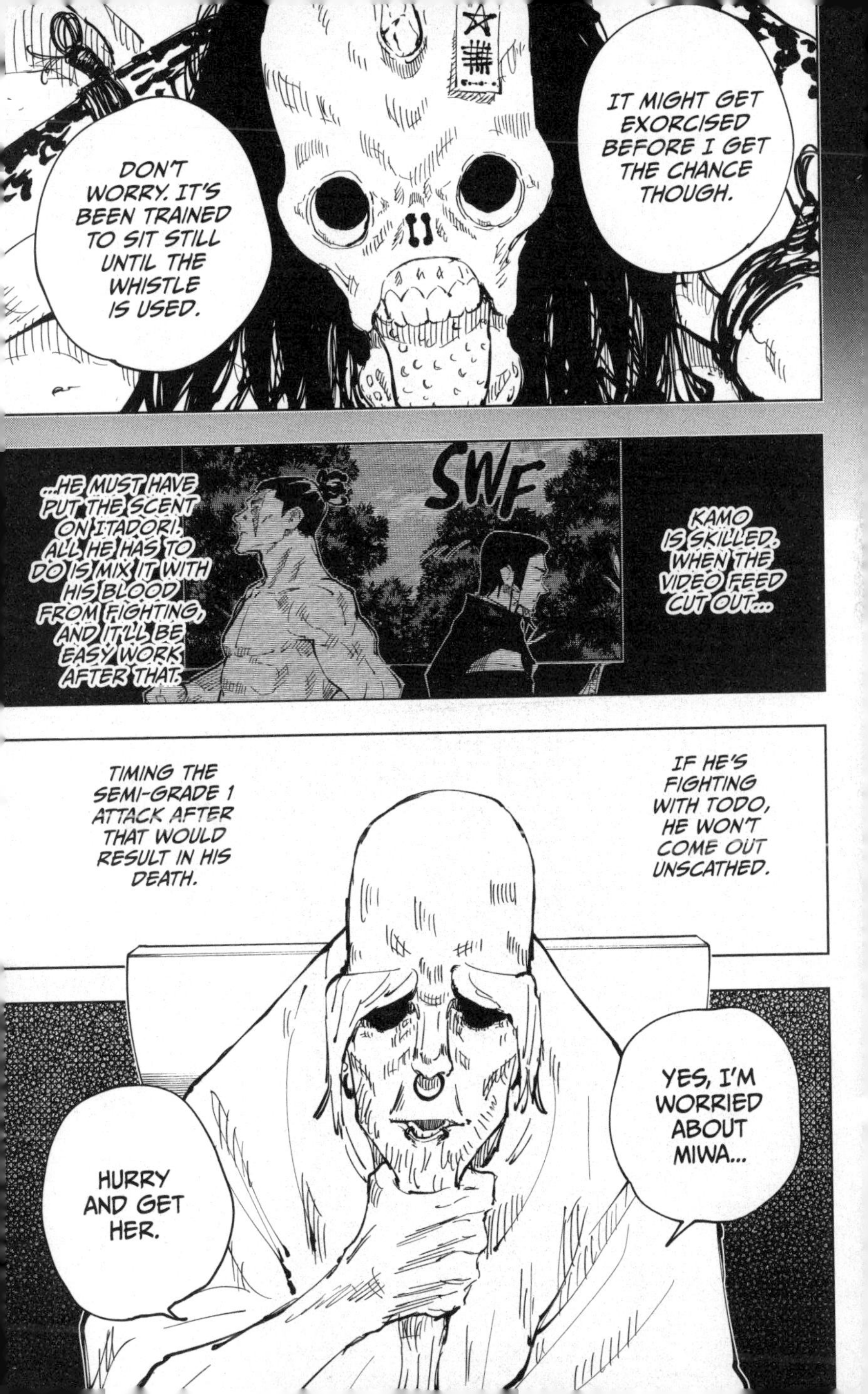
IT MIGHT GET EXORCISED BEFORE I GET THE CHANCE THOUGH.
DON'T WORRY. IT'S BEEN TRAINED TO SIT STILL UNTIL THE WHISTLE IS USED.
KAMO IS SKILLED. WHEN THE VIDEO FEED CUT OUT...
SWF
...HE MUST HAVE PUT THE SCENT ON ITADORI. ALL HE HAS TO DO IS MIX IT WITH HIS BLOOD FROM FIGHTING, AND IT'LL BE EASY WORK AFTER THAT.
IF HE'S FIGHTING WITH TODO, HE WON'T COME OUT UNSCATHED.
TIMING THE SEMI-GRADE 1 ATTACK AFTER THAT WOULD RESULT IN HIS DEATH.
YES, I'M WORRIED ABOUT MIWA...
HURRY AND GET HER.

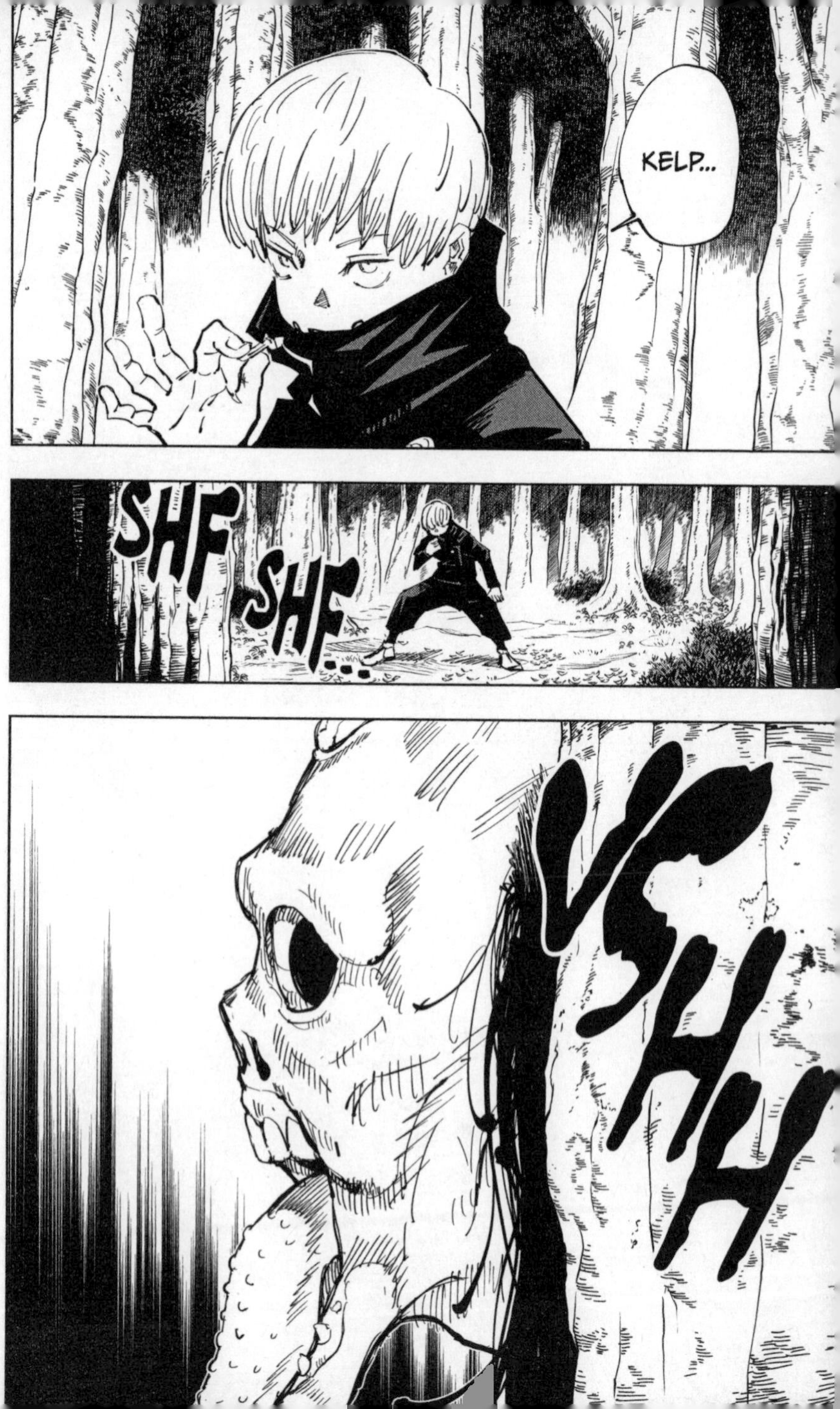
KELP...
SHF SHF...
VSHHH

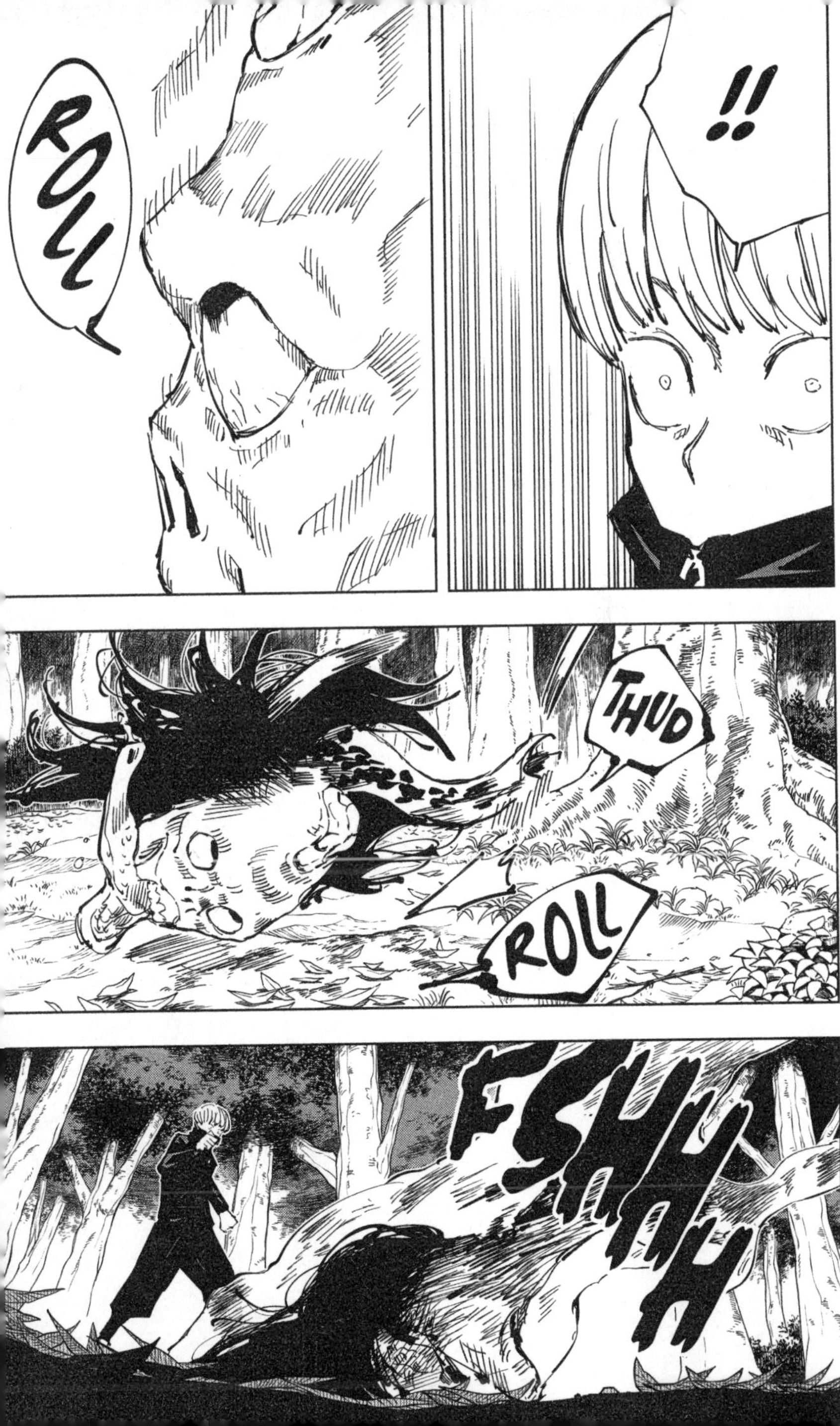
!!
ROLL
THUD
ROLL
FSHHH

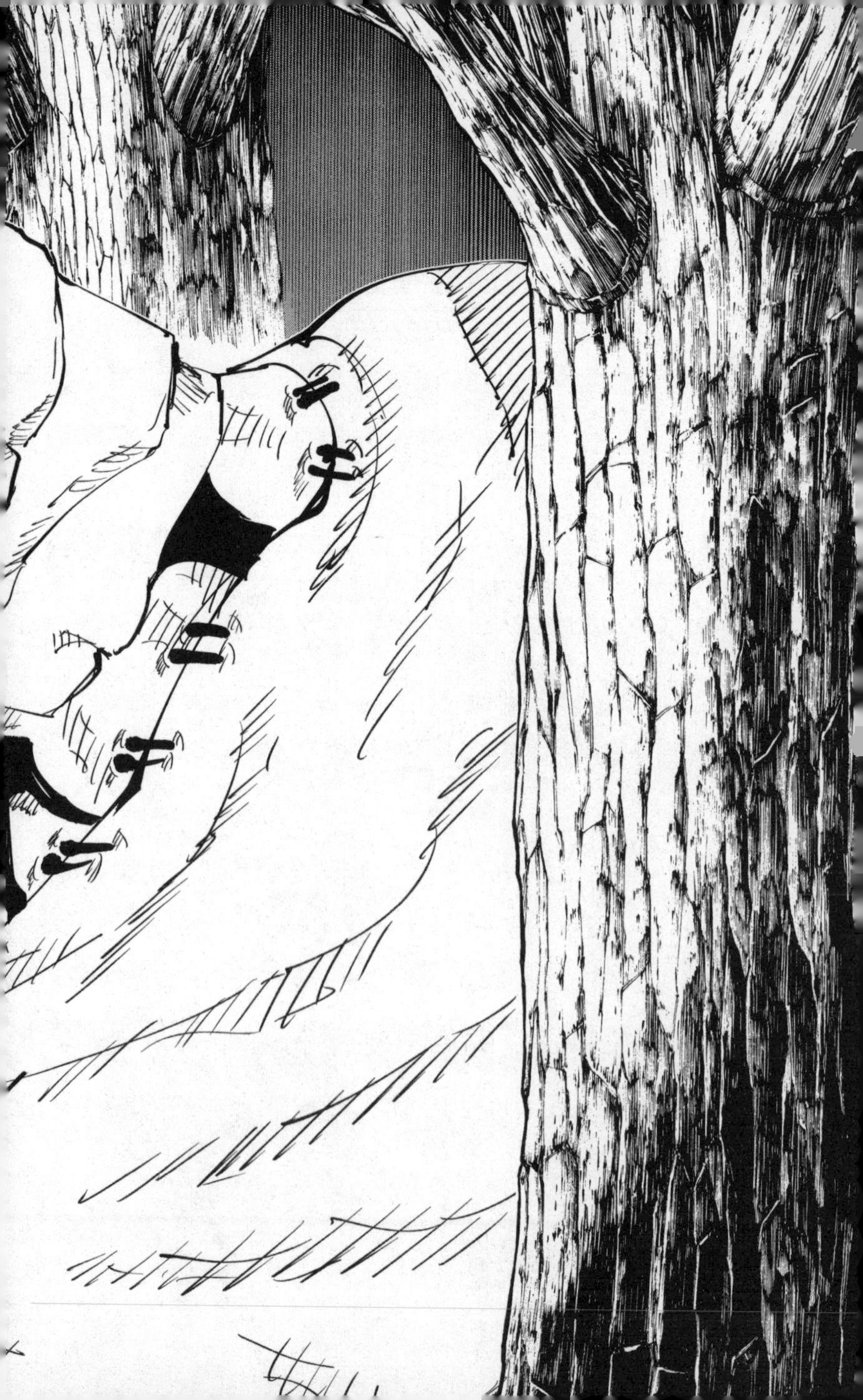

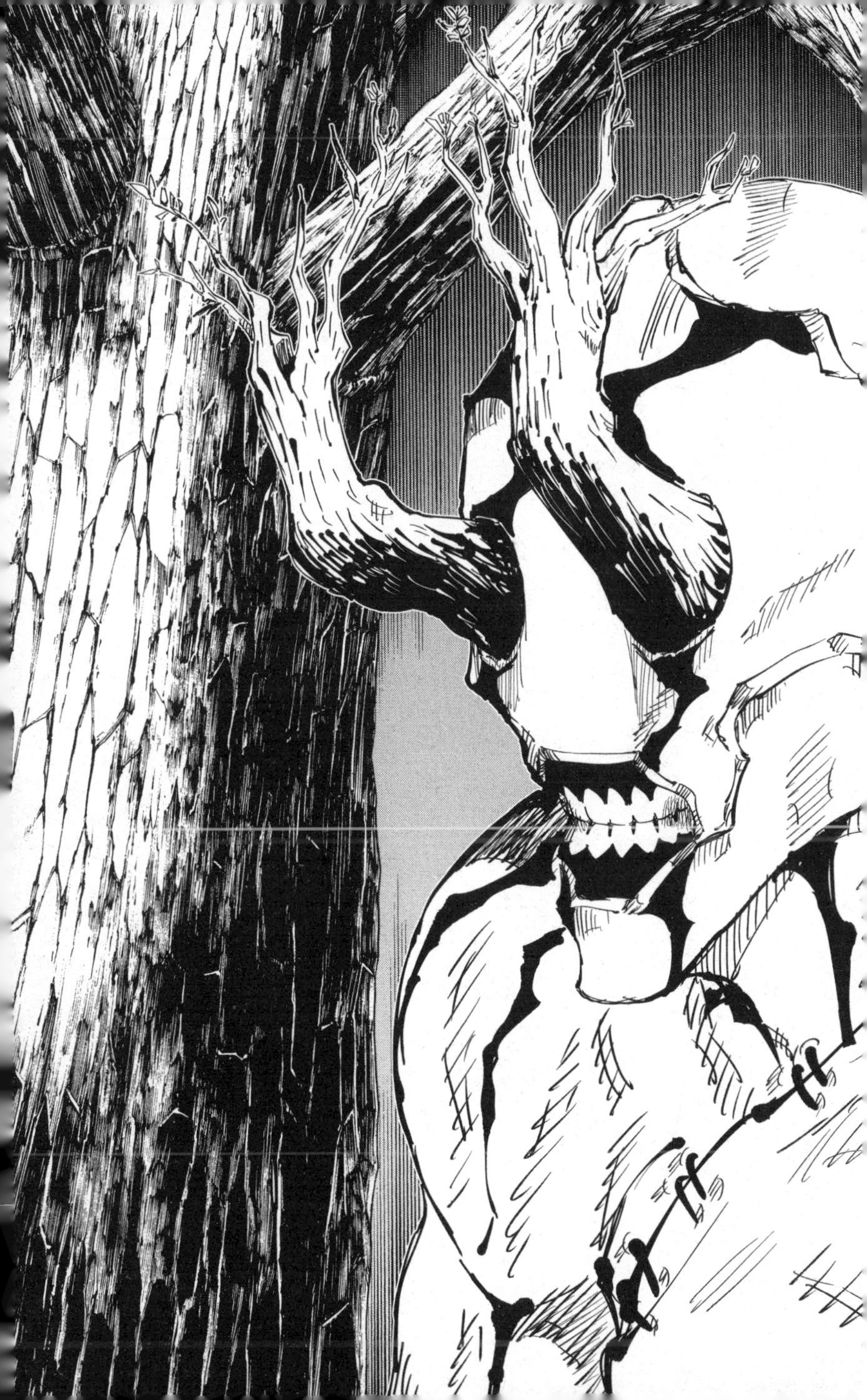

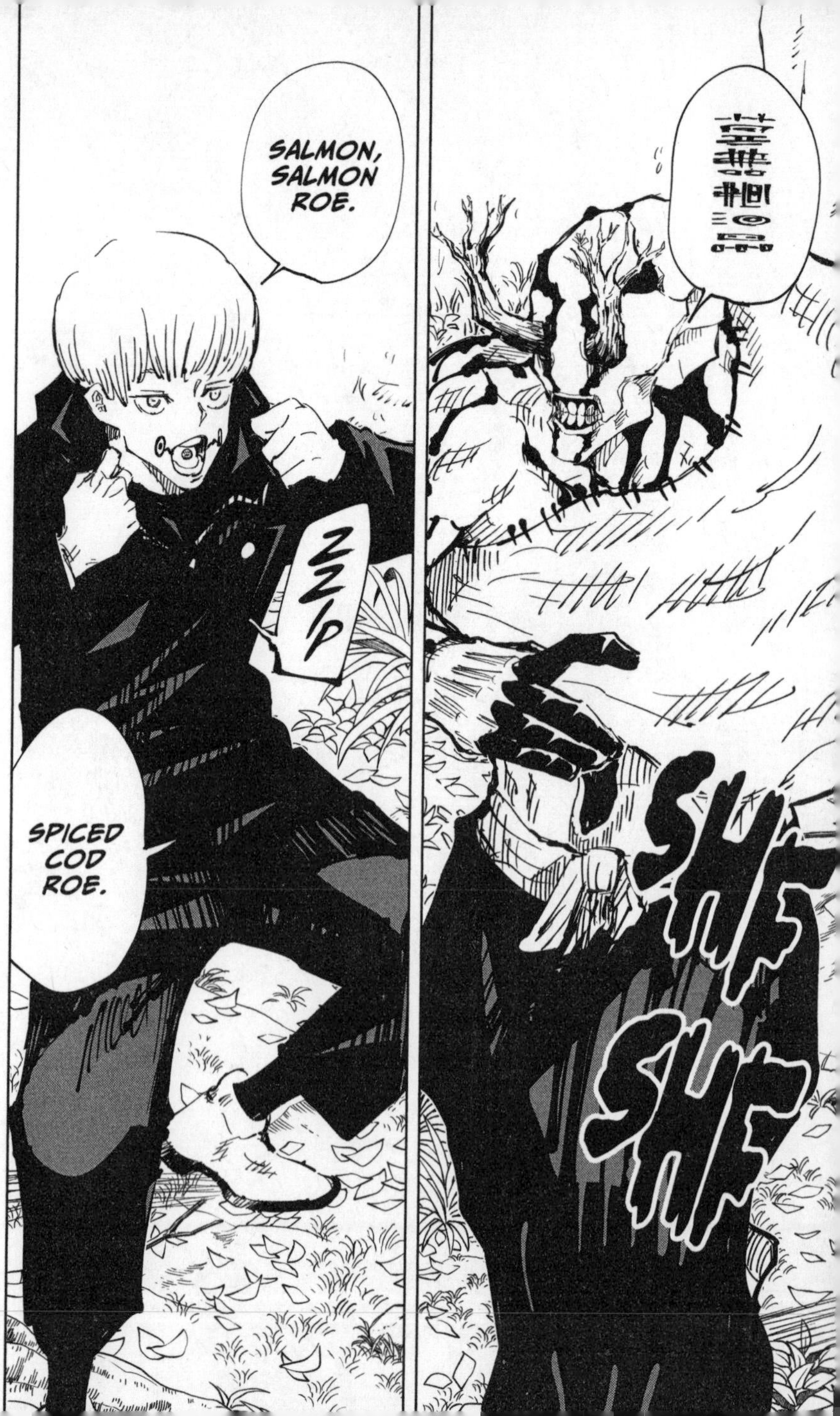
SHF
SHF
SALMON, SALMON ROE.
ZZZIP
SPICED COD ROE.

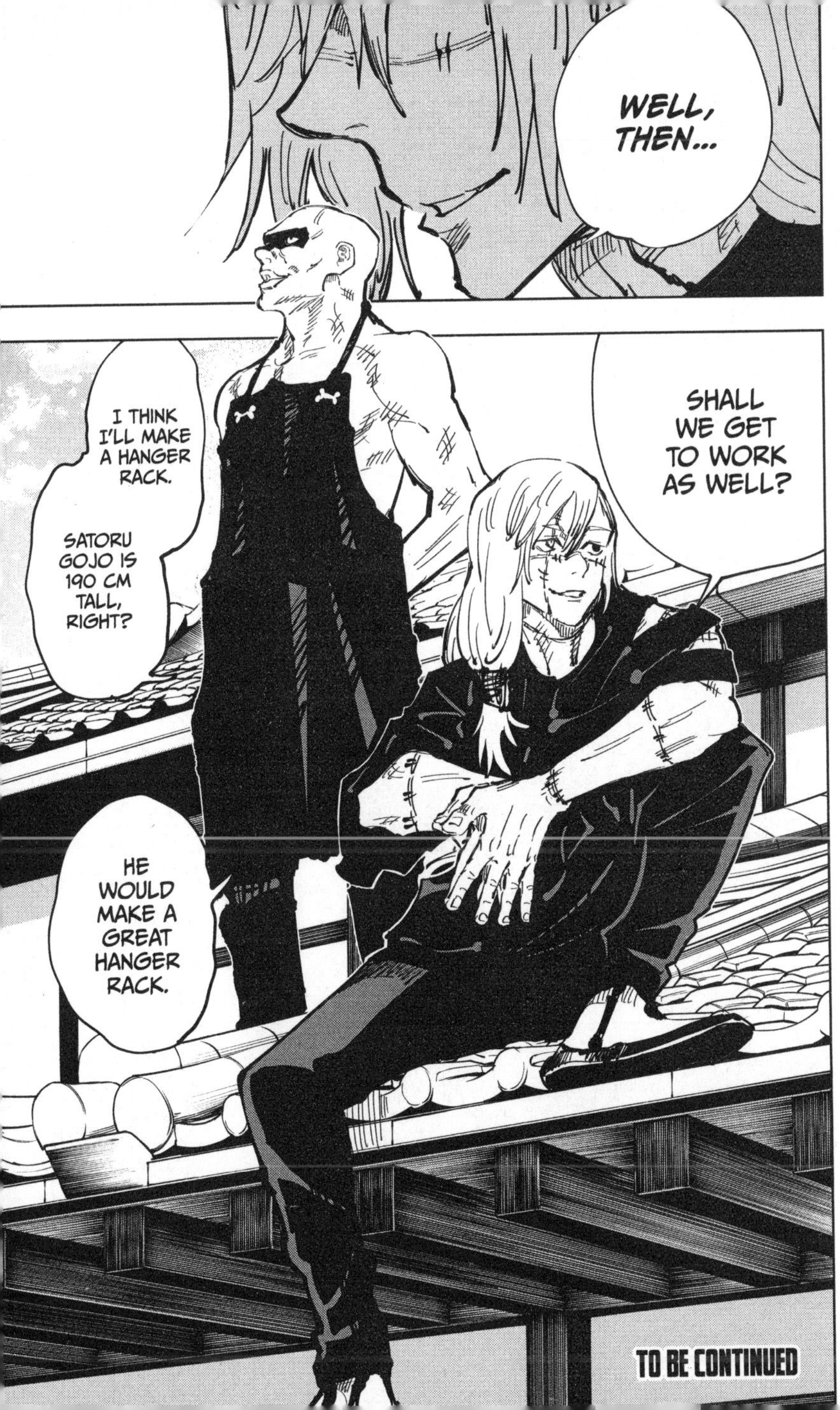
WELL, THEN...
SHALL WE GET TO WORK AS WELL?
I THINK I'LL MAKE A HANGER RACK.
SATORU GOJO IS 190 CM TALL, RIGHT?
HE WOULD MAKE A GREAT HANGER RACK.
TO BE CONTINUED

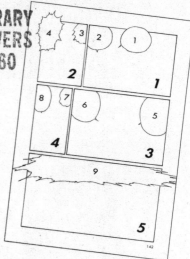

JUJUTSU KAISEN

reads from right to left,
starting in the upper-right
corner. Japanese is read
from right to left, meaning
that action, sound effects
and word-balloon order
are completely reversed
from English order.